Twentieth-Century Britain

Twentieth-Century Britain

Economic, Cultural and Social Change

SECOND EDITION

Edited by
Francesca Carnevali and Julie-Marie Strange

With a Foreword by
Paul Johnson

PEARSON
Longman

Harlow, England • London • New York • Boston • San Francisco • Toronto
Sydney • Tokyo • Singapore • Hong Kong • Seoul • Taipei • New Delhi
Cape Town • Madrid • Mexico City • Amsterdam • Munich • Paris • Milan

PEARSON EDUCATION LIMITED

Edinburgh Gate
Harlow CM20 2JE
United Kingdom
Tel: +44 (0)1279 623623
Fax: +44 (0)1279 431059
Website: www.pearsoned.co.uk

First edition published 1994
Second edition published in Great Britain 2007

© Francesca Carnevali and Julie-Marie Strange 2007

ISBN: 978–0–582–77287–8

British Library Cataloguing-in-Publication Data
A catalogue record for this book is available from the British Library

Library of Congress Cataloguing-in-Publication Data
Twentieth-century Britain / [edited by] Francesca Carnevali and Julie-Marie Strange. —
  2nd ed.
    p. cm.
  Rev. ed. of: Twentieth-century Britain / edited by Paul Johnson. London : Longman. 1994.
  Includes bibliographical references and index.
  ISBN 978–0–582–77287–8 (pbk.)
  1. Great Britain—History—20th century.   I. Strange, Julie-Marie, 1973–   II. Carnevali,
Francesca.   III. Johnson, Paul (Paul A.) Twentieth-century Britain.   IV. Title: 20th century
Britain.

DA566.T84 2007
941.082—dc22

2006053266

10   9   8   7   6
12   11

Set by 35 in 10.5/13pt Baskerville MT
Printed and bound in China

EPC/06

Contents

List of plates

List of figures

List of tables

Acknowledgements

We are grateful to the following for permission to reproduce copyright material:

Plates 2.1, 17.1 and 18.1 courtesy of Corbis; plate 3.1 courtesy of the Bridgeman Art Library; plates 4.1, 4.2, 7.1, 13.1, 16.1, 16.2 and 20.1 courtesy of Getty Images; plates 6.1 and 6.2 courtesy of the Imperial War Museum; plate 8.1 courtesy of the National Archive; plate 9.1 supplied by the Centre for the Study of Cartoons and Caricature at the University of Kent, reproduced courtesy of Mirrorpix.com; plate 9.2 courtesy of the Illustrated London News; plates 10.1, 12.1 and 14.1 courtesy of the Mary Evans Picture Library; plate 11.2 courtesy of the British Library Board; plates 13.2 and 19.1 courtesy of The Advertising Archives; plate 21.2 courtesy of Mark Simmons; plate 22.1 courtesy of NI Syndication; plate 23.1 supplied by The Centre for the Study of Cartoons and Caricature at the University of Kent, reproduced courtesy of Solo Syndication; plate 23.2 courtesy of the Liverpool Record Office; plate 23.3 supplied by the Centre for the Study of Cartoons and Caricature, reproduced courtesy of NI Syndication.

In some instances we have been unable to trace the owners of copyright material, and would appreciate any information that would enable us to do so.

Author's acknowledgements

Firstly, we would like to thank Paul Johnson for giving us the opportunity to edit the second edition of this book and for supporting our endeavour. We would also like to thank the Economic History Society for sponsoring the project. To contributors, thank you for coming on board. Thanks also to staff at Pearson, anonymous readers and colleagues at the Universities of Birmingham and Manchester.

FC & JMS

Preface

Readers of the first edition of this book, published in 1994, may well have felt short-changed by the contents. Although the title, *Twentieth-Century Britain*, promised a hundred years' worth of history, the pages contained little of substance on the 1980s and necessarily even less on the 1990s (because, though historians readily disagree about most things, they concur that history is the study of the past rather than the future). Now, more than a decade later, this newly commissioned second edition genuinely offers readers what its title claims – an up-to-date survey and analysis of economic, cultural and social change in Britain across the whole of the twentieth century.

It would be wrong to think, however, that the passage of time merely allows 'more stuff' to be included in this new volume. Although history is about the past, and this past cannot be changed, history is nevertheless a vital, living subject, continually being rewritten and reformed in the light of contemporary ideas and events. Readers of this new edition will find that, in response to changing fashions and enthusiasms in historical scholarship, the editors and contributors have produced a closer synthesis of the interrelationship between the economic, cultural and social spheres than was achieved in the first edition.

There are also more subtle changes in emphasis and interpretation that derive from authors' reactions – often unconscious – to their environment. In the early 1990s the context was that of a long-serving Conservative government, a slightly stuttering economy and a generally benign cultural environment, whereas contributors to this volume write against the backdrop of a long-serving Labour government, a thriving economy and a cultural environment characterized by newly perceived risks from international terrorism and global warming. The political, economic and cultural environments also affect how each reader navigates a passage through the text, looking for that which resonates with her or his own preferences and prejudices, and responding differently to the arguments advanced and challenges posed by each chapter. This edition of *Twentieth-Century Britain: Economic, Cultural and Social Change* therefore gives readers the opportunity to look at many of the key historical themes of the last century from a new perspective, with new insights offered by a distinguished team of new editors and contributors. The 'facts' may be old, but the history is history for today.

Paul Johnson
London School of Economics
August 2006

1

Introduction

Francesca Carnevali and Julie-Marie Strange

IN 1994 WHEN THE FIRST EDITION of this book was published, the editor Paul Johnson wrote that 'Britain [is] today a much wealthier, more comfortable place to live than it was in 1900.' The intention of this second edition is not to revise that statement but, instead, to provide the reader with further material to assess the distance and the continuities that separate and link the inhabitants of these islands in the twenty-first century from the men and women who mourned the death of Queen Victoria in 1901.

The first edition of this volume proved to be extremely successful with teachers and students alike and over the years readers have not been passive users of this book but have expressed opinions about its uses and concerns about what was left out. In this respect we are particularly grateful to our students and colleagues at the universities of Birmingham and Manchester and readers from other institutions for engaging with the book's material and pointing out its strengths and limitations.

Taking these views on board, the new edition of *Twentieth-Century Britain* does not, on the whole, endeavour to revisit and/or update the themes of the first but, rather, to address the omissions of the first volume and to represent recent shifts in historiography. Since the first edition was published, more than 10 years ago, new research has shone more light on the nature of the cultural, social and economic changes that have taken place in Britain over the course of the twentieth century; one of the aims of this edition has been to incorporate this new literature. Moreover, with this volume, we wish to develop the discussions started in the first edition to additional areas and engage with recent debates.

Class and gender, discussed in the chapter by Stephen Brookes, are just two key concepts that have attracted critical attention in recent years. Indeed, one of the most controversial shifts in contemporary historiography has been the questioning of class as a useful tool of analysis. New methodologies and theories suggested that class was far too nebulous to be used in a meaningful way. Similarly, the first edition of this book focused on women's history, reflecting the emergence of women's studies as a legitimate avenue of historical interest. Increasingly, however, studies of gender suggest that the analysis of women as a separate category is not, perhaps, the most fruitful approach to understanding the differences between male and female experiences. As this volume notes, critical analyses of masculinity are still in their inception. Yet many of the chapters are written with awareness that gender differences were embedded in multifarious experiences. Thus, Sean O'Connell examines the perception of motoring as a masculine endeavour while female drivers attracted derision and criticism. Similarly, Martin Pugh's analysis of suffrage eschews an exclusive focus on the campaign for women's votes in recognition that conceptions of citizenship were contested for numerous groups in twentieth-century society.

Likewise, the passage of time allows us to assess more fully changes that had only started to take place in the early 1990s, such as the relative decline of the trade unions, as analysed by Chris Wrigley. The opportunity to examine the twentieth century in its totality allows historians to assess the impact of policy more clearly. Nick Crafts and Julie Rugg both show how social exclusion in terms of the number of people living below the poverty line increased in the last fifth of the century while the provision of education for the socially disadvantaged has worsened, as detailed in Katherine Watson's chapter. Britain's international position at the end of the century is reassessed in Neil Rollings's in-depth chapter on Britain's troubled relationship with European integration.

As the twentieth century recedes, research is flourishing on topics previously seen as the preserve of the social sciences or media studies. For instance, Rebecca Jennings's chapter on sexuality addresses the population question and the advent of the contraceptive pill, but also considers issues such as AIDS and queer politics. The chapter on ethnicity and immigration by Panikos Panayi is situated in the context of the moral panics from the end of the 1990s about asylum seekers in Britain. It is worth noting that one chapter, John Woolfe's examination of religion and secularization, has been included from the first edition. The 1990s saw an increase in the Muslim population of Britain while the 2001 census included for the first time questions about religious identity. Given the current attention paid to issues of religion, especially in the face of an apparent revival of religious belief systems, Woolfe's chapter has been updated for this edition.

As in the first edition, each chapter includes a survey of the historical development and of the historical debate, with 'In Focus' sections. The chapters end with a brief survey of the themes that cannot be explored in depth with a guided bibliography to these themes. Compared with the first edition, one of the main changes we have introduced has been to divide the book into three parts, with the first part covering the 'long twentieth century'. The five themes included in this part provide the reader with a broad chronological and conceptual overview and allow the contributors to Parts Two (pre-1945) and Three (post-1945) to go into more depth. The five themes in Part One are also intended to convey a sense of some of the conceptual continuities across the twentieth century. So, class and gender are organizing categories which can be used across the century even though their meanings were neither static nor universally agreed. Max Jones's chapter on national identity and war examines how a sense of Britishness has tended to be defined against an external 'other'. Jones looks in particular at the ways in which British identity has galvanized around a notion of a common enemy during periods of military conflict. Similarly, Harry Cocks considers the extent to which the twentieth century represented the inauguration of a 'modern' world and whether, at the end of the century, Britain had entered a post-modern period.

Recent research also allows us to qualify our sense of the changes that have taken place in the economy. Crafts argues that, although affluence increased over the twentieth century, this was not for all. Technological and structural change benefited many as, on average, real incomes per capita rose but they also induced shifts from working-class to middle-class and from male to female employment. There was faster economic growth in the twentieth century than in the nineteenth, especially after 1945, but also relative decline compared to the other industrialized countries. Although for most of the twentieth century inequality in terms of the gap between the high and low earners narrowed steadily, by the end of the century this gap had increased again. One of the consequences of Britain's relative economic decline over the course of the century has been to scale down her relevance as a global policy maker. Catherine Schenk's analysis details how Britain lost her position as leader of the pre-1914 and interwar international economy to the United States of America after 1945.

The use of 1945 as a dividing line between Parts Two and Three suggest that we think the Second World War was a watershed in the twentieth century. Although the use of key dates to subdivide a period can sometimes be seen as arbitrary, Jim Tomlinson's chapter shows that the years after 1945 were marked by faster rates of growth and by a near-revolutionary commitment by successive governments to full employment and economic citizenship. Although full employment was abandoned in the early 1970s, the reforms of the Beveridge report of 1942 developed a collective, state system of welfare benefits that aimed at providing the population with a set of more coherent and more equitable provisions than those detailed by Martin Daunton for the previous period. The Second World War proved to be a watershed also for women. After the First World War many of the women who had become part of the workforce during the conflict left their jobs and retreated back into their traditional roles of wives and mothers. After 1945, the share of the workforce made up by women increased, with more women remaining in work after marriage. This reflected at least two changes: the first in the structure of the economy, with the progressive decline of manufacturing and the deskilling of jobs; and, second, the increase in the number of women attaining degrees and professional qualifications. However, as manufacturing has declined, other sectors have risen to greater importance such as financial and business services and health, all sectors that have given women further job opportunities.

While some chapters confirm this apparent turning point, others demonstrate continuity before and after the war. Indeed, the birth of the 'teenager' is overwhelmingly associated with the 1950s' and 60s' full employment and unprecedented youth spending power. Yet, as Penny Tinkler's chapter illustrates, many of the defining features of youth culture emerged in the 1920s and 30s. Although Britain did become a place where people 'never had it so good', to quote the Prime Minister, Harold Macmillan, in 1957, Peter Scott shows how household consumption for the middle classes and for skilled workers had increased *before* 1945, with the largest increase in spending in the 'new' consumer goods: cars, motorbikes and household equipment. A new class of consumers emerged in the interwar period, those men and women who went to populate the expanding suburbs while furnishing their homes on credit, or, as Julie-Marie Strange's chapter demonstrates, buying model railway sets and investing spare time and resources in gardens and 'home mechanics' for pleasure. Julian Greaves and Chris Price's chapters on the interwar period and Tomlinson and Michael Oliver's on the economy after 1945 give a very clear sense of how this developed without major discontinuities, although Oliver's analysis of monetarism and its influence on the Thatcher governments stands in clear contrast to Price's account of Keynesian economic policy in the interwar period.

Compared with the previous edition this volume offers fewer chapters that are explicitly chronological. However, the narrative of economic change can easily be followed by focusing on Chapters 2, 5, 9, 10, 15 and 17 even though they have a strong thematic element. A volume such as this will, inevitably, suffer from some omissions, especially in those areas where new research is just emerging. The next edition, in 10 years' time, will be able to consider more fully topics such as the development of Britain as a service economy and the challenges of affluence; the growth of a culture seemingly obsessed with youth, beauty and slimness; shifting health patterns and anxieties over increasing obesity and changes in conceptions of the family. Historiography is, as ever, in a state of flux. Recent trends include a focus on space as a historical text, visual culture and an emerging dialogue between economic and cultural methodologies. As the spate of recent television, radio and publishing ventures indicates, history is hugely popular with a broad audience. It is hoped that in presenting up-to-date research in an accessible format, this collection of essays will not only contribute to ongoing historical debates, but also raise new questions for future study.

PART ONE

The long twentieth century

2

The British economy

Nicholas Crafts

THIS CHAPTER IS DESIGNED TO provide a context for the more detailed economic history that follows in Parts Two and Three. Its primary objective is to describe the main developments in the economy over time with regard to the structure of economic activity, macroeconomic outcomes and standards of living. The chapter also reviews trends in economic policy and presents a brief introduction to the controversies surrounding relative economic decline.

Before turning to the detail it is timely to introduce the most fundamental determinant of the evolution of the British economy over the long run, namely, technological change. This has not only had a profound impact on economic life but its rapidity and pervasiveness was the distinctive feature of the twentieth century compared with earlier times. At the end of the century, the information and communications technologies (ICT) revolution was a particularly significant episode of technological change. The economic implications of the ICT revolution are the subject of the 'In Focus' section in the chapter.

Technological change is seen in the appearance of new products and processes which diffuse through the economy. Over the twentieth century the former included computers, television and antibiotics while computer-aided design, the car-assembly line and x-rays were examples of the latter. It is apparent that the impact of technological progress was much greater in the twentieth century than hitherto. The advance of technology was directly underpinned by factors such as the expansion of higher education, the spread of R&D (Research and Development) labs and advances in scientific knowledge. In addition, however, there were economic reasons for the acceleration of technological change, for example, in terms of larger markets, more sophisticated sources of external finance and much enhanced scope for multinational enterprise.

Technological change lies behind increases in labour productivity, and thus real wages, and is also the main reason for improvements in health and life expectancy in the twentieth century. In other words, technology has been the driving force behind the rise of living standards. At the same time, there is a dark side to this process in that technological progress involves exit of the old as well as entry of the new or, in Schumpeter's famous phrase, it entails 'creative destruction'. At one level this has meant the disappearance of old goods and services such as the typewriter and the horse-drawn omnibus; at another level the implication has been the elimination of particular jobs and the redundancy of old skills, for example, those of dockers and newspaper printers. Thus, technological change is not always neutral in its effects but may favour some regions or groups of workers at the expense of others.

Technological progress has also promoted globalization through reductions in transport and communications costs leading to the integration of markets and has been instrumental in successive revisions to the pattern of international production which have resulted in structural change in the British economy. First agriculture and then manufacturing contracted sharply in the face of cheap imports while, on the other hand, the financial sector expanded both in the pre-First World War period and in the recent past. These structural adjustments have been reflected in divergent regional trends. For example, after 1870, East Anglia was hard hit by agricultural imports and, after 1970, the West Midlands was exposed to severe competition from engineering imports while in both periods London flourished as a world-class financial centre.

Overall, globalization has raised real incomes in Britain through opportunities for profitable investments and reorganization of production along lines of comparative advantage to raise value-added although, here too, there have been both winners and losers. At times, however, the downside risks of exposure to the world economy have seemed unacceptable, most obviously during the world economic crisis of the 1930s which provoked a protectionist backlash. Indeed, the technological impetus to market integration was resisted by economic policy from then to the 1970s.

Growth and structural change

This section considers the growth of production, both nationally and regionally, and changes in the structure of employment. In each of these aspects of economic change, attention is drawn to the implications of technological change.

A summary of UK growth performance since 1870 based on a conventional period-ization is presented in Table 2.1 (p. 9). In 1870, although the UK was nearing the end of its unchallenged supremacy, as the first industrial nation it was still the leading economy not only in Europe but also in the world. Since then the UK has been overtaken, initially before the First World War by the United States and then after the Second World War by many European countries. Thus, the UK had slipped to third in Europe by 1950, seventh by 1973 and ninth by 2001 on a criterion of GDP per person measured at purchasing power parity (i.e., adjusted for differences in price levels). Even so,

Table 2.1 Level and growth of real GDP per person

	Level (1913 = 100)	% Western Europe	Growth rate (% per year)	
1870	65	162.8		
1913	100	142.3	1870–1913	1.01
1950	141	151.5	1913–1950	0.93
1973	244	105.3	1950–1973	2.42
2001	409	104.5	1973–2001	1.86

Source: Based on Maddison, 2003.

by 2001, as Table 2.1 reports, real GDP per person was more than six times the 1870 level; economic decline was relative to other countries which grew faster – it was certainly not absolute.

Growth in peacetime in the twentieth century was much faster than in the nineteenth century, especially after the Second World War. At no time before the First World War did the UK sustain trend growth of real GDP per person above 1.2 per cent per year whereas in the last 50 years 2 per cent per year has become a reasonable expectation. As in other OECD (Organization for Economic Co-operation and Development) countries, growth has increased as a result of stronger technological progress and, associated with this, greater investment. Whereas in the late twentieth century total factor productivity (TFP) growth, the standard measure of the contribution made by better technology and improved efficiency in the use of economic resources, was about 1.4 per cent, the best that the UK achieved in the nineteenth century was 0.8 per cent per year. Similarly, in the post-Second World War period the UK has typically devoted about 15 per cent of GDP to investment in physical capital (excluding houses) and 2 per cent of GDP to R&D, which are twice and 20 times the shares of a century earlier respectively. Whereas in 1901 the typical member of the labour force had 6.0 years of schooling, by 1951 this had risen to 9.2 and by 2001 to 12.7 years.

The fastest growth in British economic history was during the so-called 'Golden Age' of European economic growth; Table 2.1 reports a growth rate of 2.42 per cent per year between 1950 and 1973. At the same time, however, the UK lost ground against Western Europe and real GDP per person fell from 151.5 per cent of the European level to 105.3 per cent. As Table 2.1 shows, it was in this Golden Age that relative economic decline was particularly apparent. This was a period when Europe was rapidly reducing its labour productivity gap with the United States after the disruption of the World Wars and the turbulent interwar period and TFP growth in countries like France, Germany and Italy was much stronger than in the UK. In the last two decades of the century, however, productivity growth in the UK and the EU countries was very similar and relative economic decline abated.

It is conventional to talk of disparities in regional economic performance in terms of a 'north–south divide'. A historical take on this would see a traditional pattern in which London and the Home Counties was by far the most prosperous region re-emerging in the period from the late nineteenth century onwards after an Industrial Revolution interlude in which northern England led the way. The Victorian staple industries such as ferrous metals and textiles formed agglomerations located near to coalfields and ports. Subsequently, in the age of electricity and lighter consumer goods industries, proximity to markets mattered more and new agglomerated activities, such as the car industry, developed in the south and the Midlands with the southward move eventually being accentuated by the UK's accession to the EU in 1973. Moreover, the traditional service-sector strengths in international commerce and finance, which had always been concentrated in London, once again became the best basis on which to make money.

In part, Table 2.2 confirms this account of regional disparities. GDP per person has been higher in London than in the rest of Britain throughout the period since 1871 and in the later twentieth century there was a clear tendency for the south-east and East Anglia also to move up the league. By contrast, the north-west has been in relative economic decline against the rest of Britain since mid-Victorian times and since 1911 Wales has slid down and has been at the bottom of the league in the recent

Table 2.2 Regional differentials

(a) Regional GDP/head (GB = 100)

	1871	1911	1954/5	1971	2001
South-east	117.4	124.6	112.7	112.7	123.5
London	147.3	165.6	137.6	123.4	132.4
Rest of south-east	88.5	86.3	97.9	104.6	117.9
East Anglia	92.0	76.8	83.5	92.8	103.7
South-west	86.2	85.7	86.4	93.9	91.0
West Midlands	83.6	78.4	107.9	101.9	89.4
East Midlands	102.3	90.6	101.6	95.7	91.2
North-west	108.1	97.2	97.8	95.3	89.6
Yorkshire & Humberside	94.4	89.5	98.4	92.5	84.1
North	91.4	79.2	88.0	86.1	78.9
Wales	87.7	90.1	82.0	87.5	78.2
Scotland	89.9	102.1	88.1	82.2	93.5
Coefficient of variation	0.107	0.148	0.106	0.076	0.136

Note: Coefficient of variation calculated with south-east treated as one observation.

Source: Based on Crafts, 2005.

(b) Share of British population (%)

	1871	1911	1954/5	1971	2001
South-east	27.1	28.7	31.2	31.3	32.3
London	13.3	13.8	11.1	13.8	12.7
Rest of south-east	13.8	14.9	20.1	17.7	19.6
East Anglia	3.9	2.8	2.7	3.1	3.8
South-west	9.0	6.7	6.8	7.6	8.6
West Midlands	8.4	8.0	9.2	9.5	9.2
East Midlands	6.3	6.6	7.1	6.7	7.3
North-west	12.8	14.0	12.9	12.2	10.9
Yorkshire & Humberside	8.2	8.7	8.3	9.0	7.4
North	6.2	6.9	6.4	5.8	6.6
Wales	5.4	5.9	5.2	5.0	5.1
Scotland	12.7	11.7	10.3	9.6	8.8

Source: Based on Lee, 1979; 2001 Census.

past. The West Midlands reached a high point in the post-Second World War boom years but has fallen back significantly since. Table 2.2 also reflects a drift of population towards the south-east during the twentieth century, notably at the expense of the north-west and Scotland.

Table 2.2 does not tell the whole story, however, because there are no estimates for the interwar period. This was a very troubled time for 'Outer Britain' (the term used by contemporaries) as exports collapsed in the turmoil of the world depression and rampant protectionism. In 1937, a relatively good year, unemployment of insured workers was 23.3 per cent in Wales and 16.0 per cent in Scotland compared with 6.7 per cent in the south-east, whereas in 1913 the figures had been 2.4, 2.0 and 5.8 per cent respectively.

This picture of a wealthy and prosperous south compared with a poor and declining north is, however, a bit misleading. In particular, it is worth noting that in every region except Scotland real GDP per person grew more rapidly between 1911 and 1954/5 than it had between 1871 and 1911 and, similarly, in every region except West Midlands real GDP per person grew more rapidly between 1954/5 and 2001 than between 1911 and 1954/5. Thus, although during the twentieth century the rest of Britain was in relative economic decline with the south-east, this was against the background of faster economic growth than before.

In the first six decades of the twentieth century the British economy was highly industrialized. Table 2.3 (p. 12) reports that as recently as 1971 34 per cent of the labour force was in manufacturing with a further 9.3 per cent in construction, mining and

Table 2.3 Structure of employment (%)

	1911	1951	1971	1999
Agriculture	11.8	6.4	3.2	1.9
Mining	6.3	3.4	1.6	0.3
Manufacturing	32.1	33.9	34.0	15.7
Chemicals	0.9	2.7	3.0	1.9
Metal manufacture	4.1	4.6	4.8	2.1
Engineering	6.7	11.2	13.0	4.9
Textiles & clothing	12.4	7.1	4.5	1.3
Food, drink & tobacco	2.8	2.9	3.2	1.8
Other manufacturing	5.3	5.4	5.5	3.7
Construction	5.1	5.6	6.2	6.4
Gas, electricity & water	0.6	1.6	1.5	0.5
Services	44.1	49.1	53.5	75.2
Transport & communications	7.7	7.3	6.9	5.6
Distributive trades	12.1	14.8	14.1	16.7
Financial & business services	1.1	3.5	6.2	18.6
Hotel & catering	3.0	4.0	3.9	5.7
Miscellaneous personal services	12.0	7.0	6.3	6.8
Education	1.5	1.5	5.4	6.8
Health	0.7	1.7	4.1	10.2
Public administration & defence	4.1	5.3	6.5	4.8
Other services	1.9	4.0	0.1	0.0

Source: Based on 1911: Broadberry, 1997; Feinstein, 1972; manufacturing distributed as in 1907 Census of Production; 1951: O'Mahony, 1999; 1951: Census; 1971: Gallie, 2000; O'Mahony, 1999; 1999: O'Mahony, 2002; OECD, 2004.

public utilities. Since then there has been a major de-industrialization such that by 2001 only 15.7 per cent worked in manufacturing and 7.2 per cent in the remainder of industry. By the 1980s the UK had a balance of payments deficit on trade in manufactures, having been easily the world's leading exporter of manufactures a century earlier.

Within the industrial sector, the decline of the Victorian staples of textiles and mining is apparent. Until the advent of de-industrialization, this was offset by the rise of employment in new industries such as motor vehicles and electricals. The strong rise of engineering in the first half of the century followed by a sharp drop after 1971 is a notable feature of Table 2.3. These trends had regional implications. Thus, the contraction in the staples hit Outer Britain relatively hard whereas the later rundown of engineering was associated with the reversal of fortune in the West Midlands.

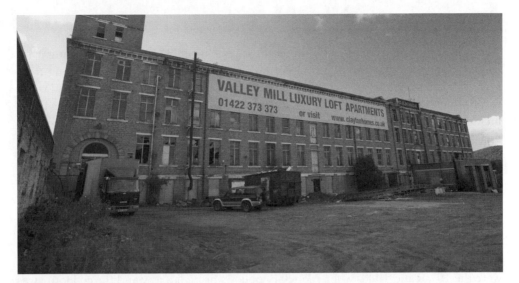

Plate 2.1 The old Gannex Factory (Valley Mill) being converted into luxury flats, Elland, West Yorkshire (© Corbis).

The service sector absorbed an increasing share of the labour force throughout the century, initially at the expense of agriculture but then as a counterpart of de-industrialization. Here the most striking advances were of employment in financial and business services and in health, both of which were prominent features of the late twentieth century. Less widely noticed is the increasing strength of employment in the distributive trades; even though Britain is no longer the 'workshop of the world' it can perhaps still be described as a 'nation of shopkeepers'.

Several forces were driving these changes in the structure of employment. First, there was a strong tendency through much of the century for labour productivity growth in manufacturing to exceed that in the service sector which meant that fewer workers were needed to produce additional output in manufacturing compared with services. Second, as the economy grew richer, spending both by households and government on services took a higher share of total expenditure. Third, as an open economy, economic activity in Britain responded to changes in comparative advantage in international trade which favoured activities intensive in the use of human capital such as financial services rather than unskilled labour-intensive sectors such as textiles. Thus, the evolution of the structure of employment reflects the direct and indirect effects of technological change.

These changes also implied a major shift over the century from working-class to middle-class and from male to female employment. In 1911 manual workers accounted for about 80 per cent of employment while professional, managerial and technical were only 14 per cent. By 1991 these groups were roughly equal in size, each representing about a third of employment. And between the first and last decades of the century the proportion of jobs filled by women had doubled to 45 per cent.

Living standards

The traditional measure of living standards is real wages. This entails collecting evidence on money wages and adjusting for changes in purchasing power resulting from inflation. It is valuable, however, also to consider broader concepts of the standard of living which include aspects of the quality of life which matter greatly to people. These include education, health and leisure. More generally, social scientists have also started to take seriously results from surveys of happiness or life satisfaction in identifying aspects of the economic environment which should be taken into account. It is, of course, possible that living standards have increased over time for the vast majority of the population but that a minority have been excluded and live in 'poverty'; in any event, the distribution of income is an important aspect of changes in economic well-being.

Table 2.4 reports estimates of peacetime inflation and unemployment by decade. Inflation prior to the second half of the century was negligible. The problem periods were the 1970s and 1980s when monetary policy was in disarray and the economy was subjected to two oil-price shocks. On a comparable basis, the 1930s and 1980s are seen to be the worst decades for unemployment followed by the 1920s and 1990s while the post-war boom in the 1950s and 1960s saw exceptionally low unemployment.[1]

These aspects of macroeconomic performance clearly do matter to people, as is suggested by voters' reluctance to re-elect governments that do not deliver on inflation and unemployment. Evidence from surveys of life satisfaction suggests that a

Table 2.4 Peacetime inflation and unemployment rates (%)

	Inflation	Unemployment
1870s	−0.2	4.9
1880s	−0.5	6.2
1890s	0.5	5.8
1900s	0.1	6.6
1920s	−4.5	8.4
1930s	1.2	12.3
1950s	4.3	1.7
1960s	3.7	2.0
1970s	14.3	4.1
1980s	6.2	11.8
1990s	3.4	9.7

Note: Inflation based on GDP deflator and unemployment rates adjusted to historically consistent definition (approximately as measured in the 1960s) throughout.

Source: Based on Boyer and Hatton, 2002; Feinstein, 1972, updated using *Economic Trends*.

one percentage point increase in unemployment is more worrying than a one percentage point increase in inflation; in 2000 prices, the former would have an effect on
well-being equivalent to taking £85 from everyone in the population (unemployed or
not) and the latter about £50.[2]

There is no reason to believe that there is an inexorable upward trend in unemployment driven by technological advance or that employment is subject to a
finite upper limit. In 2004 more people were employed in the UK economy than
ever before and it is perfectly possible to combine high labour productivity with low
unemployment as successful OECD economies have shown. However, malfunctions
of the labour market or macroeconomic policy do result in high unemployment and
when this occurs, as in the 1930s or 1980s, there are substantial costs in terms of lost
production which are additional to the costs of anxiety described above.

In other words, successful macroeconomic management has an important part
to play in delivering a high standard of living. At times during the twentieth century
policy makers seemed unable to deliver macroeconomic stability. However, recent
years have seen a long period of uninterrupted economic growth and moderate
inflation despite shocks from the stock market and oil prices. Opinion polls suggest
that there was greater confidence in future economic prospects and the ability of well-
designed monetary policy to maintain an environment of relatively low inflation and
unemployment.

Table 2.5 displays estimates of trends in real wages. They show that over the long
run real wages have increased by a bit more than real GDP per person – the level of real
wages in 2001 was just over seven times that of 1873. Growth of real wages matched or
exceeded that of real GDP per person until the last quarter of the century and was at
its most rapid in the Golden Age of growth in the 1950s and 1960s. It should also be
reckoned that real wage growth actually exceeded that reported in Table 2.5 because

Table 2.5 Level and growth of real wages

	Level (1913 = 100)		Growth rate (% per year)
1873	67		
1901	96		
1913	100	1873–1913	1.01
1938	135		
1951	173	1913–1951	1.46
1960	221		
1973	343	1951–1973	3.16
1990	406		
2001	483	1973–2001	1.23

Source: Based on Feinstein, 1995, updated using *Economic Trends*.

Table 2.6 Dispersion in male wages

	Class 1A/Class 7	90th/10th percentile
1913/4	5.21	
1935/6	4.91	
1955/6	3.54	
1970	2.54	2.46
1978	2.44	2.36
1993		3.25
2001		3.48

Note: Class 1A are higher professionals and Class 7 are unskilled workers. Wages at the 90th and 10th percentiles are those of workers whose positions in the distribution are, respectively, that 10 in every 100 earn more and 89 in every 100 earn less and that 90 in every 100 earn more and nine earn less. The data for the 1970s where both ratios can be compared suggest that they represent a comparison between similar types of worker.

Source: Based on Routh, 1980; and *New Earnings Survey*.

the price indices available to deflate money wages do not take proper account of improvements in the quality or increases in the range of goods and services on offer.

It is important also to recognize that wage differentials have changed considerably over time. As Table 2.6 reports, at the end of the century there was a large increase in the gap between the top and bottom of the male wage distribution, as reflected in the ratio of the 90th percentile to the 10th percentile which rose from 2.36 in 1978 to 3.48 in 2001, during which time real wages for the 10th percentile rose at only about 0.5 per cent per year. This was a period in which technological change and, to a lesser extent, low wage competition from Asia undermined the demand for unskilled male workers.[3]

These developments are quite recent, however, and came after several decades in which the relativity between high and low earners narrowed steadily. This is captured in Table 2.6 by the pay ratio between higher professionals (Class 1A) and unskilled workers (Class 7), which fell from 5.21 in 1913/4 to 2.44 in 1978. Thus, over the twentieth century as a whole the ratio of wages between the top and bottom of the distribution described a U-shape which reached a low in the mid-1970s and by 2001 was similar to the mid-1950s but well below that of Edwardian Britain.

Poverty is typically measured in terms of a concept based on income relative to the average which is justified by assuming that being below this poverty line implies social exclusion. Thus the required income to be out of poverty rises over time in absolute terms. Table 2.7 (p. 17) reports estimates of numbers in poverty on this basis using contemporary investigators' criteria. This would suggest that the proportion in poverty did not change greatly during the first four-fifths of the century, varying between 5 and 8 per cent, but rose markedly to about one in five persons at the end of the century.[4]

The context for this late-century surge in poverty is unemployment and wage dispersion, both of which were seriously exacerbated by poor education for the socially

Table 2.7 Poverty lines and percentage in poverty

	Poverty line (£)	In poverty (%)	Poverty line (% average disposable income)
1899: Rowntree	53.10	10	115
1936: Rowntree Class A	56.45	8	91
1953: Benefits	69.40	5	109
1979: Benefits	121.60	6	111
1979: < 0.5 mean income	155.09	8	134
2000: < 0.5 mean income	243.21	21	124

Note: Poverty line is for man, woman and three children in 2000 prices; percentage in poverty refers to persons.

Source: Poverty line from Piachaud and Webb, 2004, except 1936 from Piachaud, 1988; percentage in poverty from Hills, 2004, except 1953 from Fiegehen *et al.*, 1977.

disadvantaged. In addition, demographics played a big part in terms of more elderly and lone-parent families, as did government policies which indexed benefits to prices rather than wages after 1980.

The most important non-wage contribution to well-being of the twentieth century was the huge improvement in life expectancy that resulted primarily from improvements in medical science and public health. This was accompanied by a substantial reduction in the burden of morbidity, especially from infectious diseases such as tuberculosis. Life expectancy at birth rose from 41.3 years in 1870 to 60.2 years in 1913 and 78.1 years in 2001; infant mortality which was 145 per thousand births in the late nineteenth century had fallen to 5.4 by 2001. The evidence of happiness surveys and of market behaviour is that people attach a very high value to these improvements in mortality risks. Unfortunately, the second half of the twentieth century saw a considerable widening of health inequalities as social-class differences in lifestyle choices and ability to access health services had a greater impact on disparities in mortality. Even so, there was a continuing improvement in life expectancy for all social groups.

Other major improvements in the quality of life were seen in education and in opportunities to enjoy more leisure. Average years of schooling of the labour force rose from 6.0 years in 1901 to 9.2 years in 1951 and 12.7 in 2001. Only 5 per cent of children went on into secondary education at the start of the century but at its end about 70 per cent of 15- to 19-year-olds were in full-time education. That said, questions can reasonably be asked about the quality of some educational provision since in the mid-1990s 23 per cent of the labour force was found by the OECD to be too badly educated to participate effectively in a knowledge-based economy.

Full-time members of the labour force worked about 2700 hours per year in 1900 but about 1000 hours per year less 100 years later. Over time people worked fewer hours per week – the 54-hour week became the 37-hour week – and took more holidays, with five weeks being quite normal in 2000 compared with only two weeks 40 years earlier. This reflects an increasing demand for leisure as incomes rose and is a reflection of technological change in the sense that far fewer hours need to be worked to purchase any given amount of goods and services.

Obviously, there are other aspects of the quality of life which have not improved dramatically or may have deteriorated. For example, people may feel more exposed to anti-social behaviour or criminal violence than once they were. And there is no generally agreed way of valuing these non-wage components. Nevertheless, it seems highly likely that overall living standards grew faster than is indicated by conventional measures of real wages. On balance, technological change appears to have been a powerful force for raising economic well-being, much more so than in previous centuries.

Economic policy

During the twentieth century the government's role in economic life expanded greatly. There were several reasons for this. They included developments in economic theory, responses to bad economic outcomes, and competition for votes. Policy was directed towards improving economic performance by reducing macroeconomic instability and achieving faster economic growth, addressing market failures in the allocation of resources, and providing a social safety net through the redistribution of income.

The evolution of macroeconomic policies for the control of inflation and maintenance of low levels of unemployment can be seen in terms of a changing balance between rules and discretion. The starting point at the beginning of the century was a rules-based system in which the government was committed to balancing the budget in peacetime while monetary policy was conducted by the independent Bank of England which was committed to a fixed exchange rate with the pound fully convertible into gold while the movement of international capital was unconstrained.

The attempt to return to running the economy along these lines after the First World War ended in the world depression of the early 1930s which demonstrated that the Victorian approach to macroconomic policy left the economy exposed to massive deflation with no effective policy antidote. The crisis led to suspension of the gold standard, the introduction of capital controls and a policy of permanently low domestic interest rates but not a fully fledged Keynesian policy of seeking to manage aggregate demand through discretionary fiscal and monetary policy changes. By the 1950s, however, economic theory suggested that discretionary demand management by the government subject to the discipline of a fixed exchange rate could deliver better macroeconomic performance and win votes by keeping unemployment down. As Table 2.4 reports, for two decades unemployment was very low and inflation was dormant. Unfortunately, after the collapse of the fixed exchange rate system in 1971, faced with unprecedented wage militancy and oil-price shocks, short-termist politicians of both major parties sought votes through reckless and ultimately self-defeating expansionary policies which resulted in record peacetime inflation.

From the late 1970s onwards policy moved back towards a much more constrained discretion without going quite so far as a return to the rigid rules-based approach of Edwardian times. After unsuccessful experiments with monetary targets and exchange rate targets in the 1980s and early 1990s, the incoming Labour government restored independence to the Bank of England and gave it an explicit inflation target to be achieved through its control of interest rates in the context of a floating exchange rate. By now, post-Keynesian economic theory held that taking away the discretion of politicians over monetary policy was a means to re-establishing policy credibility while allowing some scope for the use of interest rates to stabilize demand and head off recessions. This can be seen as a framework which seeks to obviate the problems of both the 1930s and the 1970s in that it allows policy makers to respond to adverse shocks while offering safeguards against a return to the inflation that results from the manipulation of macroeconomic policy for short-term political ends.

Before the First World War, government intervened relatively little in the workings of the market economy and there was no suggestion that government should be judged on the rate of economic growth or the level of unemployment. There was neither industrial nor competition policy while taxes and government spending were minimal. In 1913, tax revenues were only 10.7 per cent of GDP compared with 21.6 per cent in 1937 and between 35 and 37 per cent in the last quarter of the twentieth century.

The main thrust of government intervention on the supply side from the 1920s until the 1970s was industrial policy which was often presented as promoting modernization but actually tended to be protectionist and aimed at saving jobs. Only in the late 1970s did Britain once again become as open an economy as it had been in the 1920s. In the interwar period a general tariff on manufactures was imposed in 1932 and cartels were encouraged. After the Second World War, tariffs were only slowly reduced prior to the major liberalization associated with entry into the European Economic Community in 1973 but cartels were basically made illegal by the Restrictive Practices Act of 1956. Nevertheless, the main thrust of policy was to spawn a variety of subsidies and tax breaks for investment and job creation which in the 1960s and 1970s had a strong bias in favour of regions outside the south and the Midlands. By the 1970s subsidies to producers amounted to 7.6 per cent of GDP and nationalized industries accounted for about a sixth of total investment. Broadly speaking, these policies were aimed at winning working-class votes and were supported by trade unions.

There was a change of direction following the election of the Thatcher government in 1979. Industrial policy in the form of subsidies, nationalization and support for the regions was largely dismantled in favour of an approach centred on privatization, industrial relations reforms and greater competition for producers while de-industrialization was allowed to take its course. The Thatcher reforms, which were not reversed when Labour regained power in 1997, can be seen as a response to the long period of relative economic decline which culminated in the crisis of the 1970s. They were also aligned with developments in economic theory which in the late twentieth century rediscovered the importance of competition in underpinning strong productivity performance.

Before the Second World War, government spending on social transfers was low; it was only 1.4 per cent of GDP in 1910 and 2.6 per cent of GDP in 1937. After the Second World War, social transfers increased by 1980 and by the end of the century, respectively, to 16.4 and 21.4 per cent of GDP. The change was from a system based on the poor law in 1900 to a welfare state based on the Beveridge Report in the 1940s with its emphasis on universal benefits indexed to wages which gave way to an era of renewed means testing and benefits that rose only in line with prices in the 1980s and 1990s. The rise of social transfers obviously resulted in large part from competition for working-class votes but was encouraged by the ageing of the population and affordable because of rising incomes.

These changes over time reflect different positions on the trade-off between efficiency and equity which arises because transfer payments and the taxation that finances them have effects on the incentives to work and save. The poor law was predicated on the notion of deterring those who might seek to dodge work by the 'workhouse test'. By the 1930s when, according to a Royal Commission, unemployment was an industrial rather than a personal problem this seemed unduly harsh. But in the Thatcher era priority was once again given to ensuring that taxation did not rise relative to GDP and to increasing incentives to seek work as unemployment came to be seen as at least partly a result of generous benefits rather than deficient aggregate demand. Estimates suggest that about half of the rise in inequality of incomes after the 1970s can be explained by the switch from indexing benefits to prices rather than wages.

In Focus

The economic implications of information and communications technology

ICT is a general purpose technology (GPT) that rivals, and will possibly surpass, steam and electricity in its economic implications. In common with those earlier GPTs, ICT has not only raised productivity growth but has also contributed to globalization. The modern computer age dates from the invention of the microchip in 1971 and its economic effects became really apparent during the 1990s.

In fact, ICT has had a noticeable productivity impact relatively quickly compared with earlier GPTs. By the late 1990s it was adding about 1 per cent per year to UK productivity growth; this was behind the United States but ahead of the EU. ICT has great productivity potential in services especially in wholesale and retail distribution. As with the whole economy, in distribution the UK has outperformed the EU but not kept up with the United States because the transport system and regulations such as planning restrictions have proved problematic. Nevertheless, the advent of the ICT era does seem to mark a period in which the UK may roll back some of its earlier relative economic decline against Europe.

> ### The economic implications of information and communications technology

ICT has not only improved productivity in the workplace, but it has also been a major benefit to consumers. In particular, it has provided new goods which offer completely new attributes. The personal computer, the mobile phone and the Internet comprise a significant improvement in living standards which will not be adequately reflected in conventional measures of real wage growth. The rapid diffusion of these goods, driven by price reductions resulting from extremely rapid technological progress, is historically remarkable.

ICT has made it possible to transmit digitalizable information across the world at virtually no cost, instantaneously. This has had interesting ramifications for international trade, especially in terms of the 'offshoring' of business services. UK businesses have been able to reduce costs of functions such as call centres and data processing by relocating the activity to remote locations. Recent examples have included national rail inquiries being offshored to India. Broadly speaking, it is routine and easily verifiable activities which do not require face-to-face delivery that can be offshored effectively. In the financial sector, for example, back-office aspects of the business can be offshored but front-office deal making still benefits hugely from the advantages of London's financial agglomeration in which specialist teams of highly skilled individuals can be readily assembled.

In principle, offshoring is 'win–win' in that the UK and India can participate in mutually beneficial trade. Just as with earlier episodes of globalization, how well this works in practice depends on the British labour market's ability successfully to redeploy displaced workers. The overall effect will probably be to add further to the recent tendency for technological change to increase the dispersion of wages between skilled and unskilled workers with, in this case, more impact on women workers as clerical employment is offshored.

Debates and Interpretations
How well did the British economy perform?

The objectives of economic policy are usually taken to be employment, growth, price stability and a fair distribution of income. These can be used as criteria to judge the performance of the UK economy during the twentieth century. The best way to implement this is to compare outcomes in the UK with those in other OECD economies since that takes account of the external economic environment and of the similar opportunities and threats coming from technological change.

Since the First World War, the UK has generally been a relatively high unemployment economy with the notable exception of the 1930s when other countries were hit much harder by the world depression. Thus, in the 1920s the UK ranked 8th out of

11 countries for which comparison can be made and 13th out of 18 both in the 25 years from the mid-1950s and the last two decades of the century. Since the Second World War, the UK has also been a relatively high inflation country. In the last 50 years of the century only three out of 18 countries had higher inflation than the UK. This makes the 1997 decision to delegate monetary policy to the Bank of England entirely understandable.

The notion of a 'fair' distribution of income is heavy with value judgements on which there is no consensus. However, many people would regard the proportion of the population below a poverty line that implies social exclusion as an important criterion by which to examine performance. On this basis, the main failure is located in the period since 1980. While income inequality rose in most OECD economies in these years the increase in the UK was relatively pronounced and at the end of the century the UK had a greater fraction of the population in poverty than all but two other countries (Ireland and the United States). In large part, this reflects policy choices with regard to social transfers – for example, the ratio of unemployment benefits relative to wages was about average for the OECD in the 1970s but had become the lowest in the 1990s – but the increase in the dispersion of earnings has also been relatively large.

This chapter set out data which show that the UK experienced relative economic decline in the sense that its economic growth was less rapid than in most other OECD countries, especially in the Golden Age after the Second World War, with the result that the level of real GDP per person in the UK fell behind that of other countries. 'Relative economic decline' and thus growth performance has been the subject of a good deal of controversy.

Among the main questions raised in the historiography are the following:

- Does relative economic decline matter?
- How far does slow growth represent an avoidable failure ?
- What could governments have done better ?

Most discussions of post-war British growth performance have seen relative economic decline as something to be seriously worried about. For example, Kitson (2004: 34) discusses the reasons for 'the UK's relatively poor growth rate' and its corollary that 'the UK's relative position had significantly deteriorated indicating that other countries had higher living standards'. However, a different take is provided by Supple (1994) who maintains that the differences in income levels with the handful of countries that have overtaken the UK are trivial and this would also be the position of researchers in the happiness tradition, such as Oswald (1997), who argue that further increases in income contribute very little to well-being when countries are as well off as the UK in the post-war period. In any event, it is important to recognize that 'decline' is an ideological construct whose rise to prominence in recent decades has been associated with the politicization of economic policy (Tomlinson, 1996).

It was not surprising that other European countries grew faster in the Golden Age since at the outset many had lower productivity levels, more scope for structural change and thus more scope for growth based on catch-up of the United States. What is debatable is how much allowance to make for this. Temin (2002) argues that once differences in the initial positions are taken into account there is no shortfall in British economic growth which is basically explained by the relatively limited ability to transfer labour to higher productivity employment given the small initial size of the agricultural sector. In contrast, Broadberry and Crafts (2003) note that other econometric analyses of comparative economic growth performance do suggest that there was a shortfall of at least 0.5 to 0.7 percentage points per year which resulted in the UK being overtaken by – not simply caught up with – other European countries, an outcome which was surely not inevitable.

Among those who share this view there is a wide range of opinions as to where economic policy went wrong, which can be seen partly as a reflection of traditional politics. Thus, Bacon and Eltis (1996) argued that a central problem was excessive growth of the public sector which crowded out private investment, while Coates (1994) lamented the failure of the state to intervene more to promote industrial modernization, and these represented 'right-wing' and 'left-wing' claims. More technical discussions have also had a similar flavour. Bean and Crafts (1996) blamed misguided supply-side policies that did not adequately address weak productivity performance including failures to reform industrial relations, to focus on incentivizing human rather than physical capital accumulation and to intensify competitive pressures on management. In contrast, Kitson and Michie (1996) saw the main problems in terms of policies that undermined investment in manufacturing, including both errors in macroeconomic management, which led to periodic economic crises, and a failure to develop a more coherent and effective industrial policy. As might be expected, after 1997 the 'New Labour' government embraced the key aspects of both these analyses.

Further reading

An overview of growth, productivity and relative economic decline can be found in Crafts (2002). More specific detail on industrial development is in Broadberry (1997). For a view of regional economic development and problems, see Armstrong and Taylor (2000). The best place to start with regard to poverty and distributional issues is Glennerster et al. (2004). There is no satisfactory long-run view of macroeconomic policy but there are relevant chapters in volumes 2 and 3 of Floud and Johnson (2004) which also can be consulted for more details on virtually all aspects of this chapter. Cairncross (2001) is an entertaining and informative introduction to the implications of ICT.

References

Armstrong, H.W. and Taylor, J. (2000) *Regional Economics and Policy*. Oxford: Blackwell.

Bacon, R. and Eltis, W. (1996) *Britain's Economic Problem Revisited*. London: Macmillan.

Bean, C. and Crafts, N. (1996) 'British Economic Growth since 1945: Relative Economic Decline . . . and Renaissance ?' in N. Crafts and G. Toniolo (eds) *Economic Growth in Europe Since 1945*. Cambridge: Cambridge University Press, 131–72.

Boyer, G.R. and Hatton, T.J. (2002) 'New estimates of British unemployment, 1870–1913', *Journal of Economic History*, 62, 643–75.

Broadberry, S.N. (1997) *The Productivity Race*. Cambridge: Cambridge University Press.

Broadberry, S.N. and Crafts, N. (2003) 'UK productivity performance from 1950 to 1979: a restatement of the Broadberry-Crafts view', *Economic History Review*, 56, 718–35.

Cairncross, F. (2001) *The Death of Distance*. Boston, MA: Harvard Business School Press.

Coates, D. (1994) *The Question of UK Decline*. London: Harvester Wheatsheaf.

Crafts, N. (2002) *Britain's Relative Economic Performance, 1870–1999*. London: Institute of Economic Affairs.

Crafts, N. (2005) 'Regional GDP in Britain, 1871–1911', *Scottish Journal of Political Economy*, 52, 54–64.

Feinstein, C.H. (1972) *National Income, Expenditure and Output of the United Kingdom, 1855–1965*. Cambridge: Cambridge University Press.

Feinstein, C.H. (1995) 'Changes in Nominal Wages, the Cost of Living and Real Wages in the United Kingdom over Two Centuries, 1780–1990', in P. Scholliers and V. Zamagni (eds) *Labour's Reward*. Aldershot: Edward Elgar, 3–36.

Fiegehen, G.C., Lansley, P.S. and Smith, A.D. (1977) *Poverty and Progress in Britain, 1953–1973*. Cambridge: Cambridge University Press.

Floud, R. and Johnson, P. (eds) (2004) *The Cambridge Economic History of Modern Britain*. Cambridge: Cambridge University Press.

Gallie, D. (2000) 'The Labour Force', in A.H. Halsey and J. Webb (eds) *Twentieth-Century Social Trends*. Basingstoke: Macmillan, 281–323.

Glennerster, H., Hills, J., Piachaud, D. and Webb, J. (2004) *One Hundred Years of Poverty and Policy*. York: Joseph Rowntree Foundation.

Hills, J. (2004) *Inequality and the State*. Oxford: Oxford University Press.

Kitson, M. (2004) 'Failure Followed by Success or Success Followed by Failure? A Re-examination of British Economic Growth since 1949', in R. Floud and P. Johnson (eds) *The Cambridge Economic History of Modern Britain*, vol. III. Cambridge: Cambridge University Press, 27–56.

Kitson, M. and Michie, J. (1996) 'Britain's industrial performance since 1960: underinvestment and relative decline', *Economic Journal*, 106, 196–212.

Lee, C.H. (1979) *British Regional Employment Statistics, 1841–1971*. Cambridge: Cambridge University Press.

Maddison, A. (2003) *The World Economy*. Paris: OEDC.

OECD (2004) *Labour Force Statistics*. Paris.

O'Mahony, M. (1999) *Britain's Productivity Performance 1950–1996*. London: NIESR.

O'Mahony, M. (2002) *The National Institute Sectoral Dataset*. www.niesr.ac.uk/research.

Oswald, A.J. (1997) 'Happiness and economic performance', *Economic Journal*, 107, 1815–31.

Piachaud, D. (1988) 'Poverty in Britain 1899 to 1983', *Journal of Social Policy*, 17, 335–49.

Piachaud, D. and Webb, J. (2004) 'Changes in Poverty', in H. Glennerster, J. Hills, D. Piachaud and J. Webb (eds) *One Hundred Years of Poverty and Policy*. York: Joseph Rowntree Foundation, 29–47.

Routh, G. (1980) *Occupation and Pay in Great Britain, 1906–1979*. London: Macmillan.

Supple, B. (1994) 'Fear of failing: economic history and the decline of Britain', *Economic History Review*, 47, 441–58.

Temin, P. (2002) 'The Golden Age of European growth reconsidered', *European Review of Economic History*, 6, 3–22.

Tomlinson, J. (1996) 'Inventing "decline": the falling behind of the British economy in the postwar years', *Economic History Review*, 49, 731–57.

Notes

1　Unemployment has been measured in many different ways, generally using evidence from unemployment benefit and insurance schemes whose rules have differed greatly over time. The estimates in Table 2.4 adjust the series to a comparable basis; in doing so, they report numbers much lower than those conventionally quoted for the 1930s and a good deal higher than the claimant count for the 1990s (about 16 per cent higher in 1999).

2　These costs represent the damage done to the average person by anxiety about the economic situation and are in addition to the direct income losses from recession or the unhappiness associated with actual unemployment.

3　These trends were much less pronounced for female workers for whom real wages at the 10th percentile rose by about 2 per cent per year over the same period while the 90th/10th percentile ratio went from 2.94 to 3.79.

4　Table 2.7 reports Rowntree's original estimate of 10 per cent in poverty in 1899; recent reworking of his data suggests this is too high and that 6 per cent is a more accurate estimate. Care needs to be exercised in the comparison of different years because, as Table 2.7 reports, the poverty lines chosen by different investigators are not a constant percentage of disposable income.

3

Modernity and modernism

Harry Cocks

WHEN ASKED TO CHARACTERIZE the twentieth century, most people would, perhaps, fall back on developments and social forms which emerged in that century. We might characterize the products of Britain's twentieth century by referring to phenomena as diverse as total world war, mass commercial leisure, democracy, the welfare state, the economic depression of the 1930s and the post-war economic boom, decolonization, women's rights, sexual freedom or consumerism; themes that are well represented in this book. However, many of these developments were not particular to the twentieth century and, indeed, pre-dated it by decades or even centuries. Can we then describe the twentieth century as 'modern' if we locate its antecedents in previous eras? What does it mean to say that we live in a 'modern age', or within a period of time which we might call 'modernity'? How did contemporaries define their age as modern, and how did they try to distinguish their present from the Victorian and Edwardian past?

Questions of modernity matter because so much of early-twentieth-century culture was preoccupied with rejecting the immediate Victorian past and redefining the world in accordance with radically new precepts and ideas. These ideas, in turn, had an enormous influence on the shape of British culture. However, in spite of the strenuous efforts of early-twentieth-century Britons to throw off the shackles of the past, the nineteenth century continued to cast a long shadow.

Many historians have argued that modernity resides in a series of social, political and economic institutions that have come into being since the eighteenth century, the influence of which has come to define our age. Others, however, have suggested that the best way to define the twentieth century is by reference to a certain kind of modern sensibility that could be found principally in the artistic movement known as modernism, which grew up in the 1890s and enjoyed its most innovative period just before the First World War. The sensibility of modernism, it is often suggested, defined a feeling that grew enormously following the catastrophe of the Great War and came thereafter to characterize European culture more generally. Among its central tenets were irony, detachment, paradox, disillusion with tradition and the repudiation of the past. Other historians have suggested that modernism remained the property of an elite avant garde in art and literature, and never reached far beyond that group. They suggest that, in spite of the rise of modernism and the attempts by writers and avant garde artists to repudiate the past and begin culture anew, there were substantial cultural and social continuities between the nineteenth and twentieth centuries. This chapter will consider the relationship between modernism and the Great War in attempts to distinguish the twentieth century as a modern period. It will conclude by examining how far the influence of modernism permeated through to the second half of the century.

What is modernity?

Historians have become interested in the idea of modernity either because it seems to be a distinct phase in human history that appeared to be drawing to a close at the end of the twentieth century, or because they see it as the constellation of forces behind a globalized economy and culture. We will not be able to deal with the question of whether modernity is intensifying or declining in any depth here, but we will examine what is usually meant by the term. The idea of modernity has been interpreted in many different ways by historians and theorists, but four interrelated themes recur in most accounts. First, modernity can be described as a set of structures, institutions, ideas and techniques which have emerged in the last 300 years or so. In another sense, modernity can be described as a set of experiences which produce a particular feeling, identity or sensibility. More recently, historians have suggested that modernity is not an inexorable process to which all societies are subject in a uniform way, and in which all societies evolve towards a market-based liberal democracy. Likewise, it is important to distinguish between modernization, the notion of evolutionary progress, and modernity, a sense of change which might be viewed as positive transformation or as rupture. Modernity, then, is better understood as a set of processes which only ever have local rather than universal application. In this reading, there are only ever localized 'sites of modernity'. Finally, modernity also describes a set of beliefs about rationality, in particular the belief that the world is inherently knowable and improvable through the application of rational thought to any problem. This idea of modernity is predominantly associated with the thinkers of the eighteenth-century European Enlightenment. Hence, faith in the improvability of the world and the possibility of progress is frequently referred to as the 'Enlightenment project' (Daunton and Rieger, 2001).

In many ways, modernity can simply be described as any culture's sense of what is new. However, in order to locate it in time, many accounts of modernity suggest that our modern world can only really be associated with the structures and institutions which have emerged since about 1700 and which represent a decisive break with a pre- or early-modern, pre-industrial past. Modernity, in this sense, is defined by the development of structures and processes which began to flourish in the eighteenth and nineteenth centuries. Central among these is the 'nation-state', defined as a political entity which is said to represent those sharing some sort of common culture, such as language or race. Similarly important here is industrial capitalism, such as that which developed in Britain in the latter decades of the eighteenth century, the features of which include the factory system, wage labour and trade unionism. Inextricable from capitalism is the rise of consumerism. After about 1880, Western Europe and America also developed techniques of mass production, which in turn made it necessary to sell to more and more people and, therefore, to advertise products as widely as possible. This feature of modern capitalism, in which branded goods are sold in mass markets using pervasive advertising techniques, is usually referred to as the consumer society.

Alongside these features of 'high' modernity, democratic political institutions and ideas also developed, including universal male and, later, female suffrage, secret ballots and political parties with national organizations. Other features of modernity include imperialism, urbanization and the rise of big cities and technological innovation based upon scientific advance. Of course, all of these processes are linked with certain cultural forms and ideas: these include the primacy of scientific over religious or spiritual accounts of the natural world, secularization, the application of bureaucratic systems, the importance of individual liberty and democracy, and the truncation of space and transformation of time through the emergence of rapid transport and international communication. These are to name but a few of the principal ideas and processes associated with modernity. In this interpretation, although modern structures like industrial capitalism or the nation-state flowered in the nineteenth and twentieth centuries they can, nevertheless, be traced back as far as the Renaissance. Indeed, it is often argued that there was no decisive break between modernity and a pre-modern world in which the structures listed above existed only minimally, if at all. If looked at in this way, modernity becomes simply a question of degree.

Modernity can also be defined as a kind of sensibility. Many Victorian writers decried modern urban life and, in doing so, defined modernity principally as humanity's alienation from nature. According to this critique, the modern world saw people walled up in cities, sealed off from natural processes, moved about with no more autonomy than a parcel, or forced to work in spirit-crushing, unhealthy and repetitive industrial labour. This sense of alienation, they argued, produced a series of pathologies ranging from crime and disease to sexual immorality and hysteria. However, this attack on the modern was accompanied by a counter-movement which faced the confusion, speed and apparent disorder of the modern world and embraced its vitality. Urban experience was central to this process. According to the nineteenth-century French poet Charles Baudelaire, the city provided the writer with the opportunity to experience the true nature of modernity, which inhered in 'the transient, the fleeting [and] the contingent' sensations of urban life (Charvet, 1972: 395). Yet feelings about the city, as about modernity as a whole, remained ambivalent. As the German sociologist Georg Simmel pointed out in 1911, the modern metropolis provided unprecedented freedoms, but was also a place of deadening anonymity. It reduced personal contacts to brief, dehumanized exchanges with other people who were usually encountered via an impersonal economic transaction. Modernity encouraged a form of detachment, but not only from fellow men and women. The chaotic urban world led people to screen out much of this over-stimulating environment. Instead, the city encouraged the development of a detached, blasé attitude. As will be explained below, artistic modernism of the early twentieth century (distinct from theories of modernity) cultivated and valued this notion of modernity as detachment, disorder and ephemerality.

Finally, modernity is also inherent in the idea that the world and its problems can be objectively known and, therefore, controlled and improved. This notion proposes that any social, cultural or political difficulty can be improved, solved or even removed by the application of reason. This faith, and the various schemes for human improvement that have been fostered by it, are often referred to collectively as the 'project of modernity' or the 'Enlightenment project'. Hence, ideas as diverse as prison reform, railway travel, military discipline or the welfare state can be said to have had their origins in this Enlightenment notion. However, some of the great theorists of modernity like Max Weber tended to see a danger in this notion. Notably, Weber argued that the essence of modernity was the capacity to order every aspect of life to be consistent with the belief that the world could be known and controlled. Modernity was, for Weber, an unstoppable force which would ultimately order every aspect of human existence. It would become an 'iron cage' of rationality and bureaucracy in which there was little or no room for human agency.

Although this type of rationality can be seen in certain places and times, historians now tend to think of modernity as a more patchy process. Schemes based on bureaucratic rationality or faith in improvement do not completely reorder the world and often only apply to particular places, sites or groups of people. Often, they fail entirely. Modernity, therefore, can be found in various places, but is by no means a set of universal or wholly successful processes. Instead, the modern world is better understood as a diverse series of 'sites', spaces or techniques which are distinctive to the nineteenth and twentieth centuries, such as the prison, liberalism, mass production, the conveyor belt or the advertising industry. At these 'sites of modernity' the ideas and processes of rationality, bureaucracy and Enlightenment are worked out, contested, resisted, reworked, abandoned or reapplied.

British modernity

So modernity is a long-term process and cannot be confined merely to the twentieth century. Neither can it be seen as something 'totalizing' which consumes the world that produced it and encages it in bureaucracy. However, in spite of these cautions, we can still use the idea to show that there are specific ways in which we might think of Britain's relationship to modernity and the modern. In short, we should investigate the various economic, social and cultural changes which Britons referred to as 'modern' at the beginning of the twentieth century. How did they understand this term?

Historians normally argue that there was something specific to the period between 1880 and 1930 which meant that Britain's transition to modernity can be located there. It is in this period, it is argued, that processes which we associate with modern life began to become especially visible. In particular, we can see in this period the decline of organized religion and the corresponding development of a Darwinian account of evolution in the natural world, the rise of a new imperialism fuelled by capitalism and racial ideologies, the rise of mass leisure and women's rights, the emergence of sexuality as a social issue and the ramifications of the Great War. In addition to this, there were a number of significant economic and technological developments and innovations. Western European economies expanded enormously between 1900 and 1914, although this was often at the expense of Britain's historic predominance. Significant inventions which arrived in Britain during this period included the automobile, the steam turbine, x-rays, aeroplanes and electric lighting. There was also a communications revolution inspired by radio, telephones, typewriters, cinema and tape recorders. The rise of mass consumerism was generated by rising real wages after 1870 and the capacity to exploit this new mass market was assisted by the rise of the department store, the advertising industry and mass literacy, leading to the establishment of the popular daily press in the 1890s. The first of these papers was the *Daily Mail*, set up in 1896.

Above all, however, Martin Daunton and Bernhard Rieger have identified a pervasive sense of crisis which animates all discussion of 'modernity' in Britain at the beginning of this period (Daunton and Rieger, 2001). This tended to focus on matters of gender, race and sexuality, often all at once. According to several cultural critics of the time, society appeared to be 'degenerating' as women threw off traditional shackles of gender and family, the nation's racial stock apparently deteriorated, Britain's empire began to be threatened by the spread of French, American and German political and economic power and homosexual men like Oscar Wilde began to be more visible, even though in his case this was because in 1895 he was tried and imprisoned for homosexual offences.

Perceptions of time, space and the physical universe also underwent a major transformation in the period leading up to the First World War. Most Western European countries standardized their internal time zones in the 1880s and 1890s. In Britain, standard time was introduced in 1880 and this was followed by the introduction of standard international time zones in 1912. The physical world was also becoming a much more confusing place, with investigations into the nature of atomic particles and of time itself which seemed to contradict common sense. In physics, the structure of the atom was described for the first time in 1911 by the British scientist Ernest Rutherford, while Einstein's special and general theories of relativity (1905 and 1915 respectively) revolutionized the understanding of time (Kern, 1983). In addition, psychology and psychoanalysis offered to explain the human mind in completely new ways. Just as Einstein demonstrated that the nature of time was dependent on how it was observed, Sigmund Freud showed that the mind was formed by the accumulated memories collected in the unconscious. Memories, especially of childhood, were therefore not simply forgotten, but continuously present to the individual and played a determining role in adult behaviour. Freud's reception in Britain, however, was limited to an avant garde minority and he met with disdain from the medical profession until after the First World War. Nevertheless, Freud's work, along with all these other scientific advances, had a crucial influence on artistic modernism in the short term and on British culture more generally in the long term.

Modernism

In spite of the revolutionary nature of these changes, British society before 1914 was nevertheless recalled by those who lived through the First World War as a time of almost stultifying stability and conservatism. No doubt these views were coloured by the trauma of the war, but they were also informed and sometimes produced by modernist artists and intellectuals who were eager to debunk what they saw as out-moded 'Victorian' convention. From the 1890s onwards, artists and writers began to try to distance themselves from the past and, in some cases, to repudiate it altogether. For perhaps the first time in the history of artistic endeavour, tradition was decisively rejected in favour of creation from first principles. This attempt to break with tradition was given enormous force by the trauma of the First World War. In a series of books during and after the conflict, the wartime generation expressed their disgust with what they saw as the outmoded and empty Victorian ideals which had led directly to pointless slaughter on a vast scale. Some historians argue that this rejection of the past represents the beginning of a truly modern sensibility, although, as we shall see, this idea is not uncontested.

In order to understand modernism, one has to accept that it is contradictory. Like the processes of modernity themselves, modernism as a cultural movement often invoked the contemporary and the new by using the motifs of the past, often the ancient past. Modernism was protean but, nevertheless, certain key themes did emerge which united its various manifestations. One of these was an attempt to break with traditional ideas about the nature of art and the standard forms of representation. As Malcolm Bradbury and James McFarlane have pointed out in *Modernism: A Guide to European Literature, 1890–1930* (1991), this sense of newness can be traced to the 1890s when a series of social trends and movements attracted the label 'new': the rebellious New Woman, the utopian New Life, the New Drama of Henrik Ibsen and George Bernard Shaw, the New Poetry and even the New Humour. These writers and artists began to reject a Victorian heritage which insisted that art should not only be a mirror of the natural world, but should also reflect morality and perform some kind of social role. In contrast, aestheticism and decadence movements, strongly associated with sexually dissident writers like Oscar Wilde, declared that art should be purely about sensation and should exist only 'for art's sake'.

Although modernism can be traced to the *fin de siècle*, its greatest period of innovation was in the years between 1900 and 1915. Part of the inspiration for modernism came from the scientific and technological changes which generated new and more complex ideas about time, space, the unconscious and the physical universe. These ideas seemed to detach art from its traditional moorings of straightforward representation and linear narrative. This movement was epitomized by trends in continental art such as the Cubism of Picasso and Braque, or the atonal music of Schoenberg. Suddenly, visual representation, narrative and musical line were broken up into non-linear chunks. Instead of depicting landscape or portraits, painting broke up the observer's view and distorted perception while literature dwelled on memory, streams of consciousness, as, for example, in James Joyce's *Ulysses* (1922), and the persistence of unconscious memories as in Virginia Woolf's *Mrs Dalloway* (1925). Modernism was also marked by its fascination with technological change. In Britain, modernist intellectuals like the poet Ezra Pound and the artist Wyndham Lewis embraced these sweeping changes in their 'Vorticist Manifesto' of 1914. They argued that language and poetry should reflect this restless spirit, should repudiate tradition, celebrate movement and change and, ideally, function like a machine. Looking back on the art of this period, the sculptor Herbert Read wrote in 1933 that it was 'not so much a revolution, which implies a turning over, even a turning back, but rather a break-up . . . some would say a dissolution' (Bradbury and McFarlane, 1991: 20). Its overriding theme was crisis, even catastrophe.

Although the restless sensibility of modernism remained confined to an avant garde in Britain before 1914, it nevertheless found echoes in mainstream culture. In particular, the spirit of novelty, change and frustration with the 'over-civilized' and even decadent social order found echoes in those who welcomed the oncoming war as an opportunity to cleanse, purge and revivify Western culture. Even poets like Rupert Brooke, who embraced tradition and romanticism, could rejoice in the war. Brooke's generation, who turned up at recruiting offices in huge numbers to volunteer in the early stages of the war, were he said, 'like swimmers into cleanness leaping' rejecting 'a world grown old and cold and weary' (Brooke, 1970: 19).

Modernity and the Great War

Many historians have suggested that the catastrophe of the First World War brought this modern sensibility, with all its love of change, ironic detachment and repudiation of the past, into focus. Initially, the war was embraced across Europe, even by those on the left, as an antidote to the enervating stasis of an increasingly bourgeois and seemingly unadventurous Edwardian society. However, as the war went on and thousands of men died to no apparent purpose, a profound disillusion with both the war and the society that had produced it set in. A furious reaction against the 'Victorian' morality that had fostered the war began in 1918 with Lytton Strachey's attack on the high ideals of the previous century in his picture of *Eminent Victorians* (1918), a collection of biographical essays on four key Victorian personalities. Although most wanted merely to forget the war in its immediate aftermath, in 1928 and 1929 the generation which had fought in it produced a series of landmark books describing their experiences in brutal detail and with savage irony. It is in these books that some historians have discerned the outline of a 'modern memory' or sensibility that is based around irony, scepticism, detachment, disillusionment and disorientation; many of the feelings apparent in artistic modernism but reinforced by the shattering experience of combat.

Lytton Strachey was part of what was known as the Bloomsbury Group (see 'In Focus'). He and his peers had begun to reject their Victorian heritage before the First World War but *Eminent Victorians* represented a full-scale hatchet job not just on four central figures of Victorian culture, but also on pre-war ideals of duty, religious enthusiasm, morality, the public school ethos and military prowess, all of which seemed empty and corrupt in a post-war context. While Strachey's feline assaults on the Victorians seem tame in comparison to modern biography, they were nevertheless sufficient for the critic Cyril Connolly to call *Eminent Victorians* a 'revolutionary textbook on bourgeois society' and to render it a sensational success (Holroyd, 1971: xi). For Strachey, the extravagantly dutiful Catholic Cardinal Manning was little more than a careerist, while the heroine of the Crimea, Florence Nightingale, is shown as a neurotic obsessive. Thomas Arnold, the great headmaster of Rugby school, was exposed as the embodiment of public school hypocrisy. Finally, General Gordon, the fallen hero of Khartoum, was portrayed as a dangerous blend of militarism and evangelical religion. In these brief biographies, Strachey tried to show that, for all their Victorian strenuousness, Herculean work and moral earnestness, the one thing that connected his subjects was that their lives ended in failure: Manning successful but soulless; Arnold the author of a preposterous cult of athleticism rather than an avatar of true learning; Gordon adrift in Khartoum in a haze of religious mysticism; and Nightingale a neurotic voice in the wilderness after her Crimean triumph. Such was his judgement on the Victorian world as a whole: its high ideals had led nowhere.

Strachey was far from alone in his typically modernist rejection of the Victorian and Edwardian past; it was a theme that echoed through much of the writing of the 1920s, especially the war memoirs produced at the end of the decade. For the poet Ezra Pound, his peers had died for no more than 'an old bitch . . . a civilization gone in the teeth' (Pound, 1975: 101). Similarly, the enigmatic modernist landmark that was T.S. Eliot's poem *The Waste Land* (1922), with its imagery of death, ruin and decay, proclaimed that the 'Son of Man' knew little other than 'a heap of broken images'. If war memoirs recalled a tranquil pre-war world, they did so in order to reiterate the fact that it had, as the modernists supposed, gone forever. For the former infantry officer Richard Aldington, the pre-war period was 'like pre-history' (Aldington, 1929: 199). Even those who recorded the pre-war world with affection as a time of peace did so with ambivalence.

For the women who, by virtue of the war, escaped the domestic confinement of middle-class life to engage in a world of work and duty, the contrast with the past was

Plate 3.1 Portrait of Lytton Strachey by Dora Carrington, 1916 (© Bridgeman Art Library).

even more compelling and their ambivalence about the effects of the war more uncertain. In the memoir *Testament of Youth* (1933), Vera Brittain, for instance, recalled her pre-war existence in provincial Buxton as a time of enervating inactivity and lack of opportunity. This was in stark contrast to her wartime experience as a nurse, shattering personal bereavements and growing political awareness. The war seemed to her, and others, to have destroyed the gender hierarchies and prudish morals of the Edwardian world. Virginia Woolf, reflecting on the war in 1929, commented that the whole tradition of romanticism had lost its force. An entire Victorian language, 'the illusion which inspired Tennyson and Christina Rossetti to sing so passionately about the coming of their loves', had become endangered. But, she continued in modernist mode, if the ideals of the past were illusions, 'why not praise the catastrophe, whatever it was, that destroyed illusion and put truth in its place?' (Woolf, 1929: 16).

Paul Fussell, himself a former Second World War infantryman, has suggested that together, all these post-war writings and memoirs demonstrate a distinctively 'modern' sensibility. For Fussell, the keynote of the war memoir was irony and, he continues, it is this sentiment which has informed British and European culture ever since. In the memoirs of former soldiers like Robert Graves and Edmund Blunden, Fussell finds not only the mordant black humour of trench wit in the face of appalling slaughter, but also a sense of 'hope abridged'. In the trenches of the Great War, gleaming ideals of Honour, Glory and Victory met the daily realities of ignominious and random death in a seemingly aimless cause. This sense of the ridiculousness of the war was picked out in soldiers' memoirs by individually tragic and ironic events: Graves singing music hall songs on the fire step before going over the top at the battle of Loos in 1915; Siegfried Sassoon capturing a German trench single-handedly and then sitting in it reading poetry before retreating for want of anything better to do; the needless deaths of an entire company insufficiently warned about the location of enemy shellfire; or the absurd image of officers going over the top at the battle of the Somme breezily kicking a football towards the enemy machine guns (Fussell, 1977). For Graves, this kind of juxtaposition was a more accurate way of recalling the spirit of the war than simple documentary realism. In remembering its strange turns and disorientating occurrences his maxim was always that 'the most painful chapters have to be the jokiest'.

The war seemed, then, to mark a complete break with the past and to have encouraged a repudiation of the traditions which had contributed to the catastrophe. In this sense, it appeared to be both an echo and reinforcement of the themes of pre-war modernism. At the very least, the war and modernist art fed off each other. At the front, the deadening activities of military discipline, the cold, the damp and the mud stripped men's consciousness down to their physical needs. Finer feelings were of little use. Many soldiers reported a sensation of returning to a primitive state in which physical safety, shelter and food were their daily preoccupations. Likewise, culture seemed to have been stripped away and replaced by the same atavistic, vital primitivism that was celebrated in modernist art, such as Stravinsky's ballet *Rite of Spring* (1913). Language became truncated and, as Woolf discerned, an existing vocabulary of sentiment seemed to lose meaning and to be rendered unnecessary in the same way that Dadaist poetry rejected all sense. Similarly, French military camouflage artists were inspired by pre-war Cubist art (Kern, 1983: 303).

However, we should be careful with ideas which seem to locate modernity or a 'modern sensibility' so accurately. As we have seen, much of the novelty of modernism was self-proclaimed and its precepts were largely confined to artistic elites like the Bloomsbury Group. It is, for instance, difficult to establish irony as a key mode of expression beyond a small group of writers and artists. Although the war saw massive social changes, such as the increased employment of women, state intervention in the economy and the beginnings of welfare measures, these shifts had either begun before 1914 or were rapidly reversed once the war was over.

Jay Winter has also argued that the idea of the war as the beginning of modernity is thoroughly overstated. Modernism, he implies, was little more than the preserve of an artistic avant garde. Moreover, ideas like psychoanalysis, which were so important to intellectuals, barely registered with the majority of the population, in spite of the fact that they caught on more strongly during the war. Winter suggests that traditional ways of thinking persisted during and after the war and were a much stronger presence in British and European culture than the paradoxes of modernism or an evanescent modern sensibility. The persistence of tradition can be found most strongly expressed just where Fussell finds the strongest presence of modernity: in the memory of war. Winter suggests several ways in which memorializing the war preserved traditional beliefs and practices, the strongest of which were the rituals of bereavement. These customs were consciously aimed at linking the present and the past by drawing upon traditional and familiar imagery. Notably, Winter argues that war memorials and their associated rituals of remembrance linked soldiers' deaths with the past by invoking an existing vocabulary of funerary symbols. War memorials made reference to a warrior tradition, highlighted the sacrifice of soldiers and the everlasting debt of the civilian population, and employed a familiar repertoire of Christian imagery. The old ideals of community, religion, romanticism, duty, honour and a worship of tradition, notions supposedly destroyed by the war, had, Winter concludes, survived relatively intact (Winter, 1995: 115).

The enduring nature of the Victorian past can also be glimpsed in the fact that, for many of the bereaved, the dead were still a vital presence in their lives. The particularly Victorian phenomenon of spiritualism enjoyed a revival during and after the war as families tried to contact their dead. Spiritualist activity attracted many famous writers and intellectuals: Sir Arthur Conan Doyle, creator of Sherlock Holmes, the poet Rudyard Kipling and respected scientists like Sir Oliver Lodge sought to contact their dead sons through the agency of a medium. Although the forces of modernity and scientific enquiry tended towards the secularization of the world, and modernism aspired to tear down such superstitions, it seemed that a faith in religious symbolism had not died out at all. In the aftermath of the war, Winter suggests, these traditional beliefs and symbols took on an even greater force than before because they were fundamentally necessary to the process of comforting the bereaved. Sites of memory were not necessarily sites of modernity, still less of irony.

In Focus

The Bloomsbury Group

The Bloomsbury Group – so called because its social world centred on the Bloomsbury area of central London – was a loose association of friends and acquaintances, writers, artists and intellectuals, who thrived in the innovative cultural atmosphere of early modernism. The best-known members of the group included writers Lytton Strachey, E.M. Forster, Leonard and Virginia Woolf, the artists Clive and Vanessa Bell, Duncan Grant, Roger Fry and Dora Carrington and the great economist John Maynard Keynes. Together, the Bloomsbury group formed a small but influential cultural avant garde which, although not explicitly political, was sympathetic to many progressive

The Bloomsbury Group

causes and, in some cases, to socialism. Many of the ideas that were promoted by Bloomsbury, such as sexual freedom, pacifism, psychoanalysis and feminism, became common features of British culture after the 1960s. This led some subsequent critics to either celebrate or denounce them as precursors of the 'permissive society'. For contemporaries, however, it was Bloomsbury's rejection of the ideals of their parents and of the Victorian world as a whole which resonated most strongly.

Some of the leading lights of the group, notably Strachey and Keynes, met as undergraduates at Cambridge University where they had been members of the secret intellectual elite known as the Apostles, supposedly made up of the 12 cleverest undergraduates. There, many of the group had been influenced by the philosophy of G.E. Moore and, in particular, his book *Principia Ethica* (1903) which preached the intrinsic worth of friendship, art and the inner life. From about 1904 onwards, Strachey began to socialize regularly with Viriginia Stephen (later Woolf), her brother Thoby and her sister Vanessa Bell at their family house at 46 Gordon Square, Bloomsbury. The group's tendency towards insularity, arrogant contempt for conventional morality and subversive humour was demonstrated when they first came to public attention in 1910 for the Dreadnought Hoax. A Bloomsbury hanger-on, Horace de Vere Cole, along with Virginia Stephen, two of her siblings and several others, disguised themselves in full make-up and costume as the 'Abyssinian royal family' and successfully demanded an official inspection of the navy's flagship, HMS *Dreadnought*.

More substantial achievements were to follow, however, and a whole host of new ideas about life and art from Cubism to psychoanalysis and literary modernism were to find their way into British cultural life through Bloomsbury's influence. In art, Roger Fry and Clive Bell were instrumental in bringing Van Gogh, Cezanne and Gaugin, as well as modernists such as Picasso and Matisse, to the attention of the British public, most notably through Fry's 1910 Post-Impressionist exhibition. Bloomsbury artists like Clive and Vanessa Bell, Duncan Grant and Fry himself helped to popularize modernism in their own work and collaborated in the Omega Workshops, founded by Fry in 1913, to explore its new aesthetic theories. In literature, Bloomsbury's influence was enormous, ranging from the novels of E.M. Forster and Virginia Woolf, through Strachey's biographies, to Bell and Fry's writings on art. In addition, Strachey's brother James and his wife Alix were pioneers of psychoanalysis to the extent that James took on the task of translating the work of Freud into English. Other notable writers, such as Rupert Brooke and Gerald Brennan, were also associated with Bloomsbury at some point in their careers. Although much of the output of the group, including the writings of Forster and Strachey, was never explicitly modernist, Woolf in particular made use of modernist motifs such as the idea of the unconscious, especially in *Mrs Dalloway* (1925).

> ### The Bloomsbury Group

For many of their conservative critics, the 'Bloomsberries' appeared to be a sinister and secretive sect who, from the comfort of upper-middle-class life, extended a subversive influence throughout British art and letters. Even fellow modernists, such as the artist Wyndham Lewis, denounced their apparent elitism and snobbery. The impression of radicalism which suggested itself to their more conservative critics was reinforced by two things: the pacificism of the group and its open disdain for moral convention in personal and sexual relationships. During the First World War, Strachey (although medically unfit for combat) was repeatedly called upon to justify his conscientious objection and abstention from any sort of war work in front of a series of military panels. When one of these tribunals asked Strachey what he would do if he saw a German soldier raping his sister, he replied with characteristic wit that he would 'try to come between them'. This pacifism later encouraged descendants of the original Bloomsberries to conscientiously object during the Second World War.

In the 1910s and 20s, Bloomsbury's unconventional attitude to morality, marriage and personal intimacy also contained a strong hint of subversion. Drawing on the teachings of G.E. Moore, they venerated the ideals of honesty and openness in personal matters, even though they did not necessarily live up to them. Many of the group were homosexual or bisexual and their ethos emphasized personal attachment without jealousy rather than marital commitment. As one anonymous observer put it, 'all the couples were triangles and they lived in squares' (Holroyd, 1971: 41). Strachey and Keynes were homosexual and the typical Bloomsbury marriage was far from ordinary. Strachey himself enjoyed a passionate friendship with Dora Carrington, with whom he set up house in the 1920s, although his main sexual interest was in her husband Ralph Partridge. Carrington was so devoted to Strachey that on hearing of his death in 1932 she took her own life.

The reputation of Bloomsbury went into eclipse after 1945 but was revived in the 1960s when their attacks on Victorian morals began to gain increasing respect. Since then, Strachey has come to be seen as the founder of modern biography while Virginia Woolf has become one of the most respected authors in the feminist canon. Although their perceived elitism has made the Bloomsbury group as a whole unfashionable in contemporary Britain, their legacy remains the same as it was when summed up by the *Times* in 1949: 'tolerance, intelligence, seriousness about art and scepticism about the pretensions of the self-important'.

Debates and Interpretations
Towards or away from modernity?

Winter argues that despite the avalanche of modernist art and trench memoir that accompanied the war and its aftermath, there were substantial continuities with the pre-war period. People clung to older, comforting images and practices as a way of dealing with the traumatic events of the war. It was not until after the Second World War, Winter suggests, that there was a decisive breach with tradition. After 1945, it became necessary to thoroughly remake Britain, to reconstruct Europe and the world as a more pacific and ordered community. The changes ushered in by post-Second World War governments were enormous: the welfare state, immigration, decolonization, the economic boom which produced the affluent society of the 1950s and 60s and the sexual revolution.

Much of this reconstruction, at least in the immediate post-1945 period, was done in the name of modernization and in the style of artistic modernism. The chief example of this was the 1951 Festival of Britain, devoted to displaying all that was best and new in British design, architecture and scientific achievement. By that point, the idea of the modern was increasingly invoked as a measure of worth and as the keynote of Britain's post-war renewal (Conekin *et al.*, 1999). The tenets of modernism, especially in architecture, urban planning and the design of household products, were also increasingly accepted, although shorn of their more revolutionary overtones. This trend was reflected in many forms, from adventurous textile designs to the remodelling of British town centres and public housing in the 1950s and 60s according to the functional principles of modernism. In practice, this often meant flat roofs, swathes of concrete, angular or 'brutalist' office blocks and shopping complexes and motorways through city centres.

The derision which the redesigned 1960s town centre now attracts shows how far we have come from the seemingly simple post-1945 faith in planning, modernist architecture and newness. There is much more scepticism concerning the idea that grand schemes of social and material reorganization will work in the manner intended. This has led some historians to question whether the age of modernity that is described above, and the faith in progress and rationality that characterized it, has come to an end. Have many of the features which were held to define modernity as a chronological period disappeared or declined to the point of inefficacy? Are we, in short, living in a 'post-modern' age? On the one hand, it would seem that the industrial capitalism of heavy industry and its associated social classes have lost their former significance in the economy and politics, that the nation-state is increasingly powerless in the face of unregulated international capital and digital communication, that secularism is on the retreat across the globe in the face of renewed religious fundamentalism, and that cities are ailing rather than vital. Moreover, we seem to live in an age where the possibility of confident progress is increasingly questioned and where faith in the application of rationality and bureaucratic systems to solve problems decisively is in decline. The only certainty, it seems, is change.

The question is whether these developments are a new kind of postmodernity or merely a reinforcement of existing trends. Some historians and theorists argue that what we now call globalization is merely the intensification of the economic and cultural processes which have characterized modernity. Capitalism, although no longer based in heavy industry in Europe and America, does take this form in China, South America and some other parts of the world. And although Europe no longer bases its political systems on class identification, it could be argued that migrant labour in Europe and labour forces within those countries which are in thrall to their European and American trading partners make up a new global 'proletariat'. Also, imperialism in the form of American foreign policy seems to have recently reinvented itself.

Yet even though this may be the case, some writers claim to detect in global culture a questioning of modernity and its processes which might be said to be integral to modernity itself. As the sociologist Zygmunt Bauman has pointed out, while modernity produces order, certainty and progress, it also generates feelings of confusion, restlessness and ambivalence, all of which highlight the limits of modernity. For Bauman, postmodernity is described as this recognition of limitations, facing up to the fact that 'certainty is not to be' and that change has no clear destination (Bauman, 1991). Maybe this set of feelings and processes, rather than the immediate disillusion of the First World War, is responsible for the tangible presence of irony and detachment within the modern sensibility. Perhaps postmodernity and modernity are not fundamentally opposed, but aspects of each other. Both try to detect and mark out a break with the past and, at some level, both have a similar ambivalent sensibility that can perhaps be located in Britain's twentieth century.

Further reading

For recent essays on modernity, see Martin Daunton and Bernhard Reiger (eds) *Meanings of Modernity: Britain From the Late-Victorian Era to World War II* (Oxford, 2001). With sections on popular culture and selfhood, historical dimensions of modernity and Empire, the collection represents a comprehensive introduction to notions of modernity and how historians have deployed them. For the later period, Becky Conekin, Frank Mort and Chris Waters (eds) *Moments of Modernity: Reconstructing Britain 1945–1964* (London, 1999) addresses themes including politics, architecture, photography and gender.

The classic theorists of modernity are Karl Marx and Max Weber, for which see Marx, *Capital* (1886, many reprints). Weber's thoughts about modernity are not all in one place, but good introductions include Stanislas Andreski (ed. and trans.) *Max Weber on Capitalism, Bureaucracy and Religion* (London, 1983) and Scott Lash and Sam Whimster (eds) *Max Weber: Rationality and Modernity* (London, 1987). Significant later theorists include Georg Simmel, for which see Kurt H. Wolff, *The Sociology of Georg Simmel* (Glencoe, 1964) and, especially for his writings on Baudelaire, Walter Benjamin, for which see Hannah Arendt (ed.) *Illuminations: Walter Benjamin* (London, 1992) and Walter Benjamin, *The Arcades Project* (Cambridge, MA, 2002). The legacy of these thinkers has been reinterpreted by many contemporary writers, the most important of whom are probably Jürgen Habermas, *The Structural Transformation of the Public Sphere: An Enquiry into a Category of Bourgeois Society* (Cambridge, 1989), Jean-François Lyotard, *The Post Modern Condition: A Report on Knowledge* (Manchester, 1984), Bruno Latour, *We Have Never Been Modern* (Cambridge, MA, 1993), Frederic Jameson, *Postmodernism, or the Cultural Logic of Late Capitalism* (London, 1991), David Harvey, *The Condition of Postmodernity: An Enquiry into Cultural Change* (Oxford, 1989) and Zygmunt Bauman, *Modernity and Ambivalence* (Cambridge, 1991).

References

Aldington, Richard (1929, repr. 1984) *Death of a Hero*. London: Hogarth.

Bauman, Zygmunt (1991) *Modernity and Ambivalence*. Oxford: Polity.

Bradbury, Malcolm and McFarlane, James (eds) (1991) *Modernism: A Guide to European Literature, 1890–1930*. Harmondsworth: Penguin.

Charvet, P.E. (1972) 'The Painter of Modern Life', in *Baudelaire: Selected Writings on Art and Literature*. London: Penguin.

Conekin, Becky, Mort, Frank and Waters, Chris (eds) (1999) *Moments of Modernity: Reconstructing Britain 1945–1964*. London: Rivers Oram.

Daunton, Martin and Rieger, Bernhard (eds) (2001) *Meanings of Modernity: Britain From the Late-Victorian Era to World War II*. Oxford: Berg.

Fussell, Paul (1977) *The Great War and Modern Memory*. London: Oxford University Press.

Holroyd, Michael (1971) *Lytton Strachey and the Bloomsbury Group: His Work, Their Influence*. Harmondsworth: Penguin.

Kern, Stephen (1983) *The Culture of Time and Space 1880–1918*. London: Weidenfeld & Nicolson.

Keynes, Geoffrey (ed.) (1970) *Rupert Brooke, the Poetical Works*. London: Faber and Faber.

Pound, Ezra (1975) *Selected Poems*. London: Faber and Faber.

Winter, Jay (1995) *Sites of Memory, Sites of Mourning: The Great War in European Cultural History*. Cambridge: Cambridge University Press.

Woolf, Virginia (1929 repr. 1977) *A Room of One's Own*. St Albans: Triad.

4

Class and gender

Stephen Brooke

CLASS AND GENDER WERE the most important categories of social identity in twentieth-century Britain, at least before post-1948 immigration ushered in a multiracial society. Class was inextricably linked to British national character. To George Orwell, writing as German bombs fell on London in 1940, Britain was the 'most class-ridden country under the sun'. Gender divisions may be less peculiar to British society than class, but they similarly structured public and private life. This chapter sets out the main factors influencing the understanding and experience of class and gender, focusing in particular upon the economy, war and political change.

Class

First of all, what do we mean by class? The traditional Marxist definition of class associated it with the economy and work, situating class in the fundamental enmity between the interests of those who owned and those who worked. In this model, class was produced by the exploitation of labour in capitalist society. The economy and work continue to influence how we think about class. Until relatively recently, the schema used by official surveys to categorize the British population was organized around occupational differences; the most important divisions were between manual and non-manual workers and between skilled and unskilled manual workers. But class cannot be fully understood only with reference to the economy and work. It is shaped by many other factors, such as family background and upbringing, education, politics and culture.

We might make three general observations about defining class. First of all, class has been used as a category for identifying and understanding social and economic difference in modern society. Second, the concept of class has been deployed to make sense of, and to challenge, the social and economic inequality that characterized British society in the twentieth century. One glimpse of such inequality is through the distribution of wealth: in 1900, the wealthiest 10 per cent of the population enjoyed 90 per cent of its total wealth; in 1990, the hold of the top 10 per cent had weakened but still stood at 51 per cent of total wealth in Britain. The final observation is that class has never been a monolithic or homogeneous thing but, rather, an uneven and shifting landscape. When speaking of working-class identity, for instance, it is important to acknowledge that the working class was made up of different groups with important divisions between skilled and unskilled workers, the employed and the poor and, more abstractly, the rough and the respectable.

However we define it, class had real purchase in the lives of twentieth-century Britons. It had far-reaching political and economic consequences involving the unequal distribution of power, authority and wealth. But the reach of class extended far beyond the public sphere. It was written on life and death: at the turn of the twenty-first century, for example, the life expectancy of professional men was 7.4 years greater than men engaged in unskilled manual jobs; infant mortality among the professional classes was 3.6 per 1000 births against 7.2 per 1000 births among the unskilled working classes. Even sex was affected by class. Before the National Health Service instituted a system of free and universal health care in 1948, there were class differences in access to contraception and sexual information meaning that reproduction (and reproductive health) and the technicalities of sexual intimacy could be very different experiences for middle- and working-class women. Nor should we forget the long psychological reach of class. In 1986, for example, the historian Carolyn Steedman wrote of the enduring legacy of class difference, even in an era where the lines between classes had blurred: 'I read a woman's book, meet such a woman at a party (a woman now, like me) and think quite deliberately as we talk: we are divided: a hundred years ago I'd have been cleaning your shoes' (1986: 2).

One of the most important questions concerning class is its effect upon social mobility in twentieth-century Britain. Were people able to move upwards, within or between classes? Can one escape class? What effect have changes in work and educational reform had on mobility? The evidence from the twentieth century has produced considerable division among historians and sociologists. In the 1980s, a major sociological survey concluded that the relationship between individuals' class position and their class origins was 'essentially the same in its extent and pattern as that which existed in the interwar period and even . . . as that which would have been found at the start of the century' (Goldthorpe *et al.*, 1987: 327). This echoed an earlier sociological survey which concluded that social status in Britain operated within 'a closed circuit' conditioned by origins and education (Glass, 1954: 51). A more recent historical examination has questioned the rigidity of class society, arguing instead that there was some fluidity in class position, certainly within the working classes and, to some extent, between the working and the middle classes (Miles, 1999). Clearly, the relationship between class and social mobility is one that demands more research.

Gender

By gender we mean the social understanding of sexual difference between men and women. If class as a category of identity arises from production, gender emerges from reproduction. A historical understanding of gender is not simply the history of men or the history of women, but the meanings that society has made, in political, economic and cultural terms, of masculinity and femininity. Like class, gender had profound social and political consequences in the twentieth century. To be a man, up to 1928, was to have more formal political rights than women. To be a man, up to and including the present day, was usually to earn more for the same job than a woman. Unequal political rights and unequal pay are but two of the meanings that British society has made of sexual difference.

As with class, the social lives of ordinary Britons have been determined by gender. A woman of 1900 or 1950 could expect that what she did and how she participated in society would be shaped by her gender, in a way that was not true of a man. In 1900, a woman could not have voted and would have found many doors closed to her in terms of work and education. Simply living independently of a man, whether this was a husband or a father, would have been difficult. Fifty years later, the public sphere was more open to women but the primary role expected of a woman remained that of motherhood. By 2000, perhaps the most basic and far-reaching change in British society was that being a woman did not necessarily hold the same limitations that it had 100 years before.

Why speak of class and gender together? The simple answer is that talking about class often involves talking about gender and vice versa. In 1963, for example, the historian E.P. Thompson offered a famous and highly gendered definition of class: 'class happens when some men, as a result of common experiences (inherited or shared), feel and articulate the identity of their interests as between themselves, and against other men whose interests are different from (and usually opposed to) theirs. The class experience is largely determined by the productive relations into which men are born – or enter involuntarily' (1963: 8–9). For Thompson, class at its most essential was a male experience, born in the workplace and nurtured in the pub and coffee house, spheres that excluded women. This reflected a long-standing and gendered understanding of what being working class meant. From the mid-nineteenth century through much of the twentieth century, for example, the economic aims of the working class, articulated through the trade union movement, focused on achieving a 'breadwinner' or 'family' wage, a wage that would enable a man to support his wife and children. The 'class' aim of obtaining a better wage from employers was thus also a statement about gender: men were meant to work and women were meant to be in the home. This has influenced many aspects of historical development, whether we think of trade union history or the formation of the welfare state. Thinking about class inevitably involves thinking about gender identity.

Class and the economy

In the twentieth century, class structure in Britain retained the same pyramidal shape it had in the nineteenth century: a small aristocracy of landed wealth sitting above a much larger mass of middle- and working-class people. What changed was the relative size and strength of each group. The twentieth century is often characterized as witnessing the decline of the aristocracy. Certainly this is true in terms of formal political power. By the 1930s, aristocrat-politicians were the exception rather than the rule. But we should not underestimate the continuing economic and social power of the aristocracy in Britain. After all, at the end of the century, a landed aristocrat, the Duke of Westminster, remained one of the richest men in Britain because of his vast property holdings in London. And the richest woman? The Queen, of course. One irony of the modern age is the persistent cultural presence of the aristocracy in British life through the popular media's obsession with the pomp, circumstance, marital woes and behaviour of the Royal Family.

There has been a clear shift in the balance of class society over the twentieth century. Between 1900 and the 1940s, the country was a working-class nation, with around three-quarters of the population classified as working class. Since the Second World War, the percentage of the labour force identified as working class has decreased from 60.6 per cent in 1961 to 49.6 per cent in 1981 to 38.4 per cent in 1991. This decline has been matched by an increase in those occupying middle-class jobs, particularly in areas of science, technology and management. In 1921, only 4 per cent of the workforce was characterized as occupying professional, scientific or managerial jobs. Sixty years later, nearly 13.6 per cent had the same jobs. Britain thus became a more middle-class nation as the century wore on.

If the balance of class society has changed over the twentieth century, its lifeblood – a sense of difference between social and occupational groups fuelled by the perception of economic inequality and opposing economic interests – has persisted. Though there has been increasing improvement in the standard of living for most Britons since the Second World War, income inequality in fact widened in the last decades of the century, leading some to argue that class differences have also sharpened (Westergard, 2001: 68–79). Other economic experiences have also thrown the lines of difference between the working and middle classes into sharp relief. The twin demons of the modern economy – inflation and unemployment – moved along class lines. Unemployment has largely been a working-class experience, whether in the interwar period or in the 1980s. Even in periods of prosperity, this experience haunted working-class memory. For middle-class people, inflation was the great threat because it undercut the security of those living on fixed salaries without the advantage of bargaining power. This was particularly apparent in the 1920s and the 1970s.

Class identity also found an institutional expression in the trade union movement. The trade unions were explicit class organizations, designed to define and protect workers' interests (over wages and conditions of work) against employers. The trade union movement showed considerable growth in the twentieth century. In 1900, there were about 1 million organized workers; by 1980, there were 12 million. Though middle-class people (particularly in the public services) joined unions in larger numbers after the 1960s, trade unionism has largely been associated with working-class economic interests. Industrial conflict between organized workers and employers was a recurrent feature of British life in the twentieth century. In three decades – the 1910s, 1920s and

Plate 4.1 Protesters on the Jarrow Crusade demonstration march by unemployed men from the shipyard town of Jarrow, Tyneside, to London to demand the right to work (© Hulton Archive /Getty).

the 1970s – such activity reached epic proportions. In 1912, there were nearly 41 million working days lost to strikes involving 1.4 million workers. Eight years later, 1.8 million workers were on strike for a total of 85.8 million working days. The picture was not so different at the end of the century. In 1979, 2 million workers were involved in 4500 strikes. By contrast, 1992 was a quiet year with only half a million days lost, involving just 148,000 workers. There were important turning points in this narrative: the General Strike of 1926, when the trade union movement faced off against the government for nine days; the series of strikes by miners, rail workers and power workers between 1972 and 1974 that led to the declaration of a state of emergency; strikes by public sector unions during the 'winter of discontent' of 1978–9 which helped set the stage for the election victory of Margaret Thatcher; and the miners' strike of 1984–5 that effectively signalled the collapse of trade union power.

If the economy often demonstrated the vibrancy of class tension, it is important to acknowledge that economic change at times also helped blunt such tensions and blur the lines between classes. In the 1950s, for example, working-class people enjoyed full employment and higher wages, a security buttressed by the new welfare state. Levels of consumer spending, once limited to middle-class people, spread through the working classes and were marked by the acquisition of televisions, washing machines, cars and even homes. This led to speculation that economic class difference was becoming less important and that the country was witnessing a 'new fluidity' in class structure (Hinden, 1960). This became known as the 'embourgeoisement' of the working classes. It is similarly believed that Margaret Thatcher's economic reforms resulted in a less constrained class society, with working-class people buying homes in record numbers and, if in work, enjoying greater consumer power. The economic line between the working and middle classes became more difficult to discern by the end of the century, leaving some to question the relevancy of class as a means of understanding British society.

Nor should we forget that economic experience brought significant changes within and not just between classes. Perhaps the most dramatic change has been the steady drop in the number of working-class people in the manufacturing industry and a concomitant increase in those in the service sector. In 1911, a third of working-class people were engaged in manufacturing. By 2002, the service sector was eclipsing manufacturing as the main employer of working-class men and women. Apart from gender, the greatest division within the working class was between skilled and unskilled workers, a divide that structured wages. As the century progressed, skilled jobs fell in number as those in unskilled or semi-skilled work rose. In the latter decades of the twentieth century, particularly with reforms enacted during the 1980s which undercut union power, changes within the working classes were accompanied by a decline of trade union membership. In 1971, the eight largest unions in Britain had 5,442,000 members; 20 years later, they had 4,301,000. Union density – the percentage of those workers represented by unions – also dropped in the same period from 47.7 per cent in 1970 to 34.3 per cent in 1991.

These changes have encouraged the belief that the working classes are in the midst of 'disintegration' (Taylor, 2005). Early in the twentieth century, it was possible to speak of a coherent working class, united in a common experience of work and represented by the trade union movement. In 1927, for example, in the *Trade Union Annual Congress Report*, George Hicks talked of the shared social topography of 'our people', one of 'labour in the mines and mills, the workshops and factories'. That landscape had changed profoundly by the late twentieth century. After eighteen years of anti-trade union legislation under a Conservative government (1979–97), trade unions' ability to represent the working classes through collective bargaining was fatally weakened. There were increasing divisions within the working classes; fewer and fewer working-class people made things, being employed, instead, in the service sector. Hicks had also talked of 'grinding poverty' uniting working people. Again, this was not true in the late twentieth century; those in work enjoyed higher standards of living. The real divide was between those in work and those who were unemployed.

In these ways, it is possible to see that class lost its unifying experiences and articulations. It might also be suggested that other ideologies have replaced collectivism as the dominant ethos shaping British society. The Thatcher and Blair years led to a greater emphasis on individualism. A longer-term change has been the rise of consumerism as a kind of social identity (Hilton, 2003). Whether particular class identities have been, or can be, constructed from consumption as much as from production needs further examination. But have the seeds of economic class difference – inequality and exploitation – disappeared? Most contemporary surveys indicate that income inequality actually increased in the late twentieth century, not decreased (Brewer *et al.*, 2005: 46). In 1927, George Hicks railed against the exploitation faced by working people. Such exploitation has not disappeared if we consider the plight of low-paid workers. But it does seem that inequality and exploitation are not read in the same way at the beginning of the twenty-first century; in particular, they do not necessarily lead to an overarching sense of class identity and difference.

Class, war and representation

If we look beyond the economy, we can see that other factors have also been critical in shaping a 'class society'. War punctuated the British experience in the twentieth century. Victory in the 'total' wars of 1914–18 and 1939–45 depended upon the mobilization of economic resources, of which the most important was labour. As a result, in both world wars, the organized working classes emerged with greater strength within British society. This was symbolized in a variety of ways, such as the presence of trade union leaders like Arthur Henderson and Ernest Bevin within the corridors of power, the new influence trade unions had with employers and the state, and the higher wages enjoyed by working people because of the high demand for labour. The rhetoric of total war also benefited the working classes. The Second World War was, for example, a 'People's War', founded on an ethos of 'fair shares' and 'equality of sacrifice'. Such rhetoric went against the grain of an unequal and divided society. The comprehensive rationing of consumer goods backed up the rhetoric of 'fair shares', representing an exercise in social levelling. Visions of a 'people's peace' that would follow the end of hostilities also promised greater material security and equality for working-class people. The welfare state and state-managed full employment that emerged under the Labour government of 1945–50 did not bring an end to class society but they substantially improved the lot of the working classes within British society.

But we should not think that war entirely dulled the edges of class tension. The First World War produced an embattled middle class, left insecure by the growing confidence and wages of the organized working classes. The Second World War is remembered for moments of social unity and communal triumph clothed in references to the spirit of Dunkirk and the Blitz but this did not stop the dissonance of class tension breaking through such harmonious choruses. The evacuation of school children and their mothers from urban to rural areas in the early years of the war may have tugged at Britons' conscience by exposing the poor conditions in which many working people lived, for example, but it was also an exercise in class tension, particularly between urban, working-class women and their rural, middle-class hosts. Class tensions continued to be played out at the workplace and in war service (Hinton, 2002; Rose, 2003).

Politics also changed class society. In a very basic way, middle-class and aristocratic people had more formal political rights than working-class people in the first half of the century. Before 1918, to vote one had to own property or pay local rates. This enfranchised many, but not all working-class men, favouring, instead, middle-class and aristocratic men. The Representation of the People Act (1918) gave the vote to all men over 21 without reference to any property or local tax qualifications. But the owner-ship of property and a university education continued to entitle some Britons to more votes than their fellow citizens. If one owned a business or was a university graduate, one was entitled to vote in more than one constituency. This was, of course, largely a privilege enjoyed by middle-class people. Such plural voting was finally abolished in 1948. One could say, therefore, that it took nearly half a century for British democracy to become, at least theoretically, 'classless'. Politics also affected the institutional expression of class. In the 1920s and the 1980s, Conservative governments limited the powers of trade unions, undermining their ability to represent working-class interests, with legislation such as the Trade Disputes Act (1927), the Employment Act (1982), the Trade Union Act (1984) and Employment Acts in 1988 and 1989.

It would be impossible to talk about class in Britain without talking about educa-tion. School and university education (or lack of) helped determine class position almost as much as work. The divisions within British education – most notably between the state and private sector, but also between the kinds of state school – have helped sustain other divisions of class and status. Educational reformers, particularly on the Left, long saw the classroom as the cauldron of class society. Although educa-tional reform in twentieth-century Britain successfully extended access to primary, sec-ondary and post-secondary education, it did little to change the relationship between class and education. In 1944, for example, the Education Act provided secondary edu-cation to the entire population. There is little question that this led to some working-class boys and girls moving upwards through British society in the 1950s and 1960s. Yet the reforms of the 1940s did not extinguish class society. Indeed, they may have helped sustain it. Private education was left virtually intact and with considerable social cachet and power. The state secondary system was organized as a 'tripartite' structure, with three kinds of school – technical, secondary modern and grammar – reflecting divisions between working- and middle-class people. That this was perceived as a problem led to the attempt in 1965 to establish a non-selective system with one kind of school, the comprehensive. At the close of the twentieth century – at a point when it was often assumed that class did not matter – education remained a sensitive subject, not least because of the acknowledged relationship between education, class position and social opportunity. Education continues to be a dividing line: working-class people still participate at much lower levels, for example, than middle-class people in university education.

Gender: women's progress and men's place

If class was one fault line in twentieth-century Britain, gender was another crucial mark of social difference. This was particularly stark in political terms. In 1900, women were not allowed to vote in national elections. Over the next half-century, perhaps the most obvious political change involving gender was the lifting of the prohibition on women formally participating in politics, either as voters or politicians. In 1907, the stage of local politics was opened to women, allowing them to run for local office. After a long campaign for the national suffrage, women over 30 and property-owning women obtained the vote in 1918. In 1928, voting equality between the sexes was fully realized when the Equal Franchise Act gave all women over 21 years the vote on the same basis as men. A further hurdle was cleared 30 years later when women were admitted to the House of Lords. If political participation was formally 'classless' in 1948, it became formally 'genderless' in 1958.

The march towards formal political equality between men and women was complemented by the lifting of restrictions on women in areas such as work, education and the law. In the nineteenth century, the ideological notion that men and women inhabited 'separate spheres' (with men traversing the public world of politics, work and economics while women were confined to a domestic sphere associated with motherhood and marriage) circumscribed women's public and productive roles. This is not to say that women did not work or have public roles before the twentieth century. Working-class women always worked and middle-class women ventured into the public sphere with philanthropic endeavours. But women's public roles remained bound by the constraints of a restrictive gender ideology. The industries in which women could be employed and the hours they could work were governed by what was called 'protective' legislation, identifying women as different employees to men. The 1850 Factory Act prohibited women from working at night; a further Factory Act in 1937 limited women to working 48 hours a week. Until the mid-twentieth century, trade unions were reluctant to allow women to take up skilled jobs and often indifferent to recruiting women workers. Life for middle-class and aristocratic women had similar limits. Though Oxford and Cambridge allowed women to read for degrees, they were not allowed to actually receive or take those degrees until the twentieth century. In the interwar period, women were required to resign from the civil service upon marriage.

In the twentieth century, the façade of such gender inequality was slowly chipped away. The two World Wars, it has been argued, had a major impact on gender. During the First World War, women replaced men in skilled jobs, thus exploding one gender-based myth about the physiological and intellectual capacity of female workers. Women also played a crucial role on the home front and in the armed services during the Second World War. The number of women in the labour force rose from 5 million in 1939 to nearly 8 million four years later. In December 1941, conscription was introduced for women. Nearly 500,000 women served in the various auxiliaries of the armed forces, the Women's Royal Naval Service, the Women's Auxiliary Air Force, and the Women Auxiliary Territorial Service. War thus helped complicate the idea of public roles based upon gender, a complication that was recognized in rhetoric across the political spectrum.

Political efforts to legislate towards equality between the sexes were uneven. In the interwar period legislation slowly extended the idea of gender equality, beginning with

Plate 4.2 The Second World War witnessed women moving into jobs perceived as typically masculine. Here, one of the first women 'dustmen' carries refuse from a house in Ilford (© Hulton Archive/Getty).

the Sex Disqualification Act (1919) which dismantled the prohibitions on women's participation in most professions. The New English Law of Property (1926) and the Law Reform (Married Women and Tortfeasors) Act (1935) gave married and single women the power to own and dispose of property like men. Inequity in the workplace was tentatively attacked with the introduction of equal pay to the civil service in 1954. The 1960s, of course, gave rise to the 'second wave' of feminism. This groundswell found legislative form with Equal Pay Acts in 1970 and 1984 and Acts that outlawed discrimination based upon gender, such as the Employment Protection Act (1975) and Sex Discrimination Acts in 1975 and 1989. 'Protective' legislation barring women from particular areas of employment, such as the mines, was finally ended in 1989. The election of Margaret Thatcher as Prime Minister in 1979 was not, by any stretch of the imagination, a feminist triumph but it did symbolize what had changed in terms of the acceptance of new roles for women in the public sphere. More generally, feminist campaigns in the early and late twentieth century challenged the idea of gender inequality.

In such ways, the understandings of femininity changed substantially. In 1900, assumptions concerning gender inequality underpinned areas such as work and politics. In 2000, the theoretical presumption in both spheres was gender equality.

Theory is, of course, different from practice. The most glaring example of a persistent inequality between the sexes comes with equal pay. Throughout the twentieth century, women's pay was a fraction of men's, solely on the basis of gender difference; at the end of the century, after thirty years of equal pay legislation, women still earned between 15 per cent and 20 per cent less than men in the same or similar work. Changes in understandings of femininity were not limited to spheres of work and politics. Perhaps the most important change of all occurred in the private sphere with women's increasing ability to control reproduction. In the late nineteenth century, middle-class women began to limit the size of their families through the deliberate use of contraception. In the twentieth century, this change spread across the class structure as birth control advocates, notably Marie Stopes, established clinics in working-class areas in the 1920s; in 1930 local authorities were allowed to circulate birth control information through maternity and infant welfare centres. Technological advances – most notably, the appearance of a safe and reliable oral contraceptive in the 1960s with the Pill – aided this change. Women's right to control their bodies was also recognized in legislation. The Abortion Act (1967) allowed women to obtain safe, therapeutic abortions. The National Health Service (Family Planning) Act of the same year meant that marital status could not affect women's right to receive contraceptive advice and contraceptives from local health authorities.

Men were, inevitably, affected by changes in women's status and rights. It is impossible to do justice to masculinity in a short chapter, but we can make some general comments. Work was, of course, a foundation of masculine identity. For middle-class men, a steady and secure job, usually with a salary rather than a wage, provided the desired status of being able to support a family and run a home. For the working-class man, independence was crucial to masculine ideals. This independence was marked, ironically, by the dependence of a wife and family. The 'breadwinner' or 'family' wage became the focus of trade union bargaining, with the worker representing his family in the economic sphere. Failure to achieve such security, status or independence, through lack of skill or unemployment, incited a sense of emasculation as well as a fear of poverty. In Walter Greenwood's famous novel of the interwar depression, *Love on the Dole* (1933), the protagonist, an unemployed youth, is mocked for his 'miserable muscles', especially when contrasted to the strapping physique of men building a new road. War also shaped masculinity. In empirical terms, a significant percentage of British men served in the armed forces. By 1945, for example, there were about 4.5 million men in the armed forces, representing nearly 20 per cent of the entire male population. Conscription was introduced in 1916 and again in 1939. The shadow of war extended into peacetime with national service claiming first 12 months and then two years of every young man's life until it ended in 1960. War as much as work helped define men's lives in the twentieth century and its influence could be seen even in the lives of those who did not see or experience it first-hand. Well into the 1970s, for example, the representation and memory of war can be seen shaping British boys and men through the popularity of hobbies associated with military endeavour, such as the building of Airfix kits.

In Focus

Did Britain have class politics?

The divergent fortunes of the Liberal and Labour parties in the first three decades of the twentieth century have provided one way of approaching this important question. The decline of the Liberal party as a force bringing together disparate class interests under one banner has suggested to some historians that class was indeed the major force shaping British electoral politics by the 1920s. Before 1918, it has been argued, the limited franchise constrained the growth of the Labour party; once all working men obtained the vote it was inevitable that they would find their 'natural' class home with Labour. Class was, then, the determinative force in politics. Electoral struggle was between two parties with clear and opposing class associations: Labour and the Conservatives. Without a clear class base, the Liberals withered and died in this new landscape of politics. For some observers, this led to the view that 'class is the basis of British party politics, all else is embellishment and detail'.

There were certainly moments when such a linear relationship between social identity and political action seemed clear. In 1945 and 1950, for example, Labour found particular favour with working-class voters. The 1960s are sometimes considered another high-water mark of class voting. But such moments are the exception rather than the rule. What is much more apparent is a disjuncture between class identity and voting. To be working class, for example, is not necessarily to be a Labour voter. In the first two decades of the century, it was the ability of the Liberals to hold on to working-class votes, against the challenge from Labour, that is most striking, an ability damaged beyond repair not by the rise of the working classes, but by the First World War. Labour grew in the 1920s not merely because of the structural shift of working-class votes, but by an array of factors, not excluding class, but including ideology, locality and circumstance. Had there been a linear relationship between class and voting in the interwar period, one would assume that, given the demographic advantage enjoyed by the working classes, the Labour party would have been the obvious beneficiary. But it was the Conservative party that reaped the fruits of democracy, a success that depended upon a substantial minority of working-class voters voting against what might be assumed to be their 'natural' class interest. For its part, Labour has also done well out of its supposed class enemies; for example, the party's historic landslide of 1945 was most striking in the way the party broke through in middle-class areas.

The post-war period bore further witness to the ambiguities between class and political behaviour. In the 1950s and early 1960s, an unbroken period of Conservative government was built upon newly affluent working-class people decamping from their 'natural' home in the Labour party to vote Conservative.

> ### Did Britain have class politics?
>
> Contemporary left-leaning accounts talked of the disintegration of the 'traditional' working classes precipitating a terminal decline in Labour's electoral fortunes. The 1970s has also been perceived as a period of 'class dealignment', when the differences between classes became more difficult to discern and the links between particular classes and parties disintegrated. This seemed to hurt the Labour party most; again, it was assumed that the decline in class matched a decline in Labour's vote. Thatcher's electoral success depended in part upon votes from a prosperous working class, even when Conservative governments were emasculating the trade union movement. Harking back to the Edwardian period, Tony Blair attempted to make Labour less of a class party by appealing to middle-class voters, nurturing ties with business and giving the cold shoulder to Labour's union partners.
>
> All of this has suggested to some observers that class is not a determinative force in politics. Instead of assuming a clear and almost structural relationship between one class and a party, we are encouraged to think about the ways that political parties construct alliances with particular groups in society, sometimes on class lines, sometimes in ways that have no reference to class. But this should not shove the idea of class politics off the agenda. First of all, recent research on the supposed period of 'class dealignment' in the 1970s and 1980s suggests that class identification and the pursuit of class interests through voting did not disappear; it simply was not, and had never been, something that was easily translatable into one political party or another.

Debates and Interpretations

Class and gender remain important ways of understanding historical change in twentieth-century Britain. As categories of social identity, they have not only been shaped by historical events, but have, admittedly in ambiguous ways, also shaped those events. A short chapter necessitates passing over some important aspects of class and gender in twentieth-century Britain. In particular, gender histories have tended to be pre-occupied with women and feminism and are only just beginning to turn their critical attention to masculinity. Gender as a category of analysis has, in itself, been the subject of debate in recent years. John Tosh, for instance, has urged historians to recognize that studies of gender must engage fully with masculinity as a social category in order to comprehend the shifting meanings of femininity through the modern period (1998).

Class has been subject to similar debates. Notably, a shift in historiography at the end of the twentieth century called for a re-evaluation of class as a historical category. In particular, some historians argued that notions of class identity were too fragmented to render class a useful analytical or descriptive tool: people saw themselves in terms of multiple identities (worker, parent, spouse, son/daughter, feminist, homosexual, vegetarian and so on), only some of which tapped into traditional socio-economic understandings of class. Often referred to as the 'linguistic turn', this school of thought explored the languages – or ways – in which people spoke about themselves and others. More recently, class has begun to regain its footing. Reclaiming class as a tool of analysis, Mike Savage and Andrew Miles have argued that the examination of language is 'unduly restrictive'. Instead, they argue that by making connections between diverse economic, social, cultural and political developments and retaining sensitivity to overlapping identities, it is possible to use class in a constructive way (1994: 17). Moreover, as this chapter has endeavoured to show, the idea of class has such broad purchase that it continues to operate as a clear organizing concept for talking about society throughout most of the modern period.

Further reading

For a comprehensive survey of research into masculinity, see Martin Francis, 'The domestication of the male? Recent research on nineteenth and twentieth century masculinity', *Historical Journal*, 45 (2002), 637–52, and Michael Roper, 'Between manliness and masculinity: the "war generation" and the psychology of fear in Britain, 1914–1950', *Journal of British Studies*, 44 (2005), 343–62. The focus on masculinity and soldiering is particularly well drawn in Graham Dawson, *Soldier Heroes: British Adventure, Empire and the Imagining of Masculinities* (London, 1994) and Matt Houlbrook, 'Soldier heroes and rent boys: homosexuality, masculinities and Britishness in the Brigade of Guards, 1900–1960', *Journal of British Studies* (2003) 42 (3): 351–88. For further material on the relationship between class and gender, see Joanna Bourke, *Working-Class Cultures in Britain 1890–1960: Gender, Class and Ethnicity* (London, 1994); Sally Alexander, *Becoming a Woman and Other Essays* (London, 1996); and Stephen Brooke, 'Gender and working-class identity in Britain during the 1950s', *Journal of Social History* 34 (2001), 773–95. Popular culture and leisure also saw intersections of class and gender. Perhaps the best example of this is the excellent book by Jonathan Rose, *The Intellectual Life of the British Working Classes* (New Haven, 2002).

The political manifestations of class have garnered considerable historical attention. For an overview of debates concerning the issue of class politics, see Keith Laybourn's 'The rise of Labour and the decline of liberalism: the state of the debate', *History* 80 (1995), 207–26. Recent works that engage with the relationship between political parties and class include Jon Lawrence, *Speaking for the People: Party, Language and Popular Politics in England 1867–1914* (Cambridge, 1998); David Jarvis, 'British Conservatism and class politics in the 1920s', *English Historical Review*, 111 (1996), 59–84; and, Lawrence Black, *The Political Culture of the Left in Britain, 1951–64: Old Labour, New Britain?* (Basingstoke, 2003). Shifts towards the end of the twentieth century are analysed in Anthony F. Heath, Roger M. Jowell and John K. Curtice, *The Rise of New Labour: Party Policies and Voter Choices* (Oxford, 2001), while Jon Lawrence and Miles Taylor (eds) *Party, State and Society: Electoral Behaviour in Britain Since 1820* (Aldershot, 1997), place those changes in a much broader context.

Examinations of the links between gender and politics can be found in Martin Francis, 'Labour and Gender' in Duncan Tanner, Pat Thane and Nick Tiratsoo (eds) *Labour's First*

Century (Oxford, 2000), and Joni Lovenduski, Pippa Norris and Catriona Burgess, 'The party and women' in Stuart Ball and Anthony Seldon (eds) *Conservative Century* (Oxford, 1994). See David Jarvis, 'Mrs Maggs and Betty: the Conservative appeal to women voters in the 1920s', *Twentieth-Century British History*, 5 (1994), 129–52, and Pamela Graves, *Labour Women* (Cambridge, 1994) for tensions in the interwar period. For studies of the gender gap in voting in the 1950s, see Ina Zweiniger-Bargielowska, 'Explaining the Gender Gap: The Conservative Party and the Women's Vote, 1945–64' in Martin Francis and Ina Zweiniger-Bargielowska (eds) *The Conservatives and British Society 1880–1990* (Cardiff, 1996), and Amy Black and Stephen Brooke, 'The Labour Party, women and the problem of gender, 1951–66', *Journal of British Studies*, 36 (1997), 419–52.

On the working classes in twentieth-century Britain, see Andrew Miles and Michael Savage, *The Remaking of the British Working Class 1840–1940* (London, 1994) and Eric Hopkins, *The Rise and Decline of the English Working Classes 1918–90* (London, 1991). Divergent views of working-class formation can be found in Michael Savage, *The Dynamics of Working-Class Politics: The Labour Movement in Preston 1880–1940* (Cambridge, 1987) and Trevor Griffiths, *The Lancashire Working Classes c. 1880–1930* (Oxford, 2001). For the middle classes, see Simon Gunn and Rachel Bell, *The Middle Classes: Their Rise and Sprawl* (London, 2003) and for the aristocracy, see David Cannadine, *The Decline and Fall of the British Aristocracy* (New Haven, 1990). A sustained study of class society in a critical period can be found in Ross McKibbin, *Classes and Cultures: England 1918–51* (Oxford, 1998). See also David Cannadine, *Class in Britain* (London, 1998) and Patrick Joyce (ed.) *Class* (Oxford, 1995). Joan Wallach Scott's *Gender and the Politics of History* (New York, 1988) is an important work discussing the history of gender and its relation to class. General surveys of women's lives in the twentieth century can be found in Ina Zweiniger-Bargielowska (ed.) *Women in Twentieth-Century Britain* (Harlow, 2001). Hera Cook's *The Long Sexual Revolution: English Women and Contraception, 1800–1970* (Oxford, 2004) is a major study of the relationship between sexuality and women's lives. Competing views of the question of social mobility are found in Andrew Miles, *Social Mobility in 19th and early 20th Century Britain* (London, 1999) and John Goldthorpe, Catriona Llewelyn and Clive Payne, *Social Mobility and Class Structure in Modern Britain* (Oxford, 1987).

References

Brewer, Mark, Goodman, Alissa, Shaw, Jonathan and Shepherd, Andrew (2005) *Poverty and Inequality in Britain: 2005*. London: Institute for Fiscal Studies.

Glass, D.V. (1954) *Social Mobility in Britain*. London: Routledge & Kegan Paul.

Goldthorpe, John H., Llewelyn, Catriona and Payne, Clive (1987) *Social Mobility and Class Structure in Modern Britain*. Oxford: Clarendon.

Hilton, Matthew (2003) *Consumerism in Twentieth Century Britain*. Cambridge: Cambridge University Press.

Hinden, Rita (1960) 'The Lessons for Labour', in Mark Abrams, Richard Rose and Rita Hinden, *Must Labour Lose?* Harmondsworth: Penguin.

Hinton, James (2002) *Women, Social Leadership and the Second World War: Continuities of Class*. Oxford: Oxford University Press.

Miles, Andrew (1999) *Social Mobility in Nineteenth and Early Twentieth-Century England*. Basingstoke: Macmillan.

Rose, Sonya (2003) *Which People's War: National identity and citizenship, 1939–1945*. Oxford: Oxford University Press.

Savage, M. and Miles, A. (1994) *The Remaking of the British Working Class, 1840–1940*. London: Routledge.

Steedman, Carolyn (1986) *Landscape for a Good Woman*. London: Virago.

Taylor, Robert (2005) 'The Rise and Disintegration of the Working Classes', in Paul Addison and Harriet Jones (eds) *A Companion to Contemporary Britain 1939–2000*. Oxford: Basil Blackwell.

Thompson, E.P. (1963) *The Making of the English Working Class*. London: Victor Gollancz.

Tosh, John (1998) 'What Should Historians do with Masculinity?' in Robert Shoemaker and Mary Vincent (eds) *Gender and History in Western Europe*. London: Arnold.

Westergard, John (2001) 'The Persistence of Class Inequalities', in Nicholas Abercrombie and Alan Warde (eds) *The Contemporary British Society Reader*. Cambridge: Cambridge University Press.

5

Britain's changing position in the international economy

Catherine R. Schenk

DURING THE LONG TWENTIETH CENTURY the international economy underwent a series of waves of integration and disintegration. In the late nineteenth century technological innovation in communications, particularly telegraph, railways and steam shipping, enhanced the integration and globalization of the international economy. Although this was a time of increasing protectionism in North America and continental Europe, Britain maintained its open free trade position up to 1914. Despite rising tariffs, this was a golden era for world trade, investment and migration that drew national economies together in an unprecedented scale of both distance and intensity. During the interwar period, by contrast, the international economy disintegrated under the pressure of the Great Depression and the economic nationalism that most states turned to in a misguided effort to ameliorate the impact on their domestic populations. Controls on flows of trade, investment and people led to a downward spiral of international incomes that was only relieved by the end of the fixed exchange rate system and rearmament. After the Second World War, British and American governments were determined to restore a well-functioning international economy to generate cooperation and a lasting peace based on the premise that freer trade and payments offered the best prospects for growth overall. This ushered in 20 years of increasing trade and growth known as the 'long boom'. Flows of investment (particularly short-term capital flows), however, remained controlled as a defence of national policy sovereignty. The 1970s marked the next wave of economic disintegration as the oil crisis and inflation fractured international economic relations and many states retreated back into economic nationalism. During the 1980s, however, the commitment to freer trade and payments was renewed and controls on investment flows were finally liberalized, leading to a deeper and more widespread era of globalization through to the end of the century. Throughout these sometimes turbulent global events, Britain was often at the centre of policy making and coordination of the international economy.

Britain's role in the international economy at the beginning of the twentieth century was one of leadership, but the dominance that had characterized the mid-nineteenth century had already eroded due to the success of newer industrial economies such as Germany and the USA. Nevertheless, the institutions providing financial services for this first era of globalization, the continuing importance of international trade and investment for Britain's economy, and the strong cultural links forged by the large-scale settlement of the empire and dominions by Britons created a legacy of connections in the international economy that continued to have influence over the next century. During the twentieth century, as the international economy expanded in size and complexity, Britain's prominence as a world economic power waned both in quantitative terms and in terms of influence in global policy making. The post-war era began with Britain exercising its still considerable influence in global policy making in close collaboration with the USA. Through the post-war years, despite heavy domestic economic burdens, Britain managed an international currency that ranked second only to the US$ and was the unit of account for half of the world's trade. As the 1950s progressed, however, the sterling area drew apart while rapid recovery and then economic integration helped other European countries to outperform the British economy. In the 1960s, Britain actively retracted its international obligations and the global role of sterling was effectively ended by devaluation in 1967. Relations with Europe came to dominate the policy side of Britain's international economic relations for the next three decades, as Britain's policy makers struggled to come to terms with the political, social and economic features of European integration. This culminated in Britain's decision not to join in the introduction of the euro in 1999.

Figure 5.1 (p. 60) gives a long-term view of Britain's relative GDP per person compared with the West European average and the USA. From this it is clear that from the turn of the twentieth century US per capita output began to exceed that of both the UK and the rest of Europe. This remained the case except during the interwar depression, which hit the USA particularly severely. Rapid recovery during and after the war, however, put the USA on a rising trajectory compared to Europe. The British economy remained larger than the European average until the end of the 1960s, although there was an acceleration of convergence between Britain and Europe during that decade. British GDP per capita then fell below the European average until the mid-1990s when it began to catch up again.

This chapter will trace the changing role of Britain in the international economy by focusing on four important international economic relations: international trade, international investment, international migration and international monetary relations. A major theme of this chapter will be to examine how Britain's trade and investment flows changed during the century as Britain receded as the dominant manufacturer in the decades running up to the First World War and then struggled through the interwar period before emerging into the new environment of the post-war era to face the challenges of the new globalization.

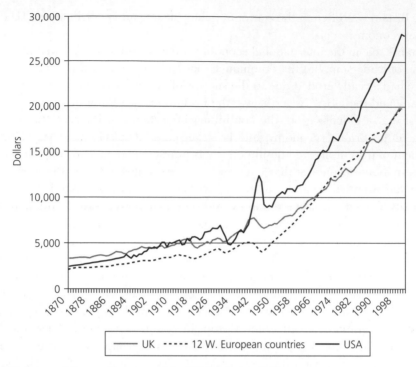

Figure 5.1 Britain, Western Europe and the USA: relative GDP per person
Note: 12 Western European countries are Austria, Belgium, Denmark, Finland, France, Germany, Italy, Netherlands, Norway, Sweden, Switzerland, UK. Unit is 1990 International Geary-Khamis dollars.
Source: Based on Maddison, 2003.

International trade

Figure 5.2 (p. 61) shows that Britain accounted for about 40–45 per cent of the world's manufactured exports from 1850 to 1870, but from 1872 this dominant position was steadily eroded as Germany and the USA industrialized, so that by 1913 Britain's share had fallen to 28 per cent. This pattern closely followed the decline in Britain's share of world manufacturing output. While other countries adopted more protectionist policies after 1880, British governments resolutely held to free trade right through to the outbreak of the First World War.

Figure 5.3 (p. 61) picks up the continuing decline of Britain's share of international trade after the disruption of the wars and interwar Great Depression. Here the data show the steady decline in Britain's share of trade in all goods (not just manufactures) during the long boom of 1950–73. These were years of rapid growth in world trade as quotas and then tariffs were reduced under successive rounds of the General Agreement on Tariffs and Trade and due to the development of the Common Market in continental

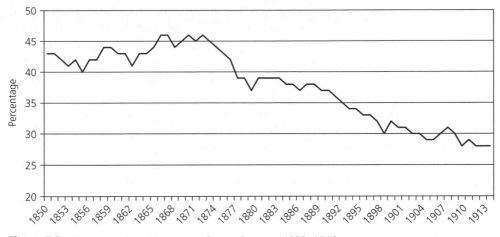

Figure 5.2 UK share of world exports of manufactures, 1850–1913
Source: Based on Mitchell, 1988.

Europe. From the time of the oil crisis, however, Britain's long-term declining share ceased and was even reversed at the beginning of the 1980s due to exports of North Sea oil. Thereafter, Britain held a remarkably steady 5 per cent of world exports of goods despite the entry of new export competitors in the Far East such as China.

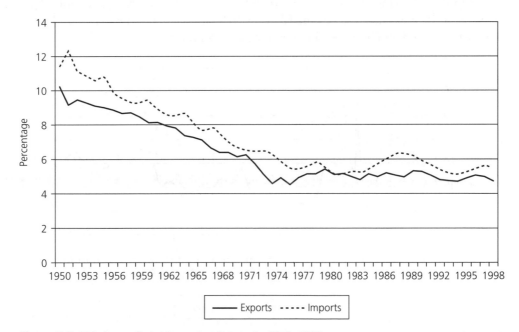

Figure 5.3 UK share of world merchandise trade, 1950–1999
Source: Based on UNCTAD, 2004.

One further observation from Figure 5.3 is the inference that Britain ran a fairly consistent deficit on the balance of trade in goods throughout the second half of the twentieth century. This deficit was offset by a growing surplus in the export of services, particularly business services. The City of London remained a prominent international financial centre providing insurance, banking and other commercial services to the growing international financial and trading community.

Figure 5.4 shows the value of international trade compared to the size of the British economy over the century. These data show that the persistent deficit in the balance of trade after 1945 noted above was by no means a new phenomenon. Indeed, the deficit on the goods account was considerably larger in the first half of the century than after, ranging from 6–10 per cent of GDP in the years 1900–18 compared to 0–2 per cent of GDP after 1950. During the early decades of the century, the trade deficit was offset by earnings from overseas investments as well as export of services. An interesting feature of Figure 5.4 is that exports in relation to GDP are almost the same at the beginning and at the end of the century. In between, however, there was considerable variation. During the heyday of the first era of globalization in the run-up to the First World War trade grew much faster than GDP. This was interrupted by the First World War and then by the Great Depression when the value of world trade collapsed. In the 1930s the nominal value of British exports fell from a peak of £1.55 billion in the restocking boom of 1920 to a trough of £416 million in 1932. During the long boom after the Second World War, both imports and exports were fairly consistently about 15 per cent of GDP as both output and trade increased steadily, but at a slower rate than world trade. Trade increased relative to GDP from 1973 to 2000 to about 20 per cent due to Britain's accession to the EEC in 1973 and the general rise in world trade during the second and more profound era of globalization.

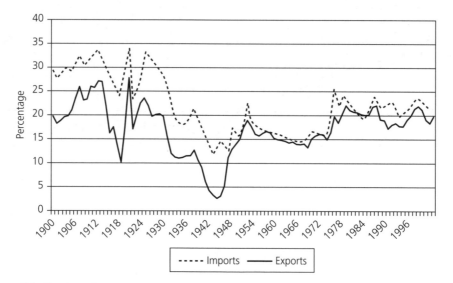

Figure 5.4 Goods trade as a percentage of GDP, 1900–2000
Source: Based on Mitchell, 1988 for 1900–1945, then Office of National Statistics.

International investment

The actual amount of foreign investment in the second half of the nineteenth century is subject to some dispute – what is not disputed is that the 60 years up to 1913 saw an unprecedented and dramatic increase in flows of capital overseas. British investments abroad were about £1 billion in 1875 and rose to £4 billion by 1913, accounting for about 43 per cent of the global total foreign investment. The reasons for the increase in overseas investment included increased financial sophistication and specialization of institutions that made it easier to invest abroad, especially through London. Technological innovations such as communications and transport also improved the awareness of opportunities for investment. In this way, the increase in international trade and migration generated increases in foreign investment and vice versa. Immigrant populations in places like Canada, the USA and Australia generated demand for investment in construction and infrastructure, particularly railroads, to bring their abundant raw materials to the coasts and thence to the European markets. About 40 per cent of British overseas investment was in railways in this period. Finally, there were relatively high domestic savings rates in industrialized countries like Britain combined with relatively low domestic investment rates.

Britain was the world's largest single source of international investment, reflecting the unrivalled financial expertise in the City of London and accumulated savings from maturing industrialization. As noted above, much of the investment was in railway shares and imperial government bonds, and the fastest growing targets were the USA and the dominions. In 1870 about one-third of British investments were in the British empire and dominions, but by 1914 this share had risen to almost half, mainly due to investment in Australia and Canada after 1880.

Two World Wars and the Great Depression interrupted flows of international investment in the same way that they disrupted trade. Both wars were accompanied by the accumulation of debt, although the outcomes were very different. During the First World War the British government lent vital cash to support the allied partners, particularly France, Italy and Russia. In turn, Britain had to borrow from the USA to help finance its own war effort and the lending to allies. The result was that, at the time of the Armistice, Britain owed almost US$4 billion to the USA and was owed US$7 billion by other allied powers (Hardach, 1973: 148). Unfortunately, Britain's debtors had few resources with which to repay their debt and this left Britain exposed in its own obligations to the USA. The result was a very damaging cycle of international debt throughout the interwar period in which the allies depended on extracting reparations from the defeated German state in order to repay their allied creditors. When the reparations were not forthcoming, the cycle broke and an international financial crisis ensued in 1931. Throughout the interwar depression international investment was severely curtailed.

Although international opinion was firmly in favour of freer trade after 1945, there was still a strong view that short-term capital flows should remain controlled in order to protect national economies from the vagaries of speculators and to support independent national economic policies. As a result, while trade restrictions were reduced dramatically in the 1950s and 1960s, investment flows were only gradually liberalized. Long-term investment and foreign direct investment were freed first during the 1950s but the final controls on short-term capital flows were not relaxed in Britain until 1979.

There were significant changes in the long-term investment position of the British economy after 1945. The 1960s marked the beginning of the American invasion, as US companies increased their presence abroad through foreign direct investment (FDI) to exploit their managerial, scale and technological advantages. In the 1950s the value of US FDI in Britain grew from $542 million to $1.6 billion. In this decade 230 new subsidiaries of foreign companies were opened in Britain, of which 187 were American (Bostock and Jones, 1994). By 1963 it was estimated that foreign companies accounted for about 10 per cent of net output of British manufacturing (Steuer *et al.*, 1973: 189). The stock of inward FDI in Britain amounted to about 6.5 per cent of GDP in 1960, rising to 27 per cent by the end of 1999 (Pain, 2001: 6). In the 1960s, British companies were responsible for about 13 per cent of the world's FDI flows but this was well behind the USA with 65 per cent of world FDI or total flows of US$57 billion from 1960 to 71. Still, outward flows of FDI amounted to 5 per cent of British gross domestic capital formation on average, compared to only 3.5 per cent for the USA in these years. Britain also had a much higher share of both inward and outward FDI than other European countries and accounted for about 40 per cent of all outward FDI from Western Europe in the 1960s.

Britain was the major target for US companies because of the similar language and familiar culture compared with other European countries. The inflow of US firms was particularly striking in the banking industry, where the culture of the City of London was rudely shaken out of its traditional values by the arrival of the more aggressive and competitive practices of American bankers. By 1971 almost 10 per cent of US outward FDI was in banking and insurance.

Figure 5.5 (p. 65) shows the trends in flows of FDI relative to domestic investment for the UK compared to Western Europe as a whole. It is clear that FDI is relatively larger for Britain than for other European economies. There was a small surge in both inward and outward FDI in the second half of the 1980s and then the huge surge in the final years of the 1990s. This reflected a few very large trans-border mergers and acquisitions particularly among telecommunications companies. The British firm Vodafone bought Airtouch in 1999 for £39 billion and then bought Mannesmann for £101 billion in 2000, making Vodafone the largest transnational corporation in the world (UNCTAD, 2002). Other major deals included BP and Amoco (£33 billion) in 1998 and Zeneca's purchase of Astra for £21 billion in 1999. Once this flurry of activity was over, however, outward FDI fell back to 14 per cent of domestic investment. The impact was to increase the stock of UK FDI but also to increase foreign holdings of UK equities since many of these deals were partly financed through swaps of shares. By 2000 the inward stock of FDI amounted to 30 per cent of GDP compared with 12 per cent in 1980.

Figure 5.6 (p. 65) puts the British position into international perspective. The USA was by far the most important source of world FDI in 1970 but this share fell dramatically through the following decade. Britain's share was fairly stable at 10–20 per cent of the

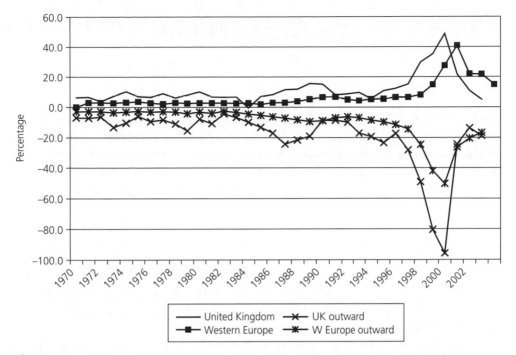

Figure 5.5 Flows of FDI as a percentage of gross domestic capital formation, 1970–2003
Source: Based on UNCTAD, *World Investment Report*, various years.

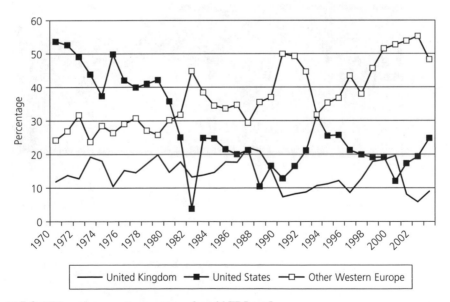

Figure 5.6 FDI outflows as a percentage of world FDI outflows
Source: Based on UNCTAD, *World Investment Report*, various years.

world total, while the share of the rest of Western Europe showed a rising trend over the period as a whole so that it had replaced the USA by 2000.

International migration

We have seen that Britain was a major contributor to the globalization of the international economy through trade and investment in the late nineteenth century. The British Isles (including Ireland) was also the leading source of emigrants in the decades from 1851 to 1880 (57 per cent of the world total), due mainly to emigration from Ireland in the wake of the famine of the 1840s. In the period 1880–1914, while the share of the world's total migrants coming from Britain fell to 28 per cent, the number increased sharply to 8.9 million people as transport became less risky and costly, information on opportunities for migrants spread and infrastructure improved. Most emigrants were destined for the USA and dominions where they settled and farmed or engaged in industrial activity in these fast growing countries, where labour was relatively scarce and incomes were higher compared to Britain. The destination of British emigrants in the years before 1914 is shown in Figure 5.7 (migrants to and from continental Europe are not included in these data).

Figure 5.8 (p. 67) shows that the number of emigrants from Britain never repeated the scale of the phenomenon in the period just before 1914. Although the UK experienced net emigration throughout most of the twentieth century, immigration recovered the

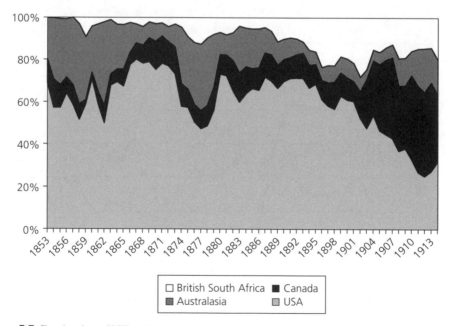

Figure 5.7 Destination of UK emigrants, 1853–1914
Source: Based on Mitchell, 1988.

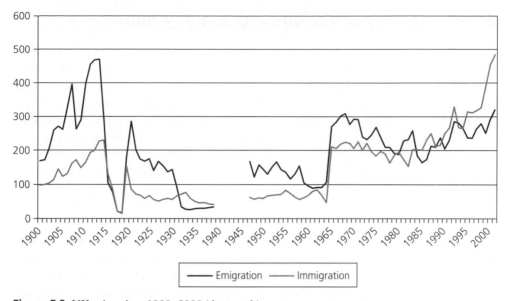

Figure 5.8 UK migration, 1900–2000 (thousands)
Source: Based on 1900–1990 Mitchell (2003); 1991–2000 Office of National Statistics. Prior to 1964 only UK and Commonwealth intercontinental migration; from 1964 including European migration.

same level as 1913 after 1950 and then increased considerably in the 1990s. Immediately after the First World War a surge in emigration was soon followed by a drop in international migration due to the depression. The falling incomes and unemployment of the interwar period reduced opportunities and resources for migration and was also accompanied by stricter controls on immigrants in many countries to protect domestic jobs. After the Second World War migration began to grow again back to the levels of the start of the century. The data before 1964 exclude British migration to and from continental Europe; however, a general trend of net emigration clearly continued. From 1983, however, there began more persistent net immigration, particularly due to immigrants from Europe with the creation of the single market. The share of total immigrants coming from Europe increased from 10.5 per cent in 1971 before Britain joined the European community to a peak of 31 per cent in 1996. Immigration from Europe was almost evenly matched by emigration to Europe. From 1964 to 1980 about 40 per cent of immigrants were UK citizens who had resided in other countries (Mitchell, 1988). In the 1980s and 1990s the number of UK citizens immigrating to the UK was fairly stable at about 100,000 per year, but they were a declining proportion of total immigrants (falling from 35 per cent in 1992 to 22 per cent in 2000) due to an increase in non-British migrants (ONS, 2001). From 1975 to 1999 about one-quarter of non-British immigrants were students coming to study at British institutions.

In the 1990s both Scotland and Northern Ireland had consistent net emigration, which contrasted with net immigration into England and Wales. Over 90 per cent of all immigrants settled in England, with London's share rising from one-third in 1992 to 46 per cent in 2000.

Britain and the international monetary system

Underlying all international transactions is the means of payment. It is only the ability to convert national currencies that allows international trade to take place on a multilateral basis. If currencies are not convertible, then trade can only take place through barter or the balancing of bilateral trade balances between two countries. When currencies are convertible, a surplus earned from exports to one country can be used to pay for imports from another country, and this allows traders to buy in the cheapest market and sell where they can get the best price, thus improving the scale and efficiency of international trade. The structure to allow convertibility is known as the international monetary system and it has taken various forms throughout the twentieth century.

By the nineteenth century Britain was the world's main trading nation and international commodities came to be marketed through London. London also became the centre for discount houses and financing of foreign trade – eventually financing the trade of goods that never touched British ports because of the security, trustworthiness and skill of London financial houses. From 1819 Britain legally identified the value of the pound sterling in terms of ounces of gold to allow international comparison of prices. The pound was valued at £4.25 per ounce of gold. In the early nineteenth century other countries fixed the value of their local currency in either silver or gold or both (bimetallism) but they ran into difficulties when the price of silver began to fall in relation to gold. In the 1870s, therefore, more countries switched to the gold standard (that is, they set a fixed price at which they would exchange their currency for gold and gold only). Germany used its indemnity for winning the Franco-Prussian War 1871–72 to buy gold and put itself on a gold standard by selling silver. This raised the international price of gold in terms of silver, making it even more difficult for other countries to sustain a bimetallic standard. At the same time, in Nevada new discoveries of silver pushed the price of silver even lower. European countries followed Germany on to gold through the 1870s and in 1879 the USA joined (legally only in 1900) followed by Japan and Russia in 1897. So, by 1880 most countries participating in the international economy had currencies convertible to gold at a fixed exchange rate. From this time, the international gold standard operated as the international monetary system, offering a fixed exchange rate and convertible currencies to ease the accelerating international trade and capital flows of the late nineteenth century.

While gold was nominally the anchor of the system, in practice sterling played a vital role in its success. Shipping gold internationally to settle outstanding balances was costly and risky, and the supply of gold was relatively fixed by the need to discover and mine it. Because of the importance of Britain in trade and also in finance, merchanting, shipping and insurance in the City of London, most trade was contracted in terms of sterling. This meant that countries did not have to compete for scarce gold supplies. Instead they fixed the exchange rates of their national currencies to sterling, which was in turn firmly pegged to gold. The period from 1880 to 1914, the Classic Gold Standard, was a period of rapid growth in international trade and payments, partly due to the high levels of confidence and reduction in transaction costs delivered by this fixed exchange rate system with Britain at its centre. It was achievable in the late nineteenth century because of the dominance of Britain and the City of London and the international confidence in the gold value of sterling that this dominance delivered.

After the disruption of the First World War, it was generally assumed that a return to a fixed exchange rate system should be the goal of all countries to resume international economic relations on the same scale as before the war. In practice, however, this proved to be difficult to achieve. Once again, Britain took a leadership role, although the British economy had suffered during the war, reducing even further its competitiveness, particularly compared to the USA. The decision to return to a revised gold standard in 1925 at the same exchange rate as had been used before the war is generally considered one of the great policy mistakes of the twentieth century. It has a particular historical significance because it showed the perils of a fixed exchange rate that was inappropriate, particularly the difficulties that ensue from an overvalued exchange rate. This experience should have taught policy makers of the future the importance of getting the rate right in any fixed exchange rate system.

The decision to return to the pre-war exchange rate was taken largely for political reasons: the public expected it, the rate had a symbolic resonance of Britain's heyday in the international economy, and a lower rate would disappoint overseas holders of sterling by devaluing their assets. At the time, moreover, expectations of a return to the pre-war rate had led the market to near that rate in any case, so it did not seem unrealistic. The extent of overvaluation is open to some dispute, but is generally agreed to have been about 10 per cent too high – thus requiring a 10 per cent reduction in domestic prices to maintain balance of payments equilibrium. The consequent need to pursue deflationary policies during the growing international economic crisis after 1925 increased the impact of the depression on British producers and workers.

After struggling through the second half of the 1920s, the government finally had to abandon the fixed exchange rate under the pressure of the international financial crisis of 1931 and the floating of the pound marked the beginning of the recovery from the depression. Nevertheless, the uncertainty and crisis of the international monetary system in the 1930s led the public and governments still to hanker after a workable system of fixed exchange rates. During the war the British and American governments agreed to start planning for the post-war era and the coordination of the international monetary system was at the forefront of their minds.

The goal for the post-war period was agreed between the British and Americans in a series of formal agreements that stemmed from aid offered by the Americans to Britain before the USA officially declared war. Under the so-called lend-lease arrangements of 1942 the USA offered munitions and supplies to Britain in return for an undertaking from the British government that they would agree to help reconstruct the international economy after the war along the lines of freer multilateral trade and payments. A requirement for multilateral trade, as we have seen above, is convertible currencies. It was also agreed that a fixed exchange rate should be the framework for the international monetary system after the war to enhance confidence and coordination, and in response to the chaos and conflict associated with the floating exchange rate system of the 1930s. Both the Americans and British began to draft the architecture for this system during 1941 and the plans were published in 1942. Both sides wanted a fixed exchange rate system policed by an international institution that would provide short-term lending as a cushion against short-term balance of payments problems. This cushion would give countries the confidence to free up controls on trade and payments and thus meet the goal of freer and multilateral trade. These plans by J.M. Keynes for Britain and by Harry D. White for the USA became the basis of discussions that culminated in the Bretton Woods meeting in New Hampshire in July 1944, when 730 delegates representing 44 members of the United and Associated Nations met to finalize a blueprint for the international monetary system.

The Bretton Woods system, as it became known, comprised two main institutions: the International Monetary Fund and the International Bank for Reconstruction and Development. The IMF was supposed to provide the short-term credit needed to give countries the confidence to free up their trade and payments at fixed exchange rates. In the event, however, currencies were generally not made convertible for 14 years after the war. Sterling was made convertible for current account transactions only, and only for residents outside the UK, from the end of 1958 along with other Western European countries. From 1960 the fixed exchange rate system began to come under strain due to persistent surpluses by West Germany and consistent deficits in the UK and the USA. The UK struggled to maintain the parity of sterling until November 1967, when it was devalued by 14 per cent. This marked the beginning of the end of the system as speculators put pressure on inappropriate exchange rates. In August 1971 the USA unilaterally devalued the US$ against gold. A brief interim system was reconstructed in December 1971 called the Smithsonian Agreement but by June 1972 sterling was forced to float. All currencies then floated free of the Bretton Woods system from the spring of 1973.

Since this time a global fixed exchange rate system has not been a goal of policy makers. Instead, countries manage their exchange rates independently, although Britain, along with other members of the G8, cooperated at times through the 1980s and 1990s to stabilize rates among the most important currencies in the world. Although a global fixed exchange rate system was out of the question, European countries sought to reduce exchange rate fluctuations among themselves. Their economies were so open to each others' trade that the transaction costs of fluctuations were very high. Even more importantly, the institutions of the EEC (in particularly the Common Agricultural Policy) did not function efficiently when exchange rates among members changed. From 1969, therefore, continental Europe progressed towards elimination of exchange rate fluctuations in a process that culminated in the introduction of the single currency in 1999. Although Britain was a member of the EEC from 1973, they did not share in the enthusiasm of others for exchange rate stability and the convergence of economic policy that this requires. Britain reluctantly joined the Exchange Rate Mechanism in 1990, pegging within +/−6 per cent to a grid of European currencies with the DM at its core. In 1992, however, the pound was spectacularly forced out of the ERM by speculators who recognized that the rate was unsustainable. This expensive experience (both financially and politically) further discouraged British governments from engaging in Europe's plans for economic and monetary union and Britain did not adopt the euro in 1999.

In Focus

Sterling as an international currency since 1945

During the Second World War, the US government was determined not to allow a repeat of this disaster and made special arrangements to 'lend-lease' vital supplies to Britain and the allies rather than force them to accumulate debt. However, as part of the war effort Britain did accumulate large debts to its colonies in South Asia. By 1945, the territories that would become the states of India, Pakistan and Ceylon held £1.3 billion of short-term British government debt denominated in sterling. These assets became known as the sterling balances and represented claims on the British economy or foreign exchange reserves. The total remained remarkably stable between £2.5 and £3.0 billion or about three times Britain's foreign exchange reserves from 1950 to 1970. However, the total figure disguises shifts in the geographical distribution of these sterling balances during the 1950s and 1960s, as is shown in Figure 5.9. After the war, the extraordinary debts to South Asia were quickly reduced, mainly through British exports to these territories and development

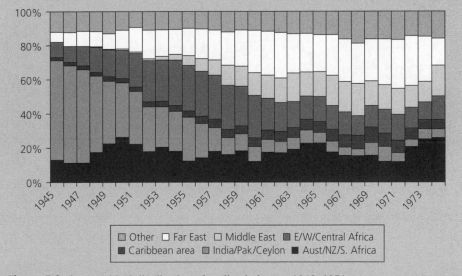

Figure 5.9 Geographical distribution of sterling balances, 1945–1974
Source: Based on Schenk, 2004.

Sterling as an international currency since 1945

spending. By the mid-1950s they were replaced by assets held in African colonies as a result of the primary materials boom associated with the Korean War. By the 1960s territories in the Middle East and Far East were accumulating sterling assets. This was due to the denomination of some oil trade in sterling, which boosted the sterling denominated foreign exchange reserves of Middle Eastern countries like Kuwait and Libya, and due to the industrialization and growth of Singapore, Hong Kong and Malaysia in the Far East. After the oil crisis of 1973, OPEC countries came to hold about 40 per cent of outstanding short-term sterling liabilities, although this share fell to 20 per cent by 1990. Another dramatic change was in the type of holders of overseas sterling assets. Until 1976, about 60 per cent of them were held by central banks or other official monetary institutions, but this share fell steadily to 20 per cent by 1980. This reflected the decline of sterling as a reserve asset and the dramatic increase in private banking and money market holdings of sterling overseas (from £10 billion in 1980 to £80 billion in 1990) due to the increase in the value of international trade and payments.

Figure 5.10 shows the decline in sterling as a reserve asset in favour of the US$ during the 1960s and mainly the German DM in the 1970s and 1980s.

Figure 5.11 (p. 73) shows how the nominal exchange rate between the US$ and sterling changed during the long twentieth century. The data are for the closing rate on the final day of each year so they disguise the shorter-term volatility of the exchange rate. However, the graph clearly shows the major features of the

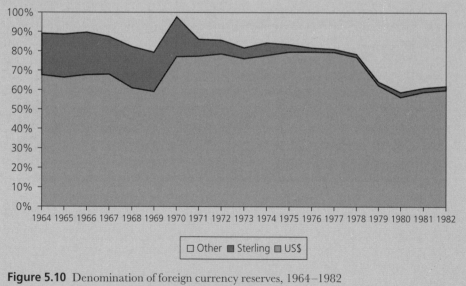

Figure 5.10 Denomination of foreign currency reserves, 1964–1982
Source: Based on IMF, *International Financial Statistics*, various years.

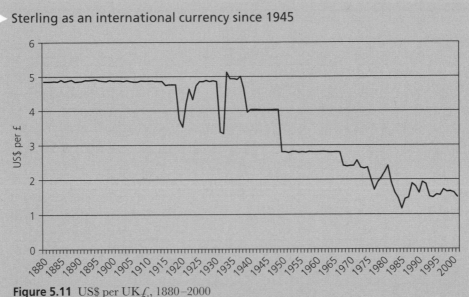

Sterling as an international currency since 1945

Figure 5.11 US$ per UK£, 1880–2000
Source: Based on Global Financial Data Inc.

international monetary system from the fixed exchange rate gold standard of
1880–1914 to the volatility of the floating period during and immediately after the
First World War. The restoration of the gold standard in 1925 was quite short-lived
and ushered in more volatility during the 1930s when the US$ left the gold standard
finally in 1933. The Bretton Woods era followed the Second World War with another
fixed exchange rate system until adjustments in the rates in 1967, 1971, 1972 and
finally the end of the system in 1973.

Figure 5.12 (p. 74) gives a better impression of the movements in the exchange
rate during the period of floating rates from 1975. This shows the real effective
exchange rate rather than merely the nominal rate against the US$ alone. This index
is adjusted for inflation and shows the exchange rate against 21 currencies weighted
by the amount of goods trade with these countries. The appreciation of sterling
during the North Sea oil boom in the early 1980s was followed by a generally
declining trend through to mid-1996 when sterling began to appreciate against
the European currencies and the US$.

In summary, Britain was the leader of the pre-1914 and interwar gold standards.
This influence shifted more towards the USA after 1945 with the design of the
Bretton Woods system. By the time that Britain re-oriented its economic relations to
Europe, these countries had already embarked on a path to economic and monetary
integration that, while not completely assured until the last minute, left Britain out of
the leadership role since these goals of policy convergence did not match Britain's
view of its role in the international economy and its domestic economic and political

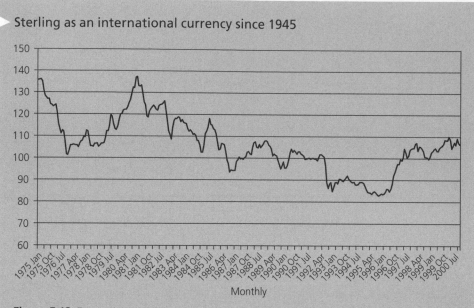

Sterling as an international currency since 1945

Monthly

Figure 5.12 Real effective exchange rate index, 1975–2000 (monthly average 1990 = 100)
Source: Based on ONS, 2001.

interests. Britain does play a key role still in the G8 and G10 organizations and has considerable influence over the determination of the direction of global policy but this role is now more commensurate with the larger and more complex international economic system at the end of the twentieth century compared to the end of the nineteenth century.

Debates and Interpretations

A central question about Britain's role in the international economy throughout the long twentieth century has been whether international economic relations and Britain's policy of openness has had a positive or negative impact on the performance of the British economy. These historical debates are reflected in the continuing disagreement today between protectionists and the anti-globalization movement, on the one hand, and advocates of free trade and free markets, on the other.

The fact that British prominence as an international investor at the end of the nineteenth century coincided with relatively low domestic investment rates compared with Germany and the USA has raised the question of whether foreign investment diverted scarce resources abroad to the detriment of the domestic economy. This was the argument put forward by Sidney Pollard in the 1980s (Pollard, 1989). He calculated that the annual outflow of capital amounted to an average of 5 per cent of national income from 1874 to 1913, and approached 9 per cent of national income in 1911–13. He blamed biases in the capital market in the City of London that channelled domestic savings towards overseas portfolio investment rather than domestic industrial investment. On the other hand, the relatively slow growth at home could be a cause as well as an effect of high rates of overseas investment, since returns on overseas assets were higher. In this way investors were reacting rationally to get the highest returns on their money.

Britain's trade policy has also been controversial. This debate pits advocates of free markets against those who believe the government should more actively support and protect domestic producers against their foreign competitors. Thus, some historians have argued that the adherence to free trade until 1932 allowed competitors to penetrate the British market, while foreign countries were protecting their producers with tariffs and so putting British industry at a disadvantage (Pollard, 1989). In 1990 Kitson and Solomou rejected the prevailing advocacy of free markets to argue that the switch to protectionism in 1932 was important for the recovery of Britain from the depression in the 1930s. Capie, however, showed that the effective protection was not on those sectors that led the recovery, which suggests that the tariffs were not instrumental in the process (Capie, 1991, 1983). Nevertheless, there were strong political pressures that explain the introduction of tariff protection of domestic industry during the economic downturn (Rooth, 1992).

After 1945, there was considerably more protection through tariffs and quotas and through preferential access to imperial markets. Some, such as Pollard, argued that this lulled British industry into an uncompetitive state and left it unable to compete with the more dynamic European market (Pollard, 1982). However, Schenk argued that this analysis overestimated the 'softness' of commonwealth markets, where British producers were increasingly encountering stiff competition from American and European producers (Schenk, 1994). Milward and Brennan calculated that controls on imports in the 1950s were more effective than contemporaries believed, and that this misapprehension led to an exaggerated view of Britain's industrial competitiveness, which in turn contributed to the governments' decision to remain outside the EEC (Milward and Brennan, 1996).

International monetary policy has also provoked historical debate. Contemporary views by authors such as Burnham and Strange have argued that the use of sterling internationally hindered British governments' freedom to adjust the domestic economy, and that this contributed to relatively slower growth rates (Burnham, 2003; Strange, 1971). They argue that higher interest rates were required to keep sterling attractive to overseas holders and that the exchange rate had to remain fixed at an overvalued rate in order to sustain the international credibility of the currency at the expense of British exporters. On the other hand, Schenk has argued that there were few realistic alternatives to the policy Britain sustained throughout the Bretton Woods era since devaluing or floating sterling would have had serious political and economic repercussions for Britain's relations with the USA and Europe (Schenk, 1994).

Another long-standing subject of debate is the relationship between economics and empire. Hobson and Lenin famously equated late nineteenth-century imperialism with economic exploitation and explained the expansion of the British empire in terms of the export of capital, the control of raw materials and the creation of captive markets for British industrial production (Eckstein, 1991; Hobson, 1902; Lenin, 1916). This view was reiterated by Hobsbawm in the 1960s, when he explored the relationship between British industrialization and imperialism (Hobsbawm, 1968). On the other hand, Robinson and Gallagher put greater emphasis on developments in the periphery rather than in Britain as a motivation for imperial expansion (Robinson and Gallagher, 1961). In the 1970s and 1980s, Davis and Huttenback and Fieldhouse revised the traditional view of the economic motivation for imperialism by emphasizing that most British investment was not aimed at the empire at the end of the nineteenth century. Moreover, the tropical colonies that became colonies in the run-up to 1914 did not offer much prospect for trade with the metropole (Davis and Huttenback, 1986; Fieldhouse, 1973). Thereafter, there emerged a general consensus among historians that political rather than economic motivations were more important for the late nineteenth-century imperial expansion, and that empire may have been a net burden on the British economy.

In the 1990s Cain and Hopkins revived economic motivations in their concept of 'gentlemanly capitalism' to explain British imperialism from the seventeenth century to the late twentieth century. They argued that the important economic driver for imperialism was not manufacturing industry (as had been suggested by Hobson and Hobsbawm) but the service sector. Thus, bankers and merchants in the City of London established economic relations with territories that did not necessarily overlap with the formal constitutional British empire. Nevertheless, due to their social and political influence in Britain the interests of these 'gentlemen' were supported through imperial political and strategic relationships (Cain and Hopkins, 1993). This thesis has subsequently been challenged by various case studies of business interests in particular territories where the link between business elites and political elites was not compelling (Akita, 2002; Dumett, 1999).

The relationship between economics and empire has also been explored for the period of decolonization in the 1950s. Krozewski argued that the financial links of empire supported the British economic recovery in these years and help to explain the timing of decolonization (Krozewski, 2001). Hinds puts more emphasis on the costs of colonial development policy in determining the pace of decolonization (Hinds, 2001). Both historians are critical of Britain's selfish failure to meet the development priorities of its colonies during the 1940s and 1950s. More recently Ferguson has controversially developed a much more positive view of the civilizing and economically benevolent influences of the British empire, with particular emphasis on the fostering of trade, migration and investment links to create an era of growth-inducing globalization (Ferguson, 2003). His thesis has in turn attracted criticism for trivializing the negative aspects of empire such as slavery and economic exploitation. Britain's international economic relations continue to generate debate, particularly over the advantages and disadvantages of European economic and monetary union, immigration and outsourcing of the service sector. These will no doubt be the foundation of the historical debates of the future.

Further reading

There are several excellent introductions to the development of the international economy, which put Britain's international economic relations into context, including A.G. Kenwood and A.L. Lougheed, *The Growth of the International Economy, 1820–2000: An Introductory Text* (London, 1999) and J. Foreman-Peck, *A History of the World Economy* (London, 1995). B. Alford, *Britain in the World Economy since 1880* (London, 1996) gives greater detail of the changes in Britain's international economic relations up to the 1980s while N.F.R. Crafts provides a succinct overview of Britain's economy in a comparative perspective in *Britain's Relative Economic Performance 1870–1999* (London, 2002).

References

Akita, S. (ed.) (2002) *Gentlemanly Capitalism, Imperialism and Global History*. London: Macmillan.

Bostock, F. and Jones, G. (1994) 'Foreign multinationals in British manufacturing 1850–1962', *Business History*, 36(1): 89–126.

Burnham, P. (2003) *Remaking the Post-war World Economy*. London: Palgrave.

Cain, P. and Hopkins, A.G. (1993) *British Imperialism: Innovation and Expansion*, and *British Imperialism: Crisis and Deconstruction 1914–1990*. London: Longman.

Capie, F. (1983) *Depression and Protectionism; Britain between the Wars*. London: Allen & Unwin.

Capie, F. (1991) 'Effective protection and economic recovery in Britain 1932–1937', *Economic History Review*, 44.

Davis, L.E. and Huttenback, R.A. (1986) *Mammon and the Pursuit of Empire: The Political Economy of British Imperialism, 1860–1912*. Cambridge: Cambridge University Press.

Dumett R.E. (ed.) (1999) *Gentlemanly Capitalism and British Imperialism: The New Debate on Empire*. London: Longman.

Eckstein, A.M. (1991) 'Is there a "Hobson-Lenin thesis" on late nineteenth-century imperial expansion?', *Economic History Review*, XLIV (2): 297–318.

Ferguson, N. (2003) *Empire: How Britain made the Modern World*. London: Allen Lane.

Fieldhouse, D.K. (1973) *Economics and Empire 1830–1914*. London: Macmillan.

Global Financial Data, www.globalfinancialdata.com.

Hardach, G. (1973) *The First World War 1914–1918*. London: Penguin.

Hinds, A. (2001) *Britain's Sterling Colonial Policy and Decolonization 1939–1958*. London: Greenwood Press.

Hobsbawm, E.J. (1968) *Industry and Empire*. London: Pelican.

Hobson, J.A. (1902) *Imperialism: An Essay*. James Nisbet & Co.

Kitson, M. and Solomou, S. (1990) *Protectionism and Economic Revival: The British Interwar Economy*. Cambridge: Cambridge University Press.

Krozewski, G. (2001) *Money and the End of Empire*. London: Palgrave.

Lenin, V.I. (1916) *Imperialism the Highest Stage of Capitalism*. Lawrence & Wishart.

Maddison, A. (2003) *The World Economy*. OECD.

Milward A.S. and Brennan, G. (1996) *Britain's Place in the World: A Historical Enquiry into Import Controls 1945–60*. London: Routledge.

Mitchell, B.R. (1988) *British Historical Statistics*. Cambridge: Cambridge University Press.

Mitchell, B.R. (2003) *International Historical Statistics: Europe, 1750–2000*. London: Palgrave Macmillan.

Office of National Statistics (ONS) (2001) *Population Trends*, Winter 2001.

Pain, N. (2001) 'The Growth and Impact of Inward Investment in the UK: Introduction and Overview', in N. Pain (ed.) *Inward Investment, Technological Change and Growth*. London: NIESR.

Pollard, S. (1982) *The Wasting of the British Economy: British Economic Policy 1945 to the Present*. London: Croom Helm.

Pollard, S. (1989) *Britain's Prime and Britain's Decline: The British economy 1870–1914*. London: Edward Arnold.

Robinson, R. and Gallagher, J. (1961) *Africa and the Victorians: The Official Mind of Imperialism*. London: Macmillan.

Rooth, T. (1992) *British Protectionism and the International Economy: Overseas Commercial Policy in the 1930s*. Cambridge: Cambridge University Press.

Schenk, C.R. (1994) *Britain and the Sterling Area*. London: Routledge.

Schenk, C.R. (2004) 'The empire strikes back: Hong Kong and the decline of sterling in the 1960s', *Economic History Review*, vol. LVII, no. 3, August.

Steuer, M.D., Abell, P., Gennard, J., Perlman, M., Rees, S., Scott, B. and Wallis, K. (1973) *The Impact of Foreign Direct Investment on the UK*. London: HMSO.

Strange, S. (1971) *Sterling and British Policy*. Oxford: Oxford University Press.

UN Centre on Transnational Corporations (1983) *Salient Features and Trends in Foreign Direct Investment*. New York: UN.

UNCTAD (2002) *World Investment Report*.

UNCTAD (2004) *Handbook of Statistics*.

6

War and national identity since 1914

Max Jones

WHO DO YOU THINK YOU ARE? British? English, Scottish, Welsh or Irish? Brummie, Cockney or Geordie? Everyone has their own answer. Often, individuals have more than one answer: people express fluid, composite allegiances, shaped by their age, gender, sexuality, class, occupation, location, whether they are married, whether they have children, whether it is wartime and so on. Historians have recently begun to ask what people in the past thought about their nations and their relationship with national identity. The answers of Britons since 1914 have tended to revolve around war.

To begin, we must establish what we mean by 'nation' and distinguish it from understandings of the state. The state can be understood as the totality of structures of governance (for instance, Parliament, civil service, local councils). The state, then, can be clearly located in institutions and administrative structures. The nation is more elusive, an 'imagined community', to use Benedict Anderson's influential phrase (1991). We never meet the vast majority of the millions of people who make up our nation, but we *imagine* we share common characteristics with them. The term 'national identity' has developed to describe these common characteristics, to describe the ways in which individuals imagine their nation, for instance, as warlike or peace-loving, religious or secular. So we can distinguish between, on the one hand, an individual's formal citizenship, that is, their legal association with a particular state, and, on the other, an individual's national identity, a personal bundle of ideas and associations.

The United Kingdom of Great Britain and Northern Ireland is a multinational state. A series of Acts of Union joined first England and Wales between 1536 and 1543, then Scotland in 1707 and, finally, Ireland in 1801. Linda Colley, in her book *Britons: Forging the Nation, 1707–1837* (1992), has argued that a new British identity emerged through the 1700s, forged around a common Protestantism during a series of wars against Catholic enemies. Some scholars have described a process of internal colonization, in which the English imposed control over their neighbours. While this interpretation works well for Ireland, many now present a more consensual relation-ship, in which Scottish and Welsh elites retained relative autonomy and benefited from union with England.

The following chapter examines the ways in which war has shaped the national imaginings of Britons since 1914. A sense of Britishness has always coexisted alongside attachments to England, Scotland, Wales and Ireland. The tensions generated by this coexistence have varied, but the union has been strongest when defined against a com-mon enemy.

The Great War, 1914–18

On 2 August 1914 the German army invaded Luxembourg and Belgium. Two days later, after the Germans refused to withdraw, the British government declared war. By the end of the month, 300,000 Britons had volunteered for military service. Within six months around 15 per cent of the industrial workforce was in uniform. Between August 1914 and the introduction of conscription in January 1916, approximately 2.4 million men enlisted.

The famous 'rush to the colours' should not be exaggerated. 'War enthusiasm' was not universal and many responded with apathy or anger to the outbreak of hostilities. But the state proved highly successful at mobilizing the nation behind the war effort. Bitter internal conflicts had marked the years before 1914, with trade unions calling an unprecedented number of strikes and an aggressive campaign to secure votes for women. The majority of workers and suffragettes, however, put aside their grievances to support the war. By mid-1915 over 230,000 miners had enlisted. Scottish regions produced some of the highest rates of volunteering, while Wales generated more recruits as a percentage of eligible males than either England or Scotland. Ex-Spurs wing-half Walter Tull, only the second black professional footballer in Britain, volun-teered for the Middlesex Regiment. He survived the Somme offensive and rose to the rank of Second Lieutenant, but was killed while leading an attack in March 1918.

Walter Tull's father was the son of a former slave from Barbados. In recent years the contribution of troops from the British Empire has been retrieved from historical obscurity. The exploits of soldiers from Australia and New Zealand during the Gallipoli campaign in 1915 and of Canadians at Vimy Ridge in 1917 remain celebrated. That over 15,000 men served in the British West Indies Regiment, seeing action against the Turkish army, is less well known.

Over 700,000 volunteers from the Indian subcontinent fought in the Middle East, while nearly 150,000 saw action on the Western Front. Gurkha rifleman Kulbir Thapa from Nepal received the Victoria Cross for risking his life to save three wounded comrades.

While the empire's massive contribution to the war effort is indisputable, the extent to which a notion of empire motivated Britons at home remains open to question. Some felt it was their patriotic duty to serve King and Country. But men volunteered for myriad reasons: to escape boring or dangerous jobs, as a way out of poverty, to see something of the world, or because they were under pressure from friends and family.

Table 6.1 Casualties sustained by the British Empire, 1914–1918

Country	Served	Killed or missing	Wounded
British Isles	5,704,500	702,410	1,644,786
Australia, Canada, New Zealand, South Africa	1,307,500	141,005	355,249
India	1,440,500	47,746	65,126
African colonies	55,000	10,000	n/a
West Indies	15,600	185	69

Source: Based on Birmingham Advisory and Support Service education pack 'We also served', accessible online though the Memorial Gates Trust website 'Links' page, http://www.mgtrust.org/links.htm.

Reasons could also be obscure. When a group of London volunteers were asked if they were fighting for the empire, many said yes – but, they were referring to the famous Empire music hall in Hackney. Nevertheless, the monarchy played a central role in galvanizing popular attitudes towards the war in Britain, offering a symbol around which diverse groups could unite. The associations were further cemented as hostilities progressed: George V made 450 military inspections, visited 300 hospitals and bestowed 50,000 medals during the conflict.

In times of peace and prosperity few people devoted much attention to questions of nationhood. War, however, forced people to think about what they were fighting for, thus reinforcing ideas of Britishness defined against enemies both abroad and at home. Notably, the conflict marked a watershed in British attitudes to immigrants. Within a few days of the declaration of war, the Aliens Restriction Act, the Defence of the Realm Act and the British Nationality and Status of Aliens Act had passed rapidly through the Houses of Parliament, drastically curtailing the rights of foreigners resident in Britain. Around 32,000 alien men were interned in 500 camps, the largest on the Isle of Wight. Germans had comprised one of the most significant immigrant communities before the war. By the end of 1919, over 23,000, more than a third of the pre-war population, had been repatriated.

Under the pressure of total war, both patriotic commentators and government propagandists contrasted a brutal, militarist Germany with a peaceful and freedom-loving Britain. 'What we are fighting for,' proclaimed the Chancellor of the Exchequer David Lloyd George, is 'that claim to predominancy of a [German] civilisation which, if once it rules and sways the world, liberty goes, democracy vanishes' (*The Times*, 21/09/1914). Reports of a succession of German atrocities reinforced this message: the killing of civilians in Belgium, the first use of poison gas, the bombardment of British cities by air and sea and the execution of Nurse Edith Cavell for helping prisoners of war to escape. Posters, cartoons and propaganda films presented German soldiers as apes or demons.

Most damaging of all was the sinking of RMS *Lusitania* by German U-boats off the coast of Ireland on 7 May 1915, with the loss of 1200 lives. The sinking of a civilian passenger liner caused outrage, most notably in the USA, as 120 Americans were among the dead. The Germans claimed the ship was carrying munitions (a claim later proved correct), and countered that the British naval blockade was starving many innocent Germans. But the incident intensified presentations of a barbaric, inhuman enemy. A few days after the disaster, the *Report of the Committee on Alleged German Outrages*, headed by James Bryce, intensified this image by publishing lurid accounts of atrocities.

The character of the German people, not just the military elite, was increasingly criticized. The editor of *John Bull* magazine, Horatio Bottomley, called for a 'vendetta against every German in Britain whether "naturalised" or not . . . you cannot naturalise an unnatural beast – a human abortion – a hellish freak. But you can exterminate it. And now the time has come' (Holmes, 1988: 97). Anti-German riots punctuated the war, with the most violent following the sinking of the *Lusitania*. George V, first cousin of Kaiser Wilhelm II, responded by changing the royal family's name from the House of Saxe-Coburg Gotha to the House of Windsor in 1917.

While the war strengthened the bond between England, Scotland and Wales, the conflict would exacerbate tensions with Ireland. Irish nationalists had long campaigned for the establishment of an independent parliament in Dublin and Herbert Asquith's Liberal government had finally introduced a Home Rule Bill in 1912. The outbreak of war postponed the passage of this controversial bill and the Irish nationalist leader John Redmond declared his support for the British war effort. Around 210,000 Irish men, both nationalists and unionists, served during the war; 27,000 were killed. However, a minority group led by James Connolly and Patrick Pearse disagreed with Redmond, declaring that 'England's extremity is Ireland's opportunity'. Around 1800 volunteers took control of Dublin's General Post Office in the Easter Rising of April 1916. Irishmen fought on both sides as the British army put down the rising. Pearse and Connolly were among the 15 rebels executed by a British government fearful of collaboration with Germany. The execution polarized Irish opinion. Disillusioned moderates split with Redmond to join the radical republican Sinn Fein party, which won a decisive victory in the post-war election.

The interwar years

Violence continued to haunt Britons after Armistice Day as the legacy of the Great War shaped representations of the nation (Lawrence, 2003). Anxieties fostered by economic problems were frequently directed against minorities, with riots involving black seamen, Irish and Chinese immigrants reaching a peak in the hot summer of 1919. The passage of a new Aliens Act later in the year extended state regulation of immigration into peacetime. 'Britain for the British socially and industrially,' declared Horatio Bottomley, the new Independent MP for South Hackney.

In 1920 the government censured General Reginald Dyer, who had ordered his troops to fire on an unarmed crowd in the Indian city of Amritsar, killing 379 and injuring 1200. While the Dyer case filled the newspapers, the government responded to increasingly violent clashes in Ireland by sending troops, nicknamed the 'Black and

Plate 6.1 A British Empire Union poster calling for patriotic shopping in the post-war years
(© Imperial War Museum).

Tans' for the colour of their uniform, to bolster the Royal Irish Constabulary. In response to the murder of undercover detectives by Irish nationalists, the 'Black and Tans' opened fire on the crowd watching a Gaelic football match at Croke Park in Dublin, killing 12 spectators. This bitter civil war catalysed the partition of Ireland in 1921, with the establishment of the Irish Free State in the south, while the six counties of Northern Ireland remained part of the United Kingdom.

Ruling elites feared the consequences of the extension of the franchise to all adult males after 1918, and these fears were compounded by the brutalization demonstrated by domestic riots, the Amritsar massacre and atrocities in Ireland. The war had demonstrated that Britishness could accommodate diverse allegiances beneath the Union Flag, securing the support both of extremists like Bottomley and of moderates such as Josiah Wedgwood, a Labour MP and decorated war veteran. Wedgwood insisted after the war that rule by force should come to an end throughout the world. His moderation would prove more attractive to Britons between the wars than the political extremism of Bottomley or Oswald Mosley, who founded the political party the British Union of Fascists in 1932. Anxieties over brutalization combined with the legacy of propaganda against Prussian militarism to enshrine liberty and freedom as the cornerstones of the British way of life.

The catalogue of waxworks on display at Madame Tussaud's in the 1920s, one of London's most popular attractions, exemplified this vision of a peaceable kingdom. A tableau of the signing of the Magna Carta decorated the front page. Inside, the catalogue singled out three war heroes for admiration: Nurse Edith Cavell, Captain Charles Fryatt, a merchant seaman captured and executed for ramming a German U-boat, and 16-year-old Jack Cornwall, who won the Victoria Cross for remaining at his machine-gun post on HMS *Chester* after being fatally wounded during the Battle of Jutland. All three were victims rather than perpetrators of aggression and had faced death bravely in a noble cause.

Within this broad emphasis on liberty and peace, historians have emphasized three trends in the development of national identity in the 1920s and 30s: first, the feminization of the nation; second, the growth of rural nostalgia; and, third, the reconfiguration of the English hero.

One in eight of the 6 million Britons who fought in the Great War was killed. Over 37,000 memorials paid tribute to their sacrifice. Thousands more men were seriously injured, with disability pensions still being paid to 640,000 veterans in 1939. Many historians have joined Alison Light in arguing that the traumatic experiences of the war initiated 'a move away from formerly heroic and officially masculine public rhetorics of national destiny . . . in "Greater Britain" to an Englishness at once less imperial and more inward-looking, more domestic and more private – and, in terms of pre-war standards, more "feminine"' (1991: 8). The experience of shellshock, on the one hand, and the increasing confidence of enfranchised women, on the other, generated a crisis of masculinity. The tales of adventure in exotic imperial settings by authors such as H. Rider Haggard, so popular before the war, were displaced by the insular detective stories of Agatha Christie in English villages.

This feminization involved a reaction against modern, urban society and promoted nostalgia for rural England, a nostalgia embodied in the character of Stanley Baldwin, who served three terms as Prime Minister between the wars (1923–24, 1924–29, 1935–37). In his most famous speech, 'On England and the West' in 1924, he offered a much quoted celebration of the:

> sounds of England, the tinkle of the hammer on the anvil in the country smithy, the corncrake on a dewy morning, the sound of the scythe against the whetstone, and the sight of a plough team coming over the brow of a hill . . . and above all, most subtle, most penetrating and most moving, the smell of wood smoke coming up in an autumn evening . . . These are the things that make England, and I grieve for it that they are not the childish inheritance of the majority of the people today in our country. (1926)

Baldwin proved a skilful radio performer, broadcasting an appealing image of a decent, moral nation.

Finally, far from dying out in the new era of universal manhood suffrage, the English hero was rejuvenated between the wars. The ordinary 'Tommy' was commemorated in war memorials throughout the land. But many of the most successful books, plays and films about the war focused on junior officers, celebrating the character of English public schoolboys. Robert Sherriff's record-breaking West End play *Journey's End* (1928), and its successful film adaptation, told the story of Captain Dennis Stanhope. Driven to drink in the trenches as his friends are killed, Stanhope continues to do his duty. All men are afraid, Stanhope confesses, but 'just go on sticking it because they know it's – it's the only decent thing a man can do'. In the wake of shellshock, Stanhope is a more complex psychological study than many of the stiff upper-lipped caricatures of the pre-war period. But *Journey's End* ultimately celebrates the traditional values of the English public schoolboy, comradeship and self-control in the face of adversity.

The problem with such generalizations about national identity is that they depend on a partial selection of sources. Baldwin celebrated the English countryside, but the son of a Worcestershire industrialist also worked to create a successful, modern Britain. The British Empire Exhibition of 1924 attracted 17.5 million visits to Wembley, celebrating the achievements of a great manufacturing nation, which exchanged its products for food and raw materials from the colonies. The Palace of Engineering, the largest concrete building in the world, showcased the latest innovations in transport and communications. Agatha Christie's novels were certainly popular, but the columns of boys' magazines like *Chums* were filled with familiar stories of warrior heroes.

A range of national images circulated in Britain between the wars. The legacy of the Great War amplified certain currents, emphasizing presentations of the British nation as a peaceable kingdom, the home of liberty and democracy. The failure of Mosley's British Union of Fascists can in part be explained by the hostility of this national culture to expressions of political extremism and violence. Many followed Baldwin in celebrating the English countryside as the heart of the nation after 1918. But the Second World War would inspire a more inclusive Britishness.

Second World War

On 3 September 1939, two days after Adolf Hitler's forces had invaded Poland, Britain declared war on Germany. Bombing raids by Zeppelins and aeroplanes had killed over 1800 people on the mainland during the First World War, but techno-logical advances since 1918 had dramatically increased the threat faced by civilians. Over 43,000 people were killed and 50,000 injured, in the nine months from September 1940. Indeed, it was not until the end of 1942 that combatant fatalities exceeded those of civilians (see Table 6.2).

The mobilization of Britons on an unprecedented scale would reconfigure ideas about national identity for a generation. War would again be presented as a moral crusade in defence of freedom against a brutal, militarist enemy. But the Second World War would be a 'People's War', presenting a more inclusive vision of the nation than ever before.

As in 1914–18, the campaign drew on the resources and manpower of the empire. India raised the largest volunteer army ever assembled and colonial troops fought in operations all over the world.

During the Allied push through Italy in 1945, Sepoy Namdeo Jadhao earned the Victoria Cross for rescuing two wounded comrades before single-handedly destroy-ing three machine-gun posts. Yet the war also encouraged colonial nationalism and exposed the fragility of Britain's global pretensions, ultimately hastening Indian inde-pendence in 1947.

For much of the 1920s and 30s, British elites had been suspicious of the masses, fearful of the consequences of universal manhood suffrage. Many located the spirit of the nation in institutions (for instance, monarchy, Royal Navy, Parliament), rather than the character of ordinary people. Indeed, Stanley Baldwin's Conservative party denounced the people-oriented rhetoric of 'socialists' as extreme and foreign propa-ganda. The Second World War, however, would place ordinary people at the centre of the national stage. While Labour MPs had filled only minor government posts during the First World War, they would be at the heart of the coalition government formed

Table 6.2 Casualties sustained by the British Empire, 1939–1945

Country	Served	Killed or missing	Wounded
UK	4,700,000	305,770	277,077
Australia, Canada, New Zealand, South Africa	1,757,000	82,600	103,500
India	2,500,000	36,092	64,354
African colonies	372,000	3387	5549
West Indies	10,000	236	265

Source: Based on Birmingham Advisory and Support Service education pack 'We also served', accessible online though the Memorial Gates Trust website 'Links' page, http://www.mgtrust.org/links.htm.

Plate 6.2 A wartime poster demonstrating the unity of Empire subjects in fighting a common enemy (© Imperial War Museum).

after Winston Churchill succeeded Neville Chamberlain as Prime Minister in May 1940: the left-wing Herbert Morrison served as Home Secretary, Ernest Bevin as Minister of Labour and Clement Attlee as Deputy PM. The state played a more active role than ever before in mobilizing the people behind an inclusive vision of Britishness, appealing to men and women, young and old, north and south, to join in the struggle.

In the dark days at the beginning of the 'Battle of Britain', Churchill used a radio interview to call on the nation to unite: 'all depends now upon the whole life-strength of the British race in every part of the world . . . doing their utmost night and day, giving all, daring all, enduring all – to the utmost – to the end. This is no war of chieftains or of princes, of dynasties or national ambition; it is a war of peoples and of causes' (1940). Churchill's inspirational rhetoric was in the vanguard of a propaganda campaign utilizing posters, pamphlets, radio broadcasts and films, coordinated by the Ministry of Information. Between 1941 and 1944 an estimated 25 million people watched documentaries such as Humphrey Jennings's *Fires Were Started*. Released in 1943, the film dramatized the work of the Auxiliary Fire Service at the height of the London Blitz, paying tribute to the camaraderie and courage of the volunteers. The film celebrated the heroism of ordinary people, in marked contrast to the focus on officers like Dennis Stanhope in tales of the Great War.

The rural elegies of the 1920s and 30s frequently focused on southern England, but the Second World War again expressed a broader national vision. The bombing raids at the centre of civilian life, strikingly captured in Jennings's film, foregrounded the experiences of the city. Another Ministry of Information film by Humphrey Jennings located the *Heart of Britain* (1941) not in the Cotswolds, but in the upland hills and moorlands of Derbyshire, Yorkshire and the Lake District. The monarchy again played a key role as a symbol of unity. The Royal Family's decision to remain at Buckingham Palace, which sustained nine direct bombings, emphasized the equality of sacrifice demanded by the war.

The unity of the British people was consolidated by hostility to foreigners. Mussolini's declaration of support for Germany prompted anti-Italian riots in London, for example. As in 1914, the government interned enemy aliens, detaining around 22,000 Germans and Austrians, and 4300 Italians; 8000 were deported. However, the sinking of the *Arandora Star* off the Irish coast in July 1940, killing 175 German and 486 Italian deportees, many of whom posed no threat to security, contributed to the relaxation of the internment policy in the later years of the war. Anti-Semitism, though, remained widespread with Jews stigmatized as foreigners who looked after their own interests rather than supporting the community. Of the 180 people interviewed by Mass Observation in 1946, 45 per cent declared themselves either 'definitely' or 'slightly' anti-Semitic.

Such surveys have prompted some to question the extent of wartime unity. Did government propaganda conceal bitterness, hatred and social conflict? Working-class evacuees generated revulsion among middle-class hosts. Far from pulling together, so the revisionists argue, morale was at breaking point during the Blitz, with blackouts providing an ideal opportunity for theft and violence. Profiteering was rife and a thriving black market allowed the wealthy to pay lip service to equality, while avoiding the worst hardships of the war.

Sonya Rose has offered an authoritative intervention in these debates, arguing that 'heroic, populist and utopian constructions of national identity and citizenship dominated public and political culture during the war years' (2003). Her book emphasizes the unstable and contested nature of these constructions. Women and men, for example, were both subject to contradictory pressures. The idealization of the soldier hero in wartime threatened the masculinity of factory workers in essential industries at home, a threat countered in part by presentations of the industrial workforce as warriors in posters and speeches. Women too provided an essential labour force during the war, but their role as wives and mothers, as guardians of family life, was usually privileged above paid work. Regardless of her actual contribution to the war effort, a woman who enjoyed herself in public was liable to be castigated as a 'good-time girl'. Many Britons did pull together, but the war also generated tensions around national identity and citizenship.

The populist rhetoric of the 'People's War' contributed to Labour's landslide election victory in 1945. Winston Churchill had proved an inspirational war leader, but the voters looked elsewhere for the architects of a brighter post-war future. 'We need the spirit of Dunkirk and of the Blitz sustained over a period of years,' proclaimed Labour's manifesto. 'The Labour Party's programme is a practical expression of that spirit applied to the tasks of peace.' The welfare state established by Clement Attlee's pioneering administrations expressed this populist, wartime vision of Britishness, combining freedom with fairness.

National identity since 1950

The British armed forces have fought all over the world since the Second World War, seeing action in Aden, Afghanistan, Borneo, Bosnia, Cyprus, Egypt, the Falkland Islands, India, Iraq, Kenya, Korea, Kosovo, Malaya, Northern Ireland and Palestine. Most of these conflicts have, however, been perceived as military actions ordered by the state, rather than expressions of the nation. Popular spy films such as *The Ipcress File* (1965) dramatized the Cold War but the demonization of the USSR was more pervasive in America than Britain. Indeed, perhaps the most striking feature of this period is the extent to which memories of the world wars continued to pervade national imaginings. Two conflicts, though, did leave their mark: the Suez Crisis and the Falklands War.

In July 1956 the Egyptian leader Colonel Nasser announced his intention to nationalize the Franco-British Suez Canal Company. In retaliation, the government colluded with France and Israel in a covert plan. Israel invaded Sinai on 29 October, offering an excuse for British and French troops to land at Port Said a few days later in the guise of peace makers. International outrage led by the USA and channelled through the United Nations, however, compelled the British and French to withdraw. The crisis precipitated the downfall of Prime Minister Anthony Eden, and offered a graphic demonstration of the decline of British power, only a decade after the defeat of Hitler.

A succession of colonies rapidly gained independence after Suez, including Nigeria (1960), Uganda (1962) and Kenya (1963). This story has largely been told as a peaceful transfer of power by a benevolent, liberal empire in marked contrast to the violence in Algeria and elsewhere which scarred the dissolution of the French empire. Popular films such as *Lawrence of Arabia* (1962) and *Zulu* (1964) offered the consolation that the British had at least managed their empire with dignity and bravery. Historians have only recently begun to expose the appalling violence of Britain's imperial sunset. Official figures state that the authorities killed around 11,000 Mau Mau fighters in the unrest following the nationalist insurrection in Kenya. Caroline Elkins has argued that this figure grossly underestimates the brutality of the British imperial regime, which murdered tens of thousands and placed between 160,000 and 320,000 Kikuyu in detention centres (Elkins, 2005). Yet such revelations appear, at present, to have had little impact on the popular memory of empire.

Newspaper columns devoted to the Mau Mau were printed alongside reports of racial tension in British cities at the end of the 1950s. The history of post-war immigration is told elsewhere, but here we must note that new arrivals generated a more racialized vision of a nation defined against these 'dark strangers'. Compulsory national service was introduced in 1947, but was not extended to black or Asian British men. They could enlist but, only 30 years after Lieutenant Walter Tull was shot leading his men into No Man's Land, were prohibited from applying for commissions.

Two-thirds of the West Indians who sailed for a new life in Britain on the *Empire Windrush* in 1948 had served during the war. Yet the contribution of immigrants was ignored in narratives of the conflict. Over 100 British war films were produced in the 1950s and 60s. The majority adopted a formulaic structure, which owed more to the stereotypes of the 1920s and 30s than the social realism of Humphrey Jennings's documentaries. Officer heroes frequently took centre stage again, as intrepid fighter pilots, stoic naval officers and ingenious prisoners of war in films such as *The Cruel Sea* (1953) and *The Colditz Story* (1955). The Home Front featured mainly as a setting for romantic encounters, with women serving largely as 'love-interest' for men. The radicalism of the 'People's War' was diluted into generic celebrations of national character.

Conservative Prime Minister Margaret Thatcher powerfully appropriated the memory of the Second World War in the 1980s. On 2 April 1982 the Argentinian military dictatorship led by General Galtieri invaded the Falkland Islands, colonized by the British since 1833 and home to around 1800 inhabitants. Thatcher swiftly despatched a task force to the South Atlantic. After intense fighting, the Argentinian forces surrendered on 14 June, having suffered around 650 fatalities. The British dead numbered 255. Reports of the war frequently referred to Churchill, the Dunkirk spirit and freedom-loving Britons standing up to dictators. Supported by a bellicose tabloid press, Thatcher presented the war as part of her broader campaign to restore British greatness at home and abroad, after Attlee's wrong turn. 'Those who believed that our decline was irreversible . . . Well, they were wrong,' she declared. 'We have ceased to be a nation in retreat. We have instead a newfound confidence – born in the economic battles at home and tested and found true 8,000 miles away' (Weight, 2002). Such patriotic rhetoric contributed to the Conservative's landslide election victory in 1983. But, as always, Thatcher's national vision was contested, not least by veterans and widows, who objected to her political exploitation of the conflict.

While the Second World War has remained the fount of British greatness for over 60 years, memories of the First World War have been very different – not glorious sacrifice, but futile slaughter. The story of brave, young soldiers sent over the top to their deaths by callous old fools has been cemented in the popular imagination by the resonant poetry of Wilfred Owen and Siegfried Sassoon, and by the hit BBC comedy series *Blackadder IV* (1989). Some historians have begun to challenge this interpretation, seeking to reclaim the forgotten victory of 1918 as the finest hour of the British army. The conflict generated pride and patriotism in the 1920s and 30s, the revision-ists argue, with the negative view of lions led by donkeys only gaining popularity in the 1960s. With *Blackadder IV* still used in secondary school history lessons, however, the negative image of the Great War remains firmly entrenched.

The collapse of empire, the declining significance of religion in public life and rela-tive economic decline have combined to call Britishness into question in the last decades of the twentieth century. Plaid Cymru and the Scottish National Party were founded in 1925 and 1928 respectively, but only began to make a major impact on British politics from the 1960s. The expansion of the European Union and an increas-ingly globalized economy have exerted further pressures, creating new relationships, which have challenged the relevance and utility of the union between England, Scotland, Wales and Northern Ireland. The outcome of this internal war over British-ness remains uncertain.

In Focus

Lawrence of Arabia

On Armistice Day in 1918, Thomas Edward Lawrence was unknown. Yet, within a few years he had become the most famous British hero of the First World War and one of the earliest examples of a modern media celebrity. Born in 1888, the slight young Lawrence developed a passion for the Arab world at Oxford University. He worked on the British Museum's excavations in Syria from 1911 to 1914, becoming fluent in Arabic. At the outbreak of war, Lawrence joined a hastily assembled military intelligence unit in Cairo. In November 1914, the Ottoman Empire declared war on the Allied Powers, and one of Lawrence's unit's aims was to encourage Arab tribes to rise up against their Turkish masters. The conflict in the Middle East struck at the heart of the British Empire, threatening both the Suez Canal and the Anglo-Persian oil pipeline.

In June 1916 Sherif Hussein of Mecca launched the Arab Revolt. Partly motivated by the death of two of his brothers in the war, Lawrence wanted action, and was attached as liaison officer to one of Hussein's sons. He played a key role in overseeing the capture of the strategic port of Akaba on the Red Sea in July 1917. The new commander of the British-led Egyptian Expeditionary Force, General Sir Edmund Allenby, greatly valued the Arab Revolt as an effective and cheap complement to assaults by larger Allied forces. For the rest of the war, Lawrence was involved in a series of guerrilla raids, blowing up important railway routes and disrupting communications behind the Turkish lines during Allenby's final victorious assault on Damascus.

'Lawrence of Arabia' was initially created by the American journalist Lowell Thomas, who had met and filmed the Englishman in 1918. Thomas's lecture 'With Allenby in Palestine and Lawrence in Arabia', copiously illustrated with photographs and films, opened at London's Royal Opera House in August 1919. The show caused

Lawrence of Arabia

a sensation and was seen by an estimated 4 million people around the world. 'The Blond Bedouin' proved the star attraction and Thomas shortened the title of his show to 'With Lawrence in Arabia'.

Britons in the 1920s were seduced by Lawrence. It had proved difficult to generate lasting heroic icons out of the mud and blood of the trenches. The Arab Revolt, on the other hand, was a war of movement in which courage, ingenuity and daring were displayed on a spectacular desert stage. And Lawrence also had sex appeal. Arabia in this period conjured images of sensuality, harnessed by the massive Hollywood blockbuster The Sheik, released in 1921, with Rudolph Valentino in the starring role.

Lawrence was both repelled and enchanted by his celebrity. He claimed to seek an anonymous life in the forces, serving in the tank corps and the RAF under pseudonyms. An increasingly intrusive press, however, relentlessly pursued this living hero, forcing him to move postings throughout the 1920s. But Lawrence also enjoyed his fame. In addition to Churchill, his circle of admirers included Thomas Hardy, Lady Astor, George Bernard Shaw, W.H. Auden, Christopher Isherwood and Kathleen Scott, the widow of 'Scott of the Antarctic'.

Lawrence carefully crafted his public image with his own account of the Arab Revolt, published privately in 1926 under the title the Seven Pillars of Wisdom, a phrase from the Book of Proverbs. An abridged version, Revolt in the Desert, achieved popular success the following year. The book has been hailed as a modernist classic. Lawrence certainly dramatized his own contribution to the revolt, but the book also offered a complex psychological portrait, which included an account of his flogging after capture by the Turks in 1917. This account, and later revelations about his predilection for regular beatings, would further intrigue his admirers.

Lawrence died suddenly in 1935 in a motorcycle accident. He was elevated to the nation's pantheon of heroes, joining Nelson, Wellington and General Gordon, with a memorial service and bronze bust in St Paul's Cathedral. His story has continued to fascinate the public ever since. Richard Aldington's savage 'debunking' biography in the 1950s, which condemned the 'Blond Bedouin's' self-aggrandisement, did more harm to the author's reputation than Lawrence's. His longevity was guaranteed in 1962 with the release of David Lean's epic film Lawrence of Arabia, with Peter O'Toole in the lead role. Hailed as a masterpiece, and the recipient of seven Oscars, the film recast Lawrence for the 1960s. Emphasizing both Lawrence's friendship with the Arabs and his brooding, complex personality, the film would serve as a vehicle for imperial nostalgia in the twilight of the British Empire.

The Imperial War Museum staged a major exhibition devoted to Lawrence's life in 2005–06. The story of Lawrence of Arabia – psychological study, tale of adventure, of heroic masculinity, of friendship in the unforgiving desert, of sexual deviance, of liberal imperialism – continues to dazzle and intrigue.

Debates and Interpretations

Paul Ward's *Britishness since 1870* (London, 2004) offers an invaluable overview of recent debates, which has informed this chapter. While Michael Paris, *Warrior Nation: Images of War in British Popular Culture* (London, 2000) and others have described a pervasive 'pleasure culture of war' in Britain before 1914, both Niall Ferguson, *The Pity of War* (London, 1998), and Adrian Gregory, 'British "War Enthusiasm" in 1914: a reassessment', in Gail Braybon (ed.) *Evidence, History and the Great War: Historians and the Impact of 1914–18* (Oxford, 2003) question the extent of 'war enthusiasm'.

Alison Light's description of a feminized post-war culture, *Forever England: Femininity, Literature and Conservatism Between the Wars* (London, 1991), has proved influential, but both Peter Mandler, 'Against "Englishness": English culture and the limits to rural nostalgia, 1850–1940', *Transactions of the Royal Historical Society*, 7 (1997) and David Edgerton, *Warfare State: Britain, 1920–1970* (Cambridge, 2005), have presented a more dynamic British encounter with modernity.

Debates about the social history of Britain during the Second World War are neatly encapsulated in a comparison between Angus Calder, *The People's War: Britain, 1939–45* (London, 1969), which emphasized wartime solidarity, and the same author's more sceptical *The Myth of the Blitz* (London, 1991). Sonya Rose, *Which People's War? National Identity and Citizenship in Wartime Britain, 1939–45* (Oxford, 2003), offers a recent intervention, which, like Nicoletta Gullace, *The Blood of Our Sons: Men, Women, and the Re-negotiation of British Citizenship during the Great War* (New York, 2002), emphasizes how gendered ideas of citizenship and national identity were contested in wartime.

Wendy Webster, *Englishness and Empire, 1939–1965* (Oxford, 2005), has retrieved the imperial echoes in this period from neglect, while Caroline Elkins, *Britain's Gulag: The Brutal End of Empire in Kenya* (London, 2005), has challenged assumptions about the gentlemanliness of Britain's imperial sunset. Gary Sheffield, *Forgotten Victory. The First World War: Myths and Realities* (London, 2001), reassesses the British military performance, while Brian Bond, *The Unquiet Western Front: Britain's Role in Literature and History* (Cambridge, 2002), argues that negative portrayals of the Great War only took hold in the 1960s.

Many have followed Tom Nairn, *The Break-up of Britain: Crisis and Neo-nationalism* (London, 1977), in arguing that the fragmentation of the United Kingdom is inevitable, but Paul Ward and others have argued that Britishness provides a suitably hybrid category to harness myriad identities of a multicultural society in the twenty-first century.

Further reading

Susan Kingsley Kent, *Gender and Power: Britain 1640–1990* (London, 1999) explores the gendered dimensions of national identity, while Andrew Thompson, *The Empire Strikes Back: The Impact of Imperialism on Britain from the Mid-nineteenth Century* (Harlow, 2005) offers an overview of debates about empire. Judy Giles and Tim Middleton (eds), *Writing Englishness 1900–1950: An Introductory Source-book on National Identity* (London, 1995), reproduce many useful texts. G.R. Searle, *A New England? Peace and War, 1886–1918* (Oxford, 2004) Part V, offers a concise introduction to the vast literature on the Great War. Both J.M. Winter, 'British National Identity and the First World War', in S. Green and R. Whiting (eds) *The Boundaries of the State in Modern Britain* (Cambridge, 1996), and Max Jones, *The Last Great Quest: Captain Scott's Antarctic Sacrifice* (Oxford, 2003), Chapter 8, consider how the Great War shaped national identity. Dan Todman, *The First World War: Myth and Memory* (London, 2005), follows the reputation of the conflict through the twentieth century, while Richard Weight, *Patriots: National Identity in Britain, 1940–2000* (Basingstoke, 2002), reviews the impact of the Second World War. For T.E. Lawrence, the website by Lawrence's authorized biographer, Jeffery Wilson, http://www.lawrenceofarabia.info/ is a good starting point, while Graham Dawson's *Soldier Heroes: British Adventure, Empire and the Imagining Masculinities* (London, 1994) offers many insights.

References

Anderson, B. (1991) *Imagined Communities: Reflections on the Origin and Spread of Nationalism.* London: Verso.

Baldwin, Stanley (1926) *On England.* London: Allen.

Colley, Linda (1992) *Britons: Forging the Nation, 1707–1837.* London: Yale University Press.

Elkins, C. (2005) *Britain's Gulag: The Brutal End of Empire in Kenya.* London: Jonathan Cape.

Holmes, Colin (1988) *John Bull's Island: Immigration and British Society, 1871–1971.* Basingstoke: Macmillan.

Lawrence, Jon (2003) 'Forging a peaceable kingdom: war, violence, and fear of brutalization in Britain', *Journal of Modern History*, 75(3): 557–89.

Light, Alison (1991) *Forever England: Femininity, Literature and Conservatism Between the Wars.* London: Routledge.

Rose, Sonya (2003) *Which People's War? National Identity and Citizenship in Wartime Britain, 1939–45.* Oxford: Oxford University Press.

Weight, R. (2002) *Patriots: National Identity in Britain, 1940–2000.* Basingstoke: Macmillan.

PART TWO

Themes pre-1945

7

Suffrage and citizenship

Martin Pugh

Citizenship

The term 'citizenship' was not very widely used in nineteenth-century Britain, even by reformers. To many the idea was a somewhat alien one, associated more with French Revolutionary thinking. When contemporaries referred to 'the people' they often meant people with property as opposed to 'the common people' who were largely, if not entirely, excluded from a formal role in the political system. However, during the course of the nineteenth and twentieth centuries the notion of citizenship became more tangible as a result of the interaction of radical movements, social class and economic inequality. The Chartists' Six Points represented one attempt at redefining citizenship, and references by politicians to bringing groups of working men 'within the pale of the Constitution' suggest a pattern of change. Yet the liberal view that all individuals enjoyed fundamental rights as members of their community remained a minority position. In 1906 the Fabian socialist Beatrice Webb explained her original opposition to women's suffrage in terms of 'my disbelief in the validity of any abstract rights'. More typical was the conservative belief that a citizen possessed not rights, but *duties* towards the state, and he would only be recognized in so far as he performed his duties. Thus, in the nineteenth century fitness for the role of a citizen as a voter was commonly associated with certain qualities such as thrift, self-help, sobriety, independence and masculinity. Consequently the emergence of militancy among women suffragists was regarded as a challenge to manliness or male honour by many men; even those who did not posses a vote took pride in their physical control of public meetings and street politics (Lawrence, 2001). But above all, voting was considered to be properly confined to those who had a stake in the country as signified by payment of rates and taxes and possession of property, especially landed property.

Social class, age and marital status

It was symptomatic of the lack of any simple conception of citizenship in Britain that by 1900 there were still seven distinct franchise qualifications for parliamentary voters, some going back hundreds of years, but largely reflecting property ownership and, thus, a stake in the community. On this basis half a million men, known as plural voters, enjoyed more than one vote because they held property in several constituencies. The majority, the householders, were required to have 12 months' continuous occupancy of a separate dwelling house or rooms before getting their names on the electoral registers. House-holders were regarded as independent members of the community; conversely, if they became dependants of the Poor Law authorities, they forfeited their right to vote.

By 1911 some 7.9 million men were parliamentary voters, representing about six out of every 10 males over 21. Yet only a few categories of men, including lunatics, aliens, paupers, peers and those convicted of electoral corruption, were formally excluded from voting; by 1914 they numbered about 1.5 million. A much larger num-ber – 3.75 million – were eligible but simply failed to get their names on the registers in any one year. Traditionally it has been assumed that those excluded were drawn dis-proportionately from the working classes. However, this view has been strongly con-tested and now looks implausible. There was, in fact, no sharp dividing line between voters and non-voters, for men frequently lost and then regained their vote as their circumstances altered or they simply changed address. In the pre-1918 system political citizenship was not determined solely by the formal qualifications enshrined in law; it was also tempered by the activity of the political parties in registering their supporters and regulated by the operation of the cumbersome registration system.

In practice it proved comparatively easy for men to register once they set up a separate household. But as this did not usually happen until they married, they often became voters later in life than the formal rules would suggest. Many men in their twenties lived with their parents or took lodgings near their place of employment and thus failed to qualify as householders. Middle-class men were especially likely to marry late because they were supposed to build their careers or businesses to the point where they could support their wives, and consequently they were heavily disfranchised when young. In this way citizenship was effectively limited by age and marital status rather than by social class. This helps to explain why there was not a major campaign to enfranchise all men in the Edwardian period; even the Labour party did not make this a priority. The explanation for this relaxed approach is that although many men were not voters, they were not absolutely excluded from citizenship; they could expect to acquire such rights at some stage in their lives.

Female enfranchisement and the reforms of 1918

Although the prejudice in favour of the married state was not explicitly enshrined in electoral law, it strongly coloured the debate over enfranchising women. During the

Victorian period many politicians had reacted against bills designed to enfranchise *single* women and regarded it as folly to reward women for staying unmarried at a time when the falling birth rate made early marriage and motherhood a matter of patriotic duty. The novelist Mrs Humphry Ward condemned suffrage bills in 1889 on the grounds that 'large numbers of women leading immoral lives will be enfranchised, while married women, who, as a rule, have passed through more of the practical experiences of life than the unmarried, will be excluded'. Conversely, the pioneer female suffragists argued that in a franchise system based on the recognition of property and taxation, it was simply illogical to exclude women; to include them, as Barbara Leigh Smith put it in a speech to the National Association for the Promotion of Social Science in 1866, would 'make our Constitution more consistent with itself'. Up to a point, this view was accepted in 1869 when female ratepayers were granted the municipal franchise without controversy. As a result, by the 1890s some 729,000 women could vote in local elections, representing almost 14 per cent of the total electorate, while many men who did not pay rates were excluded. By 1900 1147 women were serving as elected poor law guardians, 270 sat on school boards, and 170 on rural district councils. To this extent, women had already established a formal claim to citizenship in Britain before winning the parliamentary vote. For many suffragists, however, the parliamentary vote remained the chief criterion of citizenship; they sought it for its own sake rather than for any practical effects it might entail. This helps to explain why many middle-class suffragists demanded the vote on the same basis as men even though this would have meant the exclusion of most women because they were not householders.

In the course of the protracted debate over female enfranchisement, the anti-suffragists sometimes argued that women could never become citizens in the full sense because their physical inferiority made it impossible for them to fight for their country. In view of the importance placed by some historians on the impact of the First World War and the roles of men and women in that conflict, it is worth noting that this was never a major line of argument largely because in Britain, given her voluntary recruiting system, the link between military service and citizenship was weak; indeed, it ran against British tradition. Almost all soldiers failed to meet the qualifications required for voting; conversely, of those who could vote, most were confident that, under voluntary recruitment, they would never be called upon to fight for their country. The voluntary system was widely regarded as central to Britain's liberal tradition, by contrast with the unenlightened and despotic states of continental Europe whose citizens were subject to conscription.

Scholarly concentration on the controversies engendered by the suffrage campaign has obscured the fact that the Edwardian period did, in one respect, see the evolution of the concept of citizenship. The introduction of state-financed, non-contributory old age pensions in 1908 was widely interpreted, not least by its recipients, as a recognition by the state of the position and worth of the elderly in society (Pugh, 2002). Hence the use of the phrase 'senior citizens' to denote pensioners. Those who met the requirements received a pension as of *right*. It raised their status in contrast to the alternative, poor law assistance, which was generally seen as degrading. Moreover, although the pension did not directly alter the qualification for the parliamentary vote, it did impinge upon it in that the new pensioners were not disqualified as parliamentary voters as they would have been as recipients of poor law relief.

By far the most sweeping extension of citizenship came with the enactment of the Representation of the People Act in 1918. One of the most notable features of the Act was that it enfranchised women over the age of 30 (see 'In Focus'). It transformed the electorate from 7.9 million to 21.4 million including 5 million additional men and 8.4 million female voters. This involved a simplified system allowing men, at least, to register on the basis of a six-month period at their normal place of residence; their status as householders or lodgers was no longer relevant. In this way the right to vote was largely removed from the malign influence of the party agents and revising barristers and determined by the town clerks and clerks to the county councils who compiled the lists each year and acted as returning officers at elections. Moreover, the old poor law disqualification was entirely abolished, enabling many of the poorest people to join the electorate. This system eventually brought Britain about as close to full adult suffrage as is possible. In 1919 the electorate comprised 78 per cent of the adult population, by 1929 90 per cent, and by 1939 97 per cent. The 1918 Act also advanced the rights of individuals as candidates by abolishing the traditional requirement that candidates pay the expenses of returning officers and by granting a free postal delivery. However, it introduced a new impediment by requiring every candidate to place a deposit of £150 – a substantial sum in 1918 – to be forfeit by those who failed to obtain one-eighth of the votes polled.

The historiographical discussion about suffragism grew from the writing of contemporary activists including non-militant suffragists such as Millicent Fawcett and Ray Strachey and militants including Sylvia and Christabel Pankhurst. Among these Sylvia Pankhurst proved to be especially influential because hers was such a detailed account of both Pankhurst family politics and the evolution of suffragist tactics over time. But it suffered from several kinds of bias. She assumed that the women's cause made little or no progress until revived by the militant campaign in the early 1900s. Also, as a victim of the rivalry within the Pankhurst family and the Women's Social and Political Union (WSPU) itself, she painted an unfavourable picture of those with whom she disagreed and virtually wrote some people out of the script altogether. As later scholars explored the topic, their work developed along one of two, not always fully related, lines: on the one hand, research into the many aspects of the women's movement from the mid-Victorian period onwards and, on the other, studies of the suffrage question from the perspective of politicians and governments. To some extent this pattern has continued in that studies examine discrete aspects of suffragism without assessing explicitly how they relate to the overall success or failure of the movement.

Despite this it is fair to say that many writers, at least implicitly, accept the contemporary view advanced by the Pankhursts that Victorian suffragism was too conservative and cautious and that the adoption of militancy by the WSPU after 1903 forced the politicians to back down and brought enfranchisement for women. This approach was modified by Susan Kingsley Kent who argued that the suffrage and suffragette movements were really far more radical, and even subversive, in aiming not just to win the vote but to overthrow all conventional ideas about gender relations in Britain (1987). For critics of this view it was never clear that this was an accurate portrayal of the movement, or why men who refused concessions to a moderate, respectable movement were willing to make them for a truly revolutionary one. Also, detailed study of the WSPU by, for example, Andrew Rosen underlined that it was only a minority part of suffragism, even at its peak, while the release of material at the Public Record Office in recent decades has underlined how the WSPU went into a steep decline after 1911 when it alienated the public and was largely suppressed by the government (1974). Pankhurst claims about their success in mobilizing public opinion against the government were not subjected to systematic examination until Martin Pugh looked at the Edwardian by-election record, finding little evidence to justify their view (2000).

Meanwhile, many historians researched the development of the women's movement over several decades after the 1860s, thereby putting it in a more positive light. Patricia Hollis examined women's role in elective local government (1989); Jill Liddington and Jill Norris emphasized support for non-militant suffragism in the provinces (1978); Lesley P. Hume discussed the growth of the National Union of Women's Suffrage Societies (1982); and Sandra Stanley Holton, taking a diametrically opposed view to that of Kent, argued that the key development in the Edwardian period was the new alliance between the non-militants and the Labour Party, designed to offer a democratic measure of suffragism rather than the old demand to enfranchise a few women (1986). Although this body of writing does not amount to a single interpretation, it does reflect a greater emphasis on non-militant suffragism and, implicitly at least, a downgrading of the suffragettes. In a comprehensive revisionist account Martin Pugh argued that the chronology of suffragism was in need of modification; he attempted to demonstrate how the Victorian suffragists had largely won the debate on the issue by 1900, and suggested that the suffrage movement, far from being in decline in the late-Victorian period, had adapted to and benefited from changes in the agenda of politics in Britain (2000).

However, all these interpretations run up against the empirical objection that the vote was not actually won before 1914. There has, consequently, always been a strong presumption that a major, and perhaps the key, explanation for the women's vote lay in the impact of the First World War. There is certainly a *prima facie* case for interpreting the 1918 reforms as an extension of citizenship by the political establishment in recognition of the patriotic service given by men and women in the war effort. This view was put by Arthur Marwick in *The Deluge* (1965) as part of a wider interpretation of mass warfare as the key positive, progressive force in modern society. However, it was seen to suffer from major empirical flaws. The positive welcome given to women's wartime work proved to have been very superficial and short-lived. In particular, the deliberate exclusion of the munitionettes, who were largely women in their teens and twenties, from the electorate seemed inconsistent with Marwick's claims. It also flew in the face of contemporary comment by both pro-suffragists and anti-suffragists who

Plate 7.1 Two suffragettes selling copies of *The Suffragette* at Henley Regatta, 2 July 1913 (© Hulton Archive/Getty).

rejected the idea of a positive link between wartime work and political rights. In 1916 when Emmeline Pankhurst accepted an initiative by Sir Edward Carson to award the vote to men on the basis of military service, women's suffragists were appalled because of the danger that MPs would be tempted to resolve the franchise issue on the basis of a criterion that women still failed to meet.

Right-wing politicians certainly felt disposed to make special provision for the troops, if only because they wanted to maximize the patriotic vote. Thus, nineteen-year-old boys were enfranchised if they had seen active service, a novelty privately condemned by one peer as 'mischievous sentimentalism of the worst sort'. This boosted the number of military and naval electors in 1918 to 3.9 million. Novel arrangements were also made to allow soldiers to vote by post in France and Flanders and by proxy if further afield. In the same spirit, backbench members rebelled against the coalition government in November 1917 by voting to deprive the 16,000 conscientious objectors of their right to vote for a five-year period after the war.

Recently the Marwick thesis has been reworked by Nicoletta F. Gullace, who suggests that during the war women overcame their handicap in the eyes of society by demonstrating their martial qualities and thus their dedication to the national cause. She highlights the emotions and fears stirred by the reluctance of many men to volunteer by 1915–16, the campaign to distribute white feathers to men in civilian clothes, and the adoption of conscription; the effect, by 1917–18, was to make women appear to be citizens in a conventional sense (2002).

However, though supported by a wealth of contemporary material, this is open to similar objections as the earlier view. It focuses narrowly on ephemeral wartime opinion, neglecting the more enduring pre- and post-war attitudes. It is worth contrasting Gullace's view of the positive impact of war with the wholly contradictory line adopted by Susan Kingsley Kent, who argued that the war was actually responsible for the demise of feminism in Britain (1988). Gullace's thesis relies heavily upon a limited type of evidence, notably press comment, much of which went into reverse as early as 1919. There is much less evidence that those who held power and actually granted the new votes thought in the terms expressed in newspapers. Research in the parliamentary divisions shows that of the 192 MPs who voted on women's suffrage in both 1917 and 1911 only 18 had moved in favour of women's suffrage while four actually moved against (Pugh, 1978). This is a reminder that though wartime experience had an impact on the issue it was probably a marginal one and that the suffrage reforms were determined by continuity of attitude as much as by change.

There is much evidence that men reacted in a very hostile way to women's wartime role, especially where it involved wearing a uniform, which appeared to pose a threat to their masculine status. Colonel Archie Christie, whose wife Agatha Christie worked in a hospital, complained: 'It's a filthy job, nursing. I hate to think of you doing it.' After 1918 he did his best to confine her to domesticity. Indeed, the appalling loss of life in the war focused people's thoughts on the need to promote marriage and motherhood – the conventional roles of women. In the case of women's suffrage, this reinforced the pre-war bias in favour of including married women in any reform. The proposals of the Speaker's Conference, which were accepted by Parliament in 1917, reflected this in that they excluded the young women who were suspect as unmarried career girls in the eyes of politicians, and included millions of older women who were regarded as likely to be a source of stability because they were mostly wives and mothers. One member of the Speaker's Conference, Earl Grey, actually suggested granting extra votes to men and women who produced four children on the grounds that their vote was of more value and they had 'rendered a service to the state without which the state could not exist'.

A wider citizenship for women

Thus, although the 1918 reforms created a simpler and, in some ways, more equal system, they still left British citizenship replete with anomalies and oddities. For example, Jennie Lee was elected an MP at a by-election in North Lanarkshire in 1929 but was too young to vote. When Fenner Brockway contested Lancaster at the 1922 election he was disbarred from voting as a conscientious objector. Moreover, the qualifications for local government electors remained different to those for parliamentary voting; many young men and women who lived with their parents and were not ratepayers were ineligible for the municipal list. Although plural voting had been greatly reduced in 1918, some 159,000 business voters and 68,000 university voters remained. The English universities returned seven MPs, Scotland three, Wales one and Northern Ireland one. One final anomaly arose from Britain's changing relationship with Ireland. When the Union with Ireland ended in 1920 the two sides agreed to maintain 'the common citizenship of Ireland with Great Britain', which allowed citizens of the Irish Free State to vote in UK elections.

Despite these qualifications women took several major steps towards full citizenship after the war. In addition to forming 42 per cent of the electorate by 1924, they won a foothold in the House of Commons. In the summer of 1918 a separate bill had been introduced to allow women to stand for election as MPs. This was thought necessary because of uncertainty as to whether the right to vote automatically carried the right to be elected; following the creation of elected county councils in 1889 the first two women to be elected had been challenged in the courts and forced to resign. Only a handful of women stood in 1918, and the Countess Markievicz (Constance Gore-Booth), who won as a Sinn Fein candidate in Dublin, did not take her seat. As a result, Nancy Astor (Conservative), who was elected at Plymouth Sutton in 1919, became the first woman to sit as an MP, and Margaret Wintringham (Liberal), who won Louth in 1920, the second. Eight women were elected in 1923 and 14 in 1929, though by 1935 the number had diminished to nine. On first being elected in 1923, Margaret Bondfield (Labour) immediately became a junior minister and she entered the cabinet in 1929.

Women's status also improved under the 1919 Sex Disqualification (Removal) Act which allowed them to serve as jurors and magistrates. Admittedly it lay with the Lord Chancellor, who was not always sympathetic, to appoint women justices of the peace (JPs) on the advice of the Lords Lieutenant; but by 1927 749 were serving in England and Wales and over 3000 by 1934. Early JPs included Violet Markham, Mrs Lloyd George, Margaret Wingtringham and Lady Denman, President of the Women's Institutes.

Despite these advances, feminists were concerned that many women would fail to take advantage of their new status and opportunities. With this in mind the National Union of Women's Suffrage Societies changed its name to the National Union of Societies for Equal Citizenship (NUSEC) and adopted a wider programme of reforms designed to attract the mass of women who had never been involved in the campaign for the vote. Eleanor Rathbone had anticipated this need in 1913 when she pioneered a Women's Citizens' Association (WCA) in Liverpool with a view to raising political awareness among women. In 1917 this became a national organization. A major aim of the WCA was to promote female candidates in local government, though this work fell foul of the party political organizations, and the movement was largely confined to middle-class feminists in a few towns.

However, the concept of citizenship and public participation for married women was effectively promoted by the Women's Co-operative Guild (WCG), founded as long ago as 1883. Among other things, the WCG had tried to equip women with skills in public speaking, chairing meetings, taking minutes, tabling resolutions, keeping accounts and conducting correspondence that would form an apprenticeship for public work. The WCG reached its peak between the wars, membership rising from 33,000 in 1919 to 67,000 by 1931. Although less obviously political, the new Women's Institutes (WIs), founded in 1915, and the Townswomen's Guilds, founded in 1928, also promoted female citizenship. Both proved to be highly successful in mobilizing women at a time when the more overtly feminist groups were struggling. By 1937 the 5500 local WIs enjoyed a membership of 318,000. A democratic organization, the WI pressurised governments on a wide range of issues including council housing, electricity supplies, bus services, rural telephones, milk for schoolchildren, provision of midwives, women police and cinema censorship.

The process of formal political emancipation seemed to be complete when equal franchise for women was attained in 1928, making them 52.7 per cent of the total electorate. *The Times* (March 1928) confidently pronounced this 'the last of the political Reform Acts. No other in this succession is possible'. In fact, further measures were enacted after the Second World War. In 1948 the business vote, which had reached a peak of 370,000 in 1929, was finally abolished, as was the university electorate which had increased to 217,000 by 1945. By the 1960s it was increasingly claimed that improved education had promoted maturity among the young, and this led a Speaker's Conference to recommend lowering the age for voting to twenty. However, in 1969 Harold Wilson's government reduced it to 18, thereby adding 3 million extra voters to the registers. The case for 18 seemed more compelling as the Latey Com-mission had recommended it as the age of majority, the age at which a young person might marry without parental consent, for example. Even this did not end the debate. The start of the twenty-first century has seen a new interest in lowering the voting age to 16.

In Focus

The Flapper vote

Ever since the announcement of the Speaker's Conference proposals in 1917, suffragists had felt insulted by the discriminatory treatment meted out to women. Not only were they restricted by the 30-year age limit in 1918, but they were required to qualify for enfranchisement as local government voters or as the wives of local government voters. As Millicent Fawcett immediately saw, this would exclude many unmarried daughters and sisters who lived with male relatives and were thus not ratepayers, even though they were over 30 years old, not to mention widows who moved out of their own homes to live with their families. In addition, whereas a British man married to an alien could vote, a British woman married to an alien could not; one of the equal rights unsuccessfully demanded by feminist organizations

The Flapper vote

throughout the interwar period was the right for a woman to retain her British nationality on marriage to a foreigner. Yet another campaign for equal rights was waged by Lady Rhondda (Margaret Haig) who discovered that peeresses were excluded from sitting in the House of Lords. This was despite the Sex Discrimination (Removal) Act which said: 'a person shall not be disqualified by sex or marriage from the exercise of any public function, or from being appointed to or holding any civil or judicial office or post'.

From February 1920 a fresh campaign for equal suffrage was launched, led by NUSEC, the Women's Freedom League, the new Six Point Group and many other women's organizations. This involved petitions, deputations, hundreds of meetings and a resumption of processions to Hyde Park. There was, however, no return to the militant tactics of pre-war times. Emmeline Pankhurst declined an invitation to put herself at the head of the campaign, preferring to adopt the view that the whole issue had been settled.

Now that women enjoyed a formal role within the political system conventional methods of campaigning seemed more appropriate. Millicent Fawcett felt that when women appeared in the parliamentary lobbies after the war there was an immediate improvement in their standing: 'we were no longer there on sufferance, but by right . . . Democracy is a great teacher of manners.' However, the obstacles appeared formidable, partly because the sympathy towards women during the war had evaporated. Reactionary forces led by the *Daily Mail* and *Daily Express* set up a clamour of complaint about 'Flappers', young women who were alleged to be leading irresponsible lives devoted to entertainment and sexual emancipation, and thus unsuitable for the responsibilities of citizenship. Tactically women were now in the position of men after the 1885 reforms: as the majority now had the vote, many people believed there to be much less urgency about extending it to the remainder. As it was usual for Parliament to wait to see how a new reform had worked out before extending it, governments refused to see equal suffrage as a priority in the early 1920s. One of the members of the Speaker's Conference, Sir William Bull, even claimed that the suffrage societies had undertaken in 1918 to abstain from further agitation for 10 years.

On the other hand, the experience of repeated general elections in 1918, 1922, 1923 and 1924 suggested that MPs had nothing to fear from the new electors, especially as the much-feared women's party had not materialized apart from a brief experiment launched by the Pankhursts which had petered out by 1920 (Pugh, 2001). The political parties devoted their energies to recruiting female members with a view to drawing women firmly into the conventional pattern of politics. Meanwhile, backbench members of all three parties hastened to prove their sympathies by introducing bills to equalize the franchise in 1919, 1920, 1922, 1923 and 1924. This

> The Flapper vote

helped to create a feeling that the reform was inevitable, and in 1924 NUSEC finally extracted a pledge from Stanley Baldwin, the Conservative leader, to appoint a new Speaker's Conference to consider equal suffrage.

In fact, the question was referred to a cabinet committee; this was because the only real debate over women's suffrage was by now taking place *within* the Conservative ranks, and the only argument between the parties was over whether to use a franchise bill to abolish the business premises vote, as Labour wished to do. Influential ministers including Winston Churchill, Austen Chamberlain and Lord Birkenhead remained hostile to the cause. Privately, Conservative Central Office argued that the party was doing very well on the existing electorate and that there was no popular demand for further reform. However, the Tory women countered by pointing out that the party had recruited huge numbers of female members – a million by 1929 – and could not risk alienating them by reneging on Baldwin's promise. The announcement of the government's equal suffrage bill in the spring of 1927 was the signal for one last, hysterical campaign by Lord Rothermere in the *Daily Mail*. Alarmist headlines in the newspaper warned: 'Stop The Flapper Vote Folly', 'Men Outnumbered Everywhere', and 'Why Socialists Want Votes for Flappers'. Undeterred by this, the MPs approved the bill on its second reading by 387 votes to 10, though as 218 members failed to vote this probably understates the opposition. As a result, some 3.29 million women aged 21–29 gained the vote, as did a further 1.95 million who were over 30. The 'Flapper' votes thus comprised only 11–12 per cent of the total electorate of 28.85 million, and a fifth of the 15.19 million female voters eligible to vote in the election in 1929.

Debates and Interpretations
Liberalism and reaction: debates in the interwar period

The idea of citizenship continued to develop between the wars even though no further measures were enacted until after 1945. It was influenced, for example, by the marked trend towards home ownership, which increased from less than 10 per cent of properties before 1914 to 31 per cent by 1939. The notion of a 'property-owning democracy' was pioneered in the early 1920s by the Tory MP Noel Skelton, who was keen for his party to fight socialism by extending property to the masses. But it was also enthusiastically supported on the Left; for example, J.H. Thomas (Labour) also argued that home ownership 'leads to citizenship in the true sense of the word'. It was widely felt that whereas a tenant was rootless and thus prey to revolutionary propaganda, ownership conveyed a higher status, developed pride in property, promoted a sense of citizenship and thus developed the national character. Though ownership did not become a formal part of the criteria for voting, it came to be seen as a desirable attribute of citizen-ship because of the assumption that it promoted stability in the democratic system, which now appeared vulnerable to extremist influences on both Left and Right.

To some extent this view represented a counter to the sharp reaction in the press and in Parliament against the liberalization of citizenship that had taken place in 1918. During the 1920s this reaction was fuelled by widespread fears triggered by the spread of the Bolshevik Revolution, industrial militancy, the rise of the Labour party and the onset of mass unemployment from 1920 onwards. Anti-feminists alleged that Parliament had been tricked into enfranchising 8 million women in a wave of emotionalism and warned that women would use their new power to defend their temporary employment at the expense of men and to avoid marriage. Such comment gained force from a crisis of masculinity triggered by the loss of 750,000 males in the war. It was commonly claimed that the surviving men represented an inferior breed, handicapped, demoralized and shellshocked and incapable of withstanding the advance of emancipated women.

In addition to gender, age and class provoked sharp attacks on Britain's newly democratic system. Many Conservatives believed that 21-year-olds were too ignorant and impressionable to be safe voters, and suggested 25 as an alternative age; however, no one wanted to risk withdrawing the vote from the recently enfranchised men. Similarly, the creation of a working-class majority seemed to pose a threat. The Duke of Northumberland frankly claimed that mass democracy inevitably lowered political morality and promoted corruption. There was consequently some pressure to restore the old poor law disqualification for voters. 'The fact is that quite a large number of people now possess the vote who ought never to have been given it,' argued the *Daily Mail* in 1927. 'It is obviously unjust to the community . . . that persons in receipt of public relief, who are living on the taxes paid by workers out of their earnings, should have the power to dictate policy and decide elections.'

This critique of parliamentary democracy was taken much further by the many fascist organizations that emerged during the 1920s and 1930s. They disparaged democracy as a fraud, claimed that it had failed Britain and urged its replacement by a different concept of citizenship based on the corporate state. Although the formal membership of fascist organizations was small, fascist ideas enjoyed a wide currency between the wars. Front organizations such as the January Club were formed to allow members of the Establishment to discuss the transition from a parliamentary to a cor-porate system. The collapse of the Labour government in 1929 and the anticipation that the national government would fail gave some credibility to such thinking. Moreover, the replacement of democracy by dictatorships all across Europe made the surviving democracies in Britain and France appear vulnerable. Perhaps the most con-crete expression of this thinking lay in the treatment of Jews. The war had stimulated anti-alienism in general and anti-Semitism particular; in the press Jews were accused of shirking the call-up, even though 41,500 actually served in the forces. Existing pre-judices were exacerbated by post-war propaganda linking Jews with Bolshevism, and by immigration into Britain by refugees fleeing from Germany after 1933. In fact,

British citizenship was open to immigrants who obtained naturalization and by this time many Jews had become well integrated into the political system as voters, MPs and ministers. However, Sir William Joynson-Hicks, who was Home Secretary from 1924 to 1929, pandered to popular prejudice by delaying consideration of applications for naturalization and by raising the residence requirement from five years to 10 and to 15 for those coming from Russia. However, despite fascist propaganda that blamed the Jews for Britain's deteriorating relations with Germany and a fresh wave of anti-Semitism provoked by the approach of war in 1939, the conflict eventually had the effect of discrediting extremism and restoring the credibility of the system of liberal democracy.

Further reading

For a wide-ranging survey of suffrage and citizenship, see John Garrard's *Democratisation in Britain: Elites, Civil Society and Reform Since 1800* (Basingstoke, 2002) and Julia Stapleton, 'Citizenship versus patriotism in twentieth century England', *Historical Journal*, 48 (2005): 151–78. There is a valuable analysis of the interaction between individuals, the state and the legal system by K.D. Ewing and C.A. Gearty, *The Struggle for Civil Liberties: Political Freedom and the Rule of Law in Britain, 1914–1945* (Oxford, 2000). Martin Pugh's *Women and the Women's Movement in Britain 1914–1959* (Basingstoke, 1992) discusses the suffrage extensions of 1918 and 1928, women's participation and changes in feminist tactics during this period.

Among the studies of particular themes and aspects, Duncan Tanner offers an important revisionist analysis of the Edwardian electorate in 'The parliamentary electoral system, the "Fourth" Reform Act and the rise of Labour in England and Wales', *Bulletin of the Institute of Historical Research*, 56 (1983) and *Political Change and the Labour Party 1900–1918* (Cambridge, 1990); see also, Neal Blewett, 'The franchise in the United Kingdom, 1885–1918', *Past and Present*, 32 (1965). On links between pensions and citizenship, see Martin Pugh, 'Working-class experience and state social welfare, 1908–1914: old age pensions reconsidered', *Historical Journal*, 45 (2002).

The impact of the war on reform is discussed in D.H. Close, 'The collapse of resistance to democracy: Conservatives, adult suffrage, and Second Chamber reform, 1911–28', *Historical Journal*, 20 (1977); Nicoletta F. Gullace, *The Blood of Our Sons: Men, Women and the Renegotiation of British Citizenship During the Great War* (Basingstoke, 2002); Arthur Marwick, *Women At War 1914–1918* (London, 1977); and Martin Pugh, *Electoral Reform in War and Peace, 1906–1918* (London, 1978).

There is an original study of the appointment and work of women JPs by Anne Logan, 'Making Women Magistrates', unpublished PhD thesis, University of Greenwich, 2002. On participation in the parties see Pat Thane, 'Women, Liberalism and Citizenship 1918–1930' in Eugenio Biagini (ed.), *Citizenship and Community* (1996); Pamela Graves, *Labour Women: Women in British Working-Class Politics 1918–1939* (Cambridge, 1994); and G.E. Maguire, *Conservative Women: A History of Women and the Conservative Party, 1874–1997* (Basingstoke, 1998). Women's role in Parliament is examined in Susan Pedersen, *Eleanor Rathbone and the Politics of Conscience* (London, 2004); Patricia Hollis, *Jennie Lee: A Life*

(Oxford, 1997); Shelia Hetherington, *Katharine Atholl 1874–1960* (Aberdeen, 1989); Brian Harrison, *Prudent Revolutionaries: Portraits of British Feminists Between the Wars* (Oxford, 1987); Brian Harrison, 'Women in a men's house: the women MPs 1919–1945', *Historical Journal*, 29 (1986); and Elizabeth Vallance, *Women in the House* (London, 1979). On women's organizations, see Pugh (above); Dale Spender, *Time and Tide Wait for No Man* (London, 1984) which focuses on the Six Point Group; Mary Stott, *Organisation Woman: The Story of the National Union of Townswomen's Guilds* (London, 1978); Catherine Webb, *The Woman With The Basket: The History of the Women's Co-operative Guild 1883–1927* (Manchester, 1927); Maggie Andrews, *The Acceptable face of Feminism: The Women's Institute as a Social Movement* (London, 1997); and Inez Jenkins, *The History of the Women's Institute Movement of England and Wales* (Oxford, 1953).

References

Gullace, Nicoletta F. (2002) *The Blood Of Our Sons: Men, Women and the Renegotiation of British Citizenship During the Great War*. Basingstoke: Macmillan.

Hollis, Patricia (1989) *Ladies Elect: Women in English Local Government 1865–1914*. Oxford: Clarendon.

Holton, Sandra Stanley (1986) *Feminism and Democracy: Women's Suffrage and Reform Politics in Britain 1900–1918*. Cambridge: Cambridge University Press.

Hume, Lesley P. (1982) *The National Union of Women's Suffrage Societies 1897–1914*. London: Garland.

Kent, Susan Kingsley (1987) *Sex and Suffrage in Britain 1860–1914*. London: Routledge.

Kent, Susan Kingsley (1988) 'The politics of sexual difference: World War I and the demise of British feminism', *Journal of British Studies*, 27.

Lawrence, Jon (2001) 'Contesting the Male Polity: The Suffragettes and the Politics of Disruption in Edwardian Britain', in Amanda Vickery (ed.) *Women, Privilege and Power*. Cambridge: Cambridge University Press.

Liddington, Jill and Norris, Jill (1978) *One Hand Tied Behind Us*. London: Virago.

Pugh, Martin (1978) *Electoral Reform in War and Peace 1906–1918*. London: Routledge & Kegan Paul.

Pugh, Martin (2000) *The March of the Women: A Revisionist Analysis of the Campaign for Women's suffrage 1866–1914*. Oxford: Oxford University Press.

Pugh, Martin (2001) *The Pankhursts*. London: Allen Lane.

Pugh, Martin (2002) 'Working-class experience and state social welfare, 1908–1914: old age pensions reconsidered', *Historical Journal*, 45: 775–96.

Rosen, Andrew (1974) *Rise Up Women! The Militant Campaign of the Women's Social and Political Union 1903–1914*. London: Routledge & Kegan Paul.

8

Motoring and modernity

Sean O'Connell

ON 22 AUGUST 1896 a coroner's court sat to adjudicate on the death of 43-year-old Bridget O'Driscoll. Left with her brain obtruding from her head, the unfortunate O'Driscoll was to go down in history as the first pedestrian in Britain to be killed by a modern novelty, the motor car. Visiting the Crystal Palace in London with her daughter, O'Driscoll apparently became 'bewildered' at the approach of the car, which was engaged in taking visitors on 'joyrides' on the Crystal Palace terrace. O'Driscoll's daughter told the inquest that the motor car came along 'at a tremendous pace – in fact, like a fire engine, or as fast as a good horse could gallop'. A servant on board the car gave evidence that the car was 'going faster than any omnibus she had ever been on', while the car's chauffeur, Arthur James Edsall, stated that his orders were to drive slowly on busy days and that he was doing only four miles an hour. Another chauffeur, who had examined the car following the accident, reported that as it was geared the car could not have attained 'a greater speed than 4.5 miles an hour'. The jury appear to have been swayed by the technical evidence and by the reports of O'Driscoll's confusion and returned a verdict of accidental death.

Both the sad demise of Bridget O'Driscoll and the subsequent inquest provide a useful metaphor for much of what was to follow in the developing relationship between British society and motoring. The nature of that relationship was often confused and contradictory, with frequently competing perspectives. For much of the early twentieth century motoring proved contentious in terms of the obvious technical and political issues that surrounded road safety, but it was also a vehicle of cultural change and controversy. In the latter respect, its increasingly important role in the new consumerism of the early twentieth century created for the car (and, to a lesser extent, the motorcycle) a central role in the manufacturing sector of the economy. The car also simultaneously became, arguably, the most important artefact in terms of evolving gender and class relationships for middle-class Britons. Its role was played out in terms of patterns of leisure and residence and motoring came to hold a symbolic place in both critiques and celebrations of modernity.

Motoring, along with aviation, represented novelty in the early twentieth century, as railways had done for the nineteenth century. The female aviator, for example, was to prove symbolically important in terms of shifting gender concerns in the early twentieth century, as was her motoring equivalent. However, motoring was much more important in material terms. The spread of motor traffic and travel vastly outdid that of air travel in the first half of the twentieth century. The number of passenger journeys on British airlines stood at only 147,000 in 1938, at a time when car ownership was approaching 2 million, and when countless others benefited from motorcycles and motor buses. Moreover, motor traffic and the motor manufacturing industry were central to the 'new consumerism' associated with the early decades of the twentieth century. As we shall see, road transport rose in importance while the railways stagnated in the interwar decades. Passenger travel by bus equalled that for rail by the late 1930s; the numbers travelling by train stalling after 1919. The rise of motoring is reflected in the amount of attention that it has received from a variety of historians with diverse research agendas, from the environment and national identity through to crime and policing. There is, as yet, no similarly broad body of work for other forms of early twentieth century transport. Therefore, the numerous utilitarian and symbolic roles played by motor traffic in the early twentieth century and their exploration by historians will be the primary focus of this chapter, although its arguments will be placed within the context of broader developments in transport history in the penultimate section.

The spread of motor traffic

At the start of the twentieth century the car was a luxury good and, as such, the first motorists were from the very wealthiest social groups. They had to have a pioneering spirit and willingness to deal with the regular mechanical problems that car ownership brought or a good chauffeur to deal with such matters on their behalf. However, as reliability improved and the technical services offered by garages and motoring organizations such as the Automobile Association (founded 1905) proliferated, the attractions of motoring increased. It was not only the private car that took to the roads; motorcycles, buses and goods vehicles all contributed to the growth of early twentieth-century road traffic. Whereas in 1904 there were under 9000 private cars registered, by 1914 the figure had risen to 132,000, at which time a further 259,000 motor vehicles were in public, private and commercial use.

Motorcycle ownership was particularly extensive in Britain, partly as a result of the nation's strong manufacturing record in this field, which had developed out of the pedal cycle industry. In fact, in the early 1920s motorcycle ownership was greater than car ownership: there were 496,000 motorcycles and 474,000 motor cars, from a total 2.3 million motor vehicles at that point. By 1938, there were 1.94 million cars and 462,000 motorcycles on the roads, out of a total of 3.1 million vehicles (Barker, 1993: 159). These figures reflected rising real income levels and the declining costs of motor vehicle ownership in this period. They are also indicative of the design and technical improvements to cars from the 1920s that greatly improved their reliability and attraction. Motorcycle ownership levels were initially boosted by the relatively high costs of car ownership and limited income levels in the UK, particularly when compared to the market in the USA, where Henry Ford famously led the way in extending automobile ownership via mass production and low prices. By the 1920s and 1930s, however, British car manufacturers were addressing new sectors of the market and car ownership rose twenty-fold, from around 100,000 in 1919 to almost 2 million 20 years later. This equated to approximately one car for every five families and established motoring as a middle-class pastime. Cheaper, smaller cars, such as the Austin Seven, enabled this extension of car ownership and by 1936 average prices stood at 49.8 per cent of their 1924 value (at £130 as opposed to £259).

Economic analysis of the market indicates that at this point the car was at the second stage of a three-stage consumer diffusion process (Bowden, 1991). The pre-1914 period is thus associated with a luxury stage, with prices to match, and the post-1950 period is identified with the final, mass-market stage. Interwar car manufacturers concentrated on supplying vehicles for a firmly middle-class clientele. At this point, it was estimated that the purchase price and running costs of a car made ownership a practical option only for those with annual incomes above £250. This was widely viewed as the dividing line between middle- and working-class earners. As a result, the British motor industry did not adopt the modern mass-market techniques classically associated with Ford's Detroit plant. Instead, the car industry contributed to the formation of what Alison Light has labelled 'conservative modernity'. She describes this as a form of modernity taken up by the interwar British middle classes, which simultaneously looked forward and backward to accommodate the past within the present (1991). Thus, despite growing anxieties in the period about the Americanization of UK culture, the British wing of Ford was partly Anglicized. In a moment of great irony, and in response to the historical themes in British suburban architecture of the 1930s, the prime representatives of American modernity adapted to the British market by producing the Ford Tudor. By 1939 the mock Tudor home and a family car had become emblematic of a middle-class lifestyle.

As Harold Perkin pointed out, large sections of the working class were also reaping the benefits of motorized transport. While a significant minority aspired to the ownership of motorcycles and sidecars, larger numbers benefited from the extension of bus and coach services (1976: 142). Buses brought increasing numbers of working-class council tenants to suburban estates, such as Wythenshawe on the outskirts of Manchester, and coaches became an alternative to the train for day trips to Blackpool and elsewhere. At Easter 1938 more than 70,000 motor vehicles descended on Blackpool (Walton, 1978: 186). The impact of buses and coaches can be seen by the fact that between 1920 and 1938 the estimated number of miles per passenger travelled annually by bus and coach soared from 3.5 million to 19 million. During the same period, equivalent figures for railway travel stagnated at 19 million and 20 million respectively (Aldcroft, 1975: 33). Equally significant, by 1939 it was estimated that almost 1.4 million jobs were directly or indirectly dependent on the motor industry.

Middle-class criminals: policing the motorist

The emergence of motoring produced an interesting development in the history of policing. For the first time, the forces of law and order were faced with large numbers of offenders from middle- and upper-class backgrounds. This caused much embarrassment and debate among all concerned. A key issue was the speed at which motor vehicles might safely travel. From 1903 this was set at 20 miles per hour and motorists were soon in conflict with those police forces that set up speed traps to ensnare offenders. It was this practice which brought the AA into existence in 1905, with the intention of fielding an army of patrolmen whose primary task was to warn the organization's members of the presence of speed traps. Police action against motorists proved particularly popular among non-motorists on two counts. First, rural antipathy to early motorists was significant, due to the dust clouds and new dangers brought to country roads by pioneering motorists. Second, the funds raised from fines paid by speeding motorists went into the coffers of local county councils.

The responses of early motorists to the actions of the police were varied. At road level, some attempted bribery or intimidated constables who were invariably from a lower echelon of Edwardian society than the motorist. At a more general level, those speaking for motorists frequently attempted to dismiss speeding as a technical offence and a matter of interpretation. They also suggested that the lower number of cases involving offences such as dangerous driving were frequently the responsibility of chauffeurs or foreign-born drivers. Immediately after the Great War such 'road hogs' were identified with war profiteers 'who nowadays go about in cars and who, ten years ago, were riding about on buses' (*Autocar*, 1926). A sea change in attitudes towards motoring can be traced to the 1920s. As we have seen, by that stage, various forms of motorized transport were providing greater convenience for millions of travellers. Most significantly, the car was offering greater personal mobility, convenience, freedom and status to an important minority, whose significance lay with their relative wealth and status as politicians, civil servants, journalists, magistrates and senior police officers. In such a climate it was inevitable that representatives of the motor industry and of motorists (such as the AA) became increasingly influential in debates on transport and road safety in the interwar years. The former represented an increasingly vital economic interest group and the latter were a more identifiable lobby group than either cyclists or pedestrians. These groups were represented by the Cyclists' Touring Club and the Pedestrians' Association, whose memberships were comparatively small. William Plowden's classic study *The Motor Car and Politics* (1970) identified the central role of the motoring lobby in debates about the 'motor problem'. In 1909 recorded road traffic fatalities stood at 1070. During the 1920s and 1930s road casualties rose sharply and contemporaries speculated on the issue's ability to become part of a 'class war' (Perkin, 1976: 138). Average annual road fatalities during the 1920s were 4121, with an average figure for injuries of 87,255. For the 1930s the figures were 6640 and 182,834 respectively. The relative size of this problem becomes apparent when these data are contrasted with the 3221 road traffic related fatalities recorded in 2004 (Department of Transport, 2006).

The influence of the road lobby at this point was perhaps most apparent in the 1930 Road Traffic Act which, among other measures, abolished the speed limit. Not surprisingly, this did not reduce road casualties and a limit (set at 30 miles per hour) was re-introduced in 1934. However, by the 1930s attention was increasingly focused on education rather than enforcement. New units of motorized 'courtesy cops' were deployed to discuss the dangers of speeding with drivers found to be breaking the limit, in preference to instigating prosecutions. Meanwhile, schoolchildren were the subject of propaganda efforts led by the National Safety First Association (later the Royal Society for the Prevention of Accidents). Whereas schoolchildren in the 1950s, 1960s and 1970s would be advised to take care on the roads by Tufty the Squirrel, those of the 1930s were serenaded by the specially written *Look to the Left, and Look to the Right*, sung by Gracie Fields:

Listen little children, I've a tale to tell,
All you little boys and little girls as well.
When you leave the schoolroom, when you're at your play,
Don't run into danger, think of what I say.

When you cross the road by day or night,
Beware of the dangers that loom in sight.
Look to the left, and look to the right,
Then you'll never get run over.

Plate 8.1 The stolen Ford V8, driven by 17-year-old joyrider James Spindlow, London, 1938. The car was involved in an accident that killed a police constable (© The National Archive, CRIM 1/1057).

In Focus

Joyriders and motor bandits

While speeding motorists were unhappy with their potential criminalization, more identifiable lawbreakers were not slow to modernize their activities, employing motor vehicles in their crimes and making further new demands on the police. The popular press, such as the *News of the World*, were equally speedy in developing the label 'motor bandits' to identify those taking part in activities ranging from smash and grab raids on jewellers through to country house robberies. The problem became most serious in London and the Home Counties and in 1929 a number of police forces set up 'a scheme to surround London for the purpose of dealing with motor bandits . . . whereby a General Police Alarm should be given'. This Agility Alarm Scheme was to 'tackle serious crime committed with the aid of motor vehicles' and it drew upon the experience of the Metropolitan Police's Flying Squad, which had been formed in 1919 as the Mobile Patrol Experiment. Its original name emanated from the unit's ability to operate in any Metropolitan Police division.

Another, less organized, motorized crime also emerged in the early twentieth century and became known as joyriding. The vast majority of cars and motorcycles that were stolen during the early twentieth century were taken by young males. They were used primarily for activities that involved a strong element of performance in the company of other young men and were only infrequently employed in other forms of crime. Of the 5086 cars stolen from London's streets in 1931, for instance, 4869 were quickly recovered, having been dumped after use in high-speed jaunts. There is little evidence that these joyriders stole cars in order to damage them deliberately, or to engage in high-speed chases with the police (an aspect of joyriding that emerged in the late 1960s and early 1970s). Locating a police car for this purpose would have been difficult before the 1960s. But, due to joyriders' obvious taste for speed and their limited experience at the wheel, their activities led to a number of serious accidents and deaths. Among these was that of a police constable killed in an accident involving the Ford V8 stolen by seventeen-year-old James Spindlow in London in 1938 (see Plate 8.1, p. 115). The courts initially had difficulties in dealing with the offence because the Larceny Act (1916) stipulated that theft involved either the intent to keep the stolen property or to sell it on. The accused in joyriding cases frequently claimed that they took the motor vehicle involved for temporary use only, something that was clearly supported if they had only been apprehended after dumping the vehicle. As a result, a new offence – taking a vehicle without the owner's consent – was created in 1930. The courts were further confused by the fact that many young males involved in this new offence were from middle-class or 'respectable' working-class families (O'Connell, 2006).

> ### Joyriders and motor bandits
>
> The development of joyriding reveals a great deal about the relationship between gender and motoring and between legitimate and illegitimate uses of the car. Peter Stearns has argued that all major stages in the development of modern consumerism have produced a new form of theft, which he associates with a 'deviant measure of yearning' for these commodities. He notes, for example, the link between kleptomania, department stores and female thieves in the nineteenth century (1997: 105). The emergence of joyriding, in tandem with motor transport, and its association with young men is highly suggestive of the enormous symbolic value that cars and motorcycles carried in terms of gender, particularly masculinity. While the legitimate male owner of a motor car or motorcycle took part in conspicuous consumption that reflected class status (through ownership) and masculinity (through the control of the technology), the joyrider took part in a form of conspicuous theft that represented a powerful act of masculine vindication.

Gender and the motorist

An analysis of gender and motoring provides useful insights into the extent to which this new phenomenon was socially constructed around the gendered beliefs about technology that predominated in the early twentieth century. These attitudes had an impact that lasted well into the second half of the century. The most obvious example of this can be seen in the limited numbers of women who drove cars. In 1933 it was estimated that females held only 12 per cent of private licences. Significantly, even by the mid-1960s only 13 per cent of women held licences in comparison with 56 per cent of men. If cars and motorcycles were technologies that represented personal freedom and liberation, it is clear that these benefits were unequally experienced. Thus the agency that gender had in shaping motoring helped to prevent large numbers of women from taking to the driving seat.

Throughout the early twentieth century the technology surrounding motor cars and motorcycles were strongly associated with masculinity. The same held true for driving and it was widely held that it was best left to the male. For example, in 1907 *The Times* opined that it was 'difficult to reconcile the right practice of motor-driving with the feminine lot and temperament'. Of course, such opinions were not simply accepted straightforwardly and the numbers of women taking the wheel rose steadily. The Great War was one factor providing a fillip in this respect, with thousands of women being taught to drive at that time. However, this had minimal impact on the stereotypes that surrounded female drivers. The woman driver provided a powerful and contentious symbol of changing gender relations. As the editor of *Motor Magazine* put it in 1927, each time 'a woman learns to drive – and thousands do it every year – it

Plate 8.2 A female owner of a sports car poses proudly for the camera (author's private collection).

is a threat to yesterday's order of things'. This threat was nowhere more obvious than in the highly dangerous and competitive world of motor sport. Several female drivers competed successfully, but their success or failure was dependent not only on their skills, but also on the administrative hurdles that were placed before them. For example, in 1931 the authorities at the Brooklands racetrack banned Elsie Wisdom's 130-mph car, arguing that 'no woman could drive it'. Wisdom earned the satisfaction of returning the following year to triumph in a major track race and then labelled the governing body an 'anti-feminine organisation'. Many women faced similar, less public, prejudices within their own family units (O'Connell, 1998: 96).

Driving skill was consistently identified as a masculine quality and the act of driving was frequently fetishised as something of an art form. Driving could re-energise a man, it was argued. In 1927 one motoring journalist for *Autocar* wrote that 'manhood is restored by swinging into the seat of something that one can drive with precision and dexterity'. As a consequence of this almost atavistic perspective, a strong folkloric tradition emerged around women's driving, with jokes and stories circulating about their perceived inability to take the wheel safely or confidently. This tradition continued despite statistical evidence that undermined it, such as the analysis of one insurance broker in 1935: 'Do not smile. The woman driver, in many cases, is a very good risk.' He pointed out that this was particularly true in the 18–21 age group and was critical of sports cars 'driven by young men whose main ambition is to keep their feet hard down on the accelerator irrespective of road conditions'. Despite such evidence, many women appear to have been kept from the driving wheel as a result of the gender ideology circulating around the control of motoring technology. When one woman from a 1930s' car-owning family suggested to her husband that she should learn to drive, he replied, 'No. . . . You're a dreamer, you watch the scenery . . . you'd have your eyes off the road.' She accepted this even though she was 'a bit resentful really', particularly when her 17-year-old son – 'who was ham-fisted if anyone ever was' – was encouraged to take driving lessons (O'Connell, 1998: 62).

The relatively low numbers of female licence holders suggest that this was not an uncommon experience. Perhaps many women chose to take advice like that offered by the motoring journalist 'Cylanda' in *The Practical Motorist* in 1934. She urged those women drivers whose 'menfolk sit with closed eyes, waiting for the crash' to seek domestic harmony by letting the men 'do the easy part – that is the actual driving'. Women should 'swallow your pride' and carry out the tasks that enabled 'happy motoring, such as map-reading, preparing an adequate supply of cigarettes, and making hotel and restaurant reservations', the reward for which would be 'the sweetness of her lord's temper and the smoothness of the tour'.

Changing residential and leisure patterns

Developments in motor transport extended pre-existing trends both in residential and leisure patterns, notably the fillip given to suburbanization by the private car, motor cycles and buses, as well as the rediscovery of the countryside that a few years earlier had been greatly facilitated by the bicycle (Beavan, 2005: 109–113). Yet developments in motor transport also created new problems and opportunities, such as the emergence of ribbon development on main arterial routes and the not unlinked arrival of the roadhouse.

The phenomena of ribbon development and greater suburbanization were linked by the growth in motor transport. By the 1930s, the motor vehicle was proving to be 'a new and powerful dispersal agent' in and around London and other major cities. Whereas the train had never become 'a wholesale scatterer of suburban development because the tie of the station gave the spatial structure some form and coherence', the motor vehicle 'either as a private vehicle, or as a service vehicle was a new factor in promoting sprawl' (Cherry, 1970: 74). The arrival of motoring in a period that coincided with agricultural depression and significant changes in the structure of land ownership resulted in large-scale land sales on the frontage of roads between towns. The resulting development of this land for private housing and other purposes was dubbed 'ribbon development' and created the classic British suburban landscape of the twentieth century. In the interwar years, as John Lowerson has put it, cheap 'transport and cheaper finance, as well as "romantic" influences produced in many areas a lowest common denominator of design, eating up the countryside at the rate of 60,000 acres a year' (1980: 259).

As well as changing residential patterns motor transport, particularly the car, brought a degree of independence and flexibility that was unmatched by other forms of transport. This was reflected in the variety of leisure activities facilitated by the motor vehicle. Moreover, the attributes of the car dovetailed neatly with the middle-class interest in privatized leisure. In the words of *Autocar* in 1929: 'public transport, no matter how fast and comfortable, inflicts a sensation of serfdom which is intolerable to a free Briton. It dictates the time of starting, the route, the speed and the stoppages.' The car and the motorcycle, even more than the bicycle before them, provided travellers with a markedly different experience to that offered by the train. John Ruskin had bemoaned the train's transmutation of the passenger into a 'living parcel'; motoring provided liberation from this sense of commodification (Schivelbusch, 1986: 54). It also extended the speed and range of travel and facilitated the consumption of a greater range of heritage and landscape. Map production, which had been on the rise since the advent of the touring cyclist, was further boosted by the growth of motoring. Inclusions and omissions from these sources are revealing. For example, notable in Bartholomew's *Contour Motoring Map of the British Isles*, published in 1907, was a small inset map identifying industrial areas to be avoided. The AA produced a range of booklets with varying itineraries – from extensive tours to half-day drives – that reflected the differing budgets of its membership and remind us of the variety of motorists on the roads of early twentieth-century Britain.

Increasing numbers of motorists sought out resorts off the beaten track; Devon and Cornwall, west and north-west Wales and the Scottish Highlands were all popular destinations. One estimate of the impact of this new trend suggests that during the 1930s Devonshire farmers derived up to 75 per cent of their income by providing teas and accommodation to newly mobile holidaymakers. However, greater levels of middle-class mobility were not viewed favourably by all. The hotel trade publication, *Hotel*, bemoaned in 1932 the fact that in some areas 'everybody with a spare room is advertising for bed and breakfast or offering teas'. They also viewed the increasing popularity of camping and caravanning as largely a result of increased motor ownership.

Ironically, given the rhetoric about the individuality, speed and mobility of the private motorist, traffic jams were relatively commonplace on popular holiday routes from the 1920s, particularly on summer weekends or bank holidays. One motorist described a three-hour hold-up on the London to Brighton road in 1925: 'From the Brighton Aquarium to St James's Street I was not for one moment out of what can only be described as a queue of private cars, and motor bikes of every sort and size, and more chars-a-bancs than I believed existed' (Prioleau, 1925: 77).

Sunday became the most popular day for a spin in the family car and there is evidence to suggest that by mid-century is was as big a ritual as those more normally associated with the Sabbath. A Gallup poll, taken in 1949, revealed that one in seven people went motoring on Sunday, the same number as attended a church service. This trend led to more than a few concerns about the state of the nation's morals, as did fears about the potential role of the car as a venue for illicit sexual activity. In 1929 the Chief Constable of Lancashire told the Royal Commission on the Police that a law was needed to deal with 'gutter crawlers' who 'drove slowly through the streets and country lanes with a view to inducing women to go for a ride with them'. The possibilities that the car brought for erotic adventures were recognized by the motoring community, who associated certain cars with this type of activity. Thus the forerunner of the Jaguar, the SS.1, was labelled a 'cad's car' or a 'promenade Percy's car' and the Wolseley Hornet was dubbed the 'Wolseley Whore's nest' (O'Connell, 1998: 23).

Motorists and the countryside

Like thousands of cyclists before them, motorists took the opportunity that their mode of transport offered to explore the countryside. Their interest in, and impact on, rural Britain became one of the most controversial cultural issues of the early twentieth century. It also became one of the central ironies of the spread of motoring. Motor transport was a primary tool of modernity and yet cars and motorcycles were the most useful instruments in middle-class attempts to explore the countryside and to recapture a romanticized rural Britain, full of simplistic and happy folk, which no longer existed, if indeed it ever had done. Moreover, their very intrusion ensured that the world they sought was despatched further and further into the mythical past. It also facilitated an angry reaction against motoring from rural preservationists. Importantly, however, motorists were increasingly welcomed into the countryside by the large numbers of country-dwellers for whom motor traffic represented an opportunity to profit economically.

The critique of the motorist in the countryside also represents an excellent case study in the split between high-brow and middle-brow taste – reminding us of the fissures that existed within the middle classes in early twentieth-century Britain – as countless intellectuals set to work on castigating the impact of the car on rural Britain. The poet Stephen Spender, for example, bemoaned the motorist's incursion into the countryside as '*laissez faire* run mad, a huge inflation of Tudor villas on arterial roads, wireless sets, tin cars, golf clubs – the paradise of the bourgeoisie' (Cunningham, 1988: 257). Motorists were consistently lambasted for their embrace of a mechanized and materialistic culture which was, critics maintained, at odds with the traditional values of the countryside. The chief critic was the philosopher C.E.M. Joad who made many scathing assaults on the car in the countryside in the 1930s. Describing the interruption of one peaceful ramble by the noise of cars, Joad likened them to 'a series of soldiers' who 'had begun to suffer simultaneously from flatulence' and as a 'pack of fiends released from the nethermost pit'.

An equally critical commentator offered his thoughts on the commercial developments that sprang up as a consequence of the rise of motor traffic in the countryside: 'Advertisements and petrol stations and shanties ruin our villages . . . A gimcrack civilisation crawls like a giant slug over the country, leaving a foul trail of slime behind it.' Clearly, the distaste of many elitist intellectuals for social change was strongly articulated in the attacks on the motorist in the countryside. However, what these critics failed to see, or at least failed to assess fully, was the growing importance of motoring in the economic and social life of the countryside. As one historian has noted, few 'rural people were, or could afford to be, as concerned with trimness and neatness as those to whom their villages had become a solace' (Lowerson, 1980: 265).

The 1906 Royal Commission provides the largest source of evidence of the poor relationship between early motorists and rural communities. Everything from dust, caused by motor traffic, through to the danger to animals was raised. However, by the 1930s the countryside was learning to live with – and profit from – motoring. At one level, the motorized tourist was looked upon as an occupational problem. A.G. Street, the farmer, journalist and radio broadcaster, commented upon the poor behaviour of many motorists who expected access to what was, in effect, somebody's business premises. However, he concluded that any damage caused was looked upon in the same fashion as that 'done by rats or rabbits' and was, therefore, 'an unavoidable expense'. The views of Street and others were no doubt influenced by the increasing use of motor vehicles by those from rural communities. In the countryside the utilitarian benefits of motor owner-ship were, of course, greater than in urban areas where public transport was a viable alter-native. By the 1920s the majority of rural car owners were farmers. Not surprisingly, they often bought the Ford Model T, the car that was so popular with the American farming community. Cars were used for a range of practical purposes, from driving the hay sweep to gassing rats with their exhausts. It is perhaps for this reason that, unlike their equivalents of 1906, the farmers' representatives who gave evidence before the Royal Commission on Transport in 1929 did not launch sustained attacks on the motorist. As well as its uses on the farm, cars provided the farming family with many of the attractions presented to urban motorists, such as increased mobility and the expression of status. Remembering her childhood in the 1930s, Eironwy Phillips outlined what car ownership brought to her family. They lived in the Neath Valley in south-east Wales, five miles from the nearest town. When her grandmother bought a 'shimmering black' Ford 8 her life was revolutionized: 'she could go to chapel in style, deliver milk and eggs . . . even carry the occasional calf or pig, hens and ducks, all in double-quick time and come rain or shine'. For Eironwy, the family's first cars were 'magic machines' that 'seemed benevolent, giving, generous, reliable, protective, as though they loved life and had come into being to share the fun of life with us' (O'Connell, 1998: 173).

Such experiences were beyond the imagination of Joad and the other rural preservations and they seemed unable to comprehend what the car offered to the previously isolated rural family and what that revealed about the complexity of motor use in the countryside. Nor did they appreciate the economic impact of motor traffic. For those who made their living from the land, its significance usually corresponded to its use value, rather than its scenic value, and they sold and hired out pieces of it in order to aid their survival in an era of falling agricultural prices.

The Council for the Preservation of Rural England (CPRE), established in 1925, tasked itself with the role of restricting modernization in the countryside. As such, many of its efforts centred on the impact of motoring. Like Joad and others, its suggestions were often based on a limited and romantically informed understanding of the practicalities of the rural economy. Thus, while claiming to be against exaggerated rusticity, the CPRE booklet on approved designs for petrol stations in the countryside recommended building materials that included timber framing for walls and thatch for roofs. These suggestions were unsurprisingly labelled as 'incomprehensible' by the journal *Architect*. They were also ignored by the many rural entrepreneurs who began to sell petrol as a sideline to other activities, for this was a case when the urban taste for conservative modernity went too far. The owners of motor cars and motorcycles who sought an escape from city or suburban living in the countryside may often have been disturbed to see signs of modernity in rural locations but if it meant they could buy petrol outside the 'olde tea shoppe' where they had broken their Sunday spin, then so be it. They might have regretted the changes that they helped bring to the countryside, but they nonetheless wanted to motor there themselves. It was the access of others that they would have been happy to prevent, not their own. This process represented another form of conservative Britain coming to terms, rather awkwardly, with the tensions that emerged from the modernity brought by motoring.

Debates and Interpretations

Transport history grew out of business and economic history and the approaches and questions that dominated those two fields shaped the nature of knowledge that emerged from transport history until the 1990s. To a large extent the subject of the railways was predominant, primarily as a result of its role in British industrialization. The counterfactual questions about the role of the railway in the development of the North American economy that were asked by Robert Fogel were adapted and asked in the context of the nineteenth-century British economy (1964). In terms of the early twentieth century, similar approaches initially dominated the historical study of the transport technologies that emerged at that time, such as motor traffic and aviation, with histories that centred on management structures and economic performance. Thus the focus was very much on the supply side of these industries, with little related about the demand side and consumers. For example, there was a substantial and important debate about whether or not the British motor industry could have adopted Fordist production methods in the interwar period. Sue Bowden's work finally appears to have ended that debate, by indicating that the income levels in the market did not allow for such a development. Bowden's approach allied aspects of the traditional approach with insights into the nature of demand for consumer goods in interwar Britain (1991).

Over the past decade transport historians have begun to reflect more critically on their practices and to pose questions about how their enquiries might be re-energized. It has been widely acknowledged that some of transport history's traditional approaches were posited upon a whiggish interpretation of transport developments. Many summaries tended to view each new transport technology as simply replacing an earlier one. For example, views that road traffic swept aside rail traffic have been modified in recent years via more detailed research and an emphasis on the complexity of transport modes and options. For instance, John Armstrong has written that in the interwar decades the size of the average lorry and its limited speed, along with the absence of adequate arterial roads and motor roads, meant that rail transport continued to be significant. He also points out that much is still to be learned about the precise nature of the economic competition between road and rail in the early twentieth century (1998).

However, in recent years the challenges to traditional approaches to transport history have been more fundamental and have been based on developments taking place in cultural and social history. Margaret Walsh has pointed out that transport history has been slow to adopt the methods and questions of cultural and social history. In particular, she is eager to inject a strong degree of gender analysis into the historical analysis of transport and its consumption to inform what has been a male-centred discourse (2002). Gijs Mom has joined the debate to acknowledge the dominance of the economic approach in transport history to champion more dynamic approaches 'within the emerging field of the history of technology' which have adopted important insights from sociology that identify the extent to which all technologies are socially constructed. Most recently Colin Divall and George Revill have caused a stir among their more conservative counterparts by arguing that the 'cultural turn' has energized many other areas of the humanities and will have to be adopted within transport history if it is to make any relevant contributions to other fields of history (2005).

The approach urged by Walsh, Mom, Divall and Revill has been taken up by a small number of researchers and much remains to be done if their agenda is to be met. For example, there remains no study of the bicycle or motorcycle that explores the cultural and social significance of these two products that were so important in terms of individual mobility in the twentieth century. Sean O'Connell's study of the car currently stands alone in terms of the social and cultural impact of motoring in Britain. A small but growing number of studies are emerging that examine the railways in refreshing contexts. For instance, Colin Divall is developing research that begins the exploration of the twentieth-century railway from the consumer's perspective (2005). However, much of this work is still in development and because of this many of the most interesting recent insights into aspects of transport history have actually emanated from work by historians writing about subjects such as crime or national identity, whose research has led them to explore issues such as car crime or the impact of travel on conceptions of Englishness. Several of these works are cited below.

Further reading

For the current debates about potential new directions in transport history see Colin Divall and George Revill, 'Cultures of transport: representation, practice and technology', *Journal of Transport History*, 26 (2005). The best introduction to the political debates that surrounded the development of motor traffic is William Plowden, *The Motor Car and Politics* (Harmondsworth, 1973). A general overview of the historiography of motoring can be found in Theo Barker, 'Slow progress: forty years of motoring research', *Journal of*

Transport History, 14 (1993) and John Armstrong, 'Transport history 1945–1995', *Journal of Transport History*, 9 (1998). For a study of the spread of motorcycle ownership and its initial successes when compared to motor car ownership see Steve Koerner, 'The British motorcycle industry during the 1930s', *Journal of Transport History*, 16 (1995). An examination of the economics of the growth of car ownership pre-1939 is offered by Sue Bowden, 'Demand and supply constraints in the inter-war UK car industry: did the manufacturers get it right?' *Business History*, 33 (1991). Full-length studies of the social history of the car are provided by Sean O'Connell, *The Car and British Society: Class, Gender and Motoring, 1896–1939* (Manchester, 1998) and Harold Perkin, *The Age of the Automobile* (London, 1976). For a study of gender and the motor car see Margaret Walsh, 'Gendering transport history: retrospect and prospect', *Journal of Transport History*, 23 (2002). An interesting perspective on the nature of consumerism and modernity in the early twentieth century is offered by Alison Light's *Forever England: Femininity, Literature and Conservatism Between the Wars* (London, 1991). The changing relationships between the middle classes and the police brought about by car ownership are dealt with in Clive Emsley, ' "Mother, what did policemen do when there weren't any motors?" The law, the police and the regulation in motor traffic in England, 1900–1939', *The Historical Journal*, 36 (1993). Many of Emsley's views are challenged (along with many other assumptions about late nineteenth- and early twentieth-century policing) in Howard Taylor, 'Forging the job: a crisis of "modernization" or redundancy for the police in England and Wales, 1900–1939', *British Journal of Criminology*, 39 (1999). The history of joyriding has recently been addressed by Sean O'Connell, 'From Toad of Toad Hall to the "death drivers" of Belfast: an exploratory history of joyriding', *British Journal of Criminology*, 46 (2006).

References

Aldcroft, Derek (1975) *British Transport Since 1914: An Economic History*. London: David & Charles.

Armstrong, John (1998) 'Transport history 1945–1995', *Journal of Transport History*, 9: 103–21.

Barker, T.C. (1993) 'Slow progress: forty years of motoring research', *Journal of Transport History*, 14.

Beavan, Brad (2005) *Leisure, Citizenship and Working-Class Men in Britain 1850–1945*. Manchester: Manchester University Press.

Bowden, Sue (1991) 'Demand and supply constraints in the inter-war UK car industry: did the manufacturers get it right?', *Business History*, 33: 241–67.

Cherry, Gordon (1970) 'Town planning and the motor car in twentieth-century Britain', *Journal of High Speed Ground Transportation*, 4: 72–9.

Cunningham, Valentine (1988) *British Writers of the Thirties*. Oxford: Oxford University Press.

Divall, Colin (2005) 'What happens if we think of railways as a type of consumption?', Working Papers in Railway and Transport Studies, http://www.york.ac.uk/inst/irs/irshome/features/workpapr.htm.

Divall, C. and Revill, G. (2005) 'Cultures of transport: representation, practice and technology', *Journal of Transport History*, 26: 99–112.

Fogel, Robert, W. (1964) *Railroads and American Economic Growth: Essays in Econometric History*. Baltimore: Johns Hopkins University Press.

Light, Alison (1991) *Forever England: Femininity, Literature and Conservatism between the Wars*. London: Routledge.

Lowerson, John (1980) 'Battles for the countryside', in Frank Gloversmith (ed.) *Class, Culture and Social Change: A New View of the 1930s*. Sussex: Harvester.

Mom, Gijs (2004) *The Electric Vehicle: Technology and Expectations in the Automobile Age*. London/Baltimore: John Hopkins UP.

O'Connell, Sean (1998) *The Car in British Society: Class, Gender and Motoring, 1896–1939*. Manchester: Manchester University Press.

O'Connell, Sean (2006) 'From Toad of Toad Hall to the "death drivers" of Belfast: an exploratory history of joyriding', *British Journal of Criminology*, 46: 455–69.

Perkin, Harold (1976) *The Age of the Automobile*. London: Quartet Books.

Prioleau, John (1925) *Motoring for Women*. London: Geoffrey Bles.

Schivelbusch, W. (1986) *The Railway Journey*. Oxford: Berg.

Stearns, P.N. (1997) 'Stages of consumerism: recent work on the issues of periodization', *Journal of Modern History*, 69: 102–18.

Walsh, Margaret (2002) 'Gendering transport history: retrospect and prospect', *Journal of Transport History*, 23: 2–8.

Walton, John (1978) *The Blackpool Landlady*. Manchester: Manchester University Press.

9

The First World War and its aftermath

Julian Greaves

The effects of total war

The First World War did not come as a bolt from the blue: tensions between the major powers had been building for some years. But the consequences of the first general European conflagration in nearly a century were hard to predict given the growth of population and technological know-how that had occurred in the interim. The general expectation was that the fighting would not last long. Even without decisive military successes modern capitalist economies were assumed to be so interdependent that once normal channels of trade and commerce were disrupted they would rapidly cease to function, forcing governments to make peace to avoid civil collapse. In fact the vast reservoir of physical and human resources available – the fruits of industrialization and urbanization – sustained warfare of an unprecedented ferocity for over four years.

For Britain particularly, the nature and duration of hostilities forced a major overhaul of strategy. Before 1914 British politicians and their military advisers had envisaged a conflict along essentially eighteenth-century lines. The objective was to stop one state, namely Germany, dominating the continent. Britain's coalition partners, France and Russia, were to provide the bulk of the fighting troops as they already possessed large standing armies. The British military contribution was to come mainly through enforcement of a naval blockade. Beyond that Britain would underpin the allied war effort by acting as the paymaster to the anti-German coalition. Creating a mass army was not a priority. Not only would it appear too late to decisively affect the military outcome (especially as conscription was deemed politically impossible in 1914), but it would also seriously disrupt civilian production and thereby hit British overseas earnings from trade and finance, which were supposed to ensure the allies' financial solvency. Hence the slogan of 'business as usual' was coined and only a small expeditionary force sent to France.

Even when it became clear that the war would not be short-lived the 'business as usual' ethos was not jettisoned lightly and for good reason. The allied war effort depended more and more on the import of food, raw materials and industrial goods from outside Europe which had to be paid for, increasingly via borrowing. This presented a particular problem in relation to the neutral United States, by far the largest external contributor to the allied cause. Americans had to be convinced of Britain's financial soundness, which meant maintaining overseas dollar earnings as far as possible through trade. Thus domestic output could not be geared solely to war production. Concerns that Britain's creditworthiness across the Atlantic might expire were only eased when America entered the war in April 1917.

Nevertheless, the government realized even in 1914 that the war would require some augmentation of the state's role in the domestic economy. Plans had been drawn up for control of the railways and to stop hoarding of certain vital foodstuffs such as sugar, supplied hitherto mainly by Germany and her allies. Maintaining 'normal' business soon forced interventions in other ways: for example, marine insurance and the banking system had to be underwritten by the state to sustain confidence. But more important was the decision taken in 1914 to allow Lord Kitchener to raise a large army of volunteers to fight overseas. Having initially seen this as little more than a gesture – the war was supposed to be over before the question of how to feed and equip the new force arose – the government found it had taken on a commitment with widespread ramifications for the domestic economy. A belief that simply by placing orders with private firms a rapid increase in the supply of war materials could be achieved was soon shown to be naively optimistic. Munitions were a particular problem. The few state-owned factories were working to capacity and there were simply not enough private engineering firms with the requisite skills and machinery to meet a rapid increase in demand. A series of scandals highlighted by the press in 1915 concerning the quality and quantity of munitions reaching troops at the front brought matters to a head. Ministers like Lloyd George who wanted to see a greater mobilization of the domestic economy increasingly got their way.

The most significant development was the creation of the Ministry of Munitions in May 1915. By October 1916 it was directly responsible for about 2 million workers, a sixth of whom were in government-owned factories, the remainder in so-called 'controlled establishments' (mostly private engineering works). The Ministry had spent over £2 billion by the spring of 1919, developing a huge bureaucracy that employed some 20,000 people at its head office. In theory it had complete power over what items individual firms produced and how. Gradually state control spread beyond munitions to other sectors doing essential war work such as mining and shipping which came under the jurisdiction of new ministries in 1917. Food control also increased. Despite efforts to expand agriculture through re-ploughing, more than half of Britain's food supplies still had to be imported. Rationing was introduced on certain items towards the end of the war, notably meat, butter, tea, bacon, margarine and cheese. The government also took over the pricing and allocation of a growing list of raw materials and semi-finished goods. By 1918 about 80 per cent of the food consumed at home and 90 per cent of all imports were subject to state control.

The nature of state control

Historians are agreed that there was no sudden turning point away from laissez-faire towards control. Rather, the process grew up haphazardly in response to immediate needs. Regulation just tended to feed on itself as solving one bottleneck created another one further back in the supply chain. It is also important to remember the limitations of intervention. Talk of 'state control' can too easily conjure an image of an all-powerful bureaucracy directing every aspect of economic activity. But this was far from the case. Outside munitions, supervision was often lax. In coal mining, the state really did little more than regulate prices, profits and wages. Some industries only felt the effects of official activity indirectly, for example through shortages of labour and raw materials as these were directed into essential war work. Yet even in the key war industries it is misleading to see the government simply dictating to business. The British civil service was too small and lacked the managerial know-how to run large industrial ministries unaided. Hence close cooperation had to be maintained with private firms via their trade associations and many members of the business community were recruited into government service. For example, at the Ministry of Munitions E.W. Moir (head of machine-gun production and later innovations) and Alfred Herbert (in charge of machine tool provision) were head-hunted from major engineering firms, while Glyn West (in charge of artillery shell production) was a director of the armaments combine Armstrong Whitworth. To an extent therefore, the 'controlled' were in fact the 'controllers'.

The limitations of official power were even more apparent in the labour market. In any major war manpower becomes the scarce resource par excellence. And as more men joined the armed forces (some 5.7 million served at some stage between 1914 and 1918), the gaps in the factories had to be made good. This required not only fresh recruits but also changes to shop floor practices. Customary arrangements which meant certain tasks could be performed only by a specified grade of skilled worker had to be relaxed, a process known as dilution. This could be done only through discussions with the trade unions. Thus, just before the Ministry of Munitions was formed in 1915, Lloyd George negotiated the so-called 'Treasury Agreement' whereby the engineering unions suspended normal trade practices for the duration of the war and, in theory, forwent the right to strike (arbitration boards were supposed to settle disputes instead). In exchange the government promised a full restoration of old practices at the end of hostilities and that it would take action to stop profiteering. This allowed some 2.4 million new workers to be deployed on munitions and other war-related work.

The use of women attracted most attention, but they made up only about 30 per cent of the new recruits: the biggest growth in women's employment came in non-factory

Plate 9.1 Cartoon by W.K. Haselden, 'When girls take the places of men', *Daily Mirror*, 26 April 1915. The growth of female war work is usually associated with munitions factories. But this 1915 *Daily Mirror* cartoon, as well as providing a window on prevailing social attitudes, offers a useful reminder that many of the new employment opportunities came elsewhere (supplied by the Centre for the Study of Cartoons and Caricature at the University of Kent, reproduced courtesy of Mirrorpix.com).

activities such as clerical work. The majority of dilutees were men drawn from non-industrial occupations or the ranks of the casually employed. This helped maintain the size of the industrial workforce, which was only about 4 per cent smaller in 1918 than in 1914 (and, of course, in key sectors like metals and engineering employment was far higher). Remarkably little coercion was used to redirect labour. Mounting casualties saw the introduction of military conscription in 1916 (affecting all men aged 18–41) but this practice was never extended to the civilian sphere, although leaving certificates provided some check on the movement of skilled workers out of controlled factories. The government relied largely on higher wages and job availability to direct people towards essential war work. A blind eye was often turned to supposedly illegal strikes which became increasingly common in 1917–18 when over 11 million working days were lost. Instead the government tried to address the causes of discontent, notably rising prices (with rationing and controls) and profiteering (through taxation). More-over, some non-essential industries such as Lancashire cotton were allowed to hoard more labour than they really needed as it was feared the social effects of labour re-direction would be too severe.

Deference to public opinion also impacted on the financing of the war. Between 1913 and 1918 state expenditure rose from £300 million to £2800 million and its share of national income from 13 to 59 per cent. But the government was slow to raise taxes in response for fear of a popular backlash. This was particularly true of items of general consumption where higher duties would just trigger demands for higher pay. Only in the second half of the war did taxation rise sharply and then the burden fell mainly on income and profits, which accounted for 80 per cent of all revenue by 1918. In other words, the taxes paid by the better off increased the most. Even so, taxation of all types only financed about 28 per cent of the war effort. The rest had to be met by borrowing. With hindsight that was a mistake. The resulting rise in the national debt, from £650 million in 1914 to £6142 million in 1919, meant that the Treasury had to meet an enormous annual bill in interest payments for many years thereafter. More immediately, state borrowing was a prime cause of wartime inflation (retail prices roughly doubled during 1914–18). Because official spending needs went far beyond the available pool of private savings the government had to borrow large sums directly from the banks, which greatly increased the amount of money in circulation, worsening inflation.

In general, however, the government's sensitivity to public opinion was well merited. The war effort depended crucially on civilian morale, which meant avoiding unnecessary privations on individuals and creating some sense, however rough and ready, of equality of sacrifice. The dangers of getting this wrong were shown in Germany where the burdens placed on the civil population in order to maintain the army eventually brought about a collapse in morale on the home front. Hence the fact that total consumer spending in Britain fell by only about 17 per cent between 1914 and 1918 was no bad thing. Indeed, household incomes for the working classes were largely maintained. Although pay rises tended to lag behind price increases this was offset by extra overtime earnings, bonus payments and better paid jobs for female workers. Thus food intake fell very little. For some of the poorest households the availability of higher-paid work probably brought some improvement.

Demobilization and reconstruction

From about 1916 onwards the government started to think about post-war planning and a Ministry of Reconstruction was established in 1917. However, heady rhetoric about 'A Land Fit for Heroes' belied the fact that no one really knew in what circumstances the war would end. The armistice when it came was unexpected and the immediate problem confronting ministers was not how to create a better world but how to redeploy some 5 million servicemen and the similar number of civilians engaged on war-related work. To this end the government adopted a two-pronged strategy. First, it ruled out any early tightening of financial policy. Although it was clear the budget deficit would have to be addressed at some point, in 1918–19 deflation was considered politically impossible. Hence there was no rapid drive to cut spending. Interest rates were also kept low, which made it impossible to maintain the gold value of sterling (the pound was allowed to float). Second, the government decided to remove economic controls as soon as possible. Many had gone within 12 months of the armistice and most of the remainder by 1921, including those in key areas like coal and agriculture.

This approach has been the subject of much controversy. In a famous article written in the 1940s R.H. Tawney accused the government of intellectual timidity, allowing itself to be 'pushed' by vested interests into an ill-considered liberalization of economic activity. But this is to ignore the political realities of the period. The general view was that controls had been a necessary evil to meet the exigencies of war and no more. With Germany a broken reed in 1919 most British businessmen were confident about prospects, believing the needs of reconstruction both at home and abroad would provide full order books for many years ahead. All that was necessary, they claimed, was for the government to set them free. Similarly, most trade unionists wanted to see an early return to 'normal' collective wage bargaining and the restoration of pre-1914 trade practices, believing this offered the fastest route to better pay and conditions.

For its part, the government saw decontrol as the only way to create millions of new civilian jobs as demobilization gathered pace. In 1918–19 there was considerable social unrest with strikes, marches and demonstrations over pay, social conditions and employment prospects. Demobilized soldiers were seen as particularly susceptible to disaffection and rebellion. Taking its cue from events abroad, the Lloyd George coalition government feared a revolution without a rapid rise in civilian employment. Thus both practical necessity and ideology pointed in the same direction. Few doubted that British industry would be able to readjust quickly to peacetime conditions.

Initially the government's policy worked quite well. Wartime shortages meant there was a pent-up demand for goods and raw materials while the inflationary effects of war finance both at home and abroad left plenty of money in circulation.

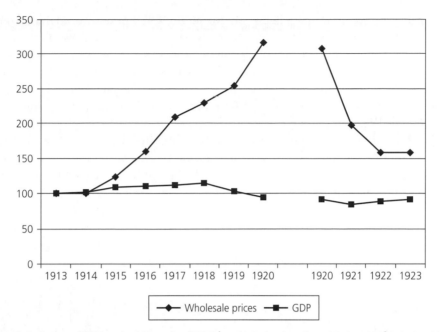

Figure 9.1 Index of UK national income (GDP)[1] and wholesale prices, 1913–1923[2] (1913 = 100)
1 GDP measured at factor cost, constant prices; 1913–20 series includes Eire; 1920–23 series excludes Eire.
2 Based on Board of Trade wholesale price index. From 1920 a new index calculated on a slightly different basis was instituted. The figures for 1913–20 use the old series; those for 1920–23 the new series.
Source: Based on Mitchell: 728–9, 836.

Businessmen and consumers were thus able to go on a spending spree. The resulting restocking boom of 1919–20 ensured labour was rapidly reabsorbed as war work ran down and military demobilization took effect. By 1920 civilian employment in Britain (excluding Southern Ireland) was higher than pre-war. Unfortunately labour productivity was much lower due to shorter working hours and because of bottlenecks in production and distribution. Industrial output was therefore slow to recover. With too much money chasing too few goods wholesale prices duly rocketed, reaching three times their 1913 level in 1920 (see Figure 9.1).

This forced a rapid rethink on the part of the government. By late 1919 a financial collapse brought about by hyper-inflation looked a more likely cause of social breakdown than rising unemployment. The Treasury and the Bank of England thus began to tighten monetary and fiscal policy. By April 1920 the bank rate was at the almost unheard of level of 7 per cent. State spending was also curtailed as the amount of official short-term debt in circulation was thought to be fuelling inflation. By now the restocking boom was slackening off anyway. Once immediate needs had been met it was clear that the war had seriously impoverished all the major belligerents apart from the United States. Thus overseas demand for British goods, particularly in Europe and the British Empire, began to collapse. By the end of 1920 prices were falling, and by mid-1921 the economy was mired in the steepest recession of the twentieth century with 2.2 million unemployed and many more on short time. However, the government continued to pursue tough financial policies as it was now committed to an early return to the gold standard at the pre-war parity against the dollar ($4.86). This required an increase in the value of sterling, which in turn required a period of prolonged fiscal and monetary restraint.

With hindsight, serious policy errors were committed between 1919 and 1921. Nothing could have prevented the collapse of the restocking boom but government actions, particularly in the financial sphere, fuelled instability by exacerbating first the boom and then the slump. But politicians were working largely in the unknown. Just as there had been no modern precedent on how to mobilize for war, so there was none on how to demobilize for peace. Moreover, most contemporaries assumed that the problems of the early 1920s were merely a temporary setback for the economy and that it would soon revive as international trade picked up again.

In Focus

The General Strike of 1926

Although the proximate cause was a pay dispute in the mining industry, the General Strike also reflected broader developments in British industrial relations over the preceding half century. It was after 1880 that effective trade union organization in Britain spread beyond skilled craft workers to embrace a growing army of the semi-skilled in manufacturing, transport and mining. By 1913 total union membership was over 4 million, about a quarter of the UK workforce. To many of the newer union leaders strength came through numbers, so they tried to organize on an industry-wide, national basis as far as possible. A few preached syndicalist doctrines (that is, the use of industrial muscle to overthrow the state), but most just sought a stronger hand when it came to negotiating better pay and conditions with employers.

In 1914 there were still distinct limits to labour solidarity. Some big, national federations did emerge but their internal structures were weak and most industries remained multi-union. Skilled workers in particular continued to insist on organizing separately. Nevertheless, a wave of nationally organized strikes in railways, docks and mining just before the First World War over pay, conditions and union recognition amply demonstrated the disruptive power of large-scale industrial action. In several instances the state intervened and put pressure on employers to compromise. Duly encouraged, union leaders sought to achieve greater cooperation across trade boundaries. In 1914 the railway, dock and mine workers formed the so-called Triple Alliance, partly in the hope that the mere threat of joint action by such a powerful

The General Strike of 1926

combination of workers would produce additional concessions from employers and the state.

The First World War prevented an early test of this theory. But the years immediately following seemed ripe for a trial of strength. The unions emerged from the war with their status and numbers enhanced. Total membership peaked at 8.3 million in 1920 and national pay bargaining was far more widespread than in 1914. Yet although there was much unrest, big disputes were short-lived and rarely spread across trade boundaries thanks to well-timed concessions by the government and employers plus inter-union bickering. The post-war slump then changed the balance of power in the labour market. By 1922 union membership had dropped to around 5.5 million and most workers were forced to accept pay cuts. The miners tried to stem this tide in 1921 by reviving the Triple Alliance but their efforts failed when other unions refused to cooperate on the miners' terms. The high tide of industrial militancy seemed to have passed.

But the coal industry remained a powder keg. Industrial relations there had been deteriorating since the 1890s over wage volatility and regional pay variations, which miners' leaders blamed on wasteful competition between owners. By 1913 the Miners' Federation (the main trade union) was arguing that nationalization was the only solution. However, an attempt to use wartime control as a springboard towards permanent state ownership was seen off by Lloyd George in 1919. The miners' subsequent refusal to consider a compromise whereby the 2500 or so pits in Britain would have been combined into district trusts gave the government a perfect excuse to return an unreconstructed industry to the mine owners during 1921. The accompanying wage cuts and lack of support from Triple Alliance partners merely added to a sense of bitterness and betrayal in the coalfields. Moreover, rising foreign competition and the emergence of alternative energy sources meant that the longer-term prospects for coal were bleak. Despite a temporary reprieve in 1923–4 when the French occupation of the Ruhr pushed up prices, it became clear that the industry as currently constituted could not be profitable. In 1925 the owners therefore sought a fresh round of pay reductions.

Knowing their position was weak the miners this time managed to elicit support from the TUC's General Council, which had replaced the Triple Alliance as the main inter-union coordinating body. Fearing a general attack on wages and feeling residual guilt over the lack of wider union support for the miners in 1921, the TUC threatened an embargo on all coal distribution. Rather than risk an immediate clash for which it felt unprepared, Stanley Baldwin's Conservative government agreed to subsidize miners' wages for nine months at current levels while an official enquiry examined the coal industry's problems afresh. Direct action appeared to have triumphed. But its success was to be short-lived. When the Royal Commission chaired by the Liberal politician Herbert Samuel reported back in 1926 it reaffirmed the need

> ## The General Strike of 1926

for immediate wage cuts, while hoping that a more efficient organization of the trade would improve pay rates longer term. The miners refused to accept this and were therefore locked out by the owners as soon as the state subsidy expired on 3 May. The TUC called a sympathy strike to begin the next day.

The General Strike involved between 1 and 2 million workers in addition to the miners themselves (they numbered over 1 million). It was never the TUC's intention to call everyone out. The focus was on groups who could cause the most immediate disruption, such as transport, power, printing and metal workers. Support was generally solid but the government was able to maintain essential services with the help of middle-class volunteers, the military and some strikebreakers. More importantly, Baldwin and his fellow ministers were unwilling to negotiate on any basis until the strike was called off. And after nine days the TUC backed down. The flimsy pretext was a new set of compromise proposals put forward by Samuel, the Royal Commission chairman. But these were not endorsed by the government and were rejected by the miners as they still involved wage cuts. Effectively the TUC had called off the General Strike unilaterally.

The miners were thereby abandoned to their fate, eventually being forced back to work on the owners' terms after a bitter nine-month struggle. Much recrimination followed. But what the General Strike demonstrated was the difficulty of using the full weight of union power for narrow industrial purposes. Although probably legal, the TUC's claim that this was just a normal dispute over miners' pay was naive. If the union movement threatened economic paralysis whenever livelihoods in a particular industry were threatened, any government, regardless of its political persuasion, would construe this as a challenge to its authority. So unless the TUC was then prepared to try to overthrow parliamentary rule, which it was not, it had to back down. Many union leaders had feared all along that they were heading towards a dead end. But to finally convince themselves that the general strike weapon was futile they probably needed to try it out just the once.

Debates and Interpretations
The post-war legacy

The longer-term impact of the war on the British economy and British society has been much debated. Did it represent a fundamental rupture or simply affect the pace of change? Inevitably this does not beget a simple answer. In terms of its effect on society the Great War forged some powerful myths. One was the notion of a 'lost generation'. True, over 700,000 adult males in the armed services lost their lives. But rather more, over a million in fact, had emigrated in the four years preceding the start of hostilities and the likelihood is that a similar number would have left between 1914 and 1918 had peace been maintained. Instead, outward migration fell to a trickle, leaving the population probably higher than it would otherwise have been. Another powerful myth was that the war transformed the lives of women. True, they gained the vote in 1918, at least if they were over 30, but this was merely a postscript to the pre-war struggle (the 1918 legislation enfranchised far more men than women) and no new cause emerged that had the same galvanizing effect. Divorce became a little easier, birth control methods a little more widespread, but this hardly constituted a social revolution. In the workplace most women accepted their wartime jobs were temporary and that men returning from the front should have first call on new work. In only a few occupations, notably clerical work, were wartime gains consolidated. By 1921 the female share of the total working population was roughly the same as in 1911.

The war affected the different social classes in myriad ways. Income inequality fell slightly. Those at the very top were hit by falling revenues from land and overseas investment plus rising direct taxation. Conversely, things got a little better for those at the very bottom. A slightly more generous welfare system, particularly for those out of work, and better pay rates for unskilled labourers helped to alleviate the extreme destitution many had experienced pre-war. A continuation of wartime rent controls and the instigation of shorter working hours in 1918–19 benefited the working classes more generally. But lessened income inequality did not translate into greater social cohesion. Those who had gained from the war (from whatever social group they came) looked to consolidate or extend what they had. Those who had lost out looked to prevent further encroachments on their position or regain ground. As a result, class divisions and class identity, while still blurred, became more distinct. People might not always have known what they were for but they knew what they were against. For the working classes it was high food prices, profiteers, rapacious middlemen and overweaning civil power; for the middle class it was general inflation, high taxes, socialism, trade unions and state bureaucrats. Yet paradoxically this negative perception of class identity also helped to keep social tensions in check. Grievances could be mediated through negotiation and legislation rather than overt conflict. All classes had too much of a stake in the existing social system to want to overthrow it (see 'In Focus' on the General Strike). Party politics provided one avenue for compromise, especially once Labour replaced the Liberals as the main alternative to the Conservatives. Although a Labour/working class, Conservatives/middle class dichotomy is far too simplistic, the two major parties provided an outlet for class-based agitation. Mediation came also through the spread of collective bargaining in the workplace; through commissions of enquiry and organized lobby groups in the wider public sphere; and through a state bureaucracy anxious to promote stability and compromise.

Did the war change the role of the state? Historians have often implied that the 1920s saw a retreat into pre-1914 laissez-faire policies. The reality was more complex. True, most economic controls had gone by 1921 and several ambitious reconstruction schemes were scrapped or scaled back on cost grounds. But by 1925 state spending was still roughly double pre-war in real terms (see Figure 9.2, p. 138). In part this was

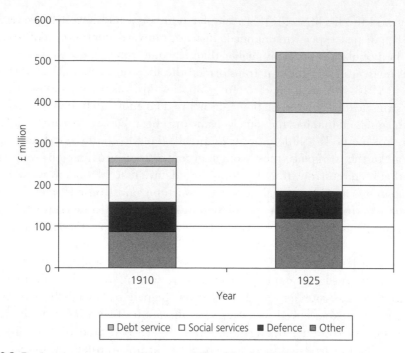

Figure 9.2 Real government expenditure, central and local (at 1900 prices)
Source: Based on Peacock and Wiseman: 164–5, 186–7.

inevitable due to the rise in the national debt. Interest payments thereon swallowed about 30 per cent of all official receipts in the mid-1920s. Yet the government spent more in other areas too, including education (where the school leaving age was raised to 14), housing and the social services. The latter accounted for about 8 per cent of national income in the 1920s compared to 4 per cent pre-war. Higher pension outlays were one reason, while the extension of unemployment insurance to cover the majority of manual workers in 1920 proved more costly than expected. The strict actuarial principles on which this plan was based, whereby benefit entitlements were related to previous contributions, had to be watered down when unemployment shot up in 1921 before most workers had had much opportunity to pay into the insurance fund. Ministers were not prepared to force large numbers of families on to the poor law and provided additional benefit help instead.

State spending accounted for roughly a quarter of national income in the 1920s, less than during the war itself but roughly double the pre-1914 ratio. This expanded outlay was possible without running further budget deficits because taxation remained far above the levels experienced in the Edwardian period (see Figure 9.3, p. 139). In 1914 many economists and politicians had genuinely believed the nation was reaching the limits of its taxable capacity. Events between 1914 and 1918 proved otherwise and the assumptions of ministers and civil servants were never quite the same again. The standard rate of income tax, for example, which stood at about 6 per cent in 1913,

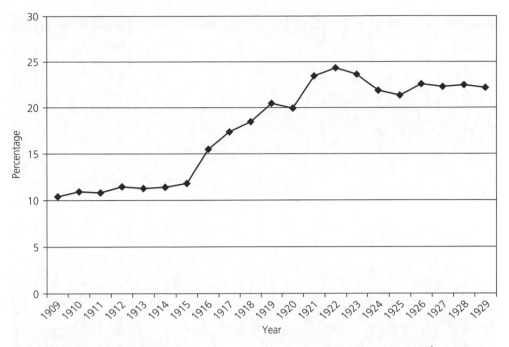

Figure 9.3 Total government receipts as a percentage of national income, 1909–1929[1]
1 Measured at current market prices.
Source: Based on Feinstein: Tables 3 and 14.

hovered between 20 and 25 per cent for most of the interwar years. This brought forth much grumbling but no economic collapse or social revolution. No doubt perceptions about 'acceptable' levels of taxation would have changed anyway, but without the war the process would have taken far longer.

The significance of budgetary enlargement was not appreciated at the time because successive governments insisted they were trying to restore the pre-war system of political economy, which was why Britain went back on the gold standard in 1925 and largely maintained a free trade policy. But this approach failed to take account of the biggest change wrought by war, namely its effect on Britain's economic relationship with the rest of the world. Exports had been curtailed, overseas assets sold, and Britain herself now had large overseas liabilities – £1241 million in March 1919 – the bulk of which was owed to the United States. The balance of payments position was thus much weaker, lessening Britain's ability to act as an international lender and banker.

Conditions in the 1920s were not conducive to any rapid restoration of former glories. Currency instability, rising protectionism and the fact that international capital flows now reflected political as well as commercial considerations sapped the global economy of its pre-war dynamism. World trade in general and British trade in particular suffered in consequence. Britain's exports in the 1920s remained below their pre-war

Plate 9.2 A traffic jam caused by the General Strike of May 1926. Although the strike succeeded in paralyzing the railway system, the government and employers were able to keep essential services going by turning to road transport (© Illustrated London News).

level, an inconceivable outcome if the war had not intervened. Not until after 1945 did the growth in global trade regain momentum. In the meantime Britain could no longer rely on international prosperity to tow the domestic economy along.

The problem of mass unemployment

Difficult overseas trading conditions posed many adjustment problems for the British economy in the 1920s. The biggest challenge of all came in the labour market. Even

Table 9.1 Employment and unemployment in the UK (thousands)

Year	Number unemployed	Working population	Percentage unemployed
(annual averages)			
1909–13[1]	828	20,388	4.1
1921–9	1,647	20,232	8.1
(individual years)			
1913[1]	430	20,740	2.1
1920	391	20,688	2.0
1921	2,212	20,120	11.3
1922	1,909	19,784	9.8
1923	1,567	19,673	8.1
1924	1,404	19,782	7.2
1925	1,559	20,147	7.9
1926	1,759	20,352	8.8
1927	1,373	20,509	6.8
1928	1,536	20,740	7.5
1929	1,503	20,982	7.3

1 Pre-1914 figures include Eire.

Source: Based on Feinstein, 1972: Table 57.

when recovery from the post-war slump was well advanced, unemployment in Britain stayed at around 1.3–1.5 million. This was about 8 per cent of the workforce according to Feinstein's estimates, roughly double the pre-war rate (see Table 9.1). Nearly two-thirds of insured workers claimed benefits at some point in the 1920s even if most were out of work only briefly. About half the unemployed came from the staple export trades: coal, textiles, iron and steel, shipbuilding and heavy engineering. Having been the backbone of British industry pre-war, these sectors suffered in the 1920s as trade barriers grew and foreign competition intensified. Overcapacity and low profitability became the norm.

While the labour force in the staple industries would have needed to contract at some point, the war truncated the process. Neither expanding newer industries, such as cars, electrical goods and fine chemicals, nor service occupations were able to take up all the slack as workers were laid off. The problems were compounded by the fact that newer trades often had different labour requirements to the old in terms of the skills, age and gender mix they needed. Moreover, the declining staple trades were found mostly in the north, Wales and Scotland, the newer industries were concentrated more in the south and Midlands.

Nevertheless, this does not mean, as some historians have suggested, that mass unemployment was simply a 'necessary' price that had to be paid while the economy re-adjusted to changing market conditions. For example, there is little evidence that businesses in the more prosperous parts of the country were suffering labour shortages in the 1920s due to workers being unwilling to move or because they could not get the type of worker they needed. There were just not enough jobs to go around nationally. More tellingly, the 1950s and 1960s saw further major structural shifts in British industry as older sectors declined and newer ones grew. Yet in this period capital and labour were able to shift rapidly between activities and the national unemployment total remained very low.

This has led some economists to argue that structural change was being inhibited by other rigidities in the economic system, particularly in the labour market itself. If wage costs had been lower, they argue, then the older industries might have shed less labour and the newer industries could have absorbed more. Proponents of this view lay particular stress on events immediately after the First World War. Major gyrations in wages and price levels accompanied by a cut in the standard working week (from 55 to 48 hours for most manual workers) left real hourly earnings about 10 per cent higher in 1923 than in 1913, even though productivity had hardly risen. Thereafter, so the argument runs, wage flexibility decreased thanks to the growth of collective bargaining and the willingness of the state to bear the burden of maintaining the unemployed. Thus, wages and productivity remained out of kilter, hampering employment growth. However, it is not clear that wage rigidity was significantly greater in the 1920s than in the Victorian/Edwardian period. Rather, the instabilities besetting both the domestic and international economies had become worse, which meant that wages would have needed to become *more* flexible if they were to act as an economic shock absorber. But the practical, not to mention social and political, difficulties raised thereby were huge, as contemporaries realized.

But what else could have been done to rebalance the labour market? Some called for steps to raise British industrial efficiency through rationalization (that is, merging firms to cut capacity and achieve scale economies). The government had no strategy to achieve this, however. Another option was more active financial management of the economy, an approach championed by the economist John Maynard Keynes. However, after 1920 expansionary fiscal and monetary policies were generally frowned upon. Interest rates stayed high in real terms to restore and then maintain the gold value of sterling, while large expenditure programmes to boost demand were rejected by the Treasury because, it was claimed, they would merely divert resources from the private sector and undermine confidence in the currency.

With hindsight, government policy was probably too deflationary after 1920. A more competitive pound and carefully targeted public works programmes would have alleviated unemployment to some degree. However, most economists now believe that reflationary policies could have worked only within fairly prescribed limits. If monetary and fiscal expansion had been pushed too far, bottlenecks and shortages would have arisen, leading to higher prices rather than higher output; while imports would have increased more than exports, worsening the balance of payments. It is also doubtful whether the private sector would have reacted very favourably to a state investment programme as most businessmen associated this with waste and profligacy.

The fundamental problem was that at a time of slow growth in the international economy there was no painless way of achieving the adjustments needed to solve unemployment. Vigorous domestic policies entailed risks and probably required sacrifices from those in work. After the upheavals of the war and its immediate aftermath no government wished to chance its arm in this way. Using the benefits system to contain the unemployment problem seemed safer. Moreover, for most of the 1920s ministers and civil servants clung to the hope that unemployment would right itself in the long run through an upturn in world trade. This brought forth Keynes's famous riposte that 'In the long run we are all dead.' But the optimistic official view was widely shared at the time. It was to take a further economic storm to finally convince policy makers that the world had fundamentally changed.

Further reading

A broad overview of the period is provided by Solomos Solomou, *Themes in Macroeconomic History: The UK Economy, 1919–1939* (Cambridge, 1996) and by R. Floud and P. Johnson (eds) *The Cambridge Economic History of Modern* Britain, vol. II (Cambridge, 2004). For a long time the standard work on the social impact of the war was Arthur Marwick's *The Deluge: British Society and the First World War* (London, 1965), but his portrayal of dramatic change has since been challenged, notably in G.J. DeGroot, *Blighty: British Society in the Era of the Great War* (London, 1996). B. Waites, *A Class Society at War: England 1914–1918* (London, 1991) provides a detailed account of how the conflict impacted on different social groups. The actual operation of the war economy has generated relatively little historical controversy. The subject is best explored via standard textbook accounts, notably P. Dewey, *War and Progress: Britain 1914–1945* (London, 1997). There has been more debate about economic policy immediately after the war, instigated by R.H. Tawney's highly critical article 'The abolition of economic controls, 1918–21', *Economic History Review*, 13 (1943): 1–30. For an effective riposte see P. Cline 'Winding Down the War Economy: British Plans for Peacetime Recovery, 1916–19', in K. Burk (ed.) *War and the State: The Transformation of British Government, 1914–1919* (London, 1982) – a volume that contains other useful essays on the impact of the war. The standard work on wartime domestic politics is J. Turner, *British Politics and the Great War: Coalition and Conflict 1915–1918* (New Haven, 1992). The politics of post-war reconstruction are debated in P.B. Johnson, *Land Fit for Heroes: The Planning of British Reconstruction, 1916–19* (Chicago, 1968) and K.O. Morgan, *Consensus and Disunity: The Lloyd George Coalition Government, 1918–1922* (Oxford, 1978) with the former taking a more pessimistic view than the latter. A useful collection of essays covering economic, social and political themes is S. Constantine, M.W. Kirby and M.B. Rose (eds) *The First World War in British History* (London, 1995).

The longer-term effects of the war on state policy are debated in J.E. Cronin, *The Politics of State Expansion: War, State and Society in Twentieth-Century Britain* (London, 1991);

M.J. Daunton, 'How to pay for the war: state, society and taxation in Britain, 1917–24', *English Historical Review*, 61 (1996): 882–919; and C.J. Nottingham, 'Recasting bourgeois Britain? The British state in the years which followed the First World War', *International Review of Social History*, 31 (1986): 227–47. D. Greasley and L. Oxley in their article 'Discontinuities in competitiveness: the impact of the First World War on British industry', *Economic History Review*, 49 (1996): 82–100, suggest that the war had a lasting adverse effect on the health of the British economy. The idea that the legacy of the war contributed to the persistence of mass unemployment in the 1920s is put most effectively in S.N. Broadberry, 'The emergence of mass unemployment: explaining macroeconomic trends in Britain during the trans-World War I period', *Economic History Review*, 43 (1990): 271–82. More general discussions of the unemployment problem can be found in W.R. Garside, *British Unemployment: A Study in Public Policy 1919–1939* (Cambridge, 1990); and S. Glynn and A.E. Booth (eds) *The Road to Full Employment* (London, 1987).

The literature on the General Strike and its aftermath is enormous. Good surveys include: H.A. Clegg, *A History of British Trade Unions since 1889: Vol. II, 1911–1933* (Oxford, 1985); M. Morris (ed.) *The General Strike* (Penguin, 1976); G.A. Phillips, *The General Strike: The Politics of Industrial Conflict* (London, 1976).

References

Feinstein, C.H. (1972) *National Income, Expenditure and Output of the United Kingdom, 1855–1965*. Cambridge: Cambridge University Press.

Mitchell, B.R. (1988) *British Historical Statistics*. Cambridge: Cambridge University Press.

Peacock, A.T. and Wiseman, J. (1961) *The Growth of Public Expenditure in the United Kingdom*. Princeton, NJ: Princeton University Press.

10

Depression and recovery

Christopher Price

THE IMPACT OF THE INTERWAR DEPRESSION, or the 'slump', on the UK has been lasting and profound. The experience dominated British economic policy making for decades after the Second World War, when successive governments of both major political parties accepted the state's overriding responsibility to ensure full employment. All but a lonely few felt that Keynes, the great economist of the interwar period, had provided them with the tools to achieve this goal. When this 'post-war consensus' broke down in the economic crises of the 1970s, commentators were quick to compare the subsequent lasting recession with its earlier counterpart. The rough symmetry of 3 million unemployed in the early 1980s and the early 1930s was suggestive of history repeating itself.

Nevertheless, while the great depression dominates recollection of the interwar period, a fact of primary importance is that the British depression was brief by international standards and shallow. Narrowly defined in terms of declining national income, it began in 1929 and ended two years later when GDP had contracted by a little over 5 per cent. National income began to rise after 1931 and regained its 1929 level by 1934. Between 1932 and 1938 the economy grew by an unprecedented 25 per cent, at which point GDP was 18 per cent larger than it had been at the time of the Wall Street Crash. Britain lost 11 per cent of her industrial output in the depression, but here the recovery was more dramatic even than that of the wider economy as industrial production increased by 53 per cent between 1931 and 1938, when it was 35 per cent higher than in 1929.

It would be unwise to imply, however, that the severity of the Great Depression has been foolishly overstated. The grim reputation of the era in Britain was not earned exclusively between 1929 and 1931, and indeed the sharper recession of 1920–21 has no enduring place in the popular memory. The lasting scar on the national consciousness was inflicted by the undeniable truth that against the broad background of increasing national prosperity, a very sizeable minority of the population, exceeding 10 million, experienced two decades of poverty, insecurity and morbidity culminating in war. It was also understood that the nation itself faced growing danger in a time when international economic and political structures fell into chaos and were replaced by threatening new orders.

The fractured world economy and British trade

The causes of the international depression are complex, but a number of factors can be identified. After the First World War and throughout the 1920s, the world economy was troubled by imbalances in the patterns of international trade, in the distribution of primary and industrial production, and in the functioning of international finance. Though impressive growth rates were achieved by many countries and an atmosphere of optimism existed by the mid-1920s, the network of international trade was clearly disintegrating by the end of the decade, even before the Wall Street Crash of October 1929. In this period, the British experience reflected the wider problems of the world economy. Britain was less dependent on foreign trade than it had been before the war, but it was still more sensitive to changes in the international economy than most industrial powers, and a determined attempt to regain control of world finance in the face of massively enhanced US wealth was to prove very costly.

The war had changed the structure of international trade in ways that had mixed effects on the UK. Britain's exporters were hampered by the loss of markets to competitors during the fighting, when industrial capacity was diverted from the export market to the war effort. The US had made gains at Britain's expense, but Japan proved to be the most serious new competitor, particularly as a bulk supplier of cheap staples to developing markets, a field in which Britain had dominated before 1914. Previous customers also demonstrated a determination to industrialize on their own account. India, for example, developed textile and iron and steel industries and introduced tariffs against British manufactures in 1919, despite being inside the Empire and possessing a government composed entirely of British officials.

The position of British exporters was worsened by structural factors. The post-war boom of 1919–20 had produced heavy investment in the staple industries in the hope that pre-war success would be repeated. The textile, shipbuilding and iron and steel industries were therefore heavily overcapitalized and possessed excess productive capacity until the late 1930s. The plight of the staples is held responsible for the fact that British unemployment in the interwar period never fell below 1 million after 1920.

Figure 10.1 (p. 147), however, shows that the British export performance in the years after 1921 was far from catastrophic by international standards. The USA and Japan did not extend their advantage over the UK, and before the return to the gold standard in 1925 and the General Strike year of 1926, British exports regained and held some of their former market share. France, however, performed dramatically well.

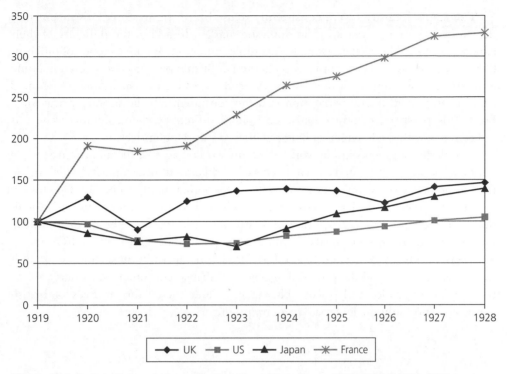

Figure 10.1 Index of export volumes for four Great War victors, 1919–1929 (1919 = 100)
Source: Based on Maddison, 1991.

Some of this growth can be accounted for by natural recovery, as French exports had been reduced to a greater extent than Britain's by the war, but the French policy of operating a devalued currency, in contrast to the British aim to return to the pre-war gold parity, is significant. Simply put, a high pound made British exports more expensive, while a low franc made French exports cheaper.

The plight of Britain's staple industries was not necessarily a problem for the world economy. It was not even a problem for the entire British economy. New industries or those that had developed during the war, such as motor vehicles, light engineering and the rising service industries, primarily served the domestic consumer and prospered. However, the notion that the British economy was divided between successful new industries and failing old ones is tidier than the reality of the situation. Some had an easier ride than others.

A number of industries were protected from foreign competition in the home market. The wartime McKenna duties remained, covering, for example, the motor vehicle industry. The Safeguarding Act of 1921 aimed to protect industries of strategic importance in case of future war. Such tariffs were a departure from Britain's guiding principle of free trade, but a narrowly defined exception to the rule. British industrial tariffs averaged 5 per cent by 1924 compared with a continental European average of 24.9 per cent and for the USA of 37 per cent.

The staple industries were consistently refused tariff protection. This meant that they were exposed to attack in the domestic market, to add to the difficulty of their export position. The steel industry, for example, suffered from the practice of differential pricing, whereby a lower price was charged in Britain by competitors than in home markets. The willingness of the British government to tolerate such abuses stemmed from an ingrained liberal perception that the consumer, not the producer, was king. From this perspective, protectionist economies ultimately damaged themselves as interference with the free market led to inefficiency and high prices.

Not all developments in the world economy worked against Britain as a free trade nation. The war had created a great excess of world agricultural capacity, which made the maintenance of export values very difficult for a great many countries. Downward pressure on prices in the late 1920s naturally affected countries dependent on agricultural production, such as Argentina and Australia, but many of the great industrial powers also retained large agricultural capacity, particularly the USA and Germany, and were also heavily affected. Britain's relatively tiny agricultural sector exempted it from this problem, and the purchasing power of British consumers was increased by the decline of world food prices. This factor counteracted the troubles of British exporters who traditionally served primary producers.

Plate 10.1 Building a bypass. The sign reads 'By-Pass work suspended, owing to National Economy requirements', presumably due to the British Depression. Curiously, these men are still at work. (© Mary Evans Picture Library).

In addition to a changed 'real' economy, the structure of international finance had also been transformed by the war. Britain's role as the financial centre of the world economy was at an end. It was not the case that the British position had collapsed, but global leadership had to be shared with the USA. The war had caused enormous disruption to currency and financial markets and the governing mechanism of international finance, the gold standard, had ceased to function. The standard was a currency regime of exchange rates fixed against the value of gold and therefore against each other. Before the First World War it had appeared to guarantee stability and transparency in international trade, and was seen to be a self-correcting mechanism which, moreover, imposed sound budgetary practice on domestic economies. The turbulent and inflationary conditions prevailing immediately after the First World War appeared to be powerful arguments in favour of the restoration of gold.

The British authorities certainly felt that the benefits of a return to gold would outweigh any pain that the process might cause, but in the immediate post-war period Britain was in no condition to resume formal operation of the standard. Nevertheless, the intention to return was announced in conjunction with the suspension of the standard in 1919. The legislation formalizing this move was set to expire in 1925, which naturally provided a target date for re-entry. However, the intention to restore the pre-war parity of $4.86 caused difficulty from the outset.

The measures required to push the pound towards $4.86 were harshly deflationary, and reflected an official desire to eradicate inflation. Heavy reductions in public spending balanced the war-inflated budget by 1919, and a combination of the 1920–21 depression and consistently high interest rates resulted in sharp price deflation. Such measures had the desired effect and the pound rose steadily against the dollar. It had reached $4.20 by 1925 and the knowledge that the government intended to restore parity in 1925 led speculators to close the gap in the time frame desired by the Treasury and the Bank of England. The Chancellor, Winston Churchill, announced the return to gold in April 1925.

The return to gold was not obviously a mistake, as modest growth was recorded in each year from 1922 to 1929. However, the drive to pre-war parity had done nothing to help Britain's exporters and the tight fiscal and monetary policies required to get sterling to $4.86 and keep it there did not encourage consumers or producers. Keynes estimated the pound to be overvalued by approximately 10 per cent.

Figure 10.2 (p. 150) shows that British GDP growth after 1919 was disappointing by international standards, though there were mitigating circumstances. The economies of France and Germany had shrunk during the war and stood at 75 per cent and 73 per cent of their pre-war level in 1919. Natural recovery, therefore, flattered their post-war growth rates compared to the UK, which finished the war with GDP at the same level as in 1913. The US and Japanese economies, however, had grown during the war and they increased their advantage relative to the UK in the 1920s, though GDP growth of all economies appeared to be flattening out in the second half of the decade.

It is safe to say that the return to gold applied a deflationary brake on the economy in the 1920s, though the extent of this can be debated. It was certainly the case that other

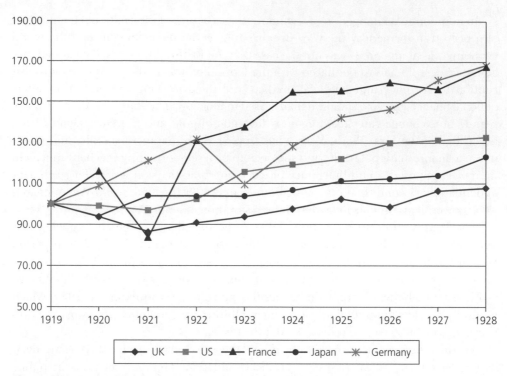

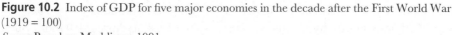

Figure 10.2 Index of GDP for five major economies in the decade after the First World War
(1919 = 100)
Source: Based on Maddison, 1991.

nations seemed to manage the return to gold without the pain experienced by Britain. France notably returned at a low parity that reflected the war-related devaluation of its currency and had no difficulty operating the standard until after Britain's departure in 1931. Germany recovered from the great inflation of 1922–3 and experienced strong growth on gold thereafter. The USA, possessing approximately half the world's monetary gold had become the world's banker, providing credit across the globe. However, each of these three nations would suffer a depression in the 1930s that made the British experience appear enviable.

War debts, reparations and US wealth

The international return to the gold standard was complicated by the twin issues of war debts and reparations. The Great War had bequeathed a heavy burden of international debt, owed mainly to the USA and Britain. Britain believed that inter-allied debts would damage recovery and aimed to write off war debt between governments, but the USA insisted on repayment of its war loans. Britain then restricted its demands on others to a sum sufficient to cover its own sizeable debt to America. The situation created considerable ill-feeling, especially in war-ravaged France where the term 'Uncle Shylock' replaced 'Uncle Sam'. France had suffered nearly 1.5 million deaths in a war fought on her own soil and believed that such sacrifice should be set against America's late arrival and modest casualties when balance sheets were drawn up.

If the European allies could get nothing from the USA, they were in a stronger position to make Germany pay. Germany, forced to accept war 'guilt', was obliged by the Treaty of Versailles to compensate its victorious enemies. Though the United States insisted that war debts and reparations were in no way connected, its debtors would not ease Germany's burden while they had in turn to repay America. This issue came to a head in 1922 when France occupied the Ruhr to extract payment in kind after a German default on reparation payments. The subsequent crisis led to Germany's famous hyper-inflation and recognition by the US that it must act. The Dawes Plan of 1924 defused the situation by allocating generous US credit to Germany, enabling the country to resume payment of reparations. A new mood of optimism prompted by the settlement and concurrent diplomatic progress, the so-called 'spirit of Locarno', disguised the fact of a dangerous and growing disequilibrium between Europe and the USA.

The international economy failed to accommodate the new dominance of the USA in the 1920s. The US economy had been easily the world's largest economy before the war, but had been an international debtor. The wartime growth of US exports and lending, however, transformed America into a major creditor. The need to repay debt to America, despite her trade surplus, created a dollar shortage. It was difficult for debtors to export to the heavily protected US economy and the USA would not tolerate discrimination against its own exports. European nations could only continue to afford US imports, therefore, if loans of dollars were forthcoming to pay for them. Consequently, all nations were vulnerable to a withdrawal of US credit, Germany particularly, but unless the US economy were opened to imports a point must one day be reached where the burden of dollar debt became insupportable.

The collapse of the world economy

The American stock market boom and subsequent crash of 1928–29 are usually perceived as the catalyst for the Great Depression. The demands of the boom saw the redirection of US capital from foreign loans to the US stock market, a trend that exacerbated the international dollar shortage. Worse was to follow when US investors actually recalled their foreign loans to cover their investments, and later their debts, at home. The attempt of the US Federal Reserve Board to contain the boom with high interest rates forced similar deflationary moves on Britain and other gold standard countries. This turbulent situation left overseas governments, particularly agricultural producers, in an impossible position whereby they had to repay rather than simply service their dollar debts at a time when their export earnings were in sharp decline. The withdrawal of American credit had predictable consequences. Nine countries were off the gold standard by 1931, and of all the countries owing war debt to the USA, only Finland did not subsequently default.

The British government could do nothing to prevent or ameliorate a catastrophe on this scale. Despite its aspiration to global leadership, it faced a desperate struggle to put its own house in order. The British depression represented a worsening of the 1920s pattern of economic disappointment. The staple industries – steel, coal, shipbuilding and textiles – faced a sharp deterioration in their already miserable condition. Export markets collapsed and unemployment, heavily concentrated in these industries, went past 3 million.

The British depression was also geographically concentrated. The plight of the north of England, Scotland, Wales and Northern Ireland contrasted sharply with the relative prosperity of the south of England and the English Midlands, though pockets of poverty and well-being were randomly distributed through Britain. However, the burden of paying for unemployment fell nationwide. The heavy increase naturally strained public finances as tax revenues fell and the burden of unemployment benefit increased. The government also faced difficulty remaining on the gold standard, an aspiration requiring continued high interest rates and a balanced budget. By mid-1931 foreign credits were required to stay on gold and when the pound was forced off in September 1931, it seemed as if the British economy was on the verge of an inflationary collapse to rival that of Germany in 1923.

Swift recovery

The expected disaster did not materialize after September 1931 and when the downward movement of sterling ceased at a competitive $3.40, British officials were commendably quick to adjust their thinking and emerge from panic, as the positive aspects of the situation soon became clear. Though the collapse in world trade had made deep inroads into Britain's export industries, the domestic economy outside the distressed areas was less badly affected and had considerable potential for growth.

The exit from gold presented the opportunity to exploit this. It severed the 'golden fetters' holding monetary and fiscal policy to a high exchange rate and during the recovery period remaining fears for the level of sterling had only a limited effect on domestic policy. The reduction of interest rates from 6 per cent to 2 per cent enabled the rescheduling of the national debt on more advantageous terms and a relaxation of fiscal policy within a continuing commitment to a balanced budget. The decision to cease repayment of the US war debt in 1932 also eased the budgetary position.

Between 1931 and 1939 the UK economy consistently achieved annual GDP growth rates of more than 3 per cent, a run of success then unmatched in peacetime and not repeated before 1992. A long housing boom and rearmament after 1935 drove the recovery, but it is clear that the strong growth of the economy after 1931 was more than a simple rebound from the depression. Figure 10.3 (p. 153) shows that the

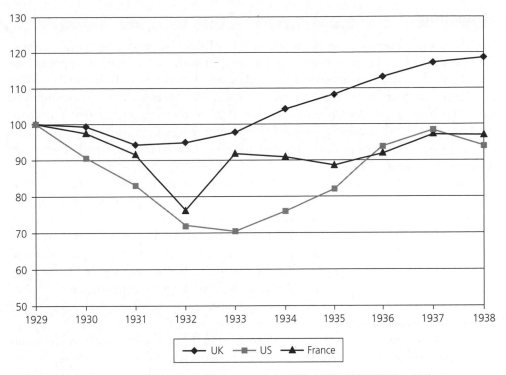

Figure 10.3 Index of GDP for the USA, France and the UK, 1929–1938 (1929 = 100)
Source: Based on Maddison 1991.

growth of Britain's GDP after a relatively shallow depression was exceptional among the largest economies that still possessed democratic governments in 1939.

In comparison with Britain's domestic revival, international trade suffered. Unemployment in export industries remained high and export growth failed to match that of imports. However, as the most prosperous of the major economies Britain attracted the capital of foreign investors, later termed 'hot' money. This resulted in a seemingly anomalous situation in which capital inflows created a demand for sterling and pushed the pound up, without reference to the state of the current account of the balance of payments. In fact, Britain had a deficit on current account for each year after 1931 except for a modest surplus in 1935, and these should have resulted in both an outflow of capital to pay for the deficits and a falling pound.

Whatever the shortcomings of the export industries it was natural that Britain's growing economy should attract more imports than could be balanced by exports to its struggling customers, and consumers continued to benefit from low commodity prices. In addition to the attraction of hot money and improved terms of trade, which might be considered accidental benefits, the results of conscious policy reinforced a tendency to sacrifice external trade balance for domestic growth.

Protection

The domestic economy was heavily influenced by Britain's abandonment of free trade. The introduction of a general tariff of 10 per cent with the Abnormal Importations Act of late 1931 was formalized in 1932 and raised to 20 per cent. Discounts from this rate known as 'imperial preference' were negotiated with colonies and dominions at the Ottawa Imperial Conference of August 1932. Protection represented a decisive symbolic break with nearly 100 years of liberal trading practice. The policy was, therefore, controversial and it provoked the resignation of Liberal ministers and others from the new national government.

Unlike the Mckenna duties of 1915 and the Safeguarding Act of 1921, the new system represented the acceptance of protection in principle and much wider application of tariffs and quotas. Nevertheless, Britain's tariffs were modest by international standards, and thus seemingly unsuitable as bargaining tools to whittle away at those of competitors. One industry's tariff protection might be offset if it had to pay increased prices to another British supplier with its own tariff. In this way it was theoretically possible for an industry such as shipbuilding to have negative net protection. Higher prices would in theory also harm British consumers, accustomed to paying the world market rate for their goods.

Positive aspects of protection also existed. After 1932 it was much more difficult for foreign manufacturers to dump goods in the British market, and in these circumstances British steel producers were able to gain membership of the lucrative European steel cartel, whereas under a regime of free trade this had been impossible. British producers could apply to the Import Duties Advisory Commission (IDAC) for increases in their tariff protection and this was often granted. It may be coincidental that the ever more heavily protected motor vehicle industry was by 1938, with a tariff of 33 per cent, Europe's largest producer by a considerable margin, but this strains credulity.

British protection can be considered as a realistic acceptance of the fact that the UK was no longer the master of the world economy. Protection was aimed primarily at the manufacturers of major rivals, particularly in Europe and the USA, and in this context had unquantifiable effects as a stimulus to negotiation and in improving the confidence of British manufacturers who now felt their home base to be secure. Whatever the merits of the case, protection became popular. Despite the fact that the Conservatives appeared to have lost the 1923 general election by advocating protection, American officials were warned repeatedly by leading British liberals in the 1930s that there was no prospect of any measure reducing British tariffs passing through the House of Commons.

The sterling area

If Britain was no longer dominant in the world economy, its web of international trading and imperial links and the collapse of American trade left it the single most important trading nation after 1929. Protection should, therefore, be viewed only as a single component of Britain's complex response to the international depression. It dovetailed with the natural development of the sterling area after the departure from gold. Originally referred to as the sterling bloc, this was a grouping of countries based on the empire, whose trading links were primarily with Great Britain, and whose currency reserves were held in London. Canada, however, was not in the sterling area, despite its importance to the Empire, because its trade was heavily dependent on the USA, but Portugal and Argentina were.

In return for the convenience of being pegged to a major reserve currency, de facto members accepted the fact that their currency transactions with non-members would have to be managed through London, in a manner approved of by the British authorities. Non-imperial members of the sterling area were usually primary producers as dependent on the British import market as the colonies, and they were usually able to negotiate trade agreements with Britain on terms comparable to imperial preference. The sterling area had practical benefits for Britain. For example, imports from within the area put no pressure on the pound. Most members were also heavily in debt to Britain and it provided another means for Britain to sustain repeated current account deficits without strain.

Despite encouraging features of the sterling area and protection, consistent current account deficits and a level of unemployment that never fell below 1.5 million, most of it in the export sector, appear to paint a picture of failure. However, by comparison America's recurrent trade surplus scarcely reflected a strong economy, simply the eradication of imports by the huge Hawley-Smoot tariff of 1930, and US per capita unemployment was much higher than in Britain.

It can be overlooked that much of the nation's external commercial and financial policy aimed to benefit the domestic economy. Producers for the home market enjoyed tariff protection the most and home consumers enjoyed the cheap imports from the sterling area that helped Britain to remain the world's largest import market while the value of the pound remained high and stable.

The world's greatest trading nation for more than 100 years, Britain believed its strength to depend on international prosperity and looked instinctively for international solutions to its economic problems in the 1920s. It was to some a bitter irony that her notably strong recovery in the 1930s seemed to be based on inward looking and selfish measures. However, such selfishness was permitted by the eventual recognition that Britain's loss of power also entailed a certain freedom from responsibility for the prosperity of others outside the British sphere of influence.

There was, however, a nagging sense of noblesse oblige. In the late 1930s Neville Chamberlain described Britain as 'a very rich and very vulnerable Empire, and there are plenty of poor adventurers not very far way who look on us with hungry eyes'. However, his government retained sufficient internationalist sentiment not to extend rearmament and turn the British Empire and its satellite economies into an autarkic bloc resembling Hitler's Germany, or even the mercantile empires which preceded the Pax Britannica of the nineteenth century. Many abroad assumed that it would.

In Focus

Keynes and how to win the war and lose the peace

The status of John Maynard Keynes as history's most famous economist has survived the eclipse of 'Keynesian' economic policies in the 1970s. As has often been pointed out, however, the *General Theory* did not appear until 1936 and exercised no tangible influence on policy before the war. It is arguable that Keynes's influence on policy might have been marginal without the accident of war. Nevertheless, Keynes's genius as an interpreter of his age remains unquestioned. His ideas crystallized over the course of the interwar period, but he quickly perceived that the problems afflicting the post-war economy could not be answered by classical economics. The laissez-faire doctrine of the time asserted that markets would correct all economic imbalances if they were allowed to function. Consequently, policy hinged on minimizing interference in the economy. This meant balanced budgets at all times at low levels of taxation and the restoration of the gold standard as a self-equilibrating tool to enforce good practice.

The experience of the British and world economies after the First World War, however, suggested to Keynes that the idea of a natural equilibrium of supply and demand, at which all factors of production were fully employed, differed increasingly from observable reality. Prices after the First World War fell as adverse conditions reinforced by classical policy forced deflation on the economy. Unemployment rose to a level of approximately 1 million by the mid-1920s and showed no signs of reduction.

In the 1920s Keynes believed in the quantity theory of money, as ironically did his monetarist critics of the 1970s, and this led him to reject laissez-faire in favour of intervention by the state in the economy. He argued that monetary policy should be used actively to promote price stability. In the circumstances then prevailing this meant monetary expansion, to reverse deflation and correct imbalances in the economy such as those which caused unemployment. As conditions worsened after 1929, however, it became clear to Keynes that activism in monetary policy alone would not be sufficient to cure mass unemployment. Keynes's theoretical work, *A Treatise on Money*, which appeared in 1931, pointed to a broader solution to Britain's problems.

In the treatise Keynes began to develop his liquidity preference theory of interest, which would be expounded fully in the *General Theory*. This suggested that monetary policy was potentially impotent in recession. A liquidity trap could develop, whereby firms feared for the future and became risk averse. They would cling to cash, preferring its liquidity to either offering or receiving credit. In these circumstances reducing interest rates to zero might have no effect on the economy,

Keynes and how to win the war and lose the peace

which would settle at an equilibrium in which money was hoarded and factors of production were underemployed. This argument seemed to be vindicated to some extent when monetary policy was finally loosened.

After the departure from gold in September 1931 laissez-faire was abandoned and an expansionary monetary policy was pursued. Though Britain's economic condition improved greatly, mass unemployment remained and Keynes came to believe that insufficient demand was at the root of the problem. If aggregate demand for goods and services could be raised, then a level must exist at which all factors of production could be fully employed, including labour.

Identifying the problem, though important, was not the same as finding a solution. Keynes had framed the Liberal party's economic programme for the 1929 General Election, based on a call for loan-financed spending on public works. This means of alleviating unemployment did not convince economists or voters. It was by no means clear that government action could raise aggregate demand, instead of simply crowding out private investment. Say's law, then dominant, argued that supply created its own demand so that a condition of deficient demand could not exist. Public spending could only increase if private spending fell, as the savings borrowed by the government would no longer be available for private investment.

The key to this problem was the income–expenditure multiplier, the concept of which was first published by Richard Kahn in 1931. The concept of the multiplier dismissed the crowding out argument by pointing out that money injected into the economy was spent again and again. The value of the input was reduced each time as a proportion of the money was saved. By the end of the process the initial spending had paid for itself in increased private savings and incomes had been increased.

The multiplier made possible the activist thesis of Keynes's famous work, the *General Theory of Employment, Interest and Money* (1936). It provided a means of lifting the economy from a depressed equilibrium to one of full employment by increasing demand. Monetary policy alone had not been sufficient to restore the economy, but the addition of fiscal policy, in the form of loan-financed deficit spending could do the trick.

By the late 1930s it seemed that Keynes's ideas were having an effect on senior Treasury officials. Though fiscal orthodoxy still prevailed, the deficit spending caused by rearmament accidentally spared Britain from the worst effects of the world cyclical downturn of 1937–38, and this was acknowledged. Keynes's victory was achieved during the war. The 1941 budget, the first to be based on national income accounting, is usually considered the beginning of Keynesian dominance. Ironically, this was achieved in wartime conditions of massive surplus consumer demand, which bore little resemblance to the depressed conditions in which the *General Theory* was devised.

Debates and Interpretations

The interwar period has a tendency to generate adversarial academic debate. Much of the literature concentrates on the significance of the period to modern issues, particularly with relation to the influence or otherwise of Keynesian economics. A second major strand of debate, related to the first, concerns the extent to which the interwar economy might be considered a success or a failure. These controversies are indicative of the importance of the period and its continued relevance to academic study.

Critics of the interwar British economy generally focus on the 'structural' causes of relatively poor per capita GDP growth. In addition to the problems caused by the over-capitalization of old staple industries and their concentration in the ailing export trades, the quality of British industrial management has been called into question. Criticism based on the work of Chandler, and echoed by others (Elbaum and Lazonick, 1986), has argued that Britain was slow to adopt 'multiform' company structures able to facilitate mass production on the American model. Broadberry and Crafts (1990, 1992) concur but go much further in arguing that anti-competitive tendencies, notably cartelization and other officially encouraged restrictive practices were instrumental in a large and growing productivity gap between Britain and the United States. Interestingly, these authors acknowledge that comparison with Germany results in a rosier British picture. They also make direct connections between their negative assessment of the 1930s and weaknesses in the post-1945 economy.

A further systemic weakness has been identified in terms of the failure of British financiers to support industry. The Macmillan Committee, appointed in 1929 to analyse the failings of the British economy, also identified a shortage of finance for small to medium-sized companies that hampered their ability to grow or even survive, the so-called 'Macmillan gap'. Although the gap was a sensation of the time, historians have considered at length whether British banks and the structure of the banking system were geared towards supplying the needs of small and medium-sized firms (Carnevali, 2005; Ross, 1996).

Structural weaknesses are not simply perceived to be a problem for managers, however. It is also argued that the new influence of trades unions also kept wages high relative to prices, potentially eroding competitiveness (Beenstock and Warburton, 1991). The relative generosity of Britain's benefit system has also been identified as a structural failing. In a famous but much criticized article (Benjamin and Kochin, 1979) it has been argued that the unemployed were a 'volunteer army', dissuaded from working by a high benefit–wage ratio.

By contrast, historians who perceive a Keynesian revolution in the making during the interwar period, generally attribute the problems of the British interwar economy to deficient aggregate demand (Middleton, 1985). This was a problem against which the most efficient economies had no defence, as the experience of the USA in the 1930s demonstrates. According to the Keynesian analysis, structural factors could have only incidental importance to the depression and the recovery.

Whereas critical historians identify structural weaknesses in the economy that persisted damagingly into the post-1945 period, historians with a Keynesian leaning can view the development of the British economy in the interwar period in terms of a positive transition to the post-war 'golden age'. In this analysis, Britain was steadily developing a managed economy capable of utilizing Keynesian policy to dramatic effect after the war, though the extent to which this was complete before the war is debated (Booth, 1989).

The issue of protectionism embraces both domestic policy and the external position. It has also excited strong and starkly opposed views. Capie (1983) approaches the British tariff policy of the 1930s from a critical perspective. However, others (Kitson and Solomou, 1990) argue that British protectionism in the 1930s was a success in its time, without making claims for protectionism as a model for other periods. They contend that protection could benefit Britain specifically in the context in which it was employed, although a wider world economy riddled with tariffs and quotas was clearly less desirable than an ideal model based on global free trade.

Historians who deal specifically with the international dimension of the British economy (Drummond, 1974, 1981) stress the post-1931 period, and the sophistication of British attempts to reorientate trade policy on the basis of the sterling area and a managed floating currency. Such writing is broadly favourable to British policy, which is considered rational and effective in the context of extraordinarily difficult times. Unfavourable assessments of British performance point to loss of overseas markets and current account deficits as features reflecting structural weaknesses in the domestic economy, rather than adverse conditions in the world economy (Alford, 1996).

The effects of rearmament after 1935 on both the British domestic economy and the external position have not yet received sufficient attention from scholars in terms of the wider development of the British economy. Thomas (1983) argues convincingly that rearmament provided a dramatic stimulus to the British domestic recovery, and even that a more determined effort might have delivered the deficit-financed Keynesian recovery before the war. Price (2001) argues that the external position offered no obstacle to such an effort. A benefit of studies based on the effects of rearmament is that they tend to analyse the interwar period on its own terms, rather than as a precursor of the triumph or disaster of the post-1945 era.

Further reading

An overview of the period is provided by Solomos Solomou, *Themes in Macroeconomic History: The UK Economy, 1919–1939* (Cambridge, 1996) and by R. Floud and P. Johnson (eds) *The Cambridge Economic History of Modern Britain*, Vol. II (Cambridge, 2004). For historians interested in the development of policy there are a number of highly regarded sources, many of which highlight the role of Keynes. These include Alan Booth, *British Economic Policy 1931–49: Was there a Keynesian Revolution?* (London, 1989) and Roger

Middleton, *Towards the Managed Economy: Keynes, the Treasury and the Fiscal Policy Debate of the 1930s* (London, 1985). The most recent study to deal specifically with Keynes is Robert Skidelsky's *John Maynard Keynes 1883–1946: Economist, Philosopher, Statesman* (London, 2004), an abridged version of his monumental three-volume biography. The relationship between Keynes and Treasury officials has been considered extensively by George Peden, most recently in *Keynes and his Critics: Treasury Responses to the Keynesian Revolution, 1925–36* (Oxford, 2004). Peter Clarke's *The Keynesian Revolution in the Making, 1924–36* (Oxford, 1990) is also essential reading.

Good Studies of Britain's role in the international economy include Ian M. Drummond's *Imperial Economic Policy: Studies in Expansion and Protection* (London, 1974) and *The Floating Pound and the Sterling Area, 1931–1939* (Cambridge, 1981). Tim Rooth, *British Protectionism and the International Economy: Overseas Commercial Policy in the 1930s* (Cambridge, 1993) is a sound analysis of the effects of British policy. An extensive treatment of the problems of political economy faced by the British economy in the 1920s can be found in R.W.D Boyce, *British Capitalism at the Crossroads, 1919–32: A Study in Politics, Economics and International Relations* (Cambridge, 1987). Barry Eichengreen provides a readable exploration of the problems of the interwar gold standard in *Golden Fetters: The Gold Standard and the Great Depression, 1919–39* (New York: 1992).

References

Alford, B.W.E. (1996) *Britain in the World Economy since 1880*. London: Longman.

Beenstock, M. and Warburton, P. (1991) 'The market for labour in interwar Britain', *Explorations in Economic History*, 28: 287–308.

Benjamin, D.K. and Kochin, L.A. (1979) 'Searching for an explanation of unemployment in interwar Britain', *Journal of Political Economy*, 87: 441–78.

Broadberry, S.N. and Crafts, N.F.R. (1990) 'The impact of the depression of the 1930s on the productive potential of the United Kingdom', *European Economic Review*, 34: 599–607.

Broadberry, S.N. and Crafts, N.F.R. (1992) 'Britain's productivity gap in the 1930s: some neglected factors', *Journal of Economic History*, 52: 531–58.

Capie, F.H. (1983) *Depression and Protectionism: Britain between the Wars*. London: Allen & Unwin.

Carnevali, F. (2005) *Europe's Advantage: Banks and Small Firms in Britain, France, Germany and Italy since 1918*. Oxford: Oxford University Press.

Chandler, A.D. (1990) *Scale and Scope*, Cambridge, MA: Belknap Press.

Elbaum, B. and Lazonick, W. (1986) *The Decline of the British Economy*. Oxford: Clarendon Press.

Kitson, M. and Solomou, S. (1990) *Protectionism and Economic Revival: The Interwar Economy*. Cambridge: Cambridge University Press.

Maddison, A. (1991) *Dynamic Forces in Capitalist Development: A Long-Run Comparative View.* Oxford: Oxford University Press.

Price, C. (2001) *Britain, America and Rearmament: The Cost of Failure.* London: Palgrave.

Ross, D.M. (1996) 'Commercial banking in a market-oriented financial system: Britain between the wars', *Economic History Review*, 49: 314–35.

Thomas, M. (1983) 'Rearmament and economic recovery in the late 1930s', *Economic History Review*, 36: 552–79.

11

Consumption, consumer credit and the diffusion of consumer durables

Peter Scott

A *mass consumption society* can be defined as one in which most people have access to a broad range of standardized, mass-produced durable goods. A related term, *consumerism*, is essentially an ideology which gives prime importance to the role of the citizen as consumer and, under some definitions, to consumption as a key economic and social activity. This chapter examines the extent to which interwar Britain moved towards being a mass consumption society and the roles of rising incomes, housing, consumer durables and consumer credit in bringing about the changes that took place.

Compared to most industrialized nations, income and wealth in pre-1914 Britain were particularly skewed towards a small proportion of wealthy individuals, producing a low ratio of real wages to national income. Over 1913–39 there was both a substantial increase in national income and some redistribution from the top 5 per cent of the population to those on middle and low incomes. Within the working class, unskilled workers gained relative to skilled workers as wage differentials between skilled and unskilled jobs narrowed markedly. However, a new income divide had emerged in the working class between those with jobs and the large army of the long-term unemployed, concentrated in the traditional industrial areas of northern Britain and south Wales.

How was this increase in incomes reflected in household consumption? Expenditure on goods can be classified by durability, into perishable goods such as food, fuel, tobacco and alcohol; semi-durables, defined here as those typically lasting between six months and three years, such as clothing; and durable goods such as furniture, personal transport and 'white goods'. Table 11.1 (p. 163) shows aggregate consumer expenditure on these categories, together with rent and other services. The data

Table 11.1 Distribution of UK consumer expenditure and its growth at constant (1938) prices (1910–1914 = 100)

	1910–14		1920–24		1935–38	
	Amount	%	Amount	%	Amount	%
Perishables	100.0	52.3	95.4	50.9	116.5	47.7
Semi-durables	100.0	11.7	99.1	11.9	121.8	11.2
Durables	100.0	4.9	133.4	6.7	233.4	9.0
Rent	100.0	9.7	110.4	11.0	141.4	10.8
Other services	100.0	21.3	89.7	19.5	127.6	21.3
Total	100.0	100.0	98.0	100.0	127.7	100.0

Source: Based on Stone and Rowe, 1966: Table 64.

are displayed in two ways, the first showing the growth in expenditure for each category over time (with 1910–14 set at 100) and the second showing the percentage distribution of total expenditure in each period.

The largest change involved an increase in spending on durable goods; by 1935–38 this stood at 2.33 times its 1910–14 level, while total consumer expenditure had only risen to 1.28 times its pre-war level. Rent was the only other expenditure category to grow faster than overall consumer expenditure. Yet durable goods still accounted for only 9 per cent of total personal expenditure, thus 'new' consumer durable assembly industries such as electrical goods and motor vehicles similarly still only made a small contribution to total employment, despite their rapid interwar growth. The expansion in durable goods consumption involved an element of substitution of goods for services – cars, motorbikes and bicycles substituted for public transport, while household equipment substituted for domestic servants. Thus expenditure on 'other services' did not rise faster than overall expenditure, contrary to the long-term trend towards a 'service-based economy'. The rise in expenditure on durables also reflected a widening of the market for such goods to new classes of consumer.

Data on aggregate expenditure do not reflect the experience of 'typical' households, as they are disproportionately influenced by the larger budgets of higher-income groups. Household budget enquiries conducted during the late 1930s provide an indication of the spending patterns of three groups which collectively constituted a large proportion of the British population and whose access to consumer goods was therefore key to the creation of any real 'mass market'. The first involved families headed by manual workers or non-manual workers earning under £250 per year (excluding agricultural workers and the long-term unemployed). These had an average weekly household budget of 85s (£4.25). The next group involved households headed by workers in Britain's lowest-wage sector – agriculture – who were further disadvantaged

Table 11.2 Average weekly expenditure for non-agricultural and agricultural working-class households, and for middle-class families with a head of household earning £250–350 per year, during the late 1930s

Mean weekly expenditure for households in the:	Non-agricultural working class		Agricultural working class		Low-income middle class	
	Shillings	%	Shillings	%	Shillings	%
Food	34.1	40.1	27.8	48.4	35.6	26.2
Accommodation	10.8	12.7	4.8	8.3	19.0	14.0
Clothing & footwear	8.1	9.5	5.3	9.2	12.4	9.1
Fuel & light	6.4	7.5	4.9	8.6	8.5	6.2
Other items:	25.6	30.1	14.6	25.5	60.5	44.5
Household items	4.1	4.8	2.3	4.1	10.9	8.0
Tobacco & cigarettes	2.5	3.0	1.9	3.3	2.8	2.0
Transport	2.3	2.6	0.9	1.5	4.1	3.0
Medical, insurance, pensions, union subscriptions	7.5	8.8	4.8	8.4	15.4	11.3
Other	9.3	10.9	4.7	8.2	27.5	20.2
Total weekly expenditure	85.0	100.0	57.3	100.0	136.0	100.0

Source: Based on The National Archives, LAB17/7, 'Weekly expenditure of working-class households in the United Kingdom in 1937–38', July 1949; Massey, 1942.

by isolation from urban amenities (including even mains water in many areas) and semi-feudal relations with their employers. For example, many lived in accommodation provided 'free' by the landowner, from which they could be evicted at will. The final group concerns some of the lowest-income middle-class households, where the household head earned £250–£350 (though, in common with the other groups shown in Table 11.2, the earnings of other family members often boosted *household* expenditure).

Agricultural households had an average weekly budget almost a third lower than other working-class families, almost half of which was spent on food. Accommodation costs were typically low, due to the provision of low-rent or 'free' farm cottages, though most of these were in a very poor condition; cold, dampness and insanitary conditions left many such families particularly vulnerable to diseases such as rheumatism, tuberculosis and bronchitis. After covering the 'essentials' of food, shelter, clothing, fuel and light, only a quarter of income was available for other items – a mere 14s 6d per week (72.5p). Non-agricultural working-class families managed to both spend substantially larger sums on 'essentials', while devoting 30 per cent of weekly income to other items – 25.6 shillings per week (£1.25). Meanwhile, households towards the bottom rung of the salaried income ladder managed to both spend substantially more on each of the essential categories than the working-class groups and devote 44.5 per cent of income to other items, spending around four times as much on 'inessentials' as agricultural workers' families – out of salaries that were 2.37 times as high.

Spending patterns were shaped both by income and 'status', as is shown by the example of housing. The lower-middle-class group devoted 14.0 per cent of expenditure to housing, compared to 12.7 per cent for non-agricultural working-class households. Yet within the non-agricultural working-class group the proportion of expenditure devoted to accommodation declined as income rose, from 16.6 per cent for those with a weekly household budget of under 40s to 7.6 per cent for those with a weekly budget of over 140s. Similarly, the proportion of income spent on housing by households in the middle-class survey (which included groups on higher incomes than the one shown in Table 11.2) also fell as income rose. The step increase in housing expenditure for low-income salaried workers compared to relatively high-income working-class families appears to have been due to the fact that a house in an appropriate middle-class neighbourhood constituted an essential part of the 'social capital' required to gain access to middle-class employment and society. As the following discussion will demonstrate, 'keeping up with the Joneses' constituted an important driver of consumption for both middle-class and working-class households.

Housing and consumption

A central element of moves towards a 'consumer society' in interwar Britain involved a radical change in the character of new housing. Prior to the First World War new working-class neighbourhoods on the fringes of towns were typically developed in long terraces, at densities of 30 or more houses per acre. Reconstruction planning in the latter years of the First World War focused on housing as a means of providing 'homes fit for heroes'. This culminated in the 1918 Tudor Walters Report on the standards of post-war local authority housing, which sought to improve economic and social conditions by creating healthier and better-designed housing and communities. Drawing on both contemporary planning ideas and the examples of garden city and model workers' village projects, the report proposed that houses should have a minimum of three ground floor rooms (living room, parlour and scullery with larder), three bedrooms (at least two of which could take two beds), plus a bathroom. They were to be built at low densities, of no more than 12 per acre, semi-detached or in short terraces, to a cottage design that included front and rear gardens.

Tudor Walters' standards embodied the basic features of both new council and owner-occupied working-class and lower-middle-class housing (private developers following them mainly on account of their popularity with purchasers). A new, more functional design of housing emerged, with lower ceilings and less space devoted to corridors. Kitchens were reduced in size, with the advent of the 'kitchenette' in many smaller houses and flats. Such houses were easier to clean and heat, had better natural lighting (and, usually, electric lighting) and were generally free of the dampness and vermin infestation typical of much inner-urban housing. The chasm that had separated pre-1914 middle- and (even better-quality) working-class houses thus narrowed considerably. As George Orwell noted in *The Lion and the Unicorn*, 'The modern Council house, with its bathroom and electric light, is smaller than the stockbroker's villa, but is recognizably the same kind of house, which the farm labourer's cottage is not.'

It has been estimated that in 1914 only around 10 per cent of families owned their own home, less than 1 per cent lived in council housing, while around 90 per cent were tenants of private landlords. After 1918 rent control led to a decline in the private rented sector, while municipal housing and owner-occupation both expanded rapidly, to around 10 per cent and 32 per cent of the 1938 housing stock respectively. Council houses generally had high standards of building and amenities; yet many were built on large estates, in 'green field' areas well beyond urban boundaries. These were often poorly situated with respect to places of work, shopping and leisure, imposing long commutes on their inhabitants.

Most new owner-occupied houses were also located in the suburbs (though generally in areas with better access to urban centres than their local authority counterparts). Middle-class households were the most active participants in the owner-occupation boom. The middle-class survey indicated that some 46.5 per cent were buying their house on mortgage and a further 18.2 per cent owned their house outright (Massey, 1942).[1] Houses designed for the Victorian middle classes had fallen out of favour, partly on account of the decline in domestic service. Lower-middle-class housewives, faced with having to do a greater share of their own housework, found houses designed to be maintained by servants too much of a burden. Instead they sought housing with labour-saving features, which would reduce their workload and allow them to make the most efficient use of the new labour-saving consumer durables. Meanwhile suburban living was seen as superior to urban life, as it offered a healthier rural environment, freedom from dangers (especially to children) such as heavy traffic and pollution, and 'exclusive' neighbourhoods – perceptions that were reinforced by estate developers' marketing campaigns.

During the 1930s falling interest rates under the government's new cheap money policy, together with liberalized mortgage terms, reductions in building costs and rising real incomes (for those in work) allowed substantial numbers of working-class households to become owner-occupiers for the first time. Of crucial importance in extending the market to families earning £2 10s to £4 per week was the introduction of 'easy terms' by building societies. Mortgage periods were extended from around 20 years to 25, or even 30, thereby substantially reducing weekly payments, while deposits were reduced from 20 to around 5 per cent, via special 'mortgage pool' arrangements with housing developers, under which the building society retained part of the house price until a substantial proportion of the mortgage had been paid off.

Developers sought to widen their market by developing houses that were affordable to lower-income groups; several offered houses priced from around £395 in London, or £350 in the provinces (equivalent to £17,765 and £15,741 in 2004 prices) which

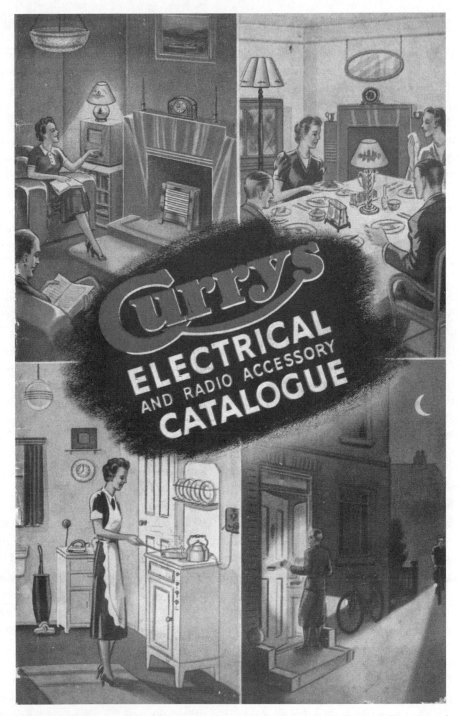

Plate 11.1 The idealised all-electric house, as shown on the cover of the 1939–40 Curry's catalogue (author's private collection).

could be purchased with a 5 per cent deposit and weekly payments of 12s or less. The Ministry of Labour's 1937/38 working-class household expenditure survey indicated that some 17.8 per cent of non-agricultural working-class families were owner-occupiers; this appears to have been at least double the proportion at the start of the decade.[2] Even almost one in eight families with weekly incomes of £2 10s to £3 (well below the urban working-class household average) were found to be owner-occupiers.

The building industry and building societies also engaged in a major promotional campaign to sell the idea of owner-occupation to a new mass market, stressing the 'easy terms' on which properties were available, together with the advantages of home ownership and suburban living. This played an important role in countering the traditional working-class aversion to taking on large debts and entering into complex legal contracts involving dealings with middle-class professionals and institutions. Mortgages were portrayed as a form of saving, rather than investment, while builders simplified the purchase process by offering 'all-in' deals that included arranging the mortgage and incorporating legal and other fees into the house price.

The housebuilding boom had a major macroeconomic impact, the increase in house building accounting for around 17 per cent of the growth in national income between 1932 and 1934. When the expansion of construction materials is added, it is estimated to have accounted for 30 per cent of the increase in employment during the first three years of the recovery (Eichengreen, 2004: 334–5). Indeed, its overall (direct and indirect) impact was even greater, as family moves to larger suburban homes were accompanied by a substantial increase in demand for consumer durables, furniture and status-related goods required to 'keep up with the Joneses' in the new, aspirational neighbourhoods. Most of this demand was met either by UK firms or US and European multinationals that had established British branch plants, such as Hoover and Electrolux. Housebuilding also accelerated the switch from coal to gas and electricity, as new housing generally had mains electricity and gas or electric cookers (and, sometimes, fires).

Narrowing differences between working- and lower-middle-class housing reflected a wider blurring between the aspirations, tastes and values of the lower middle class and the more affluent sections of the working class, influenced both by rising living standards and by the cinema and other developments in mass media that targeted the broadest possible spectrum of consumers in order to maximize their audience. An ideology of 'domesticity' – encompassing a high standard of personal and domestic hygiene, family and home-centred lifestyles even for adult males, and an increased commitment of material and psychological resources to the welfare and material advancement of children – became central to new working-class notions of respectability, as it had been to middle-class notions for several decades.

While owning and displaying prestige goods had been a recognized feature of status competition in traditional working-class communities, it had generally focused around one, or few, particularly prized possessions. In contrast, the new suburban working-class respectability generally involved adopting, or at least projecting to the outside world, a broader, coordinated material 'lifestyle' – that encompassed all aspects of observed consumption. As a social survey of the London County Council's Watling Estate noted: 'The new house needs new linoleum, new curtains and even new furniture, and all is bought on hire purchase. In the old "mean street," people were not tempted by the example of their neighbours to acquire fresh impedimentia. At Watling . . . the wireless next door becomes an obligation to bring home a wireless' (Durant, 1939: 7–8).

Evidence indicates that working-class families who moved into owner-occupation during this period made substantial changes to their consumption patterns – with a redistribution of income from items of current consumption such as food, drink, fuel and lighting to durable items connected with conspicuous consumption, such as housing, furniture and clothing. Many recall making sacrifices in daily expenditure to support their new lifestyles, such as going to bed early to save on fuel and lighting, or even going hungry so as to save on food. Such families had also begun to adopt the modern pattern of the small, planned, family – having significantly fewer children, on average, than their counterparts in rented accommodation.

Consumer durables

New interwar housing offered a good domestic environment for an expanded consumer durables market, while new aspirational working-class notions of respectability could also be expected to boost demand for durable goods. Yet the diffusion of most classic consumer durables (fridges, washing machines, vacuum cleaners, etc.) remained very limited by 1938. One major constraint on the diffusion of electrical consumer durables, the limited supply of mains electricity, was considerably eased during this period. In 1921 only around 12 per cent of British houses were wired for electricity and even in 1931 it had only reached 32 per cent of homes; yet by 1938 the figure had jumped to 65 per cent. The government boosted its diffusion via the Electricity (Supply) Act of 1926, which set up a Central Electricity Board with powers to rationalize electricity generation and distribution and create a national electricity supply grid, while encouraging suppliers to gain new customers via assisted wiring schemes and simplified tariffs. The costs of installing electric wiring fell by around two-thirds during the interwar period, while the average unit cost of domestic electricity was reduced by around 70 per cent.

Yet the adoption of consumer durables lagged considerably behind the spread of electricity supply. By 1938 radios had reached 68.8 per cent of wired households in England and Wales and electric irons were in perhaps three-quarters. The electric cooker had reached only 16.9 per cent of wired homes, though gas cookers were much more common and around three-quarters of British households are estimated to have had either a gas or electric cooker. Conversely, only 3 per cent of British households had (electric or gas) refrigerators; only 3.5 per cent had washing machines, and even vacuum cleaners were still restricted to around 27 per cent of homes.

Technological change and economies of scale generally produce both substantial price reductions and efficiency improvements in particular consumer durables over

Plate 11.2 House advertisement, from *The Birmingham and District Housing Journal* (nos 1–40, June 1936–September 1939) (© British Library Board. All rights reserved).

time, which – together with rising living standards – lead to a long-term diffusion process, initiated by 'innovative' (mainly wealthy) consumers and then spreading to middle-income, and eventually low-income, families. During this period most of the classic consumer durables were still relatively expensive, while rather than providing new services they merely offered a more efficient alternative to the housewife's existing equipment. In America consumer durables diffused more rapidly, but they were cheaper (largely due to scale economies from mass production) while, crucially, the costs of the labour they substituted for were higher. In Britain it was still relatively cheap to send washing out, at prices with which washing machines could not compete. Conversely the electric/gas cooker was harder to substitute by paid help (as it was used at various intervals spaced throughout the day); the electric iron was relatively cheap, while the radio was both affordable and provided enormous perceived value in relation to its cost. Furthermore, unlike most other consumer durables, it substituted for services that were more expensive – commercial entertainment.

Cost considerations also constrained the diffusion of personal transport. The proportion of English households owning a car in 1938 was around four times that in the early 1920s, but cars had still only reached just over 20 per cent of families. Despite the introduction of smaller, cheaper cars, and the spread of hire purchase facilities, even the cheapest models were still beyond the reach of most households. With the exception of the Ford 8 (sold for £100 during 1935–37), the minimum price for a new car was around £120, while hire purchase contracts usually required a minimum 25 per cent deposit and monthly instalments of perhaps £4 (as their high depreciation limited the length of HP contracts to two years). The 'carrying charge' of buying a car on instalments was thus greater than that for a small house. Conversely, bicycles, which could be purchased new from around £4 and offered people flexible personal transport over short distances at low running costs, had already reached the market saturation point by the late 1930s.

The diffusion of consumer durables also showed strong regional variations, take-up being particularly high in the south-east and much lower in northern Britain and Wales. For example, in 1938 average domestic electricity consumption in the north-east amounted to only 45 per cent of that in the south-east, while rates of car ownership and new housing development were also substantially lower. This was the product of mass unemployment in most provincial industrial areas, their lower rate of new house building and their lower proportion of middle-class families. Diffusion rates were also much higher in urban than in rural areas – as rural working-class incomes were substantially lower and mains electricity spread more slowly in sparsely populated areas than in urban centres.

Producers of consumer durables engaged in aggressive promotional campaigns to market their appliances to housewives. These were often portrayed as offering the key to becoming the idealized 'professional housewife' – promoted in women's magazines and other media – providing a happy, clean, home environment for her family through a combination of labour-saving devices and efficient household management practices. However, promoting the desire for consumer durables did not overcome the barrier of inability to pay. Advertising was thus accompanied by another key element of marketing – the introduction of 'easy terms'.

Consumer credit

A large proportion of durable and semi-durable consumer goods were bought on credit. According to a Board of Trade estimate, the annual value of consumer credit in Britain during the late 1930s was around £200–220 million, around 7 per cent of retail sales or 5 per cent of total personal expenditure. Some £100–120 million of this concerned hire purchase trading, while other forms of consumer credit – credit sales and 'check trading' – were estimated to amount to over £100 million.[3]

Credit sales covered a broad range of facilities, including store accounts, 'tic' at local shops, buying on credit through mail order catalogues, and clothing clubs. Clubs were often informal local arrangements where a group of neighbours or members of some organization combined to subscribe equal amounts of money each week. The total weekly subscription was then made available to one member, by drawing lots, and the winner was given a ticket, redeemable at a number of specified shops, or from a mail order firm – which paid the organizing concern a discount on its face value.

A more formal arrangement with some similarities to the club system was check trading. This was a major source of consumer credit; the president of the largest check trading company, Provident Clothing & Supply Co., claimed that the aggregate annual turnover of check traders was at least £50 million by the late 1930s.[4] 'Checks' (credit tickets) were sold on instalments, for use at certain shops that were reimbursed by the check company. This freed retailers from collecting payments, while giving customers a wider range of stores to choose from. Before receiving a check the customer had to pay the first instalment on its repayment, together with a 'poundage' fee of one shilling per pound face value – equivalent to an annual percentage rate of interest (APR) of 23.3 per cent (O'Connell and Reid, 2005: 384). Check companies also redeemed checks at 10–15 per cent below their face value, in effect taking a commission of this amount from the retailer.

Check credit appears to have been concentrated among the working classes, while also encompassing some lower-middle-class families. Checks were mainly used for clothing and household textiles. Individual purchases were generally small in value, yet customers could end up with considerable debts – Provident's customers borrowed an average of around £15–16 per year via its checks during the 1930s, equivalent to around a month's earnings for the average urban working-class family. The check system effectively involved the provision of unsecured loans on goods that could not be repossessed in the event of default. Yet the level of bad debts appears to have been low; Provident's were given as only 0.75 per cent of turnover in 1934. Potential customers were vetted, and payments monitored, via a system of local agents who made weekly home visits for collections. These were also important in persuading existing customers to take further checks and thus build an enduring customer base. Many used their familial and local connections as a major source of business, thus embedding the check trading system within working-class community networks. This community aspect also acted to discourage default, since if a person was known to have failed to meet their debts this would damage their reputation in the local community. Corner shop credit was similarly underpinned by a reciprocal social relationship of knowledge, trust and familiarity between retailers and their local customers.

While club and check credit were mainly used for items of small value, more valuable and durable items were generally sold via hire purchase (HP). Under this system the item was technically only 'hired' until the final payment was received and could be repossessed in the event of a failure to keep up the payments. HP was thus attractive to vendors of highly durable goods with an active second-hand market, the value of the initial deposit and subsequent instalments being set so as to exceed the depreciation of the item's value. The HP system is generally believed to have emerged in Britain during the second quarter of the nineteenth century. Originally confined to the more affluent sections of society, it began to diffuse to the working classes from the 1860s, when Singer used it to market its sewing machines. By the early twentieth century other consumer durables suppliers had adopted it; for example, gas companies used it as a means of boosting the diffusion of domestic gas appliances. Yet it was during the interwar period that HP became a major factor in working-class household finances; a contemporary sociological study estimated that the volume of HP trading had increased some twenty-fold between 1918 and 1938 (Hilton, 1938: 133).

HP was used for a wide variety of durable goods, including furniture and carpets, personal transport, radios and gramophones, and household consumer durables. Typical customers ranged from un/semi-skilled workers to lower-middle-class salaried employees. By the 1930s many people setting up new households used it to buy most of their furnishings; for example, the furniture retailers Drages Ltd offered the full furnishings for a house on HP for £100, with a deposit of only £2.

In Focus

HP and the expansion of the consumer durables market

By the late 1930s the majority of Britain's durable consumer goods were being sold on HP. The Board of Trade estimated that HP agreements covered more than 70 per cent of sales for cars and bicycles, working-class furniture and electrical household equipment, while trade estimates suggest that it accounted for at least this proportion of pianos and sewing machines. From the consumer's perspective HP greatly assisted access to such 'aspirational' items. As Phyllis Willmott's account of growing up in working-class Lewisham noted, the arrival of the leading HP furniture chainstore, The Times Furnishing Co., started a transformation of her family home,

> **HP and the expansion of the consumer durables market**

where the respectable, though antiquated, front room décor had hidden the spartan rooms beyond:

> Although we did not know it then, it was the death blow for Gran's front room, the piano, the solid Victorian furnishings and the aspidistras. It was also the end of Mum's solid Edwardian oak dressing table . . . bought secondhand in her early married years . . . she was only too glad to throw it out in favour of the new veneered walnut suite she could get – with matching wardrobe and chest of drawers – on the 'never never' of hire purchase. (Willmott, 1979: 133)

HP had a number of attractive features for consumers. It gave people immediate access to products which they were not able to pay for in full and made it less likely that savings devoted to them would be diverted to other uses – by imposing a contractual obligation. It thus facilitated access to such socially important goods as the radio, recorded music and personal transport, and gave large numbers of people increased opportunities to achieve their aspirations. However, despite this the system was subject to widespread condemnation, on account of the abuses with which it was rife.

HP constituted an inflexible commitment of future income and thus made those who used it extremely vulnerable to poverty in the event of illness or unemployment. Many families were likely to face this predicament, as contracts for more expensive items typically ran for between 18 months and three years. Many cases were reported where people who had their earnings interrupted through unemployment or illness found the burden of maintaining HP payments extremely onerous, pushing them into severe poverty. For example, in 1937 a social worker reported visiting a home stripped of almost all its furniture:

> This man, when about to marry – two and a half years previously – had furnished his place on the hire purchase system and had regularly paid his weekly instalments, with the exception of the last five weeks. Having been unemployed for 17 weeks with an income of 29s per week for himself, his wife, and child, paying a rent of 18s per week, it will be seen he had performed the almost impossible task of continuing his payments for 12 weeks by family privations. (Fleming, 1937)

Like house mortgages, competition among HP traders during the 1930s tended to revolve mainly around 'easy terms' – lower deposits and longer repayment periods – rather than reducing interest rates or lowering prices. HP retailers were said to both charge very high interest rates – rates in excess of 25 per cent not being uncommon – and higher prices for goods on HP, compared to those they sold for cash (similar price mark-ups were also reported in shops that accepted checks). Other abuses concerned excessive charges for 'depreciation', despite the fact that the deposit and payments

> ### HP and the expansion of the consumer durables market
>
> schedule generally exceeded any reasonable depreciation rate. In some cases customers were forced to pay several shillings weekly for years, for goods they had sent back shortly after purchase. Even if the goods were defective payments were still legally enforceable, as the HP contract usually exempted the trader from any warranty over them. One of the most notorious abuses concerned the 'snatch-back,' under which the retailer would repossess the goods towards the end of the agreement if an instalment was late by even a few hours. In such cases customers lost their deposit and accumulated payments, as until the final payment was made these were in law merely a 'hiring' charge. Attempted repossessions frequently led to violent confrontations between HP customers and 'bruisers' employed for repossession work.
>
> Perceptions that HP was rife with abuse acted to stigmatize this form of credit. In order not to embarrass potential customers, HP traders often emphasized the secrecy of transactions, advertisements using phrases such as 'No references asked for' and 'We guarantee delivery in plain vans' – which served to accentuate its disreputable image. Major stores, and other 'respectable' traders who wished to use HP to expand the consumer goods market, resented the damage that abuses by their less reputable counterparts were doing to its social acceptability. They thus collaborated with social workers in pressing for restrictive legislation, eventually introduced in the 1938 Hire Purchase Act (though in practice this failed to prevent many abuses).

Debates and Interpretations

To what extend did working-class households participate in the interwar consumer boom? As noted above, evidence suggests that the diffusion of most classic 'white goods' – consumer durables such as refrigerators, washing machines and vacuum cleaners – was confined to the middle classes and, in many cases, to the upper middle classes. This has led some scholars to conclude that, with a few exceptions such as the radio, the working classes were not participants in interwar consumerism (Bowden and Offer, 1994; Bowden and Turner, 1993). Similarly, it has been argued that before 1939 'only the elite of the working class could afford home-ownership – and even then at the cost of self-sacrifice and thrift' (Swenarton and Taylor, 1985).

The first argument, that levels of working-class ownership of consumer durables were generally very low during the 1930s, is correct from the perspective of these studies, which generally take the classic modern consumer durables – 'white goods' and cars – as their yardsticks. However, such analyses sometimes overlook less costly durable goods which did become rapidly and widely diffused among working-class households during this period. In addition to the well-known examples of the radio and electric iron, a variety of other durable goods such as gramophones; pianos; bicycles; new, mass-produced suites of furniture; new carpets; carpet sweepers; and sewing machines were to be found in many working-class homes (together with a large number of smaller items such as electric lamps, mantel clocks, manual kitchen appliances, new tableware, and similar products). The use of trade statistics on electrical consumer durables also underestimates the diffusion of all (electric plus gas) cookers and space heaters – despite the fact that gas has remained the dominant technology for these activities.

The second argument, regarding the lack of access of working-class families to new suburban owner-occupied housing, is open to more straightforward criticism, as illustrated in recent research by George Speight – which indicated that the rate of urban working-class owner-occupation at least doubled during the 1932–38 cheap money era, to around 18 per cent (Speight, 2000). Increasing working-class owner-occupation by nine or 10 percentage points during a seven-year period may not sound particularly dramatic, but it must be remembered that most purchases were made in the first few years of marriage. Relative to the rate of new household formation, owner-occupation experienced very rapid growth.

Meanwhile a significant proportion of working-class families obtained modern suburban houses on council estates, while an unknown number rented suburban houses from private landlords. While it is not possible to precisely estimate the proportion of urban working-class households that moved to modern suburban housing during the interwar period, a figure of around 25 per cent appears reasonable. The installation of electric wiring, gas, internal plumbing and, sometimes, fitted baths into inner-urban housing also gave some families in traditional working-class communities access to the new utilities and associated consumer durables.

Internal plumbing systems, with fitted internal baths and toilets and integral water heating, were probably the most important interwar 'consumer durables' from the housewife's perspective. Prior to the advent of mass indoor plumbing a large proportion of the housewife's working day was taken up in hauling water to the house, moving it within the house and heating it for cleaning, bathing and (in many rural areas lacking mains water) drinking purposes. The spread of internal plumbing, water heaters and fitted baths had a revolutionary impact on housework, both saving time and increasing quality – through the ease with which hot water for cleaning could be accessed.

Oral history and autobiographical accounts of working-class people who moved to suburban council or mortgaged houses during this period often emphasize the importance of the bath, hot water, indoor toilet and (for those households that had not previously had access to it) an indoor water supply as being central to their appreciation of their new house. A high proportion also emphasize the value of another new feature of modern suburban housing with characteristics analogous to a consumer durable – substantial gardens. These provided opportunities for growing vegetables and flowers, a place where children could play free from the dangers of traffic, and space for sunbathing and other leisure activities.

An examination of 1930s' housekeeping manuals (generally aimed primarily at lower-middle-class housewives) reveals the limited importance attached to most 'white goods' and, indeed, substantial scepticism regarding their value. For example, a 1937 *Daily Express* manual advised housewives that while labour-saving devices could reduce the volume of housework, other fundamentals included 'a lavish supply of hot water in two or three different parts of the house, an easy and clean method of heating the rooms, and a convenient system of cooking'.[5] A 1935 *Pitman's* manual warned that 'Some so-called "labour-saving" devices are not efficient in carrying out their intended purpose and are so difficult and intricate to manage that they are hindrances rather than helps' (Binnie and Boxall, 1935: 218). Its list of recommended devices consisted of such mundane items as stainless steel knives, aluminium or stainless steel pans, a gas copper, and hand-operated kitchen equipment such as egg beaters and potato peelers. Significantly the only electrical item mentioned – the electric iron – was also the only electrical labour-saving device to become widely diffused among British homes by 1939.

When viewed using a post-war lens, the 'consumer revolution' had not progressed beyond the ranks of the salaried middle class. Yet from the perspective of working-class households (and particularly those on suburban estates) a new world of bathrooms, easily accessible hot water, radios, coordinated modern furniture, bicycles and other simple luxuries had been opened up, all available on 'easy terms'. Furthermore, auto-biographical accounts and contemporary surveys indicate that the desire to present a coordinated display of material affluence, including housing, clothing and furnishings (at least in those areas visible from outside the house) were already strongly developed on new suburban working-class estates. While income constraints imposed substantial limits on interwar consumerism, the start of a transition towards a consumerist mind-set among Britain's working class was evident by the 1930s.

Further reading

For a general discussion of consumption and consumer behaviour, see Sue Bowden, 'Consumption and Consumer Behaviour', Chapter 22 in Chris Wrigley (ed.) *A Companion to Early Twentieth Century Britain* (Oxford, 2003). Paul Johnson's *Saving and Spending: The Working-class Economy in Britain 1870–1939* (Oxford, 1985) provides a good overview of changes in working-class consumption and credit, while Matthew Hilton's *Consumerism in Twentieth-Century Britain: The Search for a Historical Movement* (Cambridge, 2003) explores the political economy of consumption. For more detailed discussion of the two main avenues of interwar consumer credit, see Peter Scott, 'The twilight world of interwar hire purchase', *Past & Present*, 177 (2002): 195–225; and Sean O'Connell and Chris Reid, 'Working-class consumer credit in the UK, 1925–60: the role of the check trader', *Economic History Review*, LVIII (2005): 378–405. The diffusion of consumer durables is explored in Sue Bowden and Paul Turner, 'The demand for consumer durables in the United Kingdom in the interwar period', *Journal of Economic History*, 53 (1993): 244–58; and Sue Bowden and Avner Offer, 'Household appliances and the use of time: The United States and Britain since the 1920's, *Economic History Review*, XLVII, 4 (1994): 725–48. Studies of electrical appliances and household furnishings are provided in

T.A.B. Corley, *Domestic Electrical Appliances* (London, 1966) and Clive Edwards, *Turning Houses into Homes: A History of Retailing and Consumption of Domestic Furnishings* (Aldershot, 2005).

Useful sources on changes in the nature of housework include Caroline Davidson, *A Woman's Work is Never Done: A History of Housework in the British Isles 1650–1950* (London, 1982), and Judy Giles, *The Parlour and the Suburb: Domestic Identities, Class, Femininity and Modernity* (Oxford, 2004). One of the best contemporary surveys of life on a working-class suburban estate is Ruth Durant, *Watling: A Survey of Social Life on a New Housing Estate* (London, 1939). For a more general discussion of changes in housing, see John Burnett, *A Social History of Housing 1815–1985*, 2nd edn (London, 1986).

References

Binnie, R. and Boxall, J.E. (1935) *Housecraft: Principles and Practice*. London: Pitman and Sons.

Bowden, S. and Turner, P. (1993) 'The demand for consumer durables in the United Kingdom in the interwar period', *Journal of Economic History*, 53: 244–58.

Bowden, S. and Offer, A. (1994) 'Household appliances and the use of time: the United States and Britain since the 1920s', *Economic History Review*, XLVII: 725–48.

Durant, R. (1939) *Watling: A Survey of Social Life on a New Housing Estate*. London: King and Son.

Eichengreen, B. (2004) 'The British Economy between the Wars', in Roderick Floud and Paul Johnson (eds) *The Cambridge Economic History of Modern Britain*, Volume II: *Economic Maturity 1860–1939*. Cambridge: Cambridge University Press.

Fleming, J. (1937) 'Hire purchase', *The Times*. 19 October.

Hilton, J. (1938) *Rich Man Poor Man*. London: Allen and Unwin.

Massey, P. (1942) 'The expenditure of 1,360 British middle-class households in 1938–39', *Journal of the Royal Statistical Society*, 105: 159–96.

O'Connell, S. and Reid, C. (2005) 'Working-class consumer credit in the UK, 1925–60: the role of the check trader', *Economic History Review*, LVIII: 378–405.

Speight, G. (2000) 'Building Society Behaviour and the Mortgage Lending Market in the Interwar Period: Risk-taking by Mutual Institutions and the Interwar Housing Boom', unpublished DPhil thesis, University of Oxford.

Stone, R. and Rowe, D.A. (1966) *The Measurement of Consumers' Expenditure and Behaviour in the UK, 1920–1938*. Cambridge: Cambridge University Press.

Swenarton, M. and Taylor, S. (1985) 'The scale and nature of the growth of owner occupation in Britain between the wars', *Economic History Review*, 38: 373–92.

Willmott, P. (1979) *Growing Up in a London Village: Family Life Between the Wars*. London: Owen.

Notes

1   This survey was restricted to public-sector workers: civil servants, local government officers and teachers. This may bias owner-occupation rates upwards, given that other lower-middle-class occupations (such as small businessmen and private sector clerks) had less secure jobs and, in some cases, more volatile incomes.

2   The National Archives [hereafter TNA], LAB17/7, 'Weekly expenditure of working-class households in the United Kingdom in 1937–38', July 1949. For an estimate of the rate of owner-occupation in around 1931, see George Speight, 'Who bought the inter-war semi? The socio-economic characteristics of new-house buyers in the 1930s', University of Oxford Discussion Paper in Economic and Social History No. 38 (2000): 14.

3   TNA, BT64/3430, 'Hire purchase and consumer goods', Board of Trade memorandum, 12 November 1943.

4   TNA, LCO2/1513, President, Provident Clothing & Supply Co. Ltd, to Lord Barnby, 26 May 1938.

5   'Housewife', *The Housewife's Book* (London, 1937): 22.

12

The role of the state: Taxation, citizenship and welfare reforms

Martin Daunton

The mixed economy of welfare

IN 1900, COLLECTIVE OR PUBLIC SPENDING was only one part of a wider 'mixed economy of welfare' that included charity, self-help organizations and the market. These forms of welfare provision were financed in various ways and had different 'risk pools'. Schemes might cover the entire population in an inclusive risk pool. The finance could be based on insurance, a flat-rate payment which transferred costs from high risk individuals (say, with a serious illness) to low risk individuals (say, in good health). The funding might also come from progressive taxation and transfer benefits from rich to poor. The risk pool might be more limited or exclusive, confined to those who met criteria of eligibility such as income, gender or occupation. Private and some public insurance schemes had exclusive risk pools, and they were not redistributive between rich and poor. Entitlement could be solidarisitic, that is paying benefits as long as need continued; or contractual, depending on how much had been contributed. In order to understand how welfare provision shifted over the period, we need to place each initiative within this typology and within the 'mixed economy' of welfare. A division between public and private welfare misses many important variables. Public initiatives might be inclusive or exclusive, redistributive between rich and poor or only between sick and fit, young and old. The growth of public spending might reflect the failings of other forms of welfare – including problems with existing state institutions – and new forms of public provision might utilize the administrative capacity of non-state institutions.

At the opening of the twentieth century, public welfare was largely provided by the 'new' poor law of 1834, an attempt to reform the old Elizabethan poor law by making relief unappealing and so limiting spending. The principles of 1834 were based on deterrence or 'less eligibility': relief was conditional on entry into a workhouse, where conditions were to be worse than experienced by the lowest class of independent labourer. 'Outdoor relief' or payment to the poor in their own homes was rejected – above all, relief to able-bodied men who were in work. Political control of the poor law was changed to remove the voice of potential beneficiaries, and to increase the authority of those who were paying the bill. Before 1834, the poor law was usually managed by single parishes with a voice for all heads of household. After 1834, parishes were grouped into unions with boards of guardians elected on a franchise, giving more votes to the richer members of the community and disenfranchising any applicant for relief. The intention was clear: to give control to those who paid and not to those who received, and to limit the level of spending. Nevertheless, the new poor law continued to give relief as a right: at least in principle, it was inclusive and funded from the local property tax or rate.

Despite efforts to implement the principles of 1834, a number of pressures acted in the other direction. Could unions provide sufficient places in a workhouse to relieve large numbers of workers affected by an industrial depression? The cost was prohibitive, and the strategy of forcing men to work by deterrence was clearly pointless at a time of severe economic depression. It made more sense to separate the respectable, industrious workers who were affected by economic circumstances beyond their control from the feckless and lazy poor who needed to be reformed. Why not employ industrious workers on public works so that the poor law could be used harshly against idlers? Such an approach was found in the circular issued by Joseph Chamberlain in 1886 which urged local authorities to create public works schemes to keep the genuinely unemployed out of the reach of the poor law; it was embodied in the Unemployed Workmen's Act of 1905. Furthermore, the poor law meant institutional care for the elderly, sick and orphans, where deterrence and less eligibility were inappropriate.

By 1900, the poor law had moved away from the principles of 1834, which nevertheless remained on the statute books. Costs mounted, and fell almost entirely on the local rates which faced crisis by 1900. The government was therefore under pressure to reform the poor law, and in 1905 the Conservative administration appointed a Royal Commission on the Poor Laws and Relief of Distress to consider the future direction of the poor law – the first enquiry into the overall shape of the system since 1834.

The poor law was the largest public initiative, but was far from the only response to the social risks of sickness, death, unemployment and old age faced by all members of society. The market provided cover against death. Most middle-class families turned to commercial or mutual life insurance companies to insure against death or to provide an annuity in retirement – a practice which grew over the period, encouraged by tax breaks. Members of the lower middle class and working class were not able to accumulate sufficient personal assets to deal with social risk: their savings in the Post Office Savings Bank and other bodies were more likely to cover occasional large purchases or a seaside holiday. Far more popular than saving was insurance against death in order to pay for a decent funeral. Coverage was virtually universal in working-class families, and was dominated by large commercial concerns such as the Prudential. In all, there were 21.2 million paid-up policies in 1901. Although middle-class critics complained about the cost of these policies and urged workers to save, a pauper burial by the guardians was the ultimate indignity after a life of hardship.

The strategy of working-class families was contingency insurance against specific social risks, creating a range of institutions with exclusive risk pools for those who could afford to pay. Resources were redistributed between the working-class members of the various institutions, from young to old, fit to sick, and employed to unemployed, but not from rich to poor. Benefit was usually solidaristic, paid as long as need continued in the opinion of other members who carefully guarded against malingerers. The most popular was insurance against sickness, provided by non-profit bodies run by their members: the friendly societies such as the Manchester Unity of Oddfellows. Local branches were affiliated to a national order, and they met regularly to assess the claims of fellow members in order to prevent abuse of benefits. They developed a culture of display, status and ritual. In return for a weekly subscription of between 4d and 8d, the societies provided medical attendance and sick pay of around 10s a week. By 1910, the affiliated societies had 2.8 million members with a further 1.6 million members in 'ordinary' societies with a single branch. Clearly, many workers were not covered – and the benefits did not extend to the entire family.

Coverage against unemployment was still more limited or exclusive. Insurance was provided by trade union cover, above all in occupations susceptible to the trade cycle and with well-paid workers who could afford to pay the contributions. In 1908, 1.46 million trade union members or around 10 per cent of the male workforce were covered. The public work schemes only covered a small number of workers at times of serious depression, so that unemployed men without trade union cover had to rely on a strategy of makeshifts.

Pensions were even more rare. Friendly societies offered a sort of disguised pension in the form of sick pay to elderly members, so threatening their finances. Otherwise, pensions were limited to occupational schemes run by a few large employers and to self-help societies on the coalfields such as the Northumberland and Durham Miners' Permanent Relief Fund.

Charity was the fourth strand in the mixed economy of welfare, complementing public action, the market and self-help. Societies were created for all imaginable purposes – from the protection of cruelty to animals to the rescue of prostitutes, from orphanages to infirmaries. Although some charities had endowments to support their work, most relied on constant fund raising. Donors were attracted by the opportunity to establish their social status as well as altruism in aiding the poor. The definition of charity was contested. At one extreme stood the Charity Organization Society, formed in London in 1869 with the aim of coordinating charitable giving so that benefits were paid to the deserving poor, with the undeserving left to a deterrent poor law. In pursuit of its principles, the COS took legal action against Dr Barnardo, arguing that his children's homes encouraged the poor to abandon their offspring. By no means did everyone in the charitable world accept the Society's approach: after all, rescuing the undeserving poor was a religious duty.

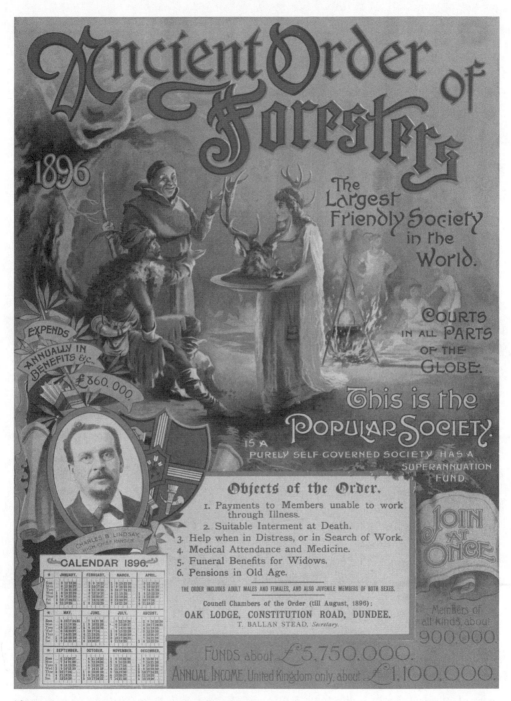

Plate 12.1 Poster for the Friendly Society of Foresters, 1896 (© Mary Evans Picture Library).

Voluntary hospitals were funded by local elites to provide care for the sick poor, with control over admissions and policy. Obviously, leading medical consultants wished to have a greater say in admissions, so there was tension between lay and professional control. At the same time, personal donations were supplemented by collections organized by local churches on Hospital Sunday and workers on Hospital Saturday, or through savings associations to buy private medical care.

Of course, many working-class families relied on an economy of makeshifts – credit from the local shopkeeper, arrears with rent, pawning of goods, assistance from kin and neighbours. They had to make hard choices. Should limited resources be used to support a sick child, even if the decision meant sending an elderly relative to the workhouse? The poor law authorities attempted to impose obligations on families to care for relatives, and working-class men and, above all, women had to negotiate their way through the available choices in order to secure the least bad outcome.

Each form of provision of relief faced difficulties at the start of the twentieth century. The tax basis of the poor law was under strain. Friendly societies were competing for members and were reluctant to increase their charges, and doctors disliked being controlled by workers. Trade union benefit funds were not distinct from strike funds and might be dissipated in an expensive labour dispute. These tensions in the existing system of welfare provided one incentive for change, but cannot be the entire explanation. After all, any system has problems which do not often lead to sweeping reform on the scale adopted by the Liberal government between 1906 and 1914.

Liberal welfare reform 1906–1914[1]

One reason for a major programme of reform was that it side-stepped the political difficulties of dealing with the poor law. The Royal Commission on the Poor Laws and the Relief of Distress did not report until 1909, and was deeply divided in its recommendations. The Majority Report expressed the views of the COS, seeking to maintain the poor law and preserve the principles of 1834. Character should always be able to rise above circumstances, and the solution to social problems was the moral regeneration of the individual. The poor law should remain precisely that – an institution dealing with the poor, and leaving the better-off to other forms of provision. The Minority Report, produced by Beatrice and Sidney Webb, argued that the deterrent principles of 1834 had been abandoned in practice and replaced by 'curative treatment' or 'greater eligibility' – a desire to improve physical and mental capacity so that the applicant for relief became fit to serve society. The Webbs wished to sweep away the poor law and create functional bodies to deal with different categories of need, regardless of social position. Furthermore, they stressed compulsion: the state should take control of the lives of individuals and compel them to become fit and direct them where to work. In their view, character was not an important consideration: their approach may be characterized as 'mechanical reform'.

The Royal Commission therefore failed to produce an agreed solution, and meanwhile a further political complication arose as a result of Joseph Chamberlain's campaign for tariff reform or imperial preference. In 1903, he proposed tariffs on non-empire goods in order to build a large, protected trade bloc on the lines of the United States and Germany. He believed that the result would be to create a strong domestic and imperial market for British manufactures which would solve the problem of poverty and unemployment. Further, some of the tariff revenue could be directed to social reform such as old age pensions. Since the Liberal party was committed to free trade, they had to devise their own free trade solution to social problems. They faced many difficulties. Where was the money to be found? If tariffs could not supply the necessary funding, income tax would have to be increased with the danger of alienating middle-class voters who might switch to the Conservative party (see 'In Focus' on the people's budget of 1909). Meanwhile, the Labour party was making its own radical proposals for a 'right to work' and redistributive taxation; the Liberal government needed to retain Labour's support in the Commons without accepting its programme.

After its election victory in 1906, the Liberal government initially used the anticipated report of the Royal Commission as a reason for delay, but by 1908 it was clear that no consensus was possible. The failure to agree gave the government freedom to make its own proposals. Both the Minority and Majority Reports were ignored, and the poor law was left unreformed. Reform of local taxation was immensely difficult, and government preferred to create a new set of institutions alongside the poor law, so removing pressure on the local rates.

The alarms of the Boer War and economic competition with Germany and the United States provided a further stimulus to action. Major-General Maurice, who was in charge of recruitment, pointed to the difficulties of finding sturdy men to defeat the Boer farmers in South Africa. As he remarked, 'it is to the condition, mental, moral and physical, of the women and children that we must look if we are to have regard to the future of our land.' His concerns led to the appointment of an Interdepartmental Committee on Physical Deterioration and to the introduction of school meals and medical inspection. More generally, the fall in the birth rate of middle-class families led to alarm that the British 'race' would be swamped by the children of the poor and less able. Would Britain be able to sustain its imperial mission? How should the quality of the racial stock be improved? One answer was offered by 'eugenics', a word derived from the Greek for 'well born'. The eugenicists argued that welfare provision allowed the poor and unfit to survive, so subverting the laws of Darwinian evolution. The eugenicists believed that the fit and clever – and they assumed that class and intelligence were intimately connected – should be encouraged to have more children. The unfit should be sterilized and mental defectives should be removed from society. Their policy was rejected in favour of an environmental approach. The conditions of towns, the standard of health care and the education of the nation should be improved to allow everyone to fulfil their full potential. Ability should be found wherever it existed in society.

In 1907, Labour introduced an Unemployed Workmen's Bill which aimed to give all unemployed men a right to work. Furthermore, the friendly societies were themselves facing financial difficulties, so they were more willing to accept state action. The response of the Liberal government was shaped by a desire to contain Labour's more radical policies which might alienate middle-class voters from the Liberal party, while at the same time maintaining Labour support in the Commons.

In Focus

The people's budget of 1909

Income tax was reintroduced in 1842 by Robert Peel, and renewed by William Gladstone in 1853. Together, they defined the nature of the tax for the rest of the century. First, it should have a single, flat rate so that money was not redistributed from rich to poor with the danger of awakening class hostility. Large incomes were considered beneficial to workers, for rich individuals saved, so leading to investment and hence to employment. The tax system as a whole should be 'proportionate', so that everyone paid more or less the same share of their income to the state. The second feature of income tax was that it should be undifferentiated, that is the same rate should apply to all types of income. Gladstone rejected the idea of charging a higher rate on 'unearned' income from property than on 'earned' income from trade, industry and other forms of employment. The proponents of differentiation argued that property survived and produced an income regardless of illness or death; earned income did not, and therefore should pay less tax to permit savings as a fund against future loss of income, and to encourage active enterprise.

The Liberal government of 1906 remade income tax, culminating in the constitutional crisis of the people's budget of 1909. Differential taxation was introduced in 1907 so that earned income paid less than unearned income. The loss of revenue was made good by an increase in taxation of estates left at death. The Liberals were using the tax system to give priority to active enterprise against passive holders of property – and the strategy was extended by an attack on landowners. The value of land and the level of rent increased as a result of the energy of other members of society, so that the income of landowners was socially created rather than earned. Society could therefore claim the 'unearned increment'. Differentiation and the land question aimed to unite active capitalists and workers against idle landowners and investors – a shrewd political response to the Conservative campaign for tariff reform, and an attempt to hold together an alliance of capital and labour within the Liberal party.

In 1909, Lloyd George went still further. He introduced graduation into income tax so that larger incomes paid a 'super-tax'. Graduation was still modest, but a new principle was introduced which was extended during the First World War. The justification was both principled and pragmatic. The principle was based on a realization that an extra pound of income produced less satisfaction for a rich person than an extra pound for a poorer person; hence a higher level of tax on large incomes

The people's budget of 1909

meant that the loss of satisfaction was considerably less. The pragmatic point was that a higher tax on large income would produce more revenue, as it did during the war. Lloyd George also introduced tax breaks for men with children so that middle-class family men with modest incomes actually paid less tax. Most controversially, Lloyd George also introduced a tax on the unearned increment in land – a proposal that outraged Conservative landowners in the House of Lords. The ensuing constitutional crisis was resolved in a general election in 1910.

Reform of the tax system threatened to alienate middle-class electors from the Liberal party, fearful of the redistributive thrust of the super-tax. Consequently, the Liberal government changed the basis of finance for welfare measures after 1909. However, the reforms did mean that Britain entered the First World War with a much stronger and more flexible tax system than in other countries.

Business and labour interests were not directly consulted on the shape of welfare reforms, which emerged from discussions between politicians, reforming civil servants and experts in the field of charity or social reform. The outcome may be characterized as 'moral reform'. Character mattered, but 'moral regeneration' was not possible unless the state removed impediments preventing the full development of character and self-reliance. 'Mechanical reform' was firmly rejected, for individuals should on no account become dependent on the state. Winston Churchill, the Liberal politician responsible for some of the reforms, explained that 'There is no chance of making people self-reliant by confronting them with problems and with trials beyond their capacity to surmount. You do not make a man self-reliant by crushing him under a steam-roller.' Churchill's aim was to prevent the growth of collectivism and socialism. People would compete in a free society if there were a safety net to catch them. 'We want to have free competition upwards; we decline to allow free competition to run downwards.'

The precise nature of the reforms was shaped by the capacity of existing institutions, the interplay of interest groups and political calculation. A serious political problem was finance. Old age pensions were introduced in 1908, and were funded from general taxation rather than contributions, so reducing the burden on the local rates and creating a need for more national taxation. The 'people's budget' of 1909 introduced a progressive income tax, and the reduced Liberal majority after the elections of 1910 meant that the government dare not alienate more voters to the Conservatives. Neither could the government afford to alienate Labour MPs whose votes were vital: their demands had to be met without losing middle-class votes. The solution adopted in 1911 was to move the funding basis from general taxation to insurance contributions. Both insured workers and employers paid a weekly contribution, with a modest supplement from the state. The national insurance schemes of 1911 were exclusive and contractual: benefits were strictly limited by the amount contributed so that the scheme was actuarially sound. Labour was caught in a dilemma. Flat-rate insurance contributions did not redistribute income from rich to poor in the same way as income tax, so the burden was proportionately heavier on unskilled workers. On the other hand, insured workers were receiving contributions from the employers and the state. Opposition was therefore difficult.

Old age pensions were administered by the state, whereas social insurance relied on the capacity of existing institutions. Friendly societies and trade unions had information on the incidence of unemployment and sickness, so allowing the state to calculate the level of contributions and benefits. They determined the coverage of the schemes. Unemployment insurance was limited to trades with trade union schemes and a susceptibility to cyclical depression. The problems of other workers were approached through minimum wages, decasualization and labour exchanges to allow them to find jobs. Health insurance applied to manual workers and, above all, men. The Liberal welfare reforms were patriarchal: the aim was to allow the male head of household to support his family by covering periods without work as a result of sickness or economic depression. Non-working wives were not provided with medical care except in the case of pregnancy.

Administration was to be left to friendly societies and trade unions with the status of approved societies, in the words of the initial proposal 'subject to the absolute control of the members, and with provision for the elections of all committees, representatives and officers by the members'. Although some historians argue that the state was capturing these institutions as a means of controlling the workers, the strategy of the Liberals was to contain the state and to leave implementation to self-governing societies. Consequently, members would have an incentive to control benefits and prevent malingering, for 'the burden of mismanagement and maladministration would fall on the workmen themselves'. However, the Liberal government's ambition was thwarted by the commercial insurance societies, which demanded that they should also become approved societies. The democratic promise was broken.

The claim that the insurance schemes of 1911 laid the foundation of the welfare state is not entirely correct: it was exclusive rather than inclusive, offering benefit according to the number of contributions with minimal redistribution. The Labour party was suspicious and argued for tax-funded redistribution. Indeed, the schemes covered only part of the population. The welfare state after the Second World War was closer to the poor law in offering benefit according to need, with an inclusive risk pool – though shorn of deterrence.

The First World War took government spending to a new level. The reasons for the increase during the war are obvious; the ability to keep taxes at a higher level after the war, without resistance on the scale of other countries, is more difficult to explain. The problems at the end of the war were potentially very serious. During the war, taxes were increased and many members of the middle class claimed that they were paying more, without the ability to raise their incomes as much as organized workers. Industrialists paid an excess profits tax on increases in their war profits, and complained that their competitiveness was reduced. Meanwhile, Labour complained that the burden of interest on war loans was crippling the economy, transferring money from active members of society to the recipients of 'unearned income'. Consequently, Labour wished to impose a 'capital levy' – a one-off tax to reduce the national debt, so relieving active enterprise of taxation and allowing revenue to be diverted to welfare. Of course, industry and property owners feared the levy might become a serious threat, not least in view of the Labour party's commitment to nationalization. The post-war coalition government of Liberals and Conservatives needed to contain the political dangers of the capital levy, and at the same time prevent a revolt by middle-class taxpayers. This difficult task was achieved by three approaches. The first strategy was a programme of retrenchment – the so-called Geddes axe – which contained middle-class revolt without making serious inroads into welfare spending. Second, the government convinced industry that it should continue to pay taxes on its profits to avoid the worse threat of a capital levy. Third, the government rejected indirect taxes which would allow Labour to claim that workers and consumers were paying for inter-est payments to rich, idle creditors of the state. The crisis passed, and the tax system retained the support of most people as fair and equitable. Taxation at the new higher level was accepted, not least as a result of Winston Churchill's budget of 1925 which reduced taxation on middle-class men with family responsibilities – a crucial electoral constituency.

The mobilization of a greater proportion of the population for warfare might be expected to lead to more generous welfare to secure commitment and to ensure that the population was fit. Some commentators argued that social reform 'failed' after the war in the face of demands for retrenchment: the proposal to raise the school leaving age was abandoned; reform of the health system was dropped; the massive council house building programme was curtailed. Is 'failure' the correct term, given the marked increase in spending on welfare? In 1913, central government spending on social services was 4.1 per cent of GNP; in 1921 it was 10.1 per cent, and the level only fell to 8.4 per cent in 1924, with a rise to 11.3 per cent in 1938. Of course, a large part of the increase in spending was a response to economic depression and the need to support the long-term unemployed. Crucially, the machinery for income support for unemployed workers was in place in Britain before the onset of economic crisis.

A more realistic way of considering the impact of the war is through the strains imposed on existing institutions of welfare provision which threatened the basis of the Liberal welfare reforms and led to shifts in policy. The approved societies failed to fulfil the hopes of 1911. In 1925, Labour informed the Royal Commission on Health Insurance that democracy was a dead letter. Commercial insurance companies under-mined the democratic nature of approved societies, and Labour recommended the nationalization of the companies. The independence of approved societies was also subverted by government control of their finances. At least in theory, the societies could offer additional benefits with the possibility of raising expectations and hence costs. The societies' finances were monitored by the government actuary and the Controller of the Health Services Division of the Ministry of Health in order to ensure that they remained solvent. These government officials could reject proposals for additional benefits on apparently technical, apolitical financial grounds. As the Controller remarked, the approved societies acted as a buffer and diverted criticism away from the government. Autonomy was therefore spurious, and members were in any case losing interest in the sociability and rituals of the societies. Might a single, national scheme be fairer, removing the divergence between the benefits of different approved societies' benefits, allowing better coordination with other health services, and extending coverage to those in greatest need?

The greatest problem was in unemployment insurance. During the war, the government planned to extend unemployment insurance to trades likely to experience post-war problems. The scheme was not ready in 1918, and the immediate response was to offer benefit or 'dole' to everyone regardless of contributions. The insurance principle of limited contractual benefits was abandoned, at least temporarily. In 1920, the government tried to return to the principles of 1911 by extending unemployment insurance to all workers except in agriculture and domestic service, and ensuring that the scheme was solvent. Unfortunately, the depression meant that many workers lost their jobs before they paid sufficient contributions to earn an entitlement to benefit, which left them with no alternative except the poor law. The government responded by paying 'uncovenanted' or 'extended' benefits beyond those covered by contributions – supposedly to be repaid in the future. As a result, two principles were in conflict: the limited and financially self-funding contractual principles of 1911; and the solidaristic payment of benefit according to need. The government introduced two measures in 1922 in order to contain the cost. First, extended benefit would only be paid to those 'genuinely seeking whole-time employment', a measure designed to deny relief to 'malingerers' and (in practice) to women. Second, a means test was imposed to deny benefit to anyone with a household income above 13s a week. The means test was abolished by the Labour government in 1924, and the genuinely seeking work clause was dropped in 1930. The apparent insolvency of the unemployment scheme contributed to the financial crisis of 1931 and the government reinstated the means test, leading to bitter resentment against intrusion into the private affairs of families and against the implication that men were dependent on the earnings of their wife and children. In the 1930s, relief of the unemployed was in the hands of two bodies, according to the insured status of workers. In 1931, unemployed workers who were not covered by insurance were passed to the public assistance committees which replaced the poor law guardians, and in 1934 to the Unemployment Assistance Board. Insured workers were covered by a newly solvent unemployment insurance scheme administered by the Unemployment Insurance Statutory Committee. As a result, there were two systems of relief, administered in different ways and with different principles.

Unemployment insurance was under pressure to become less contractual. Meanwhile, pensions moved in the opposite direction from non-contributory taxation to insurance. The Treasury had not been happy with tax funding of pensions in 1908, and its warnings were confirmed by mounting costs and by Labour's demand to reduce the age limit from 70 to 60 and to increase the weekly payment. The result would be higher taxes on the more prosperous members of society and a transfer to the elderly poor. The response of the Conservative government in 1925 was to introduce new contributory pensions for widows and orphans, for workers aged 65 to 70, and as a supplement for those aged over 70. The tax-funded basic pension survived for those over the age of 70, but the emphasis shifted to insurance.

The poor law was also in difficulties after the war. As we have seen, it was not reformed before the First World War. The introduction of old age pensions and social insurance merely reduced financial pressure without resolving the underlying problem. Difficulties mounted after the war. Workers who were not covered by unemployment insurance turned to the poor law, and in some districts the guardians were controlled by workers as a result of the extension of the franchise and the end of pauper disqualification. On the coalfields, some poor law unions paid relief to strikers or their families, much to the alarm of employers and the Conservative government. As a result, the government imposed stricter control over the guardians in 1926, and in 1929 abolished the unions. Power was handed to new public assistance committees drawn from members of local councils which covered a larger geographical area and dealt with a wider range of functions, so diluting the democratic threat of the pauper vote. Nevertheless, the danger – as the Conservative government saw it – was not entirely removed and in 1934 the Unemployment Assistance Board was created. The UAB was appointed rather than elected, and was therefore 'safe' from democratic pressure. The result was twofold: a containment of local democracy; and, more positively, a greater ability to redistribute funding between prosperous and depressed areas.

Philanthropy did not wither away between the wars. The COS redefined its role as working with the state, especially through the National Council for Social Services formed in 1919. The state had turned to voluntary bodies before the First World War to care for orphans and delinquents in approved schools, and the approach was extended between the wars. The tradition of settlement houses in the East End of London or boys' clubs was appplied to the unemployed in the depressed areas. The New Estates Committee of the NCSS provided community centres on large council estates.

The record was not one of complete success. Many charities were now working within the realm of the state, and the community centres were no more than a minor supplement to the major public investment in the council estates. The voluntary hospitals, perhaps the largest single component of the philanthropic sector, faced serious financial difficulties, forcing them into greater dependence on patient fees and hospital saving schemes. Not surprisingly, many middle-class families with modest incomes started to favour tax funding as fairer and more efficient; and the consultants realized that voluntarism limited their ability to use the latest techniques.

In 1929, the poor law hospitals were transferred either to the PACs or to local authorities, and local advisory boards could be created to coordinate the work of the voluntary and local authority hospitals. The attempt to bring together state and charitable institutions only succeeded in Manchester, and the question of coordination remained unsettled by the Second World War. One possibility was that local authorities, with their wide range of medical services, would take over the hospitals – a solution strongly opposed by the medical profession as a threat to their autonomy. In fact, the outcome was to 'nationalize' the voluntary hospitals and the local authority hospitals, so giving considerable power to the medical profession, rather than to integrate them with the other medical services in the locality. The problem was general and not confined to hospitals: welfare policies between the wars were a mass of contradictions, with different principles and different levels of benefit between schemes. Not surprisingly, the wartime government wished to coordinate the existing programmes of social insurance, and appointed William Beveridge to consider the issue. The outcome was the Beveridge Report on *Social Insurance and Allied Services* of 1942, an attempt to produce system from chaos.

Debates and Interpretations

The scale of the public sector in Britain underwent a massive transformation between 1900 and the end of the First World War. In the last quarter of the nineteenth century, total public spending in Britain amounted to between 8 and 10 per cent of GNP. By 1913, spending on the naval race with Germany and on welfare took the figure to 11.9 per cent of GDP. After this modest increase, the First World War marked a major displacement: by 1920, total government spending was 20.5 per cent of GDP. The war marked a permanent step change, for total government spending was 26.0 per cent in 1937 – and the pattern was repeated in the Second World War, with government spending at 37.5 per cent of GDP in 1951. Both world wars acted as ratchets, holding the public sector at a much higher level. The outcome was by no means inevitable, for public spending reached levels similar to the First World War during the Napoleonic wars before falling back to pre-war levels. What differed in the first half of the twentieth century so that the level of public spending did not return to earlier levels, and the boundary between the market and collective provision shifted? The largest component of the increase in public spending was social services: between 1900 and 1951, total public spending as a proportion of GDP rose by 24.2 percentage points, and social services rose by 11.8 percentage points. Why did the public sector, and especially spending on welfare, become so large in the first half of the twentieth century?

Historians have turned to a number of different explanations. The expansion of welfare provision and the role of the state have been interpreted as designed to make capitalism more efficient or to impose control over the working class. In the late nineteenth and early twentieth century, Britain was facing competition from Germany and the United States and 'national efficiency' was a serious concern. How could Britain become more efficient both as an economic and an imperial power, to retain its markets and sustain its strategic ambitions? The result might be to invest in 'human capital' through education and health, or to remake the labour market to preserve skills. Welfare could, therefore, be seen as a means towards capitalist efficiency rather than a desire to improve the conditions of the poor.

Economic efficiency and the health of the 'imperial race' were certainly central to discussions of social policy in the early twentieth century. However, did inefficiency mean that income should be redistributed from the rich to the poor in order to raise their productivity and consumption of goods, or would that strategy undermine incentives and investment? Some industrialists opposed investment in expensive welfare which would drive up their costs and lose export markets. In any case, we might wonder why few employers provided their own welfare schemes (as they did in some other leading industrial economies) rather than turning to the state. The desire for capitalist efficiency does not explain the form of welfare policy. Similarly, a desire to create an imperial race does not explain whether it should be achieved by improving their environment or sterilizing the unfit.

The interpretation of welfare reform as a search for capitalist efficiency is often connected with the view that social policy was designed to contain working-class threats to the existing order of society, incorporating their institutions and leaders into the state, and removing the promise (or danger) of democracy. On this view, trade union leaders participated in reform of the labour market in return for recognition, sacrificing the interests of the rank-and-file for control of the workplace, and assisting in the administration of state welfare measures. David Vincent argues that the extension of the franchise meant that the traditional provision of relief by local government was dangerous. Hence responsibility for relief was passed to the central state and to bodies with little direct parliamentary scrutiny. In his view, the aim of the state was to prevent the cost of welfare rising as much as might be expected given the emergence of universal manhood suffrage and the extension of the vote to women between the wars.

How far should these views be accepted? Reform of the labour market was often opposed by rank-and-file workers who feared a loss of their autonomy – but it was equally opposed by many employers who feared a loss of their freedom to hire and fire at will, and to draw on a cheap, casual workforce. Reform might depend on an alliance between trade union leaders, anxious to create a regular workforce and so increase their bargaining power on behalf of their members, and government officials or social experts anxious to remove a source of poverty and hardship. Social reform should not be seen as merely a matter of containment. Vincent admits that the elderly gained, and there were better local services for health care and maternity. Centralization was not entirely about control: national bodies could remove local discrepancies and redistribute funds between rich and poor areas. The Treasury was rightly concerned about cost, for taxes might lose their legitimacy and hence threaten welfare spending. It had to strike a balance between what could realistically be afforded in terms of political acceptability and what was socially desirable.

All advanced industrial countries experienced a rise in the level of welfare spending, reflecting the increased complexities of the economy, the greater capacity to sustain higher spending and the political circumstances of a wider franchise. But these general factors cannot explain the particular form taken by welfare policy. Many historians of welfare policy take a comparative approach, and explain the differences in terms of the nature of the political process and the interplay of interests. For example,

French welfare policy was initially directed to women and children, whereas in Britain policy was more focused on the needs of male heads of households. In some countries, welfare was funded by local government and in others by the central government; in some, based on insurance rather than taxation, and so on.

The particular outcome has been explained by some historians in terms of ideas. For example, evolutionary biology influenced policy and led at its most extreme to sterilization or even extermination of the unfit. In Britain, such beliefs had less purchase and preventive medicine was much more influential. In the opinion of Jose Harris, welfare reform did not reflect a belief in collectivism so much as a belief in the role of the state in freeing people to take control of their own lives. These ideological divergences might be explained in terms of intellectual history, through the close analysis of language and philosophy, but their influence on policy and purchase in political debate may also be explained by the different capacities of the state and of the institutions of civil society.

Many historians argue that the shaping of policy took place within the administrative capabilities and knowledge generated by existing institutions. Did the central government have the capacity to raise revenue, or did local government have more ability to extract revenue? The answer differed between societies and changed over time: one of the major changes in Britain after 1900 was a shift from local to central finance. In Britain, trade unions were generally accepted and their assumption that the male breadwinner should sustain a family was embedded in policy, frustrating the demands for family allowances paid to wives. In France, unions were opposed by many employers, and family allowances paid to women were accepted as a means of weakening unions, as well as fitting with the desire of the state to encourage larger families. Similarly, the dominance of preventive medicine in Britain reflected its acceptance by civil servants who were suspicious of the calls for sterilization and confinement of mentally unfit. In other words, the policy outcome reflected the pre-existing institutions and capacities in society.

Further reading

The changing pattern of taxation and the ability of the state to raise more revenue is outlined in two books by Martin Daunton, *Trusting Leviathan: The Politics of Taxation in Britain, 1799–1914* (Cambridge, 2001) and *Just Taxes: The Politics of Taxation in Britain, 1914–79* (Cambridge, 2002). These books emphasize the success of the British state in securing revenue without major political crisis, compared with other European countries, which allowed a greater reliance on tax-funded welfare. The changing pattern of welfare provision is explained by M.A. Crowther, *British Social Policy, 1914–1939* (Basingstoke, 1988) which provides a clear outline of the legislation and an excellent bibliography. Much writing on welfare deals with the complexities of the legislative process, without considering why it became such an important subject at some times, and without considering the wider mixed economy of welfare – a concept developed by G.B.M.

Finlayson, *Citizen, State and Social Welfare in Britain, 1830–1990* (Oxford, 1994). The
movement of welfare to the centre of political debate is explained by Jose Harris, 'The
transition of high politics in English social policy, 1880–1914', in M. Bentley and J.
Stevenson (eds) *High and Low Politics in Modern Britain* (Oxford, 1983). She also deals with
the role of ideas in shaping welfare in 'Political thought and the welfare state, 1870–1940:
An intellectual framework for British social policy', *Past and Present*, 135 (1992). Martin
Daunton, 'Payment and participation: Welfare and state formation in Britain, 1900–51',
Past and Present, 150 (London, 1996) considers the capacity of existing institutions and the
way the state drew upon them, as well as the problems faced by each form of provision.
Paul Johnson, *Saving and Spending: The Working-Class Economy in Britain, 1870–1939* (Oxford,
1985) is an excellent account of the self-help organizations created by the working class.
He also provides a typology of forms of welfare in 'Risk, redistribution and social welfare
in Britain from the poor law to Beveridge', in M. Daunton (ed.), *Charity, Self Interest and
Welfare in the English* Past (London, 1996). The impact of changes in welfare provision on
the poor is analysed by David Vincent in *Poor Citizens: The State and the Poor in Twentieth
Century Britain* (London, 1991), with an emphasis on the limitation of possibilities of
democracy – a line adopted by other historians which fails to consider the large increase
in social spending.

Note

1   Liberal welfare reforms, 1906–14: **Education (Provision of Meals) Act 1906**:
    Permitted local education authorities to provide meals at public elementary schools.
    They could finance the scheme by private contributions, charges to parents or, as a
    last resort, a rate not exceeding $^{1}/_{2}$d in £. Parents who did not pay were not to suffer
    loss of civil rights. **Education (Administrative Provisions) Act 1907**: Local
    education authorities were to provide for medical inspection of children, and to make
    arrangements for attending to the health and physical condition of children in public
    elementary schools (i.e. school medical service): **Old Age Pensions 1908**: Paid to
    everyone over the age of 70 whose income did not exceed 10s a week – this 'thrift
    clause' meant that the elderly with their own savings, earnings or occupational
    pension were penalized. The pensions were financed from general taxation.
    Labour Exchanges Act 1909: Empowered the Board of Trade to establish labour
    exchanges. No person was required to accept an appointment. Service was free for
    those unemployed or under notice to leave a job; those seeking to change jobs paid a
    fee. **Trade Boards Act 1909**: Established Boards to fix wages in certain trades where
    wages were low: tailoring, paper boxes, lace, chain making. **National Insurance
    Act Part I 1911**: This provided health insurance. Workers over the age of 16 earning
    less than £160 a year and all manual workers, whatever their income, were compelled
    to join the scheme. They paid 4d a week, the employers 3d, and the government about
    2d. For this, the insured person received medical attendance by a general practitioner;
    sickness benefit of 10s per week to insured men and 7s 6d to insured women for
    13 weeks, and then 5s for the next 13 weeks; disability benefit of 5s a week when sick
    benefit ran out; maternity benefit of 30s paid directly to an insured man's wife who

would receive a further 30s if she was also a contributor; treatment in a sanatorium for tuberculosis. **National Insurance Act Part II 1911**: Workers in building, shipbuilding, mechanical engineering, iron founding, construction of vehicles and sawmilling were compelled to be insured against unemployment. The workmen paid $2^1/_2$d a week, the employer $2^1/_2$d, and the government $^2/_3$d. A benefit of 7s a week was paid for a maximum of 15 weeks a year.

13

Leisure

Julie-Marie Strange

UNTIL RECENTLY, HISTORIES OF LEISURE focused largely on the emergence of commercial entertainment in the nineteenth century and the anxieties of the middle classes concerning how 'useful' such pursuits were. Debates about rational recreation and the 'problem' of leisure time persisted into the twentieth century, not least because the interwar period saw the expansion of a commercial leisure market that catered for increased living standards, shortened working hours and falling birth rates. This chapter examines some of the shifts in leisure pursuits and provision in the first half of the twentieth century. As we shall see, despite the emergence of a modern commercial market, leisure remained a contested concept in terms of class, gender, politics and time. Similarly, historians have not always agreed what the term 'leisure' means. Typically, leisure has denoted the period of time spent outside paid work. Yet for some groups, like the housewife, leisure time was never clearly defined. The chapter will also consider, then, how the definition of leisure has been contested.

Defining leisure

For much of the early industrial period, leisure referred to a class of people rather than a group of activities; the 'leisured classes' were people of wealth who did not need to work for a living. This group pioneered the 'Grand Tour', an extended holiday based around touring the great sites and cities of Europe and, for the particularly affluent, more exotic locations. As a middle class emerged in the late eighteenth and nineteenth centuries, one of the ways in which they sought to express their identity was through leisure pursuits: touring Europe became not only a sign of wealth, but also represented the cultural aspirations of a class that had made its fortunes in industry and commerce.

Moreover, bourgeois stereotypes of aristocratic pursuits as decadent and reckless (for instance, gambling) cultivated a middle-class notion of 'rational recreation'. Indeed, the late eighteenth and nineteenth centuries saw the emergence of a vast array of organizations which were dedicated to the pursuit of learning for pleasure: literary and philosophical societies, scientific and art associations, and clubs dedicated to the celebration of the classics. The bourgeois home was also a venue for many types of leisure pursuits, such as embroidery, musical evenings, painting, the dinner party and the social call.

For the working classes, however, leisure was much less visible. The early nineteenth-century factory system was often referred to as 'sweated labour' with entire families employed for long hours, six days a week. Gradual factory reform throughout the century meant that women and children were increasingly removed from the factory system while legislation shortened the working day; by the end of the century, most workers had Saturday afternoons off too. The decrease in working hours was matched, for many workers, by an increase in living standards and by the last two decades of the century a commercial market had grown to cater specifically for working-class leisure time and tastes. Notably, the music hall, day trips to the seaside, the pub and football clubs were all popular leisure activities with working-class consumers.

The first half of the twentieth century saw further reduction in average working hours. The most significant changes were immediately after the First World War. By 1919, the average working week dropped from pre-war levels of 54 hours to 48 hours a week, although these hours varied according to occupation, gender and region and the amount of overtime individuals chose to do. Most industries gave workers holidays away from work but, before the First World War, these were overwhelmingly holidays without pay. As many socialist commentators pointed out at the time, these breaks in employment were not 'holidays', a word resonant with pleasure, but periods of economic hardship. Trade unions had pushed from the start of the twentieth century for holidays with pay to be viewed as a fundamental right of citizenship, arguing they were good for the morale and health of the nation's workforce. Debates concerning holidays with pay gathered pace throughout the 1920s and 30s, their outcome often depending on the buoyancy of the economy. A Holiday with Pay Act was passed in 1938 but it legislated for only three consecutive days with pay and did not, therefore, substantially change the holiday experience of many people (Jones, 1986: 14–33). The Act did, however, firmly establish the right of citizens to a holiday from work with pay.

The campaign for holidays with pay indicated that while a commercial leisure market may have expanded, participation in organized pursuits often depended on disposable income. The best opportunity for indulging in commercial pleasure was in the period between leaving school and before marriage. Still living with parents, a young worker contributed to a household budget but received spends in return. Young women's 'pocket money' went largely on transport to and from work and, more excitingly, the cinema, magazines, dances and cosmetics. Young men tended to pay board and lodgings to their parents, keeping money back for leisure pursuits and luxury goods, such as cigarettes. Some studies of married working-class men suggest that many 'tipped up' wages to their wives on pay day while negotiating a sum to be kept back for their own personal pleasure, whether this be beer, gambling, reading materials and/or treating the children to sweets (Roberts, 1984). More recent surveys have called this into question, however, indicating that some Lancashire men firmly held the purse strings, deciding how much 'housekeeping' money spouses could manage on (Griffiths, 2001). Married middle- and working-class women, particularly full-time housewives, appear not to have had money for themselves, spending any spare resources on children or items for the house. Women's money was usually described as 'housekeeping' and defined as a family budget, lending an impression that to spend the money on personal items or pursuits was undeserved. Rather, women had to seek 'permission' from husbands to spend on themselves. Claire Langhamer notes, however, that few women expressed grievance at this apparent inequality of resources (2000: 159–64).

As Langhamer suggests, 'leisure' is not, perhaps, the best word to describe the activities people did in their spare time or for pleasure. Notions of leisure tend to assume that adult time is divided between paid work and time off. For many women, housework was neither paid nor governed by clear working hours. Moreover, even women in paid employment tended to oversee the domestic chores and so the workplace extended to include the home and family. Indeed, Langhamer notes that for women in the first half of the twentieth century, leisure carried specific connotations of organized and, often, commercial forms or spaces, such as the cinema or the dance hall. Notably, Langhamer's oral history respondents tended to participate in social activities that were, for instance, church based. Yet because women helped organize the events in some way, they saw them not as leisure but as an extension of a neighbourly or community role. The women derived pleasure from such pursuits but did not locate them within a vocabulary of leisure. Even holidays, especially self-catering holidays, which may seem clearly defined 'leisure' periods were, for women, typified by a continuation of childcare, cooking and cleaning.

Similarly, histories of working-class cultures have highlighted the extent to which 'leisure' for women was informal and often merged with tasks. This could be negative: a survey of *Working-class Wives: Their Health and Conditions* by Margery Spring Rice (1939) conveyed the impression that women barely ever left home; spending 'their leisure in sewing and doing other household jobs, slightly different from the ordinary work of cooking and house-cleaning'. Yet we must be careful not to paint an overly bleak picture: shopping, cleaning the front doorstep and hanging washing out all provided opportunities for gossiping with neighbours in the street. In her study *Women's Talk? A Social History of 'Gossip' in Working-Class Neighbourhoods, 1880–1960* (1995), Melanie Tebbutt located a rich but informal culture of sociability, often located in the space of the street, that did not necessarily collide with formal definitions of leisure. Such problems could also apply to middle-class women, especially in a period when domestic service was in decline: baking, cookery, sewing and playing with children might represent unpaid work but could also, for some women, bring personal pleasure and satisfaction.

The difficulty of defining leisure was not, however, confined to women. The notion of 'spare time' was particularly hard to define for groups like the unemployed who had, in a sense, lots of 'spare time'. This was rarely pleasurable but, as Walter Greenwood's novel *Love on the Dole* (1933) illustrated, more often a burden with little money to spend on pleasure and an overriding need to spend days looking for work. As Andrew Davies pointed out in *Leisure, Gender and Poverty: Working-Class Culture in Salford and Manchester, 1900–1939* (1992), unemployment might not prohibit men from participating in leisure activities altogether, but it did lead to segregation between those in and out of work: the unemployed were, for instance, more likely to attend cheap matinees at the cinema while their employed peers watched films in the evening. For young men who were 'courting' the opposite sex, there was also an expectation that the women would be paid for. The financial difficulties of the unemployed thus hampered a sense of adolescent masculinity. In Greenwood's *Love on the Dole*, girls who refuse to entertain lads when 'you've got nowt' exacerbate the unemployed young man's feelings of hopelessness. As unemployment persists, the protagonist of the novel, Harry, is unable to afford smokes (picking fag ends up from the floor instead) or take his girlfriend to the cinema; the streets become his place of 'leisure', but also a constant reminder of his failure.

Leisure and morality

The issue of money was closely tied to matters of morality too. Andrew Davies notes that many social commentators disapproved of particular forms of leisure pursuit, especially those that could be linked to poverty (1992). Hence, gambling was the antithesis of thrift while drinking represented a waste of resources and encouraged rough behaviour. Inappropriate spending and alcohol were also seen as key causes of marital dispute and social disharmony. Popular leisure had long been a contested subject. Middle-class observers fretted over how the working classes spent their leisure time and were keen to promote 'rational', that is, useful, recreation. Rational pursuits included Sunday schools and clubs such as the Boys' Brigade for children, temperance clubs and public libraries for adults, and the formation of societies for learning, such as the Mechanics Institute. Socialists also expressed concern that escapist forms of popular culture would depoliticize the working classes. Socialists saw leisure as an opportunity to unite the working classes in harmonious and educational activities that rejuvenated them, promoted family and community values, and encouraged people to strive for a better life. The most well-known example of socialist rational leisure was the rambling and cycling club. Embodied in the Clarion Club, these activities promoted good health and exercise, encouraged urban dwellers to explore the countryside and permitted groups of likeminded people to form friendships while developing their political clout.

It is unsurprising, perhaps, that with so much debate on the 'problem' of leisure, political parties were keen to include pleasure pursuits in their policies in the interwar period. At a national level, Labour advocated state intervention in shaping leisure through legislative reform. On a more local level, Conservative councillors and party workers were willing to engage in debates concerning the provision of leisure facilities and some limited leisure reforms. The right to partake in certain forms of leisure also had the potential to be political with some issues uniting left- and right-wing, working- and middle-class campaigners. For instance, hikers campaigned in the interwar years for the right to roam across private land in the countryside. Similarly, individuals combined to argue at municipal level for the provision of better leisure facilities, such as football fields, swimming baths, bowling greens or, where local councils had banned use of recreational facilities on the Sabbath, the right to play sport on a Sunday. Indeed, it was the expansion of the municipal provision of sporting facilities that enabled many working people to play games like tennis or have access to swimming facilities that had previously been the preserve of public schools and families with private courts or membership of clubs (Jones, 1986: 164–94).

In Focus

Victoria Baths

Often referred to as the city's 'water palace', Manchester's Victoria Baths opened in 1906. The Baths represented a classic municipal attempt to synthesize leisure with public health and rational recreation. Catering for all local citizens, the Baths offered first- and second-class pools, a separate female pool, 64 wash-baths, Turkish and Russian baths and laundry rooms. While the baths and washrooms may have been designed to separate the classes, society was – at least in theory – united in the pursuit of health, vitality and cleanliness. Built in breathtaking Art Nouveau style, the Baths also represented a monument to civic pride: even the second-class pool had decorative glazed tiles while the staircases and entrance hall were characterized by stained glass, fine carpentry, ornamental ironwork, mosaic floors and engraved tiling. The cost was phenomenal at over £59,000.

From the late Victorian period, the value of bath and washhouses for public health had increasingly attracted municipal attention. In a context where many terraced houses did not have bathrooms, municipal facilities offered people from less well-off backgrounds the opportunity to take a bath. One woman, born in 1918, took her first weekly bathe in Victoria Baths in her teens and never forgot the experience of submerging herself in warm water for the first time. Similarly, the provision of laundry facilities promoted hygiene even if the design of individual washing stalls meant that social opportunities were restricted. In Manchester in 1938, laundry facilities were open from six in the morning until eight at night on weekdays and from six until three in the afternoon on Saturdays.

Host to numerous swimming clubs, sports such as water polo and trophy galas, Victoria Baths also spawned some great swimming triumphs. Sunny Lowry, the first Englishwoman to swim the English Channel in August 1933, began her swimming

> ### Victoria Baths
>
> career in Victoria Baths. The municipal council were also keen to offer incentives to children to swim in their spare time. For instance, youngsters who swam their first eight lengths were rewarded with free swims. More unusually, perhaps, temporary flooring over the pools meant that the Baths could also be used as dance halls, bowling 'greens' and for other 'dry' activities. The Baths also fostered a loyalty and community in their own right, with many of the swimming clubs organizing social events and day trips.
>
> While separating the sexes was undoubtedly done in the name of modesty, it also enabled children from less well-off families to use the pools. Stories abound of boys whose families could not afford bathing trunks swimming naked while, in a separate pool, the baths loaned bathing slips to girls without swimming costumes. Mixed bathing was introduced at Victoria Baths in the 1920s but was considered quite daring.
>
> Due to the high cost of maintenance and necessity of repair, Victoria Baths closed in 1993. In September 2003 it won a BBC 'Restoration' competition where the public was invited to vote to save a historic building (http://www.victoriabaths.org.uk).

Leisure pursuits could be political in more subtle ways too. The Women's League of Health and Beauty, founded in 1930, offered relatively cheap exercise classes for pleasure and personal health. The creation of the league coincided with the growing popularity of the suntan (lauded by fashion designer Coco Chanel in the early 1920s), dieting and the explosion in the magazine market for beauty tips and hints. The League promoted 'racial health'. This was not tied to the rise of organized fascism but, rather, based on promoting relatively old-fashioned ideals of femininity: the raison d'être for the organization was to ensure the health and vitality of young women for future motherhood and the good of the Empire (Matthews, 1990). In a similar vein sport, with its clearly defined rules, element of competition and emphasis on teamwork, tended to be endorsed by a range of official institutions. For instance, Liz Oliver argues that 'rounders' was popular with millworkers in Bolton in the interwar period. Enthusiasm for the sport was encouraged by a range of institutions for specific reasons: schools endorsed rounders because it promoted good health and contributed to cultivating a generation of future mothers; Sunday schools and voluntary organizations like the Girl Guides encouraged it because it offered a healthy diversion from immoral leisure pursuits; while mill managers sponsored teams and galas to foster morale and good industrial relations (1997).

Leisure provision

In his study of leisure in the interwar years, Stephen Jones (1986) identified three key areas of leisure provision, all of which expanded in this period. First, commercial companies provided recreation for profit: sporting enterprises, holidays and the arts all offered the entrepreneur opportunities for business ventures, especially in the context of (for some) rising wages, shorter working hours and emerging notions of companionate marriage. Second, voluntary associations like the YMCA and trade unions provided a vast range of leisure activities. These ranged from brass bands, to organized rambles in the countryside, to youth clubs to literary groups. Many of these organizations had philanthropic or religious associations. Finally, Jones pinpoints leisure provision in the public sector, at both national and local levels. In particular, the establishment of public parks and playing fields enjoyed a revival after the First World War with many grounds dedicated as memorial spaces to soldiers who had fought. There was also, however, overlap between different forms of leisure. For instance, activities that took place in the home, like hobbies, depended on a commercial market making materials widely available. Likewise, leisure events such as Empire Day (a national day to celebrate Britain's imperial ambitions) or the street parties that characterized peace celebrations in the Second World War operated on a number of levels. Often initiated by the state, such events tended to take place in the street and/or a local community centre, had entertainments provided by a welter of voluntary organizations, catering was organized by local women and the canny entrepreneur could sell flags and memorabilia.

The expansion of the commercial leisure market began in the later decades of the nineteenth century. The most familiar bastion of leisure, perhaps, was the pub. By the close of the 1890s, the city of Manchester had over 1500 licensed establishments. Often these were multifunctional and, by the start of the twentieth century, a variety of commercial ventures had emerged from the public house to cater for different clientele. Hotel bars and country pubs catered for a middle-class market who were holidaying or out motoring for the day. The 'club' of the interwar period provided dancing and band music, often jazz, and were frequented by a more affluent elite, such as the Bright Young Things in the novels of Evelyn Waugh. There was a welter of music and dance venues in between the club and the pub, catering for different social groups and not all of which served alcohol.

The notion of 'classless' popular culture may have emerged in this period but would become more common in the 1960s, especially among young people through the medium of full employment and the emergence of a distinctive youth culture (in fashion, music and entertainment) and the growing interest in social realism in drama and television (Marwick, 1998). Popular culture in the interwar period (and later) remained, however, heavily gendered. This was especially the case with regard to the public house. Mostly seen as a bastion of male sociability, it was considered unrespectable for women to go the pub without a male escort or to go to the bar. Nonetheless, pubs began to compete for a female market in the twentieth century with 'lounges' designated acceptable spaces where husbands could take wives. Langhamers's study of female leisure in the twentieth century showed that the pub barely featured at all in the leisure patterns of young unmarried women until the Second World War gave women a greater sense of independence (2000).

Despite these shifts, pub sales actually declined in the interwar period. Aside from the dance hall, the chief competitor to the pub was the cinema. In 1909 the Cinematograph Act required halls and clubs to apply for a licence to show films and comply with strict fire regulations. Designated cinemas soon followed. In Manchester, the Kinemacolour Palace (now Cornerhouse Cinema) opened in 1910 with performances between 2 p.m. and 10.30 p.m. costing between 3d and 6d. While out of reach of the very poor, by the 1920s, cinema was sufficiently cheap to permit the working classes to have family outings to the cinema on Saturdays. Indeed, cinema had become hugely popular by the interwar decades. A Mass Observation survey of Bolton 1938 found that a minority of girls and young women went as often as 12 times a week. The cinema was also a fairly respectable space where women could go alone. In the film *Brief Encounter* (1945), the married but dissatisfied female lead went to see weekly matinees alone; her jaunts only became risqué when she saw movies with Alec, the man with whom she was embarking on a love affair.

The early twentieth century also witnessed the expansion of more elaborate leisure venues, notably the 'theme park', which sought to exploit the 'day tripper' market. One example of this is the development of Belle Vue Zoological and Pleasure Gardens in Manchester. Originally an inn with some gardens and a bowling green, by the start of the twentieth century, Belle Vue boasted an impressive range of animals in the zoo and a series of exotic themed gardens: Italian garden; Indian grotto; Chinese gardens; glasshouse; maze; boating lakes. Onsite dining facilities catered for different classes of visitors while the provision of dancing and music rooms, a music hall, brass band stand, annual firework displays and theatre performances meant that families could spend an entire day in the Gardens. Belle Vue soon capitalized on new technology to include an amusement fair with rides. The Gardens aimed to cater for every taste: the zoo, theatre performances and some of the restaurants openly played to a more affluent class while special events organized for traditional working-class holidays, such as Whit week, saw the survival of a less formalized culture in an organized and regulated context. By the 1930s, Belle Vue had become a pioneer theme park, with one of the biggest zoos in the UK, boxing matches, a miniature railway, a large amusement park, greyhound and speedway racing. As amusement park competition increased in the 1960s, Belle Vue began a steady decline until it closed in 1981.

For those who could afford it, the commercial holiday market also expanded in the first half of the twentieth century. When Mass Observation studied the holidays of Bolton millworkers in the late 1930s, they found that even in cases where paid holidays from work were secured, Bolton workers saved furiously to be able to afford a holiday away from their place of residence; in this case, usually at Blackpool. Most working-class people budgeted for food and fuel on a weekly basis. For extraordinary items of expenditure, such as the day trip or new clothes, savings clubs based in the neighbourhood helped families financially. In Mass Observation's study of Bolton, families saved (between 6d to 3/- per week) for the entire year in order to afford an annual holiday. Given the expense involved, it is not surprising that debate raged over the types of holiday working people enjoyed. Socialist and philanthropic organizations despaired

Plate 13.1 Wakes Week Lancashire Holidays. Children enjoying donkey rides on Blackpool beach with the famous tower in the background (© Hulton Archives/Getty).

at the escapist culture of the seaside holiday. Resorts such as Blackpool openly marketed themselves as pleasure places with Blackpool Tower, the illuminations, ballrooms, freak shows, fairgrounds, fish and chip shops all promoting a fantasy life of decadence and luxury.

Religious and socialist groups argued that the commercial seaside holiday was an extravagance that fostered shallow pleasure at the expense of solid values and communal ideals. In Walter Greenwood's novel *Love on the Dole*, the protagonist Harry wins some money on a bet and takes his girlfriend, Helen, on holiday to a romantic fishing village. As John Walton notes, Greenwood's choice of destination came straight from the Clarion Club's romantic socialism (2000: 55–6). The film version of *Love on the Dole* (1941) transported Harry and Helen to Blackpool instead, a shift that no doubt reflected the more popular working-class holiday destination. Yet the move to the commercial delights of Blackpool also highlighted some of the tensions inherent in attitudes to working-class leisure. In the film, Harry's jaunt to Blackpool, funded by the fruits of gambling and full of dances, fairgrounds, smart lodgings and opportunities for lovemaking, is potentially held out as an example of what middle-class and socialist observers frequently saw as frivolous and illogical immediate gratification, especially when set against the dire poverty Harry endures later on. In contrast, Harry's sister Sally and her boyfriend Larry go for rambles with the Labour club and eschew the culture of the pub for political meetings and reading. The film is not necessarily condemnatory of working-class pursuits, however. Rather, it highlights the appeal of escapism. The holiday stands out as an experience of unmitigated pleasure in contrast to lives characterized by struggle and hardship while Blackpool itself is held out as a land of dreams, lights and luxury in comparison to the bleak landscape of Hanky Park in Salford. Indeed, John Walton concludes that places like Blackpool traded on notions of the good humour and vitality of the common people; they were a celebration of popular culture, not an apology or a plea for rational recreation (2000).

Recognizing the difficulties of proselytizing against such pleasurable jaunts, socialist groups aimed to promote alternatives. Organizations dedicated to helping working people take improving holidays originated at the end of the nineteenth century. For instance, the Co-operative Holiday Association provided holidays in the unspoilt countryside with the companionship of likeminded people. The Holiday Fellowship, formed in 1913, organized children's camps and, later, pioneered the 'family camp'. The Toynbee Hall Workman's Travel Club flourished from 1889, offering a range of breaks including short sojourns in continental cities for £2, a cost that Susan Barton suggests was in the reach of most skilled workers. Specifically socialist camps also thrived while not necessarily promoting explicit political propaganda. For instance, the Caister Camp opened in 1906 attracting about a 1000 people each summer; by 1911 the camp provided huts and chalets for rent in addition to tents. Most of the clientele, however, were white-collar workers. Indeed, the problem with many such ventures was the failure to appeal to the broad base of working-class holidaymakers, who preferred the commercial resorts. One response to this was to run the holiday camp on a commercial basis with entertainments provided and an emphasis on fun rather than improvement. W.J. Brown, general secretary of Civil Service Clerical Association, opened the first 'modern holiday camp' in the 1920s. The camp traded on selling 'luxury' at affordable prices. While Brown's camp attracted largely white-collar clerics, other manual trade unions also built their own camps. The Derbyshire Miners Association built a camp near Skegness that opened in 1939. In the first year, 15,000 miners and their families holidayed at a cost of £1 13s a week for a couple and reduced rates for children. The union also negotiated with rail companies for special reduced fares for holidaymakers from Derbyshire to Skegness. Such camps were undoubtedly a boon to the working-class family. More commercial ventures, such as 'Butlins', which first opened in Skegness in 1936, were initially too expensive for many working-class budgets (Barton, 2005).

By 1950, 91 per cent of the UK population enjoyed paid holidays of mostly two weeks' duration. By the late 1940s, trips away from home of one-week duration had become viable for around half the population. Whereas the tyrannical landlady had ruled the Blackpool boarding house in the 1930s, families began to enjoy self-catering holidays, especially with the increasing popularity of the caravan holiday from the

1950s. Once again, however, such holidays raised the problem of defining leisure for women. Mass Observation's study of Blackpool noted that, for women holidaymakers, getting up for breakfast, with someone else having organized and cooked it, eating it knowing someone else would wash and clear up was one of the greatest joys of the holiday. The self-catering holiday slowly eroded even this simple pleasure.

Leisure in the home

Understandably, historical research has focused on the emergence of commercial leisure activities in the interwar period. Yet home-based leisure also represented a key feature of many people's lives. The idea of the home as an informal leisure space emerged at different times for different social and economic groups and, of course, partly depended upon how pleasant and spacious the domestic environment was. For early twentieth-century working- and lower-middle-class families, the home might provide a venue for having neighbours in for a cup of tea (or something stronger), holding vaguely spiritualist endeavours (reading tea leaves or contacting the dead) or hosting a 'bit of a do' for special occasions like weddings and funerals. The radio and, later on, the television cemented the sense of the home as leisure space with families sitting down to enjoy broadcasts together. In the interwar period, the notion that the home was an entertainment venue gained increasing currency among a middle-class population. Novels and films of the 1920s and 1930s highlight the extent to which bridge, afternoon tea and dinner parties formed the fabric of an affluent and culturally ambitious stratum whose notions of etiquette were highly defined. From the 1920s, women's magazines increasingly featured recipes and tips on food presentation for women who entertained neighbours and their husbands' business contacts. By the 1950s, opening one's home for entertainment had also become more common among a blue-collar society.

The interwar years also saw the emergence of the 'hobby', especially for a middle-class consumer market. The growth of the companionate marriage was integral to the growth of the hobby market: spending time together in the home was fine, but couples were urged to develop their own interests to maintain a good marriage. Once again, however, we return to the difficulty of defining women's leisure. Notions of 'family leisure' encouraged wives to create comfortable environments for husbands to relax in. Hobbies such as knitting, sewing or baking were also closely linked to housework while women's magazines, such as *Woman*, featured dress patterns that women could make at home, partly for pleasure but also as a way of economically following fashion. Reading also enjoyed a boom in the first half of the twentieth century. Located in stores like Boots rather than formal lending libraries, the 'Tupenny' library made borrowing books easy for lower-middle- and working-class women. The mass-produced paperback, pioneered by Allen Lane publishers in the 1930s, also made romantic fiction cheap and accessible. Mills and Boon, the most famous publishers of romantic fiction, began distributing their daring stories of love in the 1930s (Langhamer, 2000).

The notion of home improvement and gardening as leisure increasingly took hold too. The growth of suburban housing catering for a lower middle class who could not afford domestic help and, to a lesser degree, the emergence of council housing in new out-of-town estates for the working classes, encouraged families to invest in the appearance of their homes and gardens. On one level, this was related to an increasing market for technical goods, such as the vacuum cleaner, the washing machine and the iron, all of which were marketed as labour-saving devices but which, in practice, raised the standards of hygiene in many homes. Women were the obvious targets of these devices, helped along by the boom in magazines such as *Good Housekeeping* (1922) and *Woman's Own* (1932). Yet there was also a market for men's leisure through 'do-it-yourself' manuals. In 1936, Odhams Press published the first edition of *The Handyman and Home Mechanic: Home Repairs, Decoration and Construction Illustrated*. The book went through several editions up until 1959. The editor's introduction appealed to men's sense that their home really was their castle and spoke of the 'charm' of undertaking crafts projects for pleasure: 'This book will fill your leisure hours with pleasure and profit. Aimless leisure is unknown to the handy man . . . he has a lifetime hobby inherited from time immemorial from his forefathers – that of making and doing *real* things.' Aimed at a middle-class audience, the book also promoted a notion of masculinity that was founded on a breadwinner identity: to maintain one's family extended beyond being able to keep them financially. It also suggested that, even within the supposedly feminized space of domesticity, the home could be a location for the formation and confirmation of manliness. Indeed, the book suggested that home 'mechanics' – distinctively different to the more feminized 'home crafts' – was a key location for the formation of masculine bonds between father and son: in addition to line drawings and plans for home projects, the book included photographs of father and son, both dressed in shirt, tie and tank top, in the masculine domain of the workshop or garage, surrounded by tools.

Similarly, the growth of gardening as leisure exploded in the interwar period. Manuals such as *An Easy Guide to Gardening* (1927), *The A.B.C. of Gardening* (1935), *Modern Flower and Vegetable Culture Month by Month* (1937) and magazines such as *Popular Gardening* (1920) capitalized on a post-war culture of self-sufficiency that would boom during the Second World War. The growing interest in gardening was not confined to a middle-class market either. Many of the new council houses built in the interwar years had substantial gardens, often intended for the growth of vegetables as well as flowers. Likewise, allotments, that is, pieces of common or public land given over to the cultivation of fruit and vegetables, predated the twentieth century but it was in this period that they became much more popular. A Smallholdings and Allotments Act of 1908 established the framework for allotment holding throughout the twentieth century. A further act of 1919 was designed to assist men returning from the war in establishing kitchen gardens while the Allotments Acts of 1922 and 1925 provided allotment tenants with security of tenure on their plots. Although some allotment plots entered a period of decline after the Second World War, the closing years of the twentieth century saw a resurgence of interest in the kitchen garden and reversed this trend.

Plate 13.2 Hornby advertisement (© The Advertising Archives).

In Focus

Model railways – a masculine hobby

By 1870, there was a clear British market for toy trains, although it was not until around 1900 that the taste for realism took hold. The accurate scale model train was pioneered by the firm Bassett-Lowke and heralded the beginning of a craze for positioning the toy train within a miniature world, complete with buildings, scenery and people. By the outbreak of the Great War, Britain could boast a growing market of model engineering manuals and exhibitions, highlighting the potential adult market for toy trains. Most of the model trains on the market before the First World War originated from Nuremberg, Germany, which had a fine tradition of toy making. After the Great War, however, patriotic shoppers began to favour British goods, contributing to the growth of one of the best-known companies in the history of model trains. In 1907, Frank Hornby established his company, Mechanics Made Easy (Meccano Ltd). In 1920 he introduced the company's first 'toy train', powered by clockwork, constructed from pressed metal and built in 'O' gauge. In 1925, the first Hornby electric train appeared on the market. In 1938, Hornby Dublo was launched, featuring trains and accessories in 'OO' gauge, that is, half the size of 'O' gauge. Both the clockwork and electric varieties of the Dublo trains were made of cast metal while buildings (stations, engine sheds, stationmasters' houses and so on) were made of wood. 'OO' scale had, however, attracted the attention of adult enthusiasts for some years before the launch of Hornby Dublo. As the magazine *Model Railway News* noted in 1925, 'OO' necessitated finer modelling and held real potential for the skilled craftsmen. It also meant that an entire layout could fit on a tabletop.

Adult enthusiasm for the model railway was closely associated to engineering and technology, interests bound up with the notion that men had an inherent mechanical instinct. The growth of a market for manufactured models, parts, tools and magazines was also related to the expansion in the interwar period of the model railway club and the model exhibition. If clubs fostered a masculine space where electrical and technical engineering skills could be displayed, they also fostered competitiveness and snobbery. One contributor to *Model Railway News* in 1933 bemoaned the 'really nasty remarks' enthusiasts levelled at those who were, perhaps, less skilled or used cheaper materials. Adult enthusiasts were also sensitive to suggestions that the hobby was childish. Wives were held up as particularly guilty of deriding spouses who 'played' at being signalmen, monopolized spare rooms and neglected family commitments. Enthusiasts responded by arguing that the hobby kept men out of the pub and improved their knowledge of mechanics, thus enhancing their masculine status as 'home handyman'. The prominence of engineering in books and magazines on railway modelling of the period indicate,

> ### Model railways – a masculine hobby
>
> perhaps, a broader sensitivity to accusations that the hobby was, somehow, silly. Responding to claims that model layouts were 'over-developed nursery toys', *Model Railway News* exhorted club members in 1936 to publicize the contribution hobbyists made to industrial recovery and to emphasize the high intelligence and skill of enthusiasts. Drawing on a familiar language of 'rational recreation', the magazine not only highlighted the masculinity of the modeller, but also the 'social value' of the hobby.
>
> In 1965, Hornby Dublo merged with its main competitor, Tri-ang, to become Tri-ang Hornby. In the 1950s, the first Airfix kits of aeroplanes and railways were launched. The combination of mass production techniques and cheap plastics made the model railway more democratic, placing the hobby within reach of more affluent sections of the working class. At the end of the twentieth century, it remained a thriving industry, though still overwhelmingly masculine.

Debates and Interpretations

Much of the contemporary concern over how the working classes used their leisure time spilled over into the history of leisure. Marxist histories of leisure in the 1960s and 70s tended to see middle-class criticisms of working-class leisure in relation to the notion of 'social control'. A bourgeois class, they argued, harnessed commercial leisure in the late nineteenth and early twentieth centuries in an attempt to inculcate employees with middle-class values. Thus, football – originally an informal and spontaneous game played in the street – became increasingly organized as middle-class businessmen or, in some cases, local landowners sponsored teams who wore uniforms and played by a set of rules. Increasingly throughout the 1980s and 90s, however, the notion of 'social control' was criticized, not least because it ignored working-class 'agency', that is, the ability of working people to participate in organized leisure pursuits and invest them with their own meaning and to adapt them to specifically working-class concepts. So, as Stephen Jones notes, football may have been financially linked to the affluent classes but the location of football stadia, players, supporters and managers were overwhelmingly working class. Moreover, Jones continues, even football's crowd disturbances (violence, vandalism, fighting, pitch invasions) did not induce entrepreneurs to close grounds but, rather, to attempt to manage problems through crowd segregation, the use of stewards and the provision of better facilities. Likewise, many 'rational' pursuits – such as adult education, country walks, cycling and savings clubs – originated in a working-class culture of auto-didactism, trade unionism and friendly societies (Jones, 1986: 83–4).

More recently, gender has emerged as a key theme in studies of leisure. On one level, studies have examined questions of how particular forms of leisure activity have been 'gendered'. For instance, in what ways did cricket emerge as a specifically masculine sport? As illustrated above, Claire Langhamer has probed the difficulties of working with concepts of leisure for groups of women for whom issues of time, money and domestic responsibilities made leisure a slippery notion. The relationship between masculinity and leisure is still fairly under-researched, even though many of the early studies of leisure took masculine forms of leisure (such as football and the pub) as the keystones of working-class popular culture. One of the exceptions to this is Brad Beaven's *Leisure, Citizenship and Working-Class Men in Britain, 1850–1945* (2005). Martin Francis, meanwhile, has challenged historians to move beyond simplified notions of the increasingly domesticated male in the early years of the twentieth century. While noting the attractions that marriage, fatherhood and the home held for men, Francis urges us to look at the ways in which men also sought to escape them. Notably, he suggests that 'escapist fantasies', such as the adventure story or films about war, enabled men to indulge in a 'flight from domesticity' even if this was only in their imagination. As Francis indicates, complex histories of gender, domesticity and leisure are only just emerging and require much greater study of factors such as class, national identity, ethnicity and race before we can begin to fully understand them (2002).

Further reading

For the early part of the century, Andrew Davies's *Leisure, Gender and Poverty: Working-Class Culture in Salford and Manchester, 1900–1939* (Buckinghamshire, 1992) is a classic study. Recent work on leisure has taken up the question of gender and leisure, though admittedly, this has focused on women's leisure and femininity, asking in what ways the concept of leisure was gendered and how leisure activities differed between the sexes. Notable among these is Claire Langhamer's *Women's Leisure in England, 1920–1960* (Manchester, 2000), Brad Beaven's *Leisure, Citizenship and Working-Class Men in Britain, 1850–1945* (Manchester, 2005) and Martin Francis, 'Leisure and popular culture', in Ina Zweiniger-Bargielowska (ed.) *Women in Twentieth-Century Britain* (Harlow, 2001): 229–43. For a probing review of masculinity and domesticity, see Martin Francis, 'The domestication of the male? Recent research on nineteenth- and twentieth-century British masculinity', *Historical Journal*, 45(3) (2002): 637–52.

There is little probing work on the hobby and the home as leisure space, bizarre given the contribution the hobby industry made to the national economy in this period. For a recent history of the family, however, see the major study by M. Abbott, *Family Affairs: A History of the Family in the Twentieth Century* (London, 2002). For information on railways, see Ian Carter's *Railways and Culture in Britain: The Epitome of Modernity* (Manchester, 2001) and www.www.york.ac.uk/inst/irs/.

The seaside and tourism is one of the key areas for historical research; recent works include Susan Barton's *Working-Class Holidays and Popular Tourism, 1840–1970* (Manchester, 2005) and John Walton's *The British Seaside: Holidays and Resorts in the Twentieth*

Century (Manchester, 2000). Recent works on the cinema include Jeffery Richards, *Films and British National Identity: From Dickens to Dad's Army* (Manchester, 1997) and Alan G. Burton's *The British Consumer Co-operative Movement and Film, 1890s–1960s* (Manchester, 2005). *Music for the People: Popular Music and Dance in Interwar Britain* (Oxford, 2003) by J.J. Nott looks at a range of writers and performers, including Noel Coward, Ivor Novello, Gracie Fields and George Formby. Mike Huggins, meanwhile, highlights the importance of horseracing in British culture in *Horseracing and the British, 1919–1939* (Manchester, 2003).

References

Barton, Susan (2005) *Working-class Organisations and Popular Tourism, 1840–1970*. Manchester: Manchester University Press.

Davies, Andrew (1992) *Leisure, Gender and Poverty: Working-Class Culture in Salford and Manchester, 1900–1939*. Buckingham: Open University Press.

Francis, Martin (2002) 'The domestication of the male? Recent research on nineteenth- and twentieth-century British masculinity', *Historical Journal*, 45(3): 637–52.

Griffiths, Trevor (2001) *The Lancashire Working Classes, 1880–1930*. Oxford: Clarendon.

Jones, Stephen (1986) *Workers at Play*. London: Routledge.

Langhamer, Claire (2000) *Women's Leisure in England, 1920–1960*. Manchester: Manchester University Press.

Marwick, Arthur (1998) *The Sixties: Cultural Revolution in Britain, France, Italy, and the United States, c.1958–c.1974*. Oxford: Oxford University Press.

Matthews, Jill (1990) 'They had such a lot of fun: The Women's League of Health and Beauty between the wars', *History Workshop Journal*, 30: 22–54.

Oliver, Liz (1997) 'No hard-brimmed hats or hat-pins please: Bolton women cottonworkers and the game of rounders, 1911–39', *Oral History*, 25(1): 40–45.

Roberts, Elizabeth (1984) *A Woman's Place: An Oral History of Working-Class Women 1890–1940*. Oxford: Basil Blackwell.

Walton, John (2000) *The British Seaside: Holidays and Resorts in the Twentieth Century*. Manchester: Manchester University Press.

14

Youth

Penny Tinkler

IN THE 1950S, GOVERNMENT REPORTS and popular newspapers heralded the emergence of a distinctive youth and youth culture in Britain. As market researcher Mark Abrams explained, the 1950s were characterized by 'distinctive teenage spending for distinctive teenage ends in a distinctive teenage world' (1961: 5). Historians have often reinforced this view; one referred to an 'explosive discovery of teenage identity' in the fifties. The corollary of this belief is the assumption that youth did not figure prominently in British society prior to 1950. This view of youth history has, however, been challenged since the 1980s. As Bill Osgerby explains, 'consummate breaks in history are rare and claims to the "novelty" of the post-war British youth experience distort and exaggerate the nature of change' (1998: 5). A modern conceptualization of youth was established in the first half of the twentieth century. Further, many of the phenomena associated with youth in the 1950s can also be discerned earlier. Based on a study of working-class life in Salford and Manchester, Andrew Davies argues that elements of 'a "teenage" way of life can be traced back to 1939' and that 'generational leisure patterns' can be traced back to around 1900 (1992). David Fowler goes further and asserts that interwar young wage earners were 'the first teenagers' (1995).

This chapter explores the conditions and experiences of youth 1900–1950 and the ways these varied by social class and gender. This history reveals a tension between, on the one hand, attempts to organize and institutionalize youth and, on the other, young people's own efforts to organize and express themselves. The first part of this chapter will consider the emergence, institutionalization and 'coming of age' of adolescence and its significance for defining youth and shaping provision for young people. The second part will examine evidence of youth as a distinctive social and cultural experience. The historiography of youth is, however, skewed towards the working classes for reasons that are discussed later, and so it is this group which is the principal focus of the second section. Before proceeding further, it is useful to clarify the meaning of the term 'youth'.

Youth as a category

A long-established concept, 'youth' refers to pre-adulthood. What this means in terms of age has varied historically; in pre-industrial England, 'youth' embraced people from as young as eight years to those in their mid-twenties. Since the 1880s the term has been used in two principal ways. First, the term 'youth' refers to the period between childhood, signalled by leaving school (either the minimum school leaving age which was raised to 13 in 1899 and to 14 in 1918, or an individual's actual age of leaving school), and adulthood defined in terms of marriage or the average age of marriage (typically in the mid-twenties). Second, the term 'youth' has frequently been used inter-changeably with 'adolescence'. The word 'adolescence' was rarely used in academic and popular discourse prior to the 1890s. Although theorists have varied as to how far they attribute adolescence to biological or social factors, the term refers to a distinctive age grade between child and adult, located principally in the teenage years (although it could include the very early twenties) and characterized by a range of changes related to the onset of puberty. The interchangeable usage of the terms 'youth' and 'adolescence' is understandable because there is overlap in the age group that each term refers to, and because the experience of adolescence has been regarded as a pivotal and distinctive feature of twentieth-century youth. Adolescence emerged as a scientifically-based explanation of why people in their teens and early twenties were different from children and adults and why they deserved distinctive treatment. Given the centrality of adolescence to modern conceptions and treatment of youth, it is appropriate to reflect on why adolescence was 'discovered' and what implications this had for young people from 1900 to 1950.

Youth and the 'discovery' of adolescence

Early modern historians see adolescence as a constant feature of history; as evidence of this they point to the experiences of apprentices, monastic novices, students, and aristocratic youth in the sixteenth and seventeenth centuries. However, prior to the 1880s there was not a distinct age category understood as 'adolescence'. Indeed, there is no evidence of 'adolescence' as a mass phenomenon. Forms of 'adolescent' association and activity in early modern Europe were limited to particular groups of young people in terms of social class and gender. A modern and institutionalized conception of 'adolescence', one defined by science and perceived as a universal feature of growing up, emerged only after 1880. Indeed, 'the full crystallization of the idea and reality of adolescence as a distinct age grade is still a relatively recent occurrence' (Davis, 1990: 29).

The emergence of adolescence was inseparable from the institutionalization of a distinction between childhood and adulthood. It is widely accepted that during the Middle Ages childhood was relatively undifferentiated from adulthood in terms of provision. In the nineteenth century, due to a range of legislation, most notably the introduction of universal elementary education in 1870, childhood emerged as a distinct state. Although childhood was comparatively clearly defined and understood relative to adulthood, the transition between the two was not instantaneous, nor necessarily straightforward. It is within this ambiguous space that adolescence/youth emerged. It was among the middle classes that adolescence was first made visible and institutionalized. Gillis argues that this was 'an unintended product of the reform of the boarding schools' and the 'cloistering' of middle- and upper-class boys in these establishments. Widespread secondary education for middle-class boys provided for the institutional separation of male adolescents. It also provided the conditions for a distinctively adolescent way of life to emerge as a result of the prolonged period of dependency and segregation from adult society during which the passage from childhood to adulthood was hastened. While secondary schooling was heralded as a success in terms of controlling behaviour, 'beneath this surface calm many thought they detected an inner storm' (Gillis, 1974: 105–116). By the 1890s this observation had become the focus of psychologists.

While schooling created the 'social reality' of adolescence for middle-class young males, new ways of thinking about age and the life course contributed to the emergence of ideas about adolescence. Intellectual interest in youth was prompted by Darwin's theory of evolutionary change and progress. This provided an analogy for understanding change and development in the individual as she/he moved from 'the cradle to the grave' and focused attention on process and stages. Recognition of both the power and the responsibility of society to shape people also contributed to a preoccupation with how societal institutions could provide appropriate conditions to foster the development of youth. The most influential intellectual contribution came from the newly emerged discipline of psychology. Psychologists were keen to establish their academic and professional credentials and areas of expertise. The actions and experiences of young people became a favourite topic of theorizing and research and led to a distinctive and quite considerable body of literature on the needs of adolescence.

One of the most notable authorities on adolescence was the American psychologist G. Stanley Hall. His study, *Adolescence: Its Psychology and its Relation to Physiology, Anthropology, Sociology, Crime, Religion and Education* (1904), was widely read in Britain and the USA. Although Hall principally 'synthesized a range of themes, assumptions and arguments' in late-nineteenth-century western thought, he is widely credited with the 'discovery' of adolescence. Hall defined adolescence as a principally biological, but also socially influenced, stage that occurred between the ages of 12 and 22 years. Initiated by the onset of puberty, adolescence was presented as a period of transitions during which physical, psychological and emotional changes prepared the young person for mature and heterosexual adulthood. Adolescence was constructed as a period of 'storm and stress' for all young people but, as Carol Dyhouse notes, Hall and his contemporaries conceived adolescence in gendered ways:

For the boy, it was a time of ambition, growth and challenge. For the girl, it was a time of instability; a dangerous phase when she needed special protection from society. During adolescence, boys grew towards self-knowledge. Girls on the other hand, could never really attain self-knowledge . . . for their lives were ruled by 'deep unconscious instincts'. (1981: 122)

Around 1900 various anxieties heightened the preoccupation with young people and encouraged the belief that adolescence constituted a distinct age stage character- ized by special difficulties. As the middle-class male experience of adolescence became established as the norm, it threw into relief the very different, and seemingly un- regulated, experiences of working-class youth who usually left school at 13 years of age. During the 1890s and 1900s there were concerns about the effects of unskilled employment, in particular errand-type jobs, on 'boy labour'. These jobs were per- ceived to lack security and to thereby contribute to the instability of young males; additionally, these jobs were disapproved of because they allowed boys to roam the streets unsupervised. Anxieties about juvenile delinquency also contributed to a pre- occupation with youth. At the same time, developments in thinking about adolescence refocused perceptions of youthful deviance. The problems of youth became defined less in social terms and more in terms of individual and psychological factors; age, rather than poverty, was now the perceived cause of delinquency. Working-class young people, removed from the stabilizing and civilizing influences of schooling, were seen to exhibit the disruptive side of adolescence. This class-specific anxiety occurred within a context of concerns about the 'deterioration of the race' and the decline of economic and military efficiency, which were heightened by Britain's struggle to retain its position as a leading industrial nation and by the difficulty between 1899 and 1901 of recruiting 'fit' soldiers for the Boer War (in Manchester, 8000 out of 11000 volunteer soldiers were rejected as 'unfit') (Dyhouse, 1981: 91). Social commentators and a government interdepartmental committee on physical deterioration (which reported in 1904) attributed the problem to inadequacies in working-class schooling and family life which left young people without appropriate health, discipline and guidance.

Youth initiatives

So what were the implications of the 'discovery of adolescence' for the treatment of young people? Psychological constructions of adolescence were extremely influential 1900–50: they shaped perceptions of youth; they rationalized interventions in the lives of young people; and they shaped policy and provisions relating to education, welfare, leisure and policing (Griffin, 1993). Two main themes were common to youth initia- tives. First, young people had the potential for socially disruptive behaviour. This asso- ciation was premised on psychological constructions of the adolescent as highly volatile. This idea had particular currency after 1900 because of concerns about national stability amidst the disruptions of the First World War, the depression, interwar youth unemployment and, on the international front, the Spanish Civil War (1936–9) and then the Second World War. As in previous decades, disruptive behaviour was seen as both a classed and gendered phenomenon. Young men, particularly working-class youth, were feared to be publicly disruptive and destructive of property; young women were seen to undermine the moral foundations of society and the family through their sexual misconduct. The second theme in youth initiatives was the notion that young people were a national asset; they were the adults of the future and full of potential for good or ill.

The properties and potential of adolescence justified the extension and reorganization of education. In 1900, full-time schooling was compulsory for children aged five to 12 years (although some rural school boards allowed children to leave at 10). That schooling for most Edwardians finished before the onset of adolescence was widely regarded as a problem. Referring to the 'formative years between twelve and eighteen', a Board of Education Report in 1917 argued that adolescence should be treated as a period for full-time and then part-time education. This view was incorporated into the Education Act (Fisher) of 1918 which raised the school leaving age to 14 and proposed part-time day continuation education for 15- to 18-year-olds who were not in full-time education. Under this scheme, young people would be released from employment for a day a week (paid or unpaid) to receive the types of instruction that were thought particularly appropriate to the older adolescent – education about parental responsibilities, the body and citizenship. Experiments in part-time day continuation education were introduced in some localities but, due to the costs of the scheme for local authorities and employers, it failed to materialize on a national basis. Commitment to part-time continuation education remained throughout the interwar years and was rearticulated in the 1944 Education Act, although financial constraints again militated against the realization of this scheme (Tinkler, 2001).

Ideas about adolescence also informed the reorganization of education to provide primary education for all children up to eleven years of age and secondary education for all young people aged between 11 and 15 years. It was the Hadow Report of 1926 which first proposed this new system of education built around the distinctive needs of children versus adolescents:

> There is a tide which begins to rise in the veins of youth at the age of eleven or twelve. It is called by the name of adolescence. If that tide can be taken at the flood, and a new voyage begun in the strength and along the flow of the current, we think that it will move on to fortune . . . [Only through the reorganization of education] can children be guided safely through the opportunities, the excitements, and the perils of adolescence; only in that way can the youth of the nation be adequately trained for a full and worthy citizenship.

Subsequent education reports reinforced the distinction between the educational requirements of children and adolescents, although Hadow's proposals were not realized until the 1944 Education Act.

Although education was perceived as an appropriate and constructive way to manage and mould adolescents, in 1938 only 38 per cent of 14-year-olds were in full-time education (Davis, 1990: 70). Youth clubs were widely heralded as an alternative, although not necessarily sufficient, means of providing guidance, care and informal education appropriate to the special needs of adolescents. Government support for youth organizations is indicated by the establishment in 1916 of the Juvenile Organisations Committee to advise on how to strengthen and extend their work on adolescent welfare (this laid the foundation of the modern youth service). Youth organizations had been pioneered in the late 1800s, but their heyday was between 1900 and the 1930s with the emergence of the mass uniformed youth movements, most notably the Scouts (1908) and Guides (1909). Most youth movements sought to contain juvenile restlessness, and sexual precocity in the case of girls; they also aimed to foster the purposeful development of young people (Springhall, 1977). Until recently, historians thought the membership of these organizations was principally lower-middle and upper-working class, but Tammy Proctor has demonstrated that there was considerable regional variation in class membership and that, in general, they were 'multi-class movements' although 'the very poor were still mostly excluded' (1998: 110). While working-class troops of Scouts and Guides existed alongside middle-class ones in the interwar years, it was usual for working-class youth to abandon these clubs on leaving school; this trend also applied to other leisure organizations. The 'problem' of 'unattached' young workers was much discussed in the interwar years and during the Second World War. In 1939, amid concerns about the effects on young people of the social dislocation caused by war, the government launched the Service of Youth scheme. This scheme catered for the leisure time of 14- to 20-year-olds, particularly those removed from full-time education, through the expansion of youth clubs provided by local authorities and voluntary organizations. In 1942, less than 30 per cent of girls and 50 per cent of boys were in some form of 'approved activity' (Tinkler, 1994: 397). Despite attempts to institutionalize young wage earners through youth organizations, young workers often had other priorities.

As these examples illustrate, although the needs of adolescence were frequently mentioned and even enshrined in policy they were often slow to be implemented in practice. This changed from 1939, either in response to concerns about the effects of war on young people or because of a desire to harness the potential of youth to the task of building a better, safer and more stable post-war world. Each youth initiative was justified in terms of the needs of adolescence; at the same time, each contributed to the making of adolescence as a distinctive age category in British society. By the 1940s adolescence was firmly institutionalized. But what were the implications of these developments for young people? Did they experience a distinctive youth pre-1950?

Youthful lifestyles: Work

The experiences of working-class young people 1900–39 have recently attracted much attention. Full-time paid work has been identified as fundamental to the distinctive character of working-class youth in this period. Fowler argues that a buoyant youth labour market and improved wages was pivotal to the emergence of interwar teenage affluence and a distinctive teenage culture. On leaving full-time schooling the majority of working-class girls and virtually all working-class boys entered full-time paid employment. Unemployment affected some young people, especially males, but this was regionally variable. In November 1927, 17.5 per cent of 14- to 18-year-olds were unemployed in Liverpool, 11.2 per cent in Sheffield, 10.8 per cent in Salford and 3.4 per cent in Manchester (Fowler, 1995: 74). Areas dependent on heavy industry, such as south Wales, the north-east and central Scotland, were particularly hard hit by industrial decline and the depression. In contrast, regions such as the Midlands and the south fared better because of the expansion of the 'new' light industries such as electrical engineering and car manufacture. The significance of paid work for youth should, however, be qualified. Wage earners still experienced constraints on their time, activities and spending. Moreover, the implications of paid work differed depending on age and gender. But, paid work was not the only pathway into a distinctive youth culture.

Full-time employment signified the end of childhood and conferred heightened status, but not equality, on young people in the family. As Rose Gamble recalls of growing up in London in the 1920s: 'As long as you were at school you looked like a child in short trousers and frocks, and you were treated like one, but when you left school at the end of term after your fourteenth birthday, childhood ended. It was abrupt and final and your life changed overnight.' The young person's new status was signalled in various ways. Withdrawal from street games was one indicator, a change in appearance was another. Boys began to wear long trousers: 'often their first pair were cut-downs, the slack folded into a belt, with the crotch halfway down their thighs. They slicked their hair with water into a quiff above their foreheads, and half a comb stuck out of the top pocket of every jacket' (1982: 122). For girls, this change in status was marked in the 1920s by longer skirts and by the wearing of adult hairstyles which, for the fashionable, meant short hair with a perm. The importance of leaving school was, however, inextricably related to the young person's potential as a wage earner. It was markedly less for those who could not find paid work and, in the case of girls, those who were required to assume full-time domestic and childcare responsibilities in the family home (Tinkler, 1995: 122–4).

Young wage earners were treated differently to school children because they contributed in financially significant ways to the household purse. Better food was one benefit. A reduction in household responsibilities was another perk, but one not universally enjoyed by young wage earners. Langhamer found only one of the 16 working-class women among her oral history respondents who did not contribute to 'family duties' once she started full-time work and this was because she was the youngest of three daughters (2000: 94). This finding confirms a pattern noted by James and Moore (1940) who studied the diaries of working-class adolescents, some at school and some at work, in Manchester in the 1930s. They found that, whereas boys were exempted completely from household chores once they started full-time paid work, girls were not. It was only when girls reached 16 that domestic duties

significantly declined. The authors attributed this change to parental efforts to facilitate a daughter's pursuit of an eligible young man for marriage.

Youth was widely regarded as the most affluent period in working-class life. However, young people did not have all their wages at their disposal because it was common practice to hand over the wage packet to the mother in return for spending
money, or 'spends'. In an oral history study of women in the north-west (Preston,
Barrow and Lancaster), Elizabeth Roberts found that this practice was ubiquitous in
all but the most prosperous working-class families (1984: 42). Only a small minority
were allowed to pay 'board' and to thereby retain control of their wage packet. This
practice was also observed by both Langhamer and Davies in their oral histories of
Manchester life although they both emphasize that the amount of spends a young
person received varied according to age and gender (Davies, 1992: 84; Langhamer,
2000: 102). At 14, a young worker handed over the pay packet complete; as they got
older they kept more money back and became responsible for buying many of their
own clothes. Girls usually received less money than their brothers although they too
had more 'spends' as they got older.

Contemporary surveys confirm the significance of age. Seebohm Rowntree's *Poverty
and Progress* (1941) found that in York only the youngest workers (14- and 15-year-olds)
handed over their wage packets intact to their mothers. Surveys of working-class
families in Liverpool, Southampton, Bolton, Northampton, Reading, Stanley and
Warrington revealed that it was common practice for older wage-earning children
to retain control of their wages and contribute a fixed amount to the household budget. While practices varied by age, gender and locality, young wage earners typically
contributed a significant amount to the household exchequer but still enjoyed more
disposable income than their mothers, and often their fathers. This income was particularly important for young women because their youthful consumer power was
often short-lived. On marriage and motherhood women usually became financially
dependent on a husband and commonly had to forego personal spending in order to
manage the household budget. A 47-year-old woman with three children, surveyed in
the late 1940s by Ferdinand Zweig, lamented that 'she can't even smoke as she used to
when she was a girl, as she has no money now' (1952: 180).

While they lived at home, young people's spending and leisure was usually subject
to parental rules which were, in some instances, enforced by violence. The hour at
which a daughter or son was due home was often a focus of dispute between children
and their parents. Parents also forbade particular types of leisure or specific venues.
The appearance of daughters, and especially their use of cosmetics, was also policed.
Although she was 21, Lu's father 'threw Lu's tiny tube of tangee lip colour on the fire
and said he would beat the living daylights out of her if she mucked about with [that is,
plucked] her eyebrows again' (Gamble, 1982: 184). Employers could also restrict a
young wage earner's free time and modes of self-expression, particularly if the work
was residential as in the case of nursing and domestic service. In the interwar years
roughly a quarter of employed young women worked in domestic service, much of
which was residential. Conditions in service were notoriously constraining. Hours

were long and subject to variation on the whim of the employer, time off was limited typically to one half-day per week and alternate Sundays, while 'free time' could be subject to regulation including enforced church attendance.

Youthful lifestyles: Leisure

Leisure was a defining feature of youth; it figured prominently in how young people's lives were perceived by adults, and how this period of a person's life was subsequently remembered. The distinctiveness of youth leisure stemmed from the amount of time available and the activities engaged in. Young people were the principal beneficiaries of commercial leisure. Between 1900 and 1914 young people constituted an important segment of music hall audiences and during the interwar period, their patronage was important for dance halls and cinemas. Film and dance were key features of working-class leisure in the interwar years and a weekly diet of dancing on a Saturday and between one to three nights at the pictures was quite common. Commercial leisure was most accessible to young people with paid work but, drawing on Joan Harley's observations of unemployed young women in Manchester in 1935–6, David Fowler suggests that short-term unemployment did not significantly alter young women's lifestyles. This was partly because a young woman could rely on her male companion to finance joint leisure activities. For young men, however, lack of spending money prohibited access to commercial facilities and restricted opportunities for courting, although money was not essential to all youthful leisure activities (Fowler, 1995). There is evidence that young people experienced a reduction in leisure time during the Second World War as a result of long working hours and, in the case of girls, extra domestic responsibilities.

The distinctiveness of working-class youth leisure also hinged on the persistence of traditional non-commercial activities. These forms of leisure enabled young people to partake of a specifically youthful culture even when unemployed. Promenading, or the 'monkey parade' as it was called in Manchester and Salford, was a form of communal youth leisure that took place usually on Sundays when cinemas and dance halls were closed. Decked out in their best clothes, young men and women paraded in certain streets, attempting to catch the attention of an admirer. Other communal and informal street activities were also important features of youth leisure. Standing in groups on street corners, young men gathered to talk and play football in Manchester and Salford. Whereas the labelling of youth post-1950 has, according to Andrew Davies, often been a reflection of commercial influences, the interwar term 'corner lad', which was commonly used to refer to male youth, is testimony to the importance of street life to interwar male culture (1992: 97).

Girls sometimes joined these young men. More often, as Pearl Jephcott observed in her study *Rising Twenty: Notes on Some Ordinary Girls* (1948), a survey of girls in London, Needham (a northern industrial town) and Dowden Colliery (a pit village in County Durham), they walked around arm-in-arm with their best friend. Sociability, and especially 'talking' with friends, was an important facet of youth leisure and as much a feature of commercial entertainments as of street life. Sociability was also a feature of domestic leisure. In some localities, Friday night was 'Amami night' (named after a shampoo and setting lotion), an 'exclusively female preserve' sometimes enjoyed in isolation but often involving sisters and girlfriends making preparations for the weekend by washing and setting their hair and doing their nails (Langhamer, 2000: 95).

The distinctive lifestyle of interwar youth was due, in part, to their consumerism. David Fowler argues that the efforts of interwar 'leisure entrepreneurs' to target young people as a distinctive group constitutes evidence of the emergence of the teenager consumer. A youth market can in fact be traced back to the late 1800s. After 1900 dance halls, some films and a plethora of popular magazines targeted young wage earners. The history of magazines for young women does, however, suggest that the teenager was not a stable commercial identity before the 1940s. After introducing a range of successful papers specifically for working girls, some publishers then attempted to integrate these with magazines for women in order to rationalize production. That it was considered feasible to cater for working girls and married women in the same papers is testimony to the publishers' assumption that adolescent girls' interests dovetailed in significant ways with those of women. Adolescent girls did read papers for wives and mothers even before this rationalization, but this is not a sign that they lacked a distinctive youth identity; it is more likely an indication that working girls' magazines were lacking and, moreover, that young women read available magazines.

In Focus

The young smoker

Consumption has played an important part in young people's lifestyles and, increasingly, in media definitions of youth. The history of young people's relationship to smoking is illustrative of this. Tobacco featured in government attempts to regulate the lifestyle and self-expression of working-class male youth. In 1900, pipes and cigarettes were commonly smoked by men of all social classes. On leaving school at 10 or, after 1901, 13 years of age, smoking was also used by working-class boys to establish their maturity: 'the choice [of work] once made . . . the boy very soon falls into the routine of work and in the first fortnight ages rapidly. Hitherto the smoking of cigarettes was a furtive prank, only delightful because forbidden; now it becomes a public exhibition, denoting manhood, independence and wealth.' In 1908, however, the government attempted to suppress juvenile smoking and, under the terms of the Children's Act, it became illegal to sell tobacco to any person under the age of 16. One of the main reasons for this legislation was that boys' smoking was perceived by middle-class observers as evidence of boys' precocity and their 'lack of the correct type of adolescent upbringing' (Hilton, 1995: 594).

The young smoker

In the interwar years cigarettes featured prominently in commercial and media interest in young women. By 1920 a growing number of women, especially from the middle and upper classes, were adopting the smoking habit. In the media, the practice was heralded as one of the defining features of modern young women. National newspapers and magazines regularly printed reports, illustrations and photographs of young women smoking. Alongside a full-page photograph of two 17-year-olds perched on the arms of one chair with cigarettes joined at the tip, presumably lighting one cigarette from the other, *The Sketch* (an elite magazine) explained that:

> The modern girl has been presented on the stage, and by artists and novelists, and at times their fancy portraits of Miss 1925, with her cigarettes, her short skirts, and her 'Eton' crop, have been condemned as exaggerations. The camera, however, cannot lie, and this page presents a genuine photograph of two examples of the Modern Miss, complete with 'fags,' cropped hairs, and neat ankles and dainty knees. (1925)

Similar evidence was presented in the *Daily Express* including a photograph of a group of 'fire-and-water-nymphs' smoking while sunning themselves at the swimming baths. The media's visual preoccupation with the 'flapper' and her 'fags' represents an early example of both the 'cult' and the 'spectacle' of youth that became a key feature of media reportage after 1950. It also signals the increasingly important role of the media in defining youth and of equating it with image and consumption. The equation of smoking with the modern girl's identity and lifestyle was developed further in advertisements. By 1930 tobacco manufacturers were well aware of the commercial potential of the youth market and a proliferation of cigarette adverts were targeted at young and single women from the middle and upper classes. In these adverts smoking was aligned with a range of youthful activities such as partying, courting, swimming, tennis, golf and rambling; one young woman was portrayed with a cigarette wedged firmly between her teeth as she steered a punt down the Thames.

Interwar young women used cigarettes to say things about themselves, and this included statements about age and age relations. Like working-class boy labourers, many young women smoked to assert that they were no longer children. Ms Warrack, responding to a Mass Observation survey, 'began to smoke at about the age of seventeen . . . for effect and to appear grown-up' – i.e. at dances – 'I used to smoke a little in the evening or if I went out and was offered cigarettes . . . although actually I got no pleasure from smoking'. Smoking was also employed as a form of rebellion against the older generation. Following the Great War, 1914–18, the notion of 'generation' became of heightened significance and social commentators pointed to the emergence of a 'generation gap' between younger and older members of the middle and upper classes. Views on women's smoking became one of the symbols

> The young smoker

Plate 14.1 'Eve Adamised', Zaliouk in 'Fantasio', 15 February 1927, p. 387 (© Mary Evans Picture Library).

of generational division. While smoking increasingly achieved respectability for younger members of the middle and upper classes, older members of these class communities often operated with different, and more traditional, notions of respectability. Smoking served for some young women, therefore, as a means of shocking their elders and of asserting their independence and difference from them.

Working-class youth also engaged in other forms of consumption. Manufacturers targeted young people through magazines. A single issue of *Boys' Cinema* in 1920 included adverts for a magazine, an annual holiday, potions to increase height and curl hair, an air rifle, boxing gloves, a gramophone, a girls' hair treatment, a model railway set and a watch (Fowler, 1995: 102). In papers for working-class readers there were a number of small adverts for products including 'pink pills' to ease periods, antiseptic creams to soothe piles, facial creams, slimming aids, hair and body growth stimulators, hair removers, shampoo, chocolate, and devices to straighten noses. However, in the inter-war years young women with limited 'spends' often improvised their make-up, while the stylish costumes worn by film stars were recreated by hand (Alexander, 1994: 263). In 1945 Jephcott noted that pictures, dancing, cosmetics and smoking were the main areas of young women's spending. Much of the 'spends' of young men also went on commercial leisure, as well as on cigarettes and clothes. Frank Findley recalled that in the 1930s lads 'dressed in their thirty bob suits with 22 inch trouser bottoms [and] would stroll along emulating the screen tough guys of the day'; some spent as much as £6 on a suit for the Sunday evening promenade (Fowler, 1995: 108).

In contrast to their working-class peers, middle-class youth have attracted very little attention from historians. This is partly because between 1900 and 1914 most remained in full-time schooling or the home during adolescence. Whereas boys were sent to school until late in their teens, girls were frequently educated at home and/or in a combination of day, boarding and, for the upper classes, finishing schools, until their late teens or twenties after which it was common for them to remain in the parental home until marriage. By the 1920s it became increasingly common for both middle-class girls and boys to be sent to school until 16 years or over, typically longer for boys than girls because of parental investment in their sons' as opposed to daughters' careers. Arising from the demands of extra-curricula activities and homework, these young people had relatively little free time. They also had very little money; in contrast to the 11s 'spends' of 16-year-old working girls and boys in Birmingham in the late 1940s, the average pocket money of their school counterparts was only 4s a week (Reed, 1950).

Without the change of status and experience that followed from entering full-time employment, the lifestyle of middle-class teenagers was relatively undifferentiated by age. Secondary school pupils aged between 12 and 16 years engaged in similar activities according to the diaries analysed by James and Moore in the 1930s. This pattern contrasted with the significant change in activities experienced by children whose full-time education finished at 14. The stark contrast between 16-year-old secondary school pupils and their working counterparts is illustrated by Rose Gamble, a working-class girl who won a scholarship to her local secondary school. While at 16 she 'was still in a drill slip, which was now a bit tight around the bosom', she recalled a typical male contemporary 'in overalls, a fag end behind his ear, coming home from work' and her old girlfriends with 'perms and handbags and ear-rings' (1982: 186). Another reason why middle-class adolescents have attracted little comment from historians is because, being institutionalized until later in their teens, they attracted little comment from contemporaries; middle-class youth were, quite literally, model adolescents.

When the children of the middle and upper classes did leave school, scattered evidence suggests that many did enjoy a distinctively youthful lifestyle, especially in the interwar years. Media coverage of the antics of society's 'Bright Young Things' – a phrase used by Evelyn Waugh in his novel *Vile Bodies* (1930) – and, most notably, middle- and upper-class 'modern girls' ('flappers' as they became known) in the 1920s reinforces this impression. However, the history of middle and upper-class youth has yet to be studied closely by historians.

Debates and Interpretations

Origins are often contentious; in the historiography of youth two beginnings are debated. First there is debate about 'adolescence'. Early modern historians argue that signs of adolescence are apparent among some young men from the 1500s. Modern historians have contested this interpretation of early-modern lifestyles and insisted that while there were expressions of adolescence in early-modern societies, there was not a permanent distinct age category understood as 'adolescence' prior to the late nineteenth century. The second debate about origins focuses on the 'teenager'. Until the 1980s the teenager was regarded as a distinctively post-Second World War phenomenon. This view was challenged in the 1980s as evidence emerged of youth cultures in the late nineteenth and early twentieth centuries. There is, however, no consensus on whether the interwar years witnessed the 'birth of the teenager', or merely the emergence of 'elements' of teenage lifestyles as is more usually claimed. At the centre of this debate are questions about the degree of autonomy and affluence possessed by interwar young people.

Historical interpretations of young people and their lifestyles vary depending on how 'youth' has been conceptualized. This is particularly noticeable with regard to gender. In the 1980s Carol Dyhouse argued that 'youth' and 'adolescence' were usually defined by historians in masculine terms. Arising from this masculinist focus, historians presented male activities as characteristic of youth and young men as typical youths; the cultural life of young women was ignored and/or young women were presented as marginal to the activities of young men. This historical blind spot meant that the male orientation of early-twentieth-century approaches to youth went unchallenged. Recent research has reviewed historical sources and used oral history to reveal that youthful lifestyles were enjoyed by both sexes, although the experience of youth was differentiated by gender. Andrew Davies's exploration of street gangs in late-Victorian England has also questioned the assumption that young women were necessarily marginal to the activities of youth subcultures (1999).

Youth has preoccupied governments, the media and social commentators throughout the twentieth century. In the period 1900–50 a range of measures were introduced to organize, regulate and protect young people. These initiatives were rationalized and shaped by ideas about the distinctive characteristics, problems and potentials of adolescence. Although institutionalizing processes embraced all young people, it was often the working classes that were the focus of these initiatives because their youthful lifestyles were perceived as inappropriate for adolescents. Working-class youth developed distinctive leisure practices and modes of expression in response to their position in the labour market, family and community. Moreover, their youthful lifestyles were recognized and addressed by the leisure industry and by producers of consumables. Although the historiography of youth culture has so far focused on the working classes, and it is often claimed that early-twentieth-century youth cultures were exclusive to the working classes, evidence suggests that middle- and upper-class young people also enjoyed distinctive lifestyles. Indeed, the assumption that the 1950s and 1960s witnessed the first 'spectacle of youth' is called into question by the high media profile of middle- and upper-class 'modern girls' in the 1920s. In relation to leisure, consumption patterns, commercial recognition and media attention, the distinctiveness of youth was being established between 1900 and 1950. Most historians agree that these trends intensified after 1950 with what John Davis has called the 'full flowering' of the 'spectacle' and the 'cult' of youth (1990).

Further reading

John Gillis's *Youth and History: Tradition and Change in European Age Relations 1990–Present* (London, 1974) is a classic in the historiography of youth. So too is John Springhall's study of the emergence of adolescence as an age category in Britain, *Coming of Age: Adolescence in Britain, 1860–1960* (Dublin, 1986). These classics are, however, preoccupied with male youth. In *Girls Growing Up in Late Victorian and Edwardian England* (London, 1981), Carol Dyhouse addresses the neglect of girls and gender in an illuminating chapter on the gender dimensions of early conceptualizations of adolescence.

In recent years the historiography of twentieth-century youth has expanded considerably. Focusing on the experiences of young people, David Fowler illuminates the work and leisure of interwar youth, and especially males, in *The First Teenagers: The Lifestyle of Young Wage-earners in Interwar Britain* (London, 1995). Oral history has provided a particularly rich source for study of experience and several important studies include chapters that address youth. Importantly much of this work keeps gender to the fore and young women in focus. The most notable chapters on working-class youth are by Andrew Davies in *Leisure, Gender and Poverty: Working-Class Culture in Salford and Manchester, 1900–1939* (Buckingham, 1992), Sally Alexander in the edited collection by David Feldman and Gareth Stedman Jones, *Metropolis London: Histories and Representations since 1800* (London, 1989), and by Elizabeth Roberts in *A Woman's place: An Oral History of Working-Class Women, 1890–1940* (Oxford, 1984). Middle-class young women are addressed alongside their working-class peers in a chapter in Claire Langhamer's oral history, *Women's Leisure in England 1920–60* (Manchester, 2000). See also Brad Beaven, *Leisure, Citizenship and Working-class Men in Britain* (Manchester, 2005). Penny Tinkler also addresses both social class groups in her study of magazines for teenaged girls, *Constructing Girlhood: Popular Magazines for Girls Growing up in England 1920–1950* (London, 1995); this book also includes a chapter on the history of girlhood 1920–50. Focusing on the middle-class boy in the context of the public school, nationalism and wartime propaganda is Michael Paris, 'The Youth of our Nation in Symbol: Making and Remaking the Masculine Ideal in the Era of the Two World Wars', in Helen Brocklehurst and Robert Phillips (eds) *History, Nationhood and the Question of Britain* (Basingstoke, 2004): 289–301.

There is an extensive literature on organized youth leisure. Most studies address the boys' club movement, for example, John Springhall, *Youth, Empire and Society: British Youth Movements, 1883–1940* (Croom Helm, 1977). Recent work also addresses leisure initiatives aimed at girls, notably articles by Tammy Proctor, '(Uni)forming youth: girl guides and boy scouts in Britain, 1908–39', *History Workshop Journal*, 45 (1998) and Penny Tinkler, 'An all-round education: the Board of Education's policy for the leisure-time training of girls, 1939–50', *History of Education*, 23 (1994). Useful studies of 'deviant' youth 1900–50 are by: Stephen Humphries, *Hooligans or Rebels? An Oral History of Working-Class Childhood and Youth 1889–1939* (Oxford, 1981); Victor Bailey, *Delinquency and Citizenship: Reclaiming the Young Offender 1914–48* (Oxford, 1987); Pamela Cox, *Gender, Justice and Welfare: Bad Girls in Britain, 1900–1950* (Basingstoke, 2003); Michael Childs, *Labour's Apprentices: Working-Class Lads in Late Victorian and Edwardian Britain* (London, 1992). Moral panics about youth are explored by Geoffrey Pearson in *Hooligan: A History of Respectable Fears* (London, 1983) and by John Springhall, *Youth, Popular Culture and Moral Panics: Penny Gaffs to Gangsta-Rap, 1830–1996* (London, 1998). See also Eileen Yeo, ' "The boy is the father of the man": moral panic over working-class youth, 1850 to the present', *Labour History Review*, 69 (2004): 185–99. For recent studies of smoking and youth culture see M. Hilton, ' "Tabs", "fags" and the "boy labour problem" in late Victorian and Edwardian Britain', *Journal of Social History*, 28 (1995) and P. Tinkler, *Smoke Signals: Women, Smoking and Visual Culture in Britain* (Oxford, 2006).

A detailed study of approaches to youth throughout the twentieth century is presented by John Davis in *Youth and the Condition of Britain: Images of Adolescent Conflict* (London, 1990). Davis's book, alongside Bill Osgerby's *Youth in Britain since 1945* (Oxford, 1998), locate the period 1900–1950 in relation to later developments in the history of British youth.

References

Abrams, M. (1961) *Teenage Consumer Spending in 1959 (Part II) Middle- and Working-Class Boys and Girls*. London: London Press Exchange.

Alexander, Sally (1994) *Becoming a Woman and other Essays in Nineteenth and Twentieth Century Feminist History*. London: Virago.

Davies, Andrew (1992) *Leisure, Gender and Poverty: Working-Class Culture in Salford and Manchester, 1900–1939*. Buckingham: Open University Press.

Davies, Andrew (1999) 'These viragoes are no less cruel than the lads: Young women, gangs and violence in late Victorian Manchester and Salford', *British Journal of Criminology*, 39: 72–89.

Davis, John (1990) *Youth and the Condition of Britain: Images of Adolescent Conflict*. London: Athlone.

Dyhouse, Carol (1981) *Girls Growing Up in Late Victorian and Edwardian England*. London: Routledge & Kegan Paul.

Fowler, David (1995) *The First Teenagers: The Lifestyle of Young Wage-earners in Inter-war Britain*. London: Woburn.

Gamble, Rose (1982) *Chelsea Child*. London: Ariel.

Gillis, John (1974) *Youth and History: Tradition and Change in European Age Relations 1990–Present*. London: Academic Press.

Griffin, Christine (1993) *Representations of Youth: The Study of Youth and Adolescence in Britain and America*. London: Polity Press.

Hilton, Matthew (1995) ' "Tabs", "fags" and the "boy labour problem" in late Victorian and Edwardian Britain', *Journal of Social History*, 28: 587–607.

James, H.E.O. and Moore, F.T. (1940) 'Adolescent Leisure in a Working-Class District', *Occupational Psychology*, vol. xiv.

Langhamer, Claire (2000) *Women's Leisure in England 1920–60*. Manchester: Manchester University Press.

Osgerby, Bill (1998) *Youth in Britain since 1945*. Oxford: Blackwell.

Proctor, Tammy M. (1998) '(Uni)Forming youth: girl guides and boy scouts in Britain, 1908–39', *History Workshop Journal*, 45: 103–34.

Reed, B. (1950) *Eighty Thousand Adolescents: A Study of Young People in the City of Birmingham . . . for the Edward Cadbury Charitable Trust*. London: George Allen & Unwin.

Roberts, Elizabeth (1984) *A Woman's Place: An Oral History of Working-Class Women, 1890–1940*. Oxford: Basil Blackwell.

Tinkler, Penny (1994) 'An all-round education: the Board of Education's policy for the leisure-time training of girls, 1939–1950', *History of Education*, 23: 77–94.

Tinkler, Penny (2001) 'Youth's opportunity? The Education Act of 1944 and proposals for part-time continuation education', *History of Education*, 30: 385–403.

Zweig, Ferdinand (1952) *Women's Life and Labour*. London: Victor Gollancz.

PART THREE

Themes post-1945

15

Managing the economy, managing the people

Jim Tomlinson

THIS PERIOD EMBRACES what was undoubtedly the most successful period of British economic performance ever (the 1950s and 60s), followed by a period of crisis in the 1970s. The big question posed in this chapter is how far the successes of the first period and the problems of the second were due to economic management, or to factors beyond the control of governments. A subordinate issue is how the earlier period, despite the success recorded, came to be regarded by both contemporaries and subsequent commentators as one of failure.

These questions can only be addressed once we have a clear sense of the unfolding of events, so the first part of this chapter offers a broadly chronological account of economic management from the Second World War down to the accession of Mrs Thatcher to power in 1979.

Chronology of economic management

In 1931 Britain left the gold standard and imposed tariffs, and therefore broke decisively with the pre-1914 'liberal' international regime which minimized the role of the state in economic affairs. But between 1931 and 1940 any moves towards economic management by the government were tentative and contested. After that date this all changed, as the coalition government faced the requirements of total war, necessitating an unprecedented scale of government intervention to maximize the availability of resources for the military effort.

In the First World War, planning of the economy had grown incrementally as the war itself developed from something that would be 'all over by Christmas' into a wholly unexpected war of attrition. In the Second World War the government was much better prepared, and quickly put in place systems for rationing and allocating almost every economic resource. The aims of wartime planning included minimizing non-essential imports (to allow the maximum inflow of war supplies), minimizing investment in non-war-related industries, conscripting and allocating labour to the war industries (and other vital industries like mining and agriculture), and rationing consumer goods to provide 'fair shares' and so sustain the morale of the population.

This last aim was vital. In the First World War the military effort had at times appeared to be threatened by war weariness, so in the Second World War maintaining popular support for the war was a key aim of government. Partly this was done by an unprecedented propaganda effort, but underpinning this were measures such as rationing and measures to prevent inflation. In the First World War the rise in prices without a parallel rise in wages (but with a perceived surge in 'profiteering') had greatly affected popular opinion, so after 1940 the government was determined to keep price rises in check. In part this was done by state control of prices, but in the long run more significant was the use of the budget ('fiscal policy') to control the level of demand. In the 1920s and 1930s economists such as Keynes had advocated the use of the budget to increase demand to combat unemployment, the implication being that if necessary governments should spend more than they raised in taxation in order to expand demand. In wartime the need was quite different; the budget had to be used to stop excessive demand, which would otherwise cause inflation and also draw resources away from the war effort. In 1941, therefore, what came to be called the 'first Keynesian budget' was introduced, pioneering the use of the budget not just as a way of balancing government spending and revenue, but of balancing, or managing, the whole economy. The 1941 and subsequent wartime budgets used higher taxes to reduce non-government demand, allowing more resources to go into the war economy, while containing inflation.

If the war saw a major enhancement of the powers of government, it also saw the government taking on new political responsibilities. Driven in part by the wartime leftward shift in public opinion, the coalition began a process of expansion of state welfare provision (free secondary education under the 1944 Education Act; family allowances from 1945) that was to culminate in the measures of the Attlee government. These included the creation of the NHS in 1948 and the implementation in large part of the 1942 Beveridge Report's proposals for comprehensive social insurance, covering all contingencies 'from the cradle to the grave'. The expansion of welfare may be seen as responding to the key popular demand of the 1940s, that for greater economic security. The parallel response to this demand was the promise of 'high and stable' levels of employment, embodied in the 1944 White Paper on *Employment Policy*, and the idea of a government responsibility for 'full' employment was to be a defining feature of the next 30 to 40 years. From the end of the war down to the 1970s this goal of full employment was to be achieved, though how far this was the result of government policy is a key issue taken up in the last section of this chapter.

The Attlee government also expanded the sphere of government by a major programme of nationalization, embracing major utilities like gas and electricity, transport (especially the railways) and the coal industry. However, public ownership did not extend into the financial sector (except the Bank of England, where it had little practical significance) or manufacturing industry. In addition, the extent of government responsibility for these new 'public' industries was highly ambiguous, given that the public corporations which ran the industries had considerable autonomy. Precisely how far governments could be praised or blamed for their performance was a major issue down to the 1980s.

The welfare state created in the 1940s was in many ways built on austere lines. Benefit levels were set low, and the significant post-war reduction in poverty owed as much to full employment as it did to improved welfare provision. (Poverty tended to be worst among those without access to the labour market, notably pensioners.) While the NHS provided much needed free access to medical services, these were delivered in rundown accommodation, with practically no new hospital building. The story of the physical infrastructure was barely better in schools, where building struggled to keep pace with rising pupil numbers. Large numbers of council houses were built, but even here the provision lagged behind the growth in demand, not least because the housing stock had been subject to such major depredations during the war, both from the Blitz and the almost total cessation of new building and maintenance. This 'physical austerity' flowed from the priority given by governments to industrial and commercial building at a time when bricks, wood, construction steel and building labour were in short supply.

Total spending on welfare expanded across the war period, but less than might be expected, in part because of austerity standards, but also because the high level of employment produced an offsetting decline in spending on unemployment benefit, a huge sum in the 1930s. Conversely, spending on the military fell much less than might have been expected once hostilities ceased, partly because of the onset of the Cold War, and partly because of Britain's continuing commitment to being a world power. Throughout the 1950s and 60s Britain was to be the largest Western European spender on 'defence' (only briefly rivalled by France in the early 1960s), though right from the 1940s there were voices that questioned this level of commitment, and the compatability of this level of spending with the domestic commitments to economic security and welfare.

A key issue in managing the British economy in the 1950s and 60s was the balance of payments. The idea that Britain was suffering an almost continuous crisis in the balance of payments became central to almost all discussion of economic management in these decades The issue was in turn related broadly to two other policy concerns. First, fear of inflation; if Britain had faster price rises than other countries, competitiveness would deteriorate and trade would suffer. Second, the payments position mattered because if persistent deficits occurred this would threaten the value of the pound. But the precise nature of these crises is complex, and needs to be carefully explored.

In the war Britain had, with US encouragement, thrown caution to the winds in reducing its exports to divert resources into the war effort. The balance of payments only survived by Britain paying for its imports by selling off foreign assets; borrowing from India, Egypt and other Empire countries (by building up liabilities in the so-called 'sterling balances'); and by the receipt of lend-lease from the USA. Once the war was over a major effort went into restoring the balance between exports and imports and, helped by the damage and disorganization to the German and Japanese economies, and by devaluation of the pound in 1949, the payments position rapidly improved (though this improvement was temporarily derailed by the Korean War). In the 1950s the position was also helped by the improvement in the terms of trade (the fall in import compared with export prices), so we can say that in that decade, and for most of the 1960s, the balance of payments problem was not (as government propaganda suggested) that Britain could not sell enough abroad to pay for its imports at a full-employment level of output. Rather, the problem lay elsewhere, with the ambition of successive British governments to have a large enough surplus of exports over imports to finance the significant proportion of 'defence' spending sent overseas, and in addition to allow large-scale overseas investment. It was these expenditures, plus the vulnerability of the pound to periodic crises of confidence, due to its role as an international currency, that led to the frequency of balance of payments crises. It was not, to repeat, mainly due to some fundamental problems in British international competitiveness.

Periodic balance of payments crises became part of the policy cycle of the 1950s and 1960s, usually known as 'stop-go'. In this cycle governments used monetary and fiscal policy (especially tax changes) to expand demand and sustain low unemployment, up to the point where this threatened inflation and/or balance of payments problems, whereupon the policy was reversed until such time as the rising level of unemployment was deemed unacceptable and the cycle once again reversed. These cycles were based on hyperactive management of the economy, with governments changing direction sometimes even more often than the frequency of the annual budget, which had become the centrepiece of the new regime of economic policy. These manipulations of the economy were highly controversial and attracted much political dispute, though in the long run it may be argued that they mattered much less than the feverish contemporary discussion suggested.

By the early 1960s the 'stop-go' cycle was increasingly coming under attack, for allegedly inhibiting Britain's economic growth. From the 1950s British governments saw faster economic growth and a rise in living standards as a central part of the promise they should hold out to the electorate. But from the mid-1950s it was also evident that compared with other major economies in Western Europe British growth was slow. In part (and perhaps in large part) this gap can be explained by the fact that at the end of the Second World War Britain was significantly richer than almost all European countries, and the 1950s and 1960s was a period when these other countries were essentially catching up with Britain. But such a perspective, with the implication that there was little Britain could do to change things, was not that often articulated at the time. On the contrary, from about 1960 there was a rapidly growing tide of criticism of British economic performance, and a condemnation of almost every facet of British life which allegedly contributed to Britain's economic 'decline'. This declinist fervour was in many of its manifestations absurd. Books appeared with titles like *Suicide of a Nation?* which managed to combine high-level economic illiteracy with extraordinary scaremongering statements. But even in the more sober literature of 'decline' there was a striking absence of comparative and historical analysis, and an obsessive focus on relatively short-run manifestations of Britain's alleged shortcomings.

The result of this surge of declinism was not only much soul searching about the perceived pathologies of British society, but also a major effort to find policy instruments to increase the rate of economic growth. This imperative underlay the first significant attempts to cut back on Britain's overseas commitments (a process traceable back to the late 1950s), and the (unsuccessful) attempts to join the EEC in the 1960s. Domestically it led to a renewed interest in economic planning, dating from the early 1960s but most famously embodied in the Labour government's *National Plan* of 1965. This was intended to mobilize support for a new sense of purpose in the economy, to overcome the 'short-termism' of stop-go, and to encourage investment by promising a stable economic environment. The *Plan* embodied little in the way of mechanisms to achieve its goal, it was determinedly 'indicative' rather than coercive in character. Accompanying the modernization measures embodied in the *Plan* were a host of initiatives to, for example, expand the scale of British firms and get them to spend more on research and development and the training of labour. Most of these measures made some sense as aimed at long-term desirable goals, but none was going to deliver short-term results. Unfortunately for Labour the short term brought renewed problems with the balance of payments, culminating in devaluation in November 1967.

In economic terms devaluation may be seen as just a rational adjustment of the price of the currency to changed circumstances. The fall in the pound in 1967, 14.3 per cent, was not particularly large, and economically successful countries like France had seen not one but several such falls in their currencies in the post-war period. But in Britain the international value of the currency had been invested with enormous political importance, partly tied in with the role of the currency as an international reserve asset (this was what the 'sterling area' largely meant, as discussed in Chapters 5 and 10), but more generally as embodying some sense of that value as a measure of the country's 'greatness'. At least among the political class, therefore, devaluation was a major trauma, with significant policy consequences. In its wake, important policy decisions were taken, including speeding up the withdrawal from 'East of Suez' and the effective abandonment of the sterling area. Unfortunately, other expensive and futile symbols of 'greatness' were not given up, notably the so-called 'independent nuclear deterrent', though at one stage its future was in doubt in the discussion of budget cuts in early 1968.

The most important economic consequences of the devaluation were to (eventually) significantly improve the balance of payments, and to raise the level of inflation.

From 1968 inflation was to have an increasing significance as a policy issue. Inflation had in fact been characteristic of the economy since the war, and periodically the focus of policy. Alternating attention to inflation (and its balance of payments consequences) and unemployment had underpinned the stop-go cycle described above. But because governments perceived a trade-off between low inflation and full employment they had sought for a way out of this dilemma in the form of incomes policy, that is to say, direct intervention in the setting of prices and, above all, wages. Such intervention was first tried under the Attlee government, and met with some success until the price rises brought about by the Korean War undermined trade union support for wage restraint. In the Conservative years after 1951 the likelihood of such a policy was lessened by the enthusiasm of unions for free collective bargaining on one side and, on the other, the reluctance by Conservative governments to give any policy concessions to gain support from those always doubtful of unions.

In 1964 the new Labour government had come to an agreement with the unions on wage restraint, but this proved difficult to sustain, especially once the growth in living standards held out by the *National Plan* proved unachievable. In the face of frustration at this turn of events, the Labour government became more critical of the unions, and in 1968 tried to curb their legal powers with the ill-titled proposals of *In Place of Strife*, only to be defeated by internal party opposition. Politically the battle over this legislation was very damaging to Labour, but after they lost office in 1970 it was to be under the Conservatives that government/union conflict was to be most dramatic.

The Heath government elected in 1970 was initially committed to a significantly more liberal economic policy than its post-war conservative predecessors. It pursued tough macroeconomic policies and determined to press ahead with changes to industrial relations law, embodied in the 1971 Industrial Relations Act, despite union opposition. But the circumstances worked against such a strategy. On the one side, inflation continued to increase, in large part because of a worldwide rise in commodity prices. On the other, unemployment, edging up since the deflationary post-devaluation measures of 1968, continued to rise. This conjunction of events set the scene for policy 'U-turn' in 1972, with the government using both monetary and fiscal policy to rapidly expand the economy in order to get unemployment down, while searching for an agreement with the unions on limiting the inflationary impact of such a policy. While expansionary policy raised the short-run growth rate to 5 per cent per annum (compared with a long-run rate between 2 and 3 per cent), the search for an agreement with the unions was wholly unsuccessful, and at the end of 1973 the statutory policy, which had been imposed when that search failed, was challenged by the miners' union. This led to the biggest industrial relations crisis of the post-war period so far, and Heath called a general election (February 1974) on the issue of 'who runs the country?' but failed to secure a majority. Thus Labour inherited responsibility for economic policy at a time when the dramatic internal events noted above were being accompanied by even more important shifts in the international economic environment.

The worldwide rise in commodity prices in the early 1970s reflected the simultaneous expansion of all the major industrial economies, sucking in and raising the price of all major raw materials and agricultural produce. As already noted, this process had given a notable inflationary twist to prices across the world in the early 1970s. But in 1973 this broad picture of inflationary pressure was enormously enhanced by a quadrupling of oil prices, organized by the Organization of Petroleum Exporting Countries (OPEC). Such a huge shift in the price of a vital commodity not only raised world inflation to unprecedented levels, but also necessitated deflationary (and therefore unemployment-increasing) shifts of resources from domestic production into exports to pay for the more expensive oil. The result was a 'stagflationary' (stagnation plus inflation) crisis that adversely affected almost every country in the industrial world (see 'In Focus').

For the newly elected Labour government the crisis was immense. It had negotiated a deal with the unions prior to coming to office, aimed at defusing the industrial relations crisis of the immediate pre-OPEC period. Such a policy could not be sustained in the post-OPEC world; as the government almost immediately on coming to office was cutting expenditure and giving a higher priority to getting inflation down than to sustaining employment policies, the unions could not accept. By 1976 Britain was 'staring into the abyss' with inflation reaching 25 per cent, the budget deficit seemingly out of control, and a disastrous loss of international financial confidence which sent the pound (floated in 1972) down to unprecedented low levels on the markets.

The problem for the government was that while it had pursued increasingly tough anti-inflationary policies, it needed the stamp of approval for these policies from the IMF before international financial markets would respond – only such a stamp could restore credibility to British policy. This was only achieved after traumatic negotiations in 1976, which nearly broke the government. But once achieved, the agreement with the IMF facilitated an end to the crisis and by 1977, with inflation falling and the budget deficit declining, the pound had bottomed-out, and indeed the Bank in that year started to intervene to prevent a further rise in its value.

Part of the change in Britain's fortunes in the mid-1970s was a result of the unions' renewed support for the 'social contract', above all their agreement to limit wage increases. This worked reasonably well from 1976 to 1978, but in the bargaining year of 1978/9 the government sought to gain support for a maximum wage increase of 5 per cent, at a time when inflation was running at around 8–10 per cent. Such a policy was wholly unacceptable to the unions, especially to those in the public sector, where many union members had already seen their wages eroded by tough limits on wage increases imposed under the government's public spending cash limits. The stage was therefore set for the 'Winter of Discontent', in which public sector unions in particular struck against the 5 per cent limit, leading to widespread, if often exaggerated, disruption to public services. The boast of 1973/4, that only Labour could 'get on' with the unions, was found to be hollow and Mrs Thatcher won the election of 1979 on the back of a powerful wave of anti-union sentiment.

In Focus

Dealing with stagflation in the 1970s

The mid-1970s saw the worst economic crisis in Britain since the 1930s, but one with wholly unprecedented features, not least the combination of high inflation and high unemployment. Unsurprisingly such traumatic events have produced a great deal of contention as to what exactly happened and why. This section will look in some detail at the events of this period to try to explain what occurred.

The British economic crisis of the 1970s differed from the two previous major crises of the twentieth century (1920–22, 1929–32) in that the fall in output was small, and though unemployment rose (to over 1 million), the rise was on a much smaller scale. Thus the crisis was of a particular character, composed primarily of a loss of confidence in economic management, mainly the consequence of a broadly simultaneous rise in inflation and deterioration in the public finances. The rise in inflation, as noted above, followed a period of slowly accelerating inflation from 1968, but reached the unprecedented level of around 25 per cent in 1975/76. Such rates of inflation caused panic in some quarters. High inflation was seen as threatening stable economic and social life by undermining faith in money and hence of the economic system as a whole. Alarmists pointed to events in South America, where hyper-inflation was associated with widespread unrest, coups and military takeover. In retrospect much of this appears gravely exaggerated. While serious, Britain's inflation problem never really threatened to turn into a hyper-inflation. Government, while struggling, never lost control of the economic levers necessary to make such an outcome likely.

On the fiscal side, the problem began with the massive increases in public expenditure under the Heath government without commensurate tax increases. Initially under Labour there seemed to be a case for budget deficits to combat the recession, but such a view was very quickly overtaken by the view that in the face of inflation such deficits were unsustainable. By the budget of April 1975, the Chancellor of the Exchequer, Denis Healey, was making his priorities clear: 'I fully understand why I have been urged by so many friends both inside and outside the House to treat unemployment as the central problem and to stimulate growth in home consumption, public or private, so as to start getting the rate of unemployment down as fast as possible . . . I do not believe it would be wise to follow that advice today . . . I cannot afford to increase demand further when 5p in every pound we spend at home has been provided by our creditors abroad and inflation is running at its current rate' (House of Commons, 15 April 1975). Matching deeds to words, the government pursued expenditure cuts, albeit initially these were insufficient to offset the rise in expenditure derived from the recession. By 1976 the government had designed a system of controls, called cash limits, that quickly brought spending under

Dealing with stagflation in the 1970s

control, a process well under way *before* the visit by the IMF. Ironically, the Labour government was therefore in the summer of 1976 engaged in bitter debates about the scale of spending cuts likely to satisfy the IMF, when reductions already in the pipeline resulting from the change to the new cash limits system were larger than those advocated by even the most enthusiastic 'cutters'.

From 1976 not only did public expenditure and the budget deficit fall, but also, once the IMF agreed its package with the British government, the pound stopped declining in value. Inflation also started to come down, though the reasons for this are highly controversial. Some have argued that it followed the lagged effects from the ending of the monetary expansion that accompanied the boom under Mr Heath. Others have seen a major role for the end of the commodity price boom, which went into reverse as the world went into recession and demand for commodities dropped. Finally, there is the issue of wage inflation. The Social Contract started to have some significant effects on wage bargaining in 1975/76, as the abyss of hyper-inflation seemed to open. In the following years wage inflation fell away, and this may be regarded as an important part of the cause of the overall fall in inflation, which began at approximately the same time. However, this happy situation was soon altered when the government sought to achieve a wage inflation target of 5 per cent in 1978/9, when consumer price inflation was still running at 8–10 per cent. The Winter of Discontent that followed can thus be seen as the result of a Labour government asking for too heavy sacrifices, especially by poorly paid workers in the public sector.

In September 1976 the new Prime Minister, James Callaghan, made a famous speech to the Labour party conference where he repudiated the idea that you could 'spend your way out of a recession', claiming that 'that option no longer exists, and that in so far as it did exist it only worked by injecting a bigger dose of inflation into the economy, followed by a higher level of unemployment as a next step'. This statement was highly inaccurate as a description of what had happened in the post-war British economy. Its significance, however, was political. Made during the negotiations with the IMF, it was intended to emphasize the Labour government's repudiation of 'Keynesian' policies in order to obtain international credibility for the government's anti-inflationary and fiscally conservative policies. In this respect it may be thought successful, reinforcing the deflationary measures already noted.

By the time Labour left office in 1979 economic growth had resumed, unemployment was falling, and the balance of payments was much stronger than in 1974. In that sense the industrial relations crisis, hugely politically important as it was, should not be allowed to conceal the fact that Labour had, after a very poor start, developed polices that coped fairly well with an unprecedented crisis that left most governments in the West desperately searching for remedies. As Table 15.1 (p. 242) suggests, the British performance, while hardly outstanding, was not wholly out of line with that of the other major Western European economies.

Dealing with stagflation in the 1970s

Table 15.1 Comparative economic performance in the Western European 'Big 4' in the 1970s

	France	Italy	W. Germany	Britain
Output growth (% p.a.)				
1974–79	3.1	2.3	2.7	2.0
Unemployment (national definitions)				
1974–79	4.5	6.6	3.6	4.5
Inflation (GDP deflator)				
1974–79	10.4	16.9	4.3	16.3
Current balance (% GDP)				
1974–79	−0.6	−0.2	1.0	−1.3

Source: Based on Artis and Cobham, 1991: 267.

Debates and Interpretations

How far was economic management in the 1950s and 60s responsible for the combination of historically high growth, full employment, low inflation and commercial current account balance? One of the difficulties of answering this question is that the very success it seeks to explain is ignored or denied by much that has been written on post-war Britain. The dominant narrative dealing with these years suggests that these were years of economic 'failure' and 'decline'. This essentially political narrative is most obvious in the Thatcherite account, which seeks to represent the 1970s crisis as a logical culmination of the failed project of British 'socialism' throughout the post-war years (colluded with by Conservative governments of the period).

The fundamental difficulty with this argument is that on almost every count the British economy performed better before the 1970s than since, so that a narrative of 'rescue' of a failing economy by Thatcherite policies bears little relation to the evidence. Table 15.2 (p. 243) uses the four standard measures of economic performance, and it is evident from these how far the 1950s and 1960s were indeed a 'Golden Age' of economic performance.

Equally, far from being a culmination of long-run deterioration, the mid-1970s, although undoubtedly years of economic failure in almost all respects, were exceptional years, in many ways deviant from what had gone before. A graphic illustration

Table 15.2 Macroeconomic indicators, annual averages by government, 1945–1997

Government	GDP growth %	Change in RPI %	Unemployment %	Current payments % of GDP
Labour 1945–51	1.5	5.5	1.9	(2.1)*
Conservative 1951–64	2.9	3.4	1.8	0.2
Labour 1964–70	2.5	4.6	2.1	0.0
Conservative 1970–74	2.8	10.4	3.0	(0.3)*
Labour 1974–79	2.1	15.6	4.8	(0.9)*
Conservative 1979–97	2.1	5.8	9.2	(0.6)*

Note: *Figures in brackets indicate a deficit.

Source: Based on Middleton, 2000: 86.

of the 'deviancy' of the mid-1970s is given in Table 15.3, which compares Britain's performance with that of the high-growth West German economy, in terms of labour productivity in manufacturing, a traditional measure of efficiency. It is striking how similar the two countries growth rates were before 1973, and how quickly Britain recovered from the terrible performance of the 1973–79 period.

So in interpreting events in Britain's post-war economic history it is imperative to recognize the successes of the era from 1945 to the early 1970s.

For commentators in the 1960s one aspect of this success was most striking – full employment. In the 1940s the widespread political support for a goal of 'high and stable' employment was accompanied by major doubts, especially among economists, on whether such a goal was achievable. Certainly, many economists at the time thought that talk of a 3 per cent unemployment rate was highly optimistic. In the event, unemployment averaged 1.8 per cent in the 1950s and 1960s. Early attempts to

Table 15.3 Manufacturing labour productivity in Britain and West Germany, 1951–1989 (% per annum per person engaged)

	Britain	West Germany
1951–64	4.50	5.32
1964–73	4.18	4.52
1973–79	0.68	3.47
1979–89	4.14	1.92

Source: Based on Broadberry and Crafts, 2003: 723.

explain this success partook of a euphoric 'Keynesian optimism' which saw such low unemployment as a vindication of the policies of demand management pursued after 1945. But in 1968 R.C.O. Matthews used Keynesian techniques of demand analysis to show that post-war economic buoyancy was not largely due to any direct effect of government fiscal policies. Rather, full employment was primarily the result of a huge increase in investment, linked in large measure to wartime innovations in such areas as jet aircraft, nuclear power and pharmaceuticals, coupled to the boom in the world economy with its expansionary effects on exports. Thus, in this analysis, government played only an indirect role in creating the conditions of full employment. However, it may well be argued that governments nevertheless were important. First, by giving a political commitment to full employment they encouraged investors' confidence that profits would not be reduced by deflationary demand policies. Second, national governments designed an architecture for the international economic system which facilitated the resurgence of international economic integration, providing (down to the 1970s) a buoyant environment for national governments to operate within.

Such discussions of post-war success on the employment front were accompanied from the late 1950s by the 'declinist' literature noted above, which sought to explain the alleged failings of economic performance, especially as regards economic growth. This literature was enormous, diverse and extraordinarily variable in quality. Nevertheless, two major strands in the more serious versions may be discerned for both the intrinsic importance and longevity of their approaches. First is what may be called the 'overstretch' story, pioneered by Andrew Shonfield in his *British Economic Policy since the War*, first published in 1958. This located the cause of Britain's slow growth in low investment, itself mainly the consequence of 'stop-go', a policy which resulted in his view from Britain's excessive overseas commitments, both to military expenditure and to the sterling area. In his view, the second of these created a 'sword of Damocles' poised over the British economy, always likely to fall at times of crisis because of the imbalance between Britain's international reserves and her liabilities.

The alternative narrative had a more internal focus. Pioneered as an overall approach by Michael Shanks in his *Stagnant Society*, first published in 1960, it saw the roots of Britain's malaise in the conservatism of both its management and workers, reinforced by an outdated trade union system. This was essentially a cultural diagnosis, in which faster growth would require a major attitudinal shift, not least on the part of the working class.

Both of these accounts of Britain's problems emanated from the centre-Left of the political spectrum. But while Shonfield's approach can be seen as founding a long line of broadly Left-leaning critiques (Pollard, Cain and Hopkins, etc.), the Shanks story could easily resonate with the anti-union prejudices of the Right. Not dissimilar in approach are conservative accounts of decline to be found in the work of those such as Wiener and Barnett.

Barnett's work is the more interesting politically, as it seeks to combine an essentially 'Prussian' view of the failure of Britain's policy makers to deliver a 'national industrial strategy' with an anti-welfare, anti-union, and anti-liberal polemic that is close to the politics of Thatcherism. Much more sophisticated and qualified is the work of Broadberry and Crafts, who, while significantly modifying the story of whole-sale decline to be found in the work of writers such as Barnett, nevertheless diagnose a significant degree of 'government failure' in Britain's post-war political economy. For them, governments gave too much emphasis to short-run economic stability and full employment, at the expense of enhancing competition and cutting subsidies, which they believe would have improved long-run growth prospects.

The declinist narrative of Britain's post-war economy has recently come under challenge from a range of perspectives. These include detailed re-assessments of economic performance; the placing of declinism as the product of very specific political and historical contexts; and broad 'revisionist' accounts of post-war Britain which seek to create alternative 'meta-narratives'. Of the latter the most interesting is undoubtedly David Edgerton's notion of a 'militant and technological nation'. None of these challenges is without its own problems, but together they have shifted the consensus about how far 'decline' provides a helpful assumption about post-war Britain. Logically, once decline is regarded as a problematic description of events, the idea of government failure as an explanation of that decline is also called into question. Perhaps, therefore, it is time to bring out the successes of post-war economic management, alongside the undoubted failings.

Interpretations of post-war Britain as in 'decline' and the idea of government as failing initially became fashionable in the 1960s, at a time of a broad political/social/cultural crisis in Britain about the country's place in the world and its future as a post-imperial power. These angst-ridden discussions, then, underpinned attempts under both Labour and Conservative governments to improve economic performance, which 'failed' in the sense that they created unrealistic expectations of how fast living standards could rise, though, as noted above, down to the early 1970s British performance was perfectly adequate by historic standards. The failures of the 1970s reinforced the 'declinist' understanding of Britain, with both the Left and Thatcherite Right claiming that events in that decade vindicated their view of an underlying economic sickness in Britain. With the centre of politics finding it hard to resolve the crisis, the way was open for radical attacks to succeed – and it was that from the Radical Right, under Mrs Thatcher, that succeeded, very much helped, of course, by the Winter of Discontent.

Further reading

A variety of views on the post-war British economy can be found in the *Cambridge Economic History of Modern Britain, Vol. III: Structural Change and Growth, 1939–2000* (Cambridge, 2004). On macroeconomic policy, J.C.R. Dow, *The Management of the British Economy, 1945–60* (Cambridge, 1964) and F. Blackaby (ed.) *British Economic Policy 1960–74* (Cambridge, 1978). On growth, see Steve Broadberry's *The Productivity Race* (Cambridge, 1997) and Steven Broadberry and Nick Crafts, 'UK productivity performance from 1950 to 1979: a restatement of the Broadberry-Crafts view', *Economic History Review*, 56 (2003). Though also see Booth, 'The manufacturing failure hypothesis and the performance of British industry during the long boom', *Economic History Review*, 56 (2004): 1–33. Nick Crafts's work is central to the debate on post-war Britain; see, for example, *Britain's Relative Economic Decline 1870–1995* (London, 1997). Broadly a 'declinist', Crafts has done important work in contextualizing 'decline', especially in his 'The golden age of economic growth in Western Europe, 1950–1973', *Economic History Review*, 48 (1995): 429–47. Andrew Shonfield's *British Economic Policy since the War* (Harmondsworth, 1958) is still worth consulting as a foundation text of declinism, as is Michael Shanks, *The Stagnant Society* (Harmondsworth, 1961). For more recent declinism, see (from the Right) Correlli Barnett's work, for example, *The Audit of War* (Basingstoke, 1986) or, from the Left, Sidney Pollard, *The Wasting of the British Economy* (Croom Helm, 1984). On the historical context of declinism, see Jim Tomlinson, 'Inventing "decline": the falling behind of the British economy in the post-war years', *Economic History Review*, 49 (1996): 734–60, and for alternative 'narratives', see David Edgerton, *England and The Aeroplane* (Basingston, 1991). For a coruscating account of aspects of the debate, see Theo Nichols, *The British Worker Question* (London, 1996). All these themes can be developed further by reading the following books: Michael Artis and David Cobham, *Labour's Economic Policies 1974–79* (Manchester, 1991); Alan Booth, *The British Economy in the Twentieth Century* (Basingstoke, 2001); Kathleen Burk and Alec Cairncross, *Goodbye Great Britain: The 1976 IMF Crisis* (New York, 1992) and Roger Middleton, *The British Economy since 1945* (Basingstoke, 2000).

16

Immigration, multiculturalism and racism

Panikos Panayi

ALTHOUGH IMMIGRATION HAS PLAYED a central role in the evolution of Britain, historians have only begun to devote attention to it as a phenomenon in recent decades. After 1945 Britain certainly witnessed a scale of immigration which it had not previously experienced, with profound consequences for all aspects of British life. But migration into Britain is not a new phenomenon. An acceptance of the concept of the English as a people would have to recognize that they themselves originate from a migratory movement which made its way to the British Isles during the fifth and sixth centuries. Since then a series of other groups entered the country, increasing especially during the nineteenth century, with an influx of close to 1 million Irish and several hundred thousand Jews fleeing persecution from Eastern Europe. During the late 1930s a new group of Jews arrived in Britain, fleeing Nazi Germany. The outbreak of the Second World War meant further influxes of refugees from the continent, although very few Jewish ones, together with some West Indian and Asian people to join the small numbers of these communities already present in Britain. A significant percentage of the ethnic majority would have had no contact with migrants and their offspring before 1945, as the latter tended to remain focused in large cities.

The post-war influxes altered this state of affairs as large numbers of migrants moved to Britain from throughout Europe and the world between 1945 and 2000. While much of the settlement remains in conurbations, ethnic minority communities have now spread to cities and parts of the country which had previously experienced little migration. At the same time, the impact of immigration upon British life has been transformative: the evolution of the country since the Second World War cannot be understood without considering the importance of migrants. The influence of immigration upon Britain has taken place despite the hostility which all groups of newcomers have faced upon arriving in the country. As the narrative below will demonstrate, multiculturalism has evolved alongside the existence of racism.

Despite the centrality of immigration in the evolution of modern Britain, especially since 1945, historians have tended to shy away from studying this subject. Some of the most substantial groups have a long historiographical tradition, especially the Irish and Jewish communities, although the attention which the former have received has largely ignored the post-war period. Similarly, the history of the settlement of black people in Britain has also received much attention, although the same does not apply to Asians. Much of the work which has occurred has dealt with the period before 1945, so that it has mostly been left to social scientists to look at the post-war migrants. Only during the last two decades have historians begun to examine immigration in post-war Britain. However, with the exception of the first edition of this volume, most general histories of Britain pay little attention to the history and impact of immigration either before or after 1945 (Burrell and Panayi, 2005: 5–8).

Migration to post-war Britain

The lack of attention paid to immigration in most general histories of Britain strikes us because of the level and regularity of movement to the country since the end of the Second World War, encompassing a variety of groups. In order to understand these streams we need to place Britain within the world economy and consider developments both within Britain and outside. Migration to the country divides into a series of chronological periods.

The first of these consists of the immediate post-war years, when the British government strove to attract migrants from Europe in order to help with reconstruction. The largest influxes originated in Ireland, a traditional supplier of labour for the British economy since the middle of the nineteenth century. By 1971 over a million Irish people lived in Britain. In addition, the government also attracted people from Italy, from where emigrants moved to a series of European states during this period. The Ministry of Labour further recruited 91,151 displaced persons in the late 1940s, consisting of individuals who did not wish to return to their homelands in the Soviet bloc. To these we need to add approximately 145,000 Poles, who essentially consist of members of the Polish army and government in exile who chose to remain in Britain when Poland fell under Stalin's control. Immigration policy remained selective as the government aimed to keep out European Jews during this period.

Despite the influx of peoples which would occur from the Empire and Commonwealth, the government displayed an initial reluctance to allow migration from these destinations because of the desire, as Kathleen Paul (1997) and Ian Spencer (1997) have demonstrated, to keep Britain white. However, the British Nationality Act of 1948 allowed persons with Imperial or Commonwealth citizenship to settle in Britain. The initial influx occurred from the West Indies, a part of the world experiencing significant levels of unemployment and where living standards remained significantly lower than those in the 'mother country' as the migrants viewed it. British companies, including London Transport, recruited here. But many accounts point to the fact that chain migration (whereby immigrants send for other adults, usually relatives, to join them) developed bringing, for instance, Nevisians to Leicester (Byron, 1994). Chains also developed from other parts of the Empire including Cyprus, where movement based on family and village occurred, and Hong Kong, from where labour supplies for emerging Chinese restaurants originated. But after the West Indies, the most significant provider of migrants consisted of South Asia, by which we mean India and Pakistan. In fact, in these cases, migration occurred from particular areas. Most Indian migrants to Britain originated either in Punjab or Gujarat, while many Pakistanis actually came from Sylhet, which would subsequently become part of Bangladesh. While chain migration played a large role here, migrants again left undeveloped regions often in the hope of working, accumulating capital and then returning home. This second phase of immigration ended in 1962, when, following a press campaign echoed in parliament, the Conservative government of Harold Macmillan passed the Commonwealth Immigrants Act of 1962 which restricted entry from former Imperial territories to individuals who received a voucher to work in areas which needed recruitment from abroad.

This measure did not, however, prevent immigration from the Empire and Common-wealth because two further streams continued to move into the country into the 1970s. In the first place, some movement occurred under the voucher system, although the numbers entering fell from 30,130 in 1963 to 2290 in 1972. A second stream consisted of the relatives of those men who had moved to Britain before 1962, especially those from India, which significantly increased the size of the South Asian communities in the UK. In the third place, the 1962 Act did not prevent a migration of 155,000 people of Indian origin who had previously settled in East Africa but still had a British passport, which meant a further augmentation of the Gujurati, Sikh and Indian Muslim popula-tion of Britain. These three groups had differences from people of the same ethnic group who came directly from India because of their status as 'twice migrants' (Bhachu, 1985). But this final movement ceased following hostility which emerged in the popular press, fuelled by the speeches of Enoch Powell and leading to the passage of the Common-wealth Immigrants Act of 1968 and the Immigration Act of 1971, which meant that the only British passport holders who could move to Britain consisted of those who had at least one parent or grandparent born, adopted or naturalized in the UK, a blatant example of discrimination which prevented Asians from moving to the country.

We might see the fourth and final period of migration to Britain covering the decades from the early 1970s until the end of the century, because the main move-ments remained the same throughout this long period, even though their constituent parts may have altered. In the first place, some family migration continued, especially of South Asians. Linked to this, some second-generation South Asian immigrants chose (and were very rarely, despite media hype about this subject, forced into mar-riages with) husbands or wives from their land of origin.

A series of refugee movements also made their way to Britain from the early 1970s. One of the first of these consisted of the Ugandan Asians fleeing from the dictatorship of Idi Amin, who initially received a hostile reception, but have more recently been celebrated as a refugee success story. The 1970s also witnessed an influx of about 10,000 Greek Cypriots escaping the Turkish invasion of their country and about 15,000 Vietnamese, mostly ethnic Chinese, who fled after the American defeat in their country. Relatively few refugees moved to Britain during the 1980s, but this changed after the end of the Cold War and the nationalistic and ethnic tensions which this released, which has created an international refugee crisis. Some exiles, particularly from Yugoslavia, the Middle East and Africa moved to Britain, where they faced vilification as 'asylum seekers', a label that increasingly developed into a term of abuse.

A third important group of migrants to Britain since the 1970s consists of citizens of the European Union, entering the country under the 1957 Treaty of Rome clause allowing free movement of labour. One of the largest groups has actually consisted of Germans, whose numbers reached over 200,000 by the 1990s, working in a range of predominantly middle-class occupations, including school and university teaching (Kettenacker, 1996).

Finally, the concluding decades of the twentieth century also witnessed an increase in the number of illegal immigrants in Britain, particularly in London, to as many as one million people. Originating from a variety of destinations and surviving in the black economy, they have played a vital role, especially in the capital, performing tasks which Britons have shunned (Hall, 2003). During the post-war period, despite the hostility which virtually all groups of newcomers have faced, Britain has attracted millions of people to its shores. They have arrived as economic migrants, refugees, illegal migrants and families of people already here. The freedoms and economic success of Britain, especially in comparison with their own countries, have acted as the magnets.

Multiculturalism

By the time the Labour government of Tony Blair had taken power in 1997, the concept of a multicultral Britain had increasingly become accepted in public and governmental discourse. This would become even more the case under New Labour. This discourse essentially acted as an inclusive ideology which focused upon enfranchised and increasingly empowered West Indian and South Asian migrants and their descendants. This viewpoint suggested that we had moved away from the dark age of racism which had greeted the arrivals from the West Indies and South Asia from the 1950s to the 1970s. It operates upon four assumptions: first, that the Commonwealth migrants and their descendants have had a significant measure of economic success; second that the British state has made political space for them; third, that they have become fully integrated; and finally, that the newcomers have enriched British life. Are these assumptions true?

If we begin with the level of economic success of newcomers to post-war Britain, we find a complex picture, with some groups and individuals demonstrating high levels of economic entrepreneurship and business triumph while others have had a standard of living and success below the national average. Thus, while statistics indicate high levels of self-employment among most Commonwealth immigrant groups, some immigrants have done better than others, particularly Greek Cypriots and South Asians. Among South Asians, Indians demonstrate the highest levels of success, whether measured in terms of wealth, entrepreneurship or higher education, while, at the other end of the scale, Bangladeshis and Pakistanis have suffered high levels of unemployment. A similar pattern would emerge for West Indians. Meanwhile, a group such as the Greek Cypriots have a social and economic structure which reflects British society, meaning that members of this minority fit on to all parts of the class, employment and educational spectrum. The Germans, however, have a predominantly middle-class profile.

How do we explain these variations? In the first place, most sociological studies which appeared from the 1980s, especially the work of John Solomos (2003), which focused upon black youth, stressed racism. While this goes a long way to explaining the discrimination faced by African-Caribbeans, it probably also helps us to explain the level of success of 'white' Greek Cypriots and Germans, although it would be foolish to suggest that neither of these groups has faced hostility. Nevertheless, how do we explain the higher social status of Indians compared with Pakistanis and Bangladehsis? We might point to some form of Islamophobia, but this was not really an issue until after 2001, although 'Paki bashing' of the 1970s did seem to have some focus upon people originating in Pakistan rather than India. But we need to add another element here in the form of the class origins of newcomers to Britain so that Indians, often entering as professionals, could maintain their social standards, while those from the Caribbean, Bangladesh and Pakistan tended to enter unqualified and simply slipped into an urban proletariat. On the other hand, Germans usually came with qualifications. But this is a simplification: Greek Cypriots often entered as unskilled and uneducated, while many West Indians never attained the levels of employment they had in the Caribbean. Thus, class and race issues operate together. We need to add one other element here: the level of entrepreneurship among ethnic minorities received partial explanation from the fact that they faced racial discrimination in the wider job market, which impacted upon their chances of success, which meant that they chose to take their own path.

What does this tell us about 'multicultural' Britain? Clearly, some post-war migrants, especially those of Asian origin have had a high degree of business success, but this finds partial explanation in the fact that mainstream occupations, initially at least, remained more or less closed to them, forcing many migrants into alternative employment. Some ethnic minorities remain towards the lower end of the social scale, some find themselves spread across it and others are focused at the top. In terms of economic position, we can speak of multiculturalism operating, but we need to bear in mind obvious inequalities.

If we turn to state attitudes, we have already seen that a succession of governments have made efforts to control immigration. On the other hand, certainly if we focus upon migrants from the Commonwealth, the Labour governments of 1966–70, 1974–9, together with the Blair regime, have implemented a series of measures aimed at preventing racial discrimination. This policy is summed up by Roy Hattersley's classic statement that 'Integration without limitation is impossible; limitation without legislation is indefensible' (quoted in Solomos, 1988). Perhaps the most important of piece of legislation consisted of the Race Relations Act of 1976, which established the Commission for Racial Equality (CRE) with the aim of policing incidents of discrimination. In addition, since the middle of the 1960s, local councils have also established units to promote better inter-ethnic relations. While this indicates a readiness on the part of Labour governments to tackle discrimination, the passage of legislation cannot prevent it from taking place.

Part of the reason why Labour governments have led the way in the implementation of 'race relations' legislation lies in the fact that many of their inner-city parliamentary seats depend upon the votes of ethnic minorities. Thus, while Labour initially fielded parliamentary candidates with black and Asian backgrounds, especially in the 1987 general election, the other main parties followed suit. At the same time, ethnic minorities have increasingly played a role in the local councils where they find themselves concentrated, again consisting mainly of Labour supporters. On one level this indicates multiculturalism, but political realities also play a role here, with the Labour party in particular looking after its own constituency.

The level of integration of ethnic minorities in British society also represents a measure of whether Britain has become multiculturalized. Ethnic segregation, lack of friendships with members of different groups and endogamy might suggest an absence of integration, as might separate schooling. We can consider each of these issues. Certainly, ethnic segregation exists as it has done throughout twentieth-century Britain, as we could see if we went back to examine East European Jewish concentrations before 1945. In the immediate post-war period, newcomers from the Empire and Commonwealth also focused upon specific areas, as did Europeans. These have sometimes broken down, as the example of Notting Hill as an area of West Indian settlement indicates, while others have consolidated, as Brixton suggests. Similarly, many northern towns with Asian communities have faced high levels of segregation (Cantle, 2001). Still other areas act as home to changing ethnic minority communities over time, as the example of the East End suggests, moving from overwhelmingly Jewish to predominantly Bangladeshi. The reasons for concentration, especially in the inner city, include fear of racism, economic position and desire for ethnic consolidation. Change certainly takes place over time, as the example of the Jews who moved out of inner-city areas indicates, but in terms of residence patterns, it seems difficult to speak of a multicultural Britain.

A report from the CRE in July 2004 claimed that 94 per cent of 'white people' had 'few or no ethnic minority friends', which seemed again to indicate a lack of integration and interaction, although the statistics and methodology seem flawed. It is highly likely that friendships have developed in the workplace in Britain. But statistics of intermarriage from the 2001 census seem to support the CRE figures, as they suggest that 98 per cent of marriages involved people from the same ethnic group. However, this rate was much higher for ethnic minorities than it was for the majority. While only 1 per cent of the latter entered into such marriages, the figure for black Caribbean men and Chinese women, for instance, was close to a third.

In terms of integration, we appear to have had a mixed picture, with residential segregation, apparent lack of friendships and variable rates of intermarriage. The existence of faith schools would also seem to confirm such ethnic separation, although we need to remember that these have operated for a variety of groups over the past century. While they may prevent contact with members of other minorities, much of the syllabus remains similar, certainly in terms of ultimate qualifications.

While segregation, perpetuated by both the majority and minority communities, seems to exist, especially in housing, and while it cannot be ignored, this does not change the fact that the overwhelming majority of ethnic minorities have become integrated into British society and, in fact, form an important part of it. The cultural sphere would seem to indicate that multicultural Britain exists. Since 1945 minorities have transformed fundamental aspects of British life. In the first place, they have introduced new religions, notably Hinduism, Islam, Sikhism and Greek Orthodoxism, although none of these has had an impact upon the ethnic majority. The same applies to the countless new languages which have arrived in Britain on a large scale, particularly from South Asia and Europe. But migrants have brought aspects of their lives with them which have influenced the British. We can say this, for example, of dress, where South Asian influences have certainly played a role in the clothing of ethnic majority women, witnessed, for instance, by the rise of the *Monsoon* chain of female clothes stores. At the same time, most second-generation women, with British citizenship, wear traditional dress at social functions of their own community. Migrants from the Caribbean in particular have also influenced the development of British popular music and also play a large role on the 'club scene'. By the end of the twentieth century, top-flight English football teams had become dominated by migrants and their offspring. Similarly, some of the leading novelists in the country, including Monica Ali, Salman Rushdie and Zadie Smith, have migrant origins. Finally, newcomers have played a central role in transforming the eating patterns of Britain, introducing all manner of cuisines, from pizza to curry, and providing the staff for establishments of all sizes, from Chinese takeaways to the Ritz.

In Focus

The history of curry in Britain

Perhaps no other aspect of post-war British life symbolizes the rise of multiculturalism as the spread of curry. While popular studies have speculated upon the origins of this dish, the names of the fare served within Indian restaurants in post-war Britain essentially have their origins in an exercise in unofficial culinary mapping which took place during the nineteenth century involving members of the Raj. By the end of the nineteenth century, English language cookbooks about Indian food contained recipes

> ## The history of curry in Britain

for 'kormas', 'jalfarezis' and 'tikkas'. At the same time, most general cookbooks also listed at least one curry dish.

But only a handful of Indian restaurants had come into existence in Britain by the end of the Second World War, meaning that most Britons had not tasted Indian food, certainly not in a restaurant. However, by the end of the twentieth century, around 8000 Indian restaurants existed in Britain and curry had become part of the everyday diet. Not only did these restaurants serve the dishes invented by the British in India, the owners of these establishments created new ones, above all chicken tikka massala and balti.

How did the expansion take place? Many of the early owners and chefs consisted of cooks originating in Sylhet, which would become part of Bangladesh, who had worked in the British merchant navy. Over time, a type of ethnic clustering in employment occurred, whereby the opening of an 'Indian' restaurant became an entrepreneurial opportunity for Bangladeshis, who have owned the overwhelming majority of such establishments. But the spread of Indian food also suggests a receptive audience among Britons, perhaps because of the relatively bland diet which existed for the majority of the population in the early post-war decades. Just as important was increasing disposable income among the British population in the final few decades of the twentieth century, which meant that eating out became increasingly normal, as did the purchase of takeaway meals. But curry consumption did not simply rely on Bangladeshi cooks and takeaways, as it gradually became a staple item on supermarket shelves as national retailers and multinational food producers jumped on the bandwagon of the taste for exotic food, which encompassed not simply Indian, but a range of other products, including those with origins in Italy, China and Thailand.

What does the spread of Indian food tell us about multiculturalization? On the one hand, it would suggest that Britons, by embracing such a foreign food so wholeheartedly in the post-war years, have demonstrated their tolerance of foreign 'cultures'. Nevertheless, this seems rather simplistic, for a number of reasons. In the first place, eating in a Bangladeshi restaurant has required little interaction with the community from which the food has evolved. At the same time, we also need to emphasize that the Indian food served in the restaurants does not represent the same as that eaten by Indian immigrants at home, which has strict dietary controls, whether we are talking about Sikhs, Hindus or Muslims. While members of the ethnic majority dominate the custom base of Bangladeshi restaurants, they rarely venture into Indian grocery stores and certainly not into halal butchers, which symbolize ethnic separation in Britain. The Indian food eaten by the ethnic majority represents a multicultural compromise, a symbol of a superficial level of exchange between the majority and one particular minority. The dishes were imagined and constructed by the British in India or Bangladeshis in Britain and represent what these two groups view as acceptable fare.

The history of curry in Britain

Plate 16.1 The exterior of the Madras Indian restaurant in 1974 demonstrating the multicultural dining experience of twentieth-century Britain: Indian curry with American Coca-Cola (© Hulton Archive/Getty).

Racism

Multiculturalism remains a problematic concept in Britain after 1945. In purely cultural terms it exists, but trying to prove that it functions in other ways becomes problematic because of so much contradictory evidence. While we might suggest that the post-war period may have seen the 'irresistible rise of multiracial Britain' (Phillips and Phillips, 1999), certainly in cultural terms, the personal experiences of most migrants would question such celebratory language, as would many aspects of state policy. In many ways, the history of attitudes towards migrants in post-war Britain follows the patterns established from the end of the nineteenth century, whereby hostility always focuses upon a particular group, consisting of Jews between *c.*1880–1914, Germans during the First World War, and then Jews again until 1945. In the immediate post-war decades attention initially went towards those from the Caribbean, then focused more particularly upon South Asians, as their numbers increased. As these two groups have become increasingly integrated and have gained increasing influence, a new dehumanized out-group has developed, towards which hostility has become legitimate in the form of 'asylum seekers' (Kushner, 2006), so that we now almost have multicultural racism. While the above might represent the main groups to face hostility, others have also suffered, especially the Irish during the height of the IRA bombing campaigns during the 1970s and 1980s (Hickman and Walter, 1997).

Post-war racism and discrimination in Britain manifests itself in a wide variety of ways. We can only focus upon a small number of these. First, the role of the state is central. We have seen that Labour governments have introduced a series of measures for the purpose of lessening discrimination and increasing multiculturalism and integration. Nevertheless, we need to remember, in this context, Roy Hattersley's statement quoted above. The various Race Relations Acts have come into being in parallel with the passage of a series of highly selective immigration control measures, again continuing precedents established at the end of the nineteenth century. Although the post-war governments welcomed migrants from the Empire and Commonwealth for a short time, they also subsequently introduced measures to keep them out. More recently, a whole series of asylum and immigration acts have come into operation to deal with refugees. On the other hand, Europeans, under the Treaty of Rome have had right of entry to Britain, as have white Commonwealth citizens with origins in the UK.

Another indication of state racism, which a succession of scholars have pointed to, particularly John Solomos (1988), consists of the actions of the police, particularly towards black youth. An early indication of such hostility occurred in August 1948, when, following a racist attack upon a hostel for black sailors in Liverpool, the police arrested 60 black men and only 10 white men (Panayi, 1996: 16). Such discriminatory policing occurred during the entire post-war period, reaching a head during the early 1980s, especially in Brixton, but also elsewhere in the country, leading to the publication of the Scarman Report (1981), which pointed out that such practices had alienated inner-city black youths to such an extent that they felt that rioting had become the only way to defend themselves. Despite recommendations made by the Scarman

Report, discriminatory policing continued in Britain over the following decade, as revealed by the report which looked into the murder of Stephen Lawrence, published in 1999 (MacPherson, 1999).

While a multiracial culture may have evolved over several decades, this has had to overcome an Anglocentric one which, especially in the early post-war decades, displayed hostility towards migrants from the Commonwealth, as evidenced, for instance, in working-class humour, which focused particularly upon Pakistanis and the Irish, although the passage of race relations legislation has made such humour disreputable, if not illegal.

The most persistent hostility towards migrants has probably come from the right-wing press on both a local and national level which, throughout the post-war period, has devoted attention to whichever group it viewed as the main threat. Thus, during the 1950s attention focused particularly upon newcomers from the Caribbean and played a role in the outbreak of the Notting Hill and Nottingham race riots of 1958. The intense focus upon immigration continued and helped to create the atmosphere which led to the passage of the Commonwealth Immigrants Act of 1962. This hostility towards immigration continued into the 1960s and 1970s, reaching a series of peaks,

Plate 16.2 Firemen and onlookers beside a burnt-out building on the second day of the Brixton riots, London, April 1981 (© Hulton Archive/Getty).

including the autumn of 1972, as Ugandan Asians fleeing Idi Amin moved towards Britain. Much press attention during the 1970s and 1980s focused upon illegal immigrants, especially those of South Asian origins. By the end of the century, the focus turned towards 'asylum seekers', dehumanized in many sections of the press.

Against such a background, it is not surprising that migrants have faced direct experiences of discrimination since 1945, especially in housing and employment. During the early post-war years, until the passage of the Race Relations Act of 1968, no legislation existed to prevent discrimination, so that many people of Caribbean and Asian origin faced direct discrimination in both of these areas. Prejudice from landlords and estate agents, as well as a desire to live near or together with people from the same ethnic group, played a large role in determining the concentrated housing patterns of ethnic minorities, especially those from the Caribbean and South Asia, as revealed in a number of contemporary studies, including Dilip Hiro's *Black British, White British* (1971). However, the passage of the Race Relations Acts of 1968 and 1976 could not prevent racial discrimination in either of these areas. One of the functions of the CRE is precisely to investigate examples of racial discrimination. As we have seen, many members of ethnic minorities prefer to launch their own firms rather than face institutional racism. In terms of housing patterns, movement has often taken place out of the initial areas of settlement, but this has sometimes occurred *en masse*, so that inner-city areas of settlement have sometimes simply moved into the suburbs, as the example of Leicester would indicate. Perhaps even more worrying for the future of race relations and integration is the fact that Asians, particularly of Gujurati origin, have been moving to Leicester because it has become known as a centre of Indian settlement (Singh, 2003).

As well as 'subtle' forms of discrimination in housing and employment, many migrants to post-war Britain have experienced racist violence. In the years immediately after 1945 rioting against migrants occurred in a series of locations, culminating in the Nottingham and Notting Hill riots in 1958, and followed by further outbreaks of disorder in Middlesbrough, Dudley, Accrington and Wolverhampton into the middle of the 1960s. Most of these disturbances focused upon people of Caribbean origin. During the 1970s and 1980s Pakistanis and Bangladeshis, concentrated in inner-city areas, became the main victims of attacks perpetuated by white working-class youths, especially in the East End of London. Even as late as 1993 official statistics suggested that between 130,000 and 140,000 attacks took place per annum (Panayi, 1996). By the end of the twentieth century, against the background of press and official hostility, 'asylum seekers' were becoming the victims of racist attacks (Kushner, 2006).

In this section on racism we finally need to look at extreme Right parties, which have always existed in Britain since the end of the nineteenth century. In the early post-war years the largest group consisted of Oswald Mosley's Union Movement, running parallel with the smaller League of Empire Loyalists, out of which would emerge the National Front and the British National Party. The former reached its highpoint in the early 1970s, but had its thunder stolen by Margaret Thatcher, who spoke of a Britain 'swamped' by immigrants just before the 1979 election. Only during the 1990s did the far Right, in the form of the British National Party, find its feet again. Although extremist groups have had no national electoral success in the second half of the twentieth century and only gained one local council seat in Wapping in 1993, they influenced the debate on immigration because of their perceived potential to steal voters from the mainstream (Copsey, 2004).

Debates and Interpretations

Despite the threat of the overt racists it seems tempting to accept the dominant Blairite narrative on 'the irresistible rise of multiracial Britain' (Phillips and Phillips, 1999). Such a narrative focuses upon the upward mobility of Caribbean and Asian people from the deprivations which they faced when they first arrived in the country during the early post-war decades. It would certainly seem unwise to dismiss this analysis, especially if we consider the success which many members of minorities from the Commonwealth have achieved. Similarly, newcomers and their offspring have also achieved some political power, especially in local councils, if not at the centre of government. Further, we could also point to the fact that migrants have had a significant impact upon popular culture, sport and eating patterns.

Nevertheless, we also need to look at the other side of the coin. This would show that, while some ethnic minorities have demonstrated considerable levels of success, with economic indicators better than the majority, this does not apply to others, for whom the same statistics point to a social and economic status below the majority. The narrative about the rise of multiracial Britain does not take a broad enough view. It focuses particularly upon the successes of Commonwealth migrants. It also ignores the rise of a new form of racism which evolved at the end of the twentieth century, involving government and local and national press, which fed into popular views and which dehumanized people seeking asylum into the country.

Perhaps Britain at the end of the twentieth century had become a multicultural racist state. This meant that, on the one hand, some of those who originated in the early post-war migrations from the Commonwealth, especially those from middle-class backgrounds, had experienced social and economic success. At the same time, in purely cultural terms, Britain had become far more diverse than it had been in 1945. On the other hand, some ethnic minorities experienced high levels of unemployment, immigration laws discriminated against particular racial groups and 'asylum seekers' had become the new pariahs.

Further reading

While social scientists have devoted much attention to migration in post-war Britain, historians have not. The most important historical works still include the relevant sections in two books by Colin Holme, *John Bull's Island: Immigration and British Society, 1871–1971* (Basingstoke, 1988) and *A Tolerant Country? Immigrants, Refugees and Minorities in Britain*

(London, 1991). Other general books include Jim Walvin, *Passage to Britain: Immigration in British History and Politics* (Harmondsworth, 1984) and Panikos Panayi, *The Impact of Immigration: A Documentary History of the Effects and Experiences of Immigrants and Refugees in Britain Since 1945* (Manchester, 1999). A very useful general survey is John Solomos, *Race and Racism in Modern Britain* (Basingstoke, 2003). For material addressing the migrant experience, see Kathy Burrell and Panikos Panayi, 'Immigration, History and Memory in Britain', in *Histories and Memories: Migrants and their History in Britain* (London, 2005). See also Kathleen Paul, *Whitewashing Britain: Race and Citizenship in the Post-war Era* (New York, 1997).

For refugees, see Tony Kushner, *Refugees – Then and Now* (Manchester, 2006). For the rise of multicultural Britain, see Mike and Trevor Phillips, *Windrush: The Irresistible Rise of Multi-Racial Britain* (London, 1999). For post-war racism, see especially Robin Cohen, *Frontiers of Identity: The British and the Others* (London, 1994); Paul Gilroy, *There Ain't No Black in the Union Jack: The Cultural Politics of Race and Nation* (London, 1987); and Dilip Hiro, *Black British, White British* (London, 1971). For an introduction to the history of Indian food in Britain see Panikos Panayi, 'The Spicing Up of English Provincial Life: The History of Curry in Leicester', in Anne J. Kershen (ed.) *Food in the Migrant Experience* (Aldershot, 2002): 42–76.

References

Bhachu, Parminder (1985) *Twice Migrants: East African Sikh Settlers in Britain*. London: Tavistock.

Burrell, Kathy and Panayi, Panikos (2005) 'Immigration, History and Memory in Britain', in *Histories and Memories: Migrants and their History in Britain*. London: Tauris Academic Studies.

Byron, Margaret (1994) *Post-war Caribbean Migration to Britain: The Unfinished Cycle*. Aldershot: Avebury.

Cantle, Ted (2001) *Community Cohesion: A Report of the Independent Review Team*. London: Home Office.

Copsey, Nigel (2004) *Contemporary British Fascism: The British National Party and the Search for Legitimacy*. Basingstoke: Palgrave Macmillan.

Hall, Malcolm Macalister (2003) 'The gangs of new Britain', *Independent*, 14 August.

Hickman, Mary and Walter, Bronwen (1997) *Discrimination and the Irish Community in Britain*. London: Commission for Racial Equality.

Hiro, Dilip (1971) *Black British, White British*. London: Eyre & Spottiswoode.

Kettenacker, Lothar (1996) 'The Germans after 1945', in Panikos Panayi (ed.) *Germans in Britain Since 1500*. London: Hambledon.

Kushner, Tony (2006) *Refugees – Then and Now*. Manchester: Manchester University Press.

MacPherson, William (1999) *The Stephen Lawrence Inquiry*. London: The Stationery Office.

Panayi, Panikos (1996) 'Anti-Immigrant Violence in Nineteenth and Twentieth Century Britain', in *Racial Violence in Britain in the Nineteenth and Twentieth Centuries*. London: Leicester University Press.

Paul, Kathleen (1997) *Whitewashing Britain: Race and Citizenship in the Post-war Era*. Ithaca, NY: Cornell University Press.

Phillips, Mike and Phillips, Trevor (1999) *Windrush: The Irresistible Rise of Multi-Racial Britain*. London: HarperCollins.

Scarman, Leslie George (1981) *The Brixton Disorders of 10–12 April 1981*. London: HMSO.

Singh, Gurharpal (2003) 'Multiculturalism in contemporary Britain: reflections on the "Leicester model" ', *International Journal on Multicultural Societies*, 5: 40–54.

Solomos, John (1988) *Black Youth, Racism and the State: The Politics of Ideology and Policy*. Cambridge: Cambridge University Press.

Solomos, John (2003) *Race and Racism in Modern Britain*. Basingstoke: Palgrave Macmillan.

Spencer, Ian R.G. (1997) *British Immigration Policy: The Making of Multi-Racial Britain*. London: Routledge.

17

The retreat of the state in the 1980s and 1990s

Michael J. Oliver

REVOLUTIONS IN ECONOMIC POLICY were rare events in twentieth century economic history, despite the all too frequent promises made by politicians that, if elected, they would transform the economy and society of the UK. With a quarter of a century of hindsight, however, it is clear that the election of the Conservative government in May 1979 ushered in a period of widespread economic change that had profound long-term effects on the economy and society of the UK and changed the political landscape. The incoming government believed that a series of policy mistakes in the 1970s, particularly between 1974 and 1979, had led to a crisis of the state which the existing economic philosophy could not adequately address. Several influential Conservatives believed that the root cause of the crisis was Keynesian social democracy, which had caused the build-up of fundamental problems within the UK since 1945. Over the next five years, the post-war consensus was not so much shaken up as torn apart by a government which adopted economic policies that were the antithesis of those which had formed the basis for policy making since 1944. Ironically, although her political opponents vehemently opposed many of the reforms introduced by the Conservatives in the 1980s, New Labour later came to embrace a lot of the ethos, if not the rhetoric, of Margaret Thatcher.

The new economic strategy

The rise of the new economic strategy from the mid-1970s and its association with the monetarist press, the City, businessmen and think-tanks such as the Institute of Economic Affairs was fuelled by a desire to totally transform the British economy. Behind much of the thinking lay the belief that successive post-war British governments had suppressed the role of the free market and had allowed the growth of government and its associated bureaucracy to become too invasive in people's lives. A further concern, which arose out of the particular economic circumstances of the 1970s, was that macro-economic instability was caused by inflation (which incomes policies could not control) and microeconomic inefficiency was caused by the excessive power of the trade unions which had stifled innovation, disrupted productivity and retarded economic growth.

To address these concerns, it was intended that the first priority would be to estab-lish a firm discipline for monetary policy to control inflation and provide macroeco-nomic stability. A series of policies would then be introduced to remove the state from as many areas of the economy and society as it was possible to do. This would involve 'freeing up' many of the constraints which had been placed by governments in the markets for labour, money, and goods and services. Once the shackles of government had been removed, personal and corporate taxes could be significantly reduced. This, the proponents of the new policies argued, would enable the growth of private enter-prise to resume on a scale not seen since the late nineteenth century and would be at the expense of government provision. Entrepreneurs would thrive in this new environ-ment and be encouraged to produce for consumers who would be given a far greater choice about where they purchased products, be it consumer durables, stocks and shares, education and health. For some neo-liberals there were very few places where market forces should not be allowed to go and it was the intention that government would therefore play a minimalist role in this transformed economy (gradually people would be weaned off their reliance on the state) and would ultimately be replaced by a creative, efficient and dynamic private sector.

The justification for these ideas came from theories that had undergone most of their development in the USA. One was supply-side economics, the central tenet of which is that if taxes are cut, entrepreneurs can invest their tax savings, which creates higher productivity, jobs and profits. Consumers would have more disposable income, which they would spend in the private sector. In the British context, supply-side economics came to embrace more than just tax cutting, and included reductions in trade union power, privatization, liberalization and reforms to the labour market. However, the most controversial economic theory, and one that is frequently misappropriated to describe all economic policy making after 1979, was monetarism.

Monetarists believe that inflation is always and everywhere a monetary phenomenon and argue that to control inflation it is necessary to control the money supply. In the UK, monetarism received a great deal of attention in the mid-1970s, from politicians, officials in the Bank of England and the Treasury, academics and the media, partly because the published data for the monetary aggregate £M3 (which consists predom-inantly of bank deposits in sterling) had been an excellent indicator of the rise in inflation at the time. In 1976, money supply targets had been published for the first time by the Labour government, just before the negotiations with the IMF after the sterling crisis.

The extent to which these ideas and developments fed into the reformation of economic policy within the Conservative party between 1974 and 1979 is an ongoing area of research by historians. It is clear that at least three prominent Conservatives,

Margaret Thatcher, Keith Joseph and Geoffrey Howe, played an important role in the evolution of the ideas, though Joseph acted as the leading proselytizer. Each of them believed that a counter-inflationary posture be stated and defended and made to stick. This reflected political as well as economic reasoning: they knew that the necessary measures would only be forthcoming from a government divided on almost every key economic question if its prestige was irretrievably pledged. The think-tanks, media, City experts and businessmen provided Thatcher and Joseph with a refreshing sense that there was no reason not to 'think the unthinkable' as they contemplated policies which challenged the Keynesian consensus. However, it would be quite wrong to suggest that the majority in the Conservative party shared the views that Keith Joseph was expressing and throughout the 1980s there were a group of detractors (the 'wets') who remained implacably hostile to the implementation of the bulk of the economic programme.

At the start of the 1980s, the government's economic strategy had five features:

1. Macroeconomic policy would be conducted within a medium-term perspective and not concerned with short-term issues. This would be done through a framework known as the medium-term financial strategy (MTFS).
2. The government would secure a deceleration of the growth in the money supply.
3. There was to be a more active use of monetary policy. The authorities were to announce a target aggregate for the money supply (£M3) and would raise interest rates if monetary growth appeared excessive.
4. There would be greater emphasis on controlling the public sector net cash requirement (PSNCR), which was then known as the public sector borrowing requirement. The authorities intended to use fiscal policy as a means of influencing interest rates for a given money target: by reducing the PSNCR as a percentage of gross domestic product (GDP), the money supply would not grow so quickly, and interest rates could be kept low. The PSNCR was thus an important link between monetary and fiscal policy. However, fiscal policy was not seen as a short-term policy instrument (it would be subordinate to monetary policy) and Keynesian full-employment policies would be abandoned.
5. It was believed that the instruments which previous governments had used to try to create economic growth had failed and that microeconomic policies – with an emphasis on the free market rather than state intervention and central planning – could improve the growth rate of the economy. The government would introduce a series of microeconomic reforms to strengthen the supply side of the economy. Although the supply-side strategy had not been perfectly formulated by the 1979 General Election, the government quickly provided greater incentives to work (through reductions in marginal income tax rates, reductions in unemployment and social security benefits); required more flexible wages and working practices (curtailing union power); encouraged occupational and geographical mobility of labour through government retraining schemes; and attempted to achieve a more efficient market for goods and services (facilitated by privatization).

Chronology of macroeconomic strategy

British policy makers believed that as inflation had taken a long time to become established in the UK economic system, only a gradual implementation of monetarism would prevent a big loss in output and rise in unemployment. The monetarist experiment between 1979 and 1985 was an attempt to introduce, in Chancellor Nigel Lawson's words, 'a wholly new approach to economic policy'. However, during the first 18 months of the government's first term, the ideological niceties of monetarism were quickly replaced by a political realism that recognized that permanent price stability would be an arduous struggle and not without some expensive side-effects.

The government's anti-inflation stance seemed anything but gradual: £M3 grew rapidly because of several distortions in the financial system and the authorities responded to the upward growth by raising Bank rate by two percentage points in June 1979 and a further three percentage points in November to stand at 17 per cent (a new post-war high). The economy entered a steep recession and unemployment doubled between the end of 1979 and mid-1981. For most people this was arguably a huge price to pay for the government attempting to attain its monetary targets.

Unlike the Heath government, however, the Thatcher administration was determined not to do a 'U-turn' and reverse its economic strategy. In response to its critics it unveiled the 1981 budget, where taxes were raised by 2 per cent of GDP during the steepest recession of the post-war years. This further rebuttal of Keynesian economics prompted an infamous letter to the *Times* newspaper with 364 signatories denouncing the entire monetarist strategy. As the economy began to recover from the second quarter of 1981 and inflation finally fell to single figures by 1983, the supporters of monetarism could claim that they had been vilified unjustly. However, there were a number of economists who questioned whether the fall in inflation was due to the monetarist policy and who claimed that the slowdown in inflation could be explained by the fall in world commodity prices and the contraction in aggregate demand. Moreover, it needs to be stressed that the overshooting of the money supply targets during 1980–81 and 1981–82 coupled to the upward revisions in the target ranges in the budgets of March 1982 and March 1983 greatly undermined the credibility of the government's monetary strategy. Further damage was done when new targets were introduced after Nigel Lawson became Chancellor in 1983. In essence, it appeared that the government could not control £M3 and whenever it faced difficulties, it either choose to move the target range or redefine how the money supply was measured. Consequently, monetarism lost credibility in financial markets.

By 1985, not only had the macroeconomic policy instruments evolved from their initial stance but also the overall goal of policy seemed to have wavered. Control of inflation, given pride of place in the 1980 budget, had been distilled to represent only the 'judge and jury' of monetary policy by the time of the Chancellor's Mansion House speech in October 1985. Between 1985 and 1989, economic policy exhibited all the old tendencies of Keynesian (discretionary) management: a variety of targets, poor forecasts and disagreements over policy.

With the abandonment of monetary targets in 1987, Chancellor Lawson needed a lodestar for monetary policy and he believed that joining the Exchange Rate Mechanism (ERM) of the European Monetary System would provide this. The ERM was a fixed exchange rate system and as the Prime Minister was ideologically attracted to a floating exchange rate, she did not support Lawson. Between March 1987 and March 1988 Lawson began to 'shadow' the Deutschmark, which was the lynchpin of the ERM, by pegging the rate at roughly DM3 to the pound. The extent to which the Chancellor hid the shadowing exercise from Mrs Thatcher is a moot point, but the legacy of the episode was that Mrs Thatcher relied more frequently on the advice of her personal economic adviser, Sir Alan Walters. A corollary was that the Prime Minister was alienated from Lawson and led to the financial markets doubting the instruments and objectives of policy. In October 1989, Nigel Lawson resigned and was replaced by John Major who within a year had taken the pound into the ERM. By the time Thatcher resigned the premiership in November 1990, the economy had already entered its second recession within 10 years as monetary policy was successively tightened to curb inflationary pressures of the late 1980s. At this time, it was Britain's commitment to membership of the ERM, rather than monetary targets, which proved the constraint (although membership was supported by few, if any, monetarists). Arguably, the UK entered the ERM with an overvalued exchange rate but it was not until 16 September 1992, when sterling's membership was 'suspended', that the pound was free to find its own level again.

A new monetary framework was put in place over the next two years, the most significant of which was inflation targets in 1992, but the monetary framework was made more rigid when New Labour granted independence to the Bank of England in 1997 and established a Monetary Policy Committee (MPC) charged with, and held accountable for, setting interest rates to meet the government's inflation target. The authorities had learnt from some of the criticisms directed at the MTFS in the 1980s and introduced a series of procedures that promoted openness, transparency and accountability (e.g. the publication of voting records, minutes of the monthly MPC meetings and the quarterly *Inflation Report*).

Upon taking office in May 1997, New Labour bound themselves to the spending plans outlined in the last Conservative budget in November 1996. Not content with continuing to tighten the public finances for the first two years, New Labour also published a 'Code for Fiscal Stability' in June 1998, announcing that it would follow two fiscal rules. The 'golden rule' stated that over the economic cycle, the government would only borrow to invest and not to fund current spending. The sustainable investment rule stated that over the economic cycle, the ratio of net public sector debt to GDP would be set at a 'stable and prudent' level, defined by the Chancellor as 40 per cent of GDP.

The performance of the economy

The scorecard for the Conservative government's economic record is very patchy (Table 17.1 (p. 267)). Inflation peaked at 22 per cent in May 1980 but it was not until

Table 17.1 Macroeconomic outcomes, 1975–2000

	GDP growth (%)	Inflation (RPI %)	Current account (% GDP)	Exchange rate (2000 = 100)
1975	−0.5	24.2	−1.6	115.6
1976	2.7	16.5	−0.8	100.5
1977	2.4	15.8	−0.2	96.2
1978	3.3	8.3	0.5	97.4
1979	2.7	13.4	−0.5	103.1
1980	−2.1	18.0	0.8	113.7
1981	−1.4	11.9	1.9	115.9
1982	1.9	8.6	0.8	111.5
1983	3.5	4.6	0.4	104.8
1984	2.6	5.0	−0.4	100.7
1985	3.6	6.1	−0.2	100.8
1986	4.0	3.4	−0.9	93.3
1987	4.6	4.2	−1.8	92.3
1988	5.0	4.9	−4.2	97.9
1989	2.2	7.8	−5.1	94.7
1990	0.8	9.5	−4.0	93.1
1991	−1.4	5.9	−1.8	93.8
1992	0.2	3.7	−2.1	90.5
1993	2.3	1.6	−1.9	83.0
1994	4.4	2.4	−1.0	83.5
1995	2.9	3.5	−1.3	79.9
1996	2.8	2.4	−1.0	81.0
1997	3.3	3.1	−0.2	93.7
1998	3.1	3.4	−0.5	97.1
1999	2.9	1.5	−2.7	96.9
2000	3.9	3.0	−2.6	100.0

Note: RPI inflation: average of 12-month growth rates; exchange rate: nominal effective.

Source: Based on National Statistics online (http://www.statistics.gov.uk); *International Financial Statistics*.

June 1982 that interest rates were below 10 per cent. Higher interest rates caused a sharp appreciation of sterling between 1979 and 1981, and partly as a result of higher interest rates and partly because of the second oil-price shock, the economy rapidly contracted. Although inflation fell from 1980, price stability was never obtained after 1985 and inflation ended up higher in 1989 than it had been in 1982. The UK's current account deficit widened from the mid-1980s but by 1988, the government was making the case that this was the result of private-sector decisions.

The fiscal side of the MTFS wore better than the monetary side. Although the government saw a budget deficit as poor housekeeping, it was not until 1987 that the national debt was reduced by a negative PSNCR. Contrary to the aspirations of the Prime Minister, absolute spending in real terms rose after 1979 and while spending as a percentage of GDP fell slightly, it increased again following the recession in the early 1990s. Thereafter, while general government expenditure (GGE) continued to rise, it did so at a lower rate than GGE/GDP ratio. Until 1984–85, the PSNCR remained above 3 per cent of GDP, but gradually fell to just below 1 per cent of GDP in 1986–87. During the budgets of 1987 and 1988, Lawson introduced two new fiscal directives: first, the '1 per cent borrowing rule' in 1987 (whereby a PSNCR of 1 per cent of GDP was deemed 'an appropriate destination' for the MTFS path); and, second, a commitment made in 1988 to balance the budget over the medium term. As the public finances improved from the mid-1980s (in 1987–88, the UK had its first budget surplus since 1969–70), Lawson was able to introduce a series of tax cuts in the budgets of 1986, 1987 and 1988. In March 1988 he cut taxes by over £6 billion. In March 1989 taxes were cut by a further £3.5 billion so as to achieve a gradual return to a balanced budget over the medium term. The long-term objective of fiscal policy remained a balanced budget but the fiscal position deteriorated, contributing to a higher net government debt (rising from −1 per cent of GDP in 1988–89 to 7.8 per cent of GDP in 1993–94) and a big jump in GGE.

The Conservatives believed that the performance of the British economy would be improved by competition policy and not industrial policy, which had characterized microeconomic reforms pre-1979. Privatization was a vital component of this (see 'In Focus'). Two key policies to create employment incentives in the labour market were cuts in the marginal rate of income tax and reductions in the relative value of benefits to income for the unemployed.

The incentives were badly needed as the nature of employment shifted away from manufacturing to services. This did enable more opportunities for women to enter the labour market, but there was a substantial growth in part-time work. As far as unemployment is concerned (Figure 17.1, p. 269), after 1979 there was a big rise in joblessness for men, which persisted until 1987 when a short-lived sharp fall was followed by a significant rise during the early 1990s' recession. Since 1981 unemployment has been higher among males than females, with the biggest gap appearing in 1993. Since 1993, there has been a drop in unemployment for both sexes, which was particularly significant among men. At the end of the century, however, unemployment rates were higher for males than they were in 1979, whilst for females they were falling towards their lowest level on record.

The legislative attack on trade unions dismantled many of the pre-1979 collective structures and employment regulations and led to some wide-ranging changes in labour relations. There was a sharp fall in membership between 1979 and 2002, the halving in the number of trade unions and a fall in the number of strikes. However, to

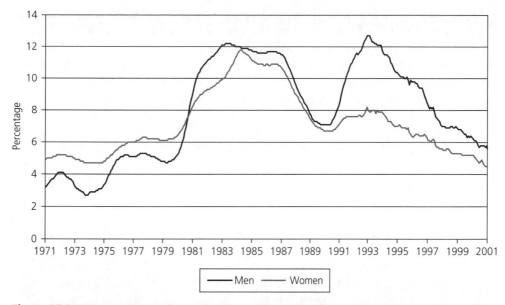

Figure 17.1 UK unemployment rates for all people aged 16 and over by sex, January–March 1971 to January–March 2001
Source: Based on *Labour Force Survey*, Historical Data (http://www.statistics.gov.uk).

focus on the decline in trade union membership since 1979 and to draw the conclusions that this was solely a product of anti-union legislation would be to ignore some other important long-term factors contributing to membership changes. For instance, both increased unemployment and the changing composition of the workforce contributed to a crisis within the trade union movement as traditional areas of union membership were disrupted by the growth in new occupations, changes in employment patterns and increasing gender mobilization.

There were some positive effects on the rate of productivity growth in the UK because of 25 years of reform, which grew substantially between 1979 and 1995 (tending to slow between 1995 and 2000), and growth is particularly marked when compared to the slowdown in growth in France, Germany, Japan and the United States. Detailed work by economists has shown this was achieved by more efficient use of physical capital, human capital and research and development. The rapid growth of productivity in manufacturing followed on from the restructuring after the 1979–81 recession and the changes in industrial relations. More generally, there was an improvement in the training of the workforce between 1979 and 2000 and a substantial increase in those with a higher or intermediate qualification.

The supply side of the economy continued to be strengthened post-1997: between 1997 and 1999 the number of small businesses in the economy grew by 170,000; literacy levels at age 11 had improved by nearly a third between 1997 and 2000; and the UK had been consistently rated by the OECD as having the lowest barriers to entrepreneurship of any major economy. In terms of halting relative economic decline (i.e. compared to OECD countries) it would be fair to say that by 1997 the pace of Britain's fall down the league table was not so evident as it had been in the 1970s; however, in terms of sustaining a non-inflationary growth rate higher than the British economy's historic long-run growth of 2 to 2.5 per cent per annum, there is no evidence that by 1997 the reforms had managed to achieve this.

In Focus

Privatization

Thatcherism became synonymous with privatization in the 1980s and the fact that more than 100 countries were adopting some variant of it led Margaret Thatcher to comment in 1992 that it was Britain's best export. Privatization in the UK was specifically about denationalization (taking industry out of the state's hands), and ownership (placing industry into the hands of shareholders). The aim of privatization tied in with the government's aspiration to liberalize the economy, which in essence meant greater competition and improved efficiency. The scale and scope of the sell-off was significant.

Between 1979 and 1997 there were around 80 firms and state-owned enterprises which were privatized with the main sectors being energy, telecommunications, water, transport equipment and services. The most popular method of privatization was to place a corporation on the stock exchange with an initial fixed price for public offering or with a minimum price tender (e.g. Rolls-Royce, the electricity companies and Railtrack). The other means comprised an employee or management buyout, trade sales and private placements. In 1979, 1.5 million people worked in public firms but with the large majority of British public firms sold off, over a million employees were transferred to the private sector. The success in the take-up of shares is revealing: between 1979 and 1993, the number of individual shareholders in British corporations rose from 3 million to over 11 million (from 7 per cent to 22 per cent of the total adult population).

It is important to note that in 1979 there was no long-term coherent plan for privatization on the scale which later took place. However, privatization came to be seen by the Conservatives as a politically useful device for accruing votes. The intention was that privatization would create a 'capital owning democracy', a phrase which complemented the desire for a 'property owning democracy'. In essence, the message to the electorate was that the Conservative party would continue to give the individual opportunities for ownership in contrast to the Labour party which was ideologically committed to state ownership of all the means of production,

Privatization

distribution and exchange. After its election victory in 1997, Labour abandoned any plans for re-nationalization and merely imposed a windfall tax on privatized utility companies.

Aside from the ideological and political niceties associated with privatization, selling off nationalized industries had two direct benefits for the state's coffers. First, it would substantially reduce the PSBR. In 1979, £3 billion was provided to public firms by way of loans but by 1989, receipts from privatization accounted for 4 per cent of the British public debt. Second, the sales would generate revenue. It has been estimated that the government's gross receipts from privatization is around £86 billion.

Although there were significant reductions in prices for the consumer and improvements in the quality of many services which had formerly been provided by state-run industries, looking a little more deeply at the economic outcomes does not paint an altogether rosy picture. In those firms which operated in a relatively competitive environment, such as the National Freight Corporation and Cable & Wireless, privatization led to an improved performance. However, with companies such as British Telecom and British Gas little initial thought was given to limiting the abuse of monopoly power and did not stem the disquiet from critics who argued that public monopolies had merely become private monopolies. For instance, British Telecom was privatized in 1984 but it was not until 1991 that its duopoly with Mercury ended and until the end of the 1990s it owned more than 90 per cent of local lines in the UK.

One of the perceived key benefits to the consumer from privatization was lower prices for goods and services. In some sectors, such as electricity, gas and coal, there were price decreases after privatization but in others, particularly water, there were considerable price rises. Some economists have suggested that ownership change might not have been the key driver for price movements but was the result of changes in market structure, exogenous changes in costs and the regulatory agencies (e.g. Ofwat, Oftel and Ofgas).

Although it would not sit comfortably with the beliefs of new Conservatism, economic historians have found that that long-term trend of productivity in Britain's nationalized industries was no lower than that for private firms. What might be even more disconcerting for supporters of privatization is recent evidence that privatization *per se* had a limited overall impact on long-term productivity trends. To be sure, there were increases in output per capita for some industries, but much of this can be explained by changes in technology. Firms were not always made more efficient once privatized, frequently because the new ownership did not provide strong incentives for innovation, productivity growth or cost savings and a price cap protected monopoly rents and eliminated the need for efficiency savings.

Persistence of social democratic values

The 1980s and 90s are frequently cited as a time when inequality widened, the public sector underwent deep cuts in expenditure and the welfare state was under constant threat by a government that was ideologically opposed to its existence. However, one of the most thorough academic assessments by Glennerster and Hills paints a more nuanced picture. Indeed, far from rolling back the welfare state, by 1996, the share of GDP spent on state-funded welfare services was greater than in 1974. Cuts were instigated in some sectors, for instance housing, but in other areas such as social security, there was growth.

One of the problems facing the Conservatives was that despite their desire to rein in public expenditure and cut taxes, concerns were expressed by the public that there were priority areas which should receive more money during successive public spending rounds and mixed evidence that cutting taxes resulted in a greater willingness to buy public goods in the private sector (e.g. health care). Evidence from the *British Social Attitudes Survey*, for example, reveals that support for the proposition that the government should 'increase taxes and spend more on health, education and social benefits' rose from 32 per cent of respondents in 1983 to 58 per cent in 1994. However, as some commentators have noted, individuals were not asked in the surveys if they themselves were willing to pay extra taxes and political parties who did espouse the arguments for higher personal taxation did not do well in successive general elections in the 1980s.

One vote-catching scheme, which worked very well for the Conservatives among the working class, was the 'right to buy' policy initiated in 1980. Tenants of council housing were given the opportunity to purchase their property from the local authority and, depending on the length of their occupation, they would qualify for a discount on the market value of the property. The 'right to buy' programme was an important element in the wider desire among senior Conservatives to create a 'property-owning democracy'. By 1995, about 1.7 million tenants had purchased a quarter of the 1980 stock of housing. As private ownership rose, so public spending on housing and housing benefit fell dramatically. The total amount spent in 1996/97 represented half the share of national income that it had in 1974/75.

Contrary to the expectations of some, the National Health Service (NHS) remained safe in Conservative hands during the 1980s and there were no attempts to introduce widespread privatization and real expenditure as a share of GDP increased by 1.1 percentage points between 1978/79 and 1995/96. However, a combination of demography and medical advance meant a widening gap between demand and supply for treatment. There were some significant changes in the organization of the NHS in the 1980s to encourage greater efficiency. One tier of administration was removed after 1982 and greater use was made of professional management techniques. There were some modest moves to encourage private medical care through loosening up of regulation designed to regulate private practice, contracting out of catering and cleaning services and providing consultants with greater opportunity for private practice. There was also the withdrawal of entitlement to free dental and eye checks and the introduction of tax relief for private medical insurance for the over sixties. From the end of the 1980s there was a more marked shift to implement private sector management techniques, the introduction of competition through an internal market and a plethora of performance targets (hospital league tables, the Patient's Charter and targets for major public health risks such as heart disease and HIV/AIDS). Even by the end of the Conservative's period in office, there was little sign of any dismantling of the NHS and of its being replaced by private health care.

An area, which for many supporters of neo-liberalism epitomized the 'dependency culture' was social security. However, despite the strong desire to reduce spending, governments after 1979 were forced to respond to increased demands on social security because of rising unemployment, a rise in economic inactivity (caused by illness, disability and early retirement), increases in the number of poor employed people and pensioners living longer. Between 1974 and 1994 there was a spectacular increase in social security spending, rising from 18 per cent of all government spending to 31 per cent respectively. The key thing to note about social security expenditure over 1979–97 was the rise in means-tested spending which fitted in with the emphasis by the Conservatives on the long-term goal of targeting welfare more effectively to the poor. Coupled to an increase in means testing, the government wanted to ensure adequate work incentives by reducing the relative value of benefits to income for the unemployed, which would close down the unemployment trap.

By 1997 there had been considerable progress made in mitigating the effect of the unemployment trap but, at the same time, the poverty trap had become more pronounced again. The poverty trap is caused by the extension of means testing which reduces benefit as income rises and simultaneously increases the incidence of tax and social security contributions. Although the worst excesses of the poverty trap were reduced over the period, the number of families that faced a tax rate of over 50 per cent increased.

Finally, there is the rise in inequality after 1979. A number of factors influenced this including the change in the taxation system towards indirect tax (which was more regressive on the poor), the abolition of earnings-related unemployment benefit and more stringent conditions which were attached to benefit payments. The most cited indicator of inequality is the Gini coefficient, which has an estimated value between 0 and 1, where 0 corresponds with perfect equality (where everyone has the same income) and 1 corresponds with perfect inequality (where one person has all the income, and everyone else has zero income). Figure 17.2 (p. 274) plots the Gini coefficient and an alternative indicator, the 90:10 ratio (the ratio of the incomes of households at the 90th and 10th percentiles), between 1961 and 2002/03. The Gini coefficient shows that the level of inequality was fairly stable throughout the 1960s and most of the 1970s but began rising from 1978 and rose sharply in the 1980s and peaked under the Conservatives in 1992. However, after stabilizing in the mid-1990s it continued its upward rise under New Labour, peaking during 2000/01 before falling slightly. The 90:10 ratio shows a steeper increase in inequality between 1985 and 1991, a sharper fall between 1992 and 1996/97 and only a marginal fall after the election of New Labour.

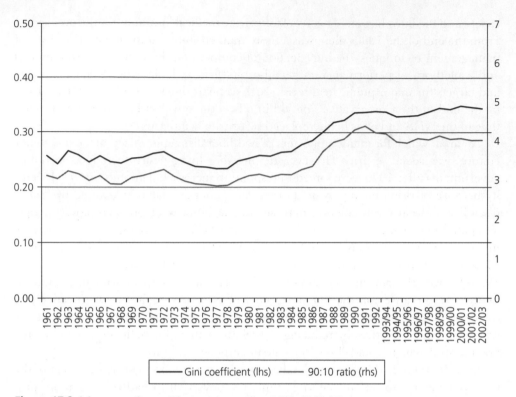

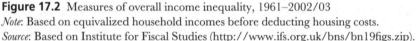

Figure 17.2 Measures of overall income inequality, 1961–2002/03
Note: Based on equivalized household incomes before deducting housing costs.
Source: Based on Institute for Fiscal Studies (http://www.ifs.org.uk/bns/bn19figs.zip).

Debates and Interpretations

The distinctive features about economic policy making in this period was the emphasis placed by policy makers on focusing on the medium term (through the MTFS) rather than the short term; the belief that money supply targets could control the growth of inflation rather than incomes policies; and the emphasis placed on rules and discipline as opposed to the discretion of the Keynesian regime.

The government's economic strategy rejected the post-war consensus but it was not until the Mais Lecture in 1984 that Chancellor Nigel Lawson provided its most cogent intellectual justification. Lawson argued that job creation could not be left to government macroeconomic policies; indeed, government could not guarantee full employment. The conquest of inflation, not the pursuit of unemployment, should be the objective of macroeconomic policy. *Per contra*, microeconomic (or supply-side) policy should be designed so as to create conditions conducive to growth and employment. Given the practical demonstration by the Thatcher government of such a credo from a very early stage, the considerable amount of public comment which this lecture provoked might seem surprising but it attracted such interest for two reasons.

First, it was a restatement of the government's approach to the conduct of economic policy. Why this should have been necessary is interesting. Perhaps Nigel Lawson wanted to make clear that he was as committed a 'monetarist' as his predecessor; although, ironically, Lawson became considerably less so within a year of the Mais Lecture. Alternatively, perhaps the Chancellor wished to make it clear that in spite of the economic recovery, the government did not propose any 'job creation' measures on traditional Keynesian lines.

The second reason was that this speech turned the post-war consensus once and for all on its head. At the time, there were many who accused the government of standing idly by and watching unemployment rise to levels not seen since the early 1930s and there were even those who argued that the policies of the Thatcher government were the sole cause of the sharp rise in unemployment. It was not the case that the government deliberately aimed to create mass unemployment, but the government's tough stance on unemployment (most notably exemplified by Norman Tebitt's comments in 1981 that the unemployed should 'get on their bikes' to look for work) created a new realism in the labour market.

The Conservative government made a more intense effort to focus on the supply side of the economy after the 1983 election victory, although some would point to the legislation that was introduced to roll back the frontiers of the state as conflicting with the philosophy espoused by the Conservatives that the best government was the least government. The government did not intend to add to 'red tape', however, but wished to remove what it saw as major obstacles to economic growth.

Trade union reform, for instance, was undertaken to restrict and regulate union activity in British society. The way to do this was to remove the 'special privileges' enjoyed by unions (e.g. closed shops) and expose them to common law (e.g. mandatory elections and ballots). *Conservative policy did not seek to abolish or outlaw the unions*; policy makers saw the issue more in terms of choice, albeit regulated choice. Employees must be free to choose whether they wished to join a union and union members must freely make decisions about union policy and activities, but the decision-making procedures must accord with the new legal framework, imposed by the government.

To be sure, the arguments will continue over the extent to which the supply side of the economy was improved, whether the spirit of individual free enterprise was revived, how far socialism was destroyed, whether Britain's economic status was transformed and so on. Yet many social and cultural changes cannot be picked up by an economic balance sheet alone and some defy quantitative assessment. How, for instance, can it be ascertained whether neo-liberalism produced a greedier society, which is the claim of some critics? The fact that annual charitable giving in the UK doubled in real terms between 1979 and 1997 would perhaps not satisfy the detractors who would rather focus on the persistence of inequalities in society and the interests of the individual over the needs of a community. The question of how much of this is caused or can be cured by 'the state' (whether in retreat or otherwise engaged) and how much is due to wider forces outside the remit of government remains an unresolved question.

Plate 17.1 Demonstrator in a Margaret Thatcher mask. Prime Minister Margaret Thatcher announced her resignation in November 1990 (© Corbis).

Even in areas of distinct economic success, such as the pre-eminence of London as a financial centre, negatives can be found. One experienced dealer, reflecting on his time at a City firm between 1983 and 1988, noted that:

> The occupants of our offices were a strange mixture, combining dynamically ruthless but bright Americans, a mixture of extremely clever Englishmen and other Europeans, and a number of barrow-boys who, with their cockney accents and flash suits, were making fortunes as traders. This was a typical reflection of the Thatcher years when talent in any form was amply rewarded on the basis of merit and it was no bar to success that a young trader, when entertaining a client to lunch, might stick his half-masticated chewing-gum under the dining-room table. (Kynaston, 2001: 716–17)

Yet for those who decry this probably atypical description of change in the City during the 1980s, there will be others who argue that in a microcosm, this was the whole purpose of the reforms after 1979: to encourage increases in social mobility, the break-up of closed shops and vested interests, the rise of individualism and the spirit of entrepreneurship.

Further reading

There have been a number of interesting studies done on the post-1979 period although, for obvious reasons, many have been written without recourse to archival sources and when the full implications of the reforms have yet to be felt. For a publication that has used some of the material in the Thatcher archive at Churchill College, see E.H.H. Green, *Thatcher* (London, 2006). On changing the climate of opinion, see R. Cockett, *Thinking the Unthinkable: Think-tanks and the Economic Counter-revolution, 1931–1983* (London, 1995). On the political economy of the Conservative years, see Andrew Gamble, *Free Economy and the Strong State* (Basingstoke, 1994) and Simon Jenkins, *Accountable to None: Tory Nationalization of Britain* (Edinburgh, 1995). Although it only covers the first eight years after 1997, Andrew Britton, *Macroeconomic Policy in Britain 1974–1987* (Cambridge, 1991) is essential reading on the evolution of macroeconomic policy. On the important changes to monetary policy in this period, see Michael J. Oliver, *Whatever Happened to Monetarism?* (London, 1998) and David Cobham, *The Making of Monetary Policy in the UK, 1975–2000* (Chichester, 2000). On the changes to the labour market, see D. Card, R. Blundell and R.B. Freeman (eds) *Seeking a Premier Economy: The Economic Effects of British Economic Reforms, 1980–2000* (Chicago, 2004). On privatization, see M. Florio, *The Great Divestiture: Evaluating the Welfare Impact of the British Privatisation, 1979–1997* (New York, 2004). For an assessment of one of the most successful sectors of the economy post-1979, see David Kynaston, *The City of London – Volume 4, A Club No More: 1945–2000* (London, 2001). For a series of annual surveys since 1983 charting continuity and change in British social, economic, political and moral values in relation to other changes in society, see *British Social Attitudes Survey* (http://www.britsocat.com). On the welfare reforms between 1979 and 1997, see Howard Glennerster and John Hills (eds) *The State of Welfare: The Economics of Social Spending* (Oxford, 1998) and Rodney Lowe, *Welfare State in Britain since 1945*

(Basingstoke, 2004). For an account which places the post-1979 changes into a long-run perspective, see Nick Crafts, *Britain's Relative Economic Performance, 1870–1999* (London, 2002). For an assessment of the post-1945 period, see Roger Middleton, *The British Economy since 1945* (Basingstoke, 2000). For an insider's view, see Nigel Lawson, *View from Number 11* (London, 1992) and Margaret Thatcher, *The Path To Power* (London, 1995).

References

Kynaston, David (2001) *The City of London – Volume 4, A Club No More: 1945–2000.* London: Pimlico.

18

Trade unions: Rise and decline

Chris Wrigley

IN 1979 UK TRADE UNIONISM reached its peak membership of 13,289,000 of whom 71.8 per cent were male. After that its decline was longer than in previous set-backs and was marked by a substantial collapse in the private sector of the economy. When it stabilized at the start of the twenty-first century it was still stronger than trade unionism had been at its peak in France, a country where trade unionism had been historically weak (UK union density in 2003 being 29 per cent whereas French density had only reached 21.4 per cent, in 1975) (see Table 18.1, p. 280).

This chapter provides an analysis of the rise and decline of British trade unions since 1945 and a discussion of the explanations that have been offered.

The pattern of union membership in the period of growth

One of the major reasons given for trade union decline after 1979 is major changes in the structure of the workforce. While this is true, it is less commonly commented that the years of major growth after the Second World War also saw changes in the structure of the workforce, with the labour forces of many of the heavily unionized sectors of earlier years diminishing markedly in the three decades after the Second World War. Table 18.2 (p. 280) reports the substantial shrinkage in employment in several sectors of traditional trade union strength between 1948 and 1974, in which the overall number of trade unionists in the occupations in Table 18.2 dropped by 52.5 per cent yet the high trade union density in each case rose a little. In terms of British trade unionism these five areas had amounted to 11.2 per cent of the total in 1913, 7.2 per cent in 1948 but only 3.0 per cent in 1974.

Nevertheless, there was growth in employment in numbers of trade unionists in some sectors of traditional trade union strength. These included metals and engineering,

Table 18.1 UK trade union membership (thousands)

(a) Certification Officer data

Year	Males	Density	Females	Density	Total	Density (of all)
1950	7,605	54.6	1,684	23.7	9,289	44.1
1960	7,884	54.2	1,951	25.4	9,835	44.2
1970	8,444	58.2	2,743	32.1	11,187	48.5
1980	9,162		3,790		12,947	52.9
1990	6,195		3,753		9,947	40.5

(b) Labour Force Surveys data

Year	Total	(a) density (of employees only)	(b) density (of all)
1990	9,100	38.1	
2000	7,580	29.5	27.1
2001	7,550	29.1	26.8

Note: The Certification Officer's data includes retired members, overseas members and counts twice those in two unions. The *Labour Force Surveys* eliminate that but can count staff association members as trade unionists. In Britain usually density is the proportion of trade unionists among all employees and those unemployed; but the LFS figures on density as a proportion of employees is useful in comparisons, as some other countries only measure this.

Source: Based on Bain and Price, 1980: 38; Visser, 1989: 241; *Labour Market Trends*, May 1995: 191–209, and July 2002: 349.

Table 18.2 Employment and trade union strength in selected sectors in Britain

	Employment (thousands)		Trade union density (%)	
	1948	1974	1948	1974
Coal mining	800.1	314.1	86.4	96.1
Cotton[1]	350.1	147.7	78.3	100.0[3]
Ports[2]	150.7	79.2	92.9	94.4
Railways	535.3	223.2	88.7	92.8
Sea transport	150.5	89.8	74.9	96.3

1 Includes also flax and man-made fibres.
2 Includes also inland water transport.
3 Overstated because retired and unemployed counted by some smaller textiles unions.

Source: Based on Bain and Price, 1980: 39–40, 45, 51, 67 and 69–70.

where, between 1948 and 1974, trade union membership grew from 1,913,700 to 2,805,700 (with the density rising from 54.5 to 69.0 per cent), with the rise for printing and publishing being from 206,700 to 332,200 (75.8 to 92.2 per cent), chemicals, 141,500 to 233,600 (35.3 to 48.4 per cent) and electricity, 101,000 to 190,000 (64.2 to

Table 18.3 Trade unionism in selected sectors of white-collar work in Britain, 1948–1974

	Membership (000s)			Density (%)		
	1948	1968	1974	1948	1968	1974
Local government and education	860.9	1,366.8	1,831.6	69.4	61.5	67.9
Central government	400.3	493.3	593.2	56.5	81.1	100.0
Insurance, banking and finance	138.9	250.7	328.8	29.2	33.1	37.9

Source: Based on Bain and Price, 1980: 74, 76 and 78.

100.0 per cent). There were also notable rises in bricks and building materials, glass, pottery, water, air transport and distribution.

Yet the most notable development was the rapid expansion of white-collar trade unionism, especially after 1964. Between 1951 and 1979 there was a rapid expansion of white-collar employment, rising from just under a third to a half of the British labour force. Between 1951 and 1968 white-collar trade unionism grew by nearly 30 per cent but did not keep up with the expansion in such jobs, but from the mid-1960s unionization accelerated and the proportion of the white-collar workforce who were trade unionists went up. By 1979 about 44 per cent of all white-collar workers were in trade unions, and the characteristic trade unionist was now a white-collar worker, not a miner, engine driver or docker. Between 1948 and 1974 unionization in central government rose from a density of 56.5 per cent to 100 per cent, while in insurance, banking and finance it rose from 29.2 to 37.9 in the same period (see Table 18.3). The Association of Scientific, Technical and Managerial Staffs (ASTMS), under the dynamic and publicity-conscious Clive Jenkins, was the fastest growing union in the TUC in 1968 to 1974, increasing its membership by 531 per cent. While part of its increase in size stemmed from its merger with smaller unions, it was notably successful in recruiting in engineering and also the aircraft and chemical sectors.

The late 1960s also saw the start of the rapid catching up of unionization among women. There were more women in paid work, perhaps a third more than in the late 1940s. The proportion of women workers unionized had hovered between 23 and 26 per cent between 1945 and the late 1960s, but from 1968 moved upwards, reaching an average of 40 per cent in 1976–80.

Explaining growth, 1945–79

Substantial trade union growth in what has been called 'the golden age' of the international economy (1950–73) was common in many industrialized economies. European and US labour had prospered in the economic boom after the First World War, with trade unionism in Britain reaching a density of 48.2 per cent in 1920, which was not surpassed until 1974. Trade unionism also prospered in most industrialized countries for much of the 1950s, 60s and early 70s (see Table 18.3, p. 281).

Decline in union density did not set in for Denmark or Sweden in these years. Britain and Germany peaked in 1979, whereas Austria had peaked in 1971 and France in 1975, with Italy later, in 1980, and Norway in 1981 (after an earlier peak in 1964). In terms of numbers the Netherlands peaked in 1978, but in terms of density its trade unionism experienced a slow slide down from 1951.

Most explanations of trade union growth have involved a mixture of economic causes with more particular ones such as government actions, employers' policies and changing industrial structures. Various econometric studies of the rate of change of trade union membership have found that the rates of change of retail prices, wages and unemployment are the most significant of the economic causes. During 1968–79, as during 1915–19, marked inflation seems to have been the motivation for unionization among groups hitherto weakly unionized as they felt their wages were being left behind by more strongly organized groups of employees. However, earlier in the post-Second World War period there was inflation, albeit less severe, in 1950–2 and 1959–62, which was not accompanied by rapid trade union growth. Perhaps, it takes a certain level of inflation to provide the required motivation. With regard to employment, a strong labour market has usually been a prerequisite for trade union growth.

Another suggested general encouragement to trade union growth has been a favourable political environment. Bruce Western, in a study of trade union growth between 1950 and 1990 in 18 industrialized countries, argued that trade unionism was strongest where it was helped by working-class parties holding office and favouring the trade unions, where national collective bargaining enabled the unions to coordinate their efforts and where trade union management of welfare schemes enabled them to hold the loyalty of their members. In Britain the public sector had been extended by the nationalization, notably of coal, steel and the public utilities, and the setting up of the National Health Service. By 1979 nearly 30 per cent of employees were in the public sector and in it there was widespread national collective bargaining. Between 1945 and 1970, and 1974 and 1979 (or perhaps 1945 and 1979) both Labour and Conservative governments recognized trade unions as a major interest in the state and through the National Economic Development Council (NEDC) from 1961 consulted them on broad economic issues.

There was also a correlation between levels of strike activity and trade union membership. Good economic conditions and low unemployment are favourable conditions for strikes, especially if the employees are suffering from a squeeze on their real wages (the level of wages relative to the level of the cost of living). Often people join a union for the safety of numbers when a strike seems imminent and also people are encouraged to join after successful strikes deliver higher wages and better conditions of work. Trade unions which deliver success are likely to grow. Trade unions operating in political climates favourable or neutral to trade unions are more likely to be successful.

Trade union success is also more likely when public opinion and popular culture is favourable to them. British trade unions emerged from the Second World War with

Plate 18.1 Members of the Electrical Trades Union march through London to demonstrate against the refusal of their pay claims, 1954 (© Corbis).

considerable public prestige. Ernest Bevin, the powerful Secretary of the Transport and General Workers Union, had been Minister of Labour and National Service, 1940–45, and, after Churchill, one of the most powerful wartime ministers, and the trade unions generally were considered to have played a major role in the mobilization of the domestic economy for war. Churchill in 1947 referred to the unions as 'a long established and essential part of our life' and 'pillars of our British society' and for many years the Conservative party sought cooperation from the trade union movement.

However, public and political perceptions of the trade unions changed during the 1950s and 60s. In this period the interwar malaise of high unemployment had not recurred but concern grew about increasing inflation in an economy of near full employment. There was also much public alarm at persistent wildcat strikes in several industries, notably docks, car making and print. Strike-happy workforces and hide-bound trade unionists were memorably portrayed in such British films as *Chance Of A Lifetime* (1950), with its theme of the need for both sides of industry to work together, the popular Peter Sellers film *I'm All Right Jack* (1960), which made the same point satirically and more chilling, and *The Angry Silence* (1960), about a man whose fellow workers 'sent him to Coventry' (avoided speaking to him). These stereotypes of trade unionists were also reinforced by a range of comedies, including the 1960s television series *The Rag Trade* (with the shop steward's catchphrase 'Everybody out') to such films in the 'Carry On' series as *Carry On Cabby* (1963) and *Carry On At Your Convenience* (1971). Public opinion polls showed rising proportions of respondents saying that trade unions had too much power: from 62 per cent in 1964 to 73 per cent in 1970 and 81 per cent in October 1974 and in 1979. The later figures reflected concern over clashes between Edward Heath's government (1970–74) and the unions and the widespread strikes of early 1979 ('the Winter of Discontent'). Such signs of popular alienation during the later years of growth were to contribute to the conditions enabling hostile governments after 1979 to act against the trade unions.

As well as general reasons for trade union growth, there have been more specific reasons suggested for parts of the workforce. In the case of white-collar workers George Bain in his classic study *The Growth of White-Collar Unionism* (1970) stated that the degree of concentration of employment, the willingness or otherwise of employers to recognize trade unions, and the extent to which government action promoted trade union recognition boosted membership. He also argued that white-collar workers joined unions 'not so much to obtain economic benefits as to be able to control more effectively their work situation'. However, the serious inflation of the early 1970s greatly encouraged trade union membership as many white-collar workers were fearful that their real wages would be squeezed and that other comparable groups would secure better pay rises, leaving them behind.

The pattern of trade union membership in the years of decline

British trade union membership fell for more years and much further between 1979 and 1998 than even during the bad interwar years. Membership fell by around 40 per cent, but as the basis of the figures changed in the late 1980s some caution needs to be exercised in being precise. Trade union density fell from 53 to about 30 per cent and stabilized within about 1 per cent lower over the next six years. At 29 per cent it was higher than in 1926–36 and any time before 1917.

There was a continued contraction of the old bastions of trade unionism. There was a substantial loss of jobs in much of manufacturing industry, mining and the docks. The most dramatic fall was in coal mining, from a workforce of 235,000 in 1979 to some 2,600 in 2003. Yet, even when privatized, trade union membership held up better in such areas than much of the private sector. In 1999 union density in electricity, gas and water supply was 52 per cent, transport and communications 42 per cent, mining and quarrying 37 per cent and manufacturing 28 per cent. However, by the early twenty-first century trade unionism was generally weak in the private sector. The government-sponsored *Workplace Employment Relations Survey* in 2004 found that in workplaces with 10 or more employees union density ranged from 22 per cent in the private sector to 64 per cent in the public sector.

The period after 1979 also saw a very marked shrinkage in the number of employees covered by collective bargaining. Between 1984 and 1990 the percentage of those covered fell from 71 to 54 and by 2001 it was at 36. There were wide variations, with coverage in 2001 in the private sector at 22 per cent of the workforce whereas in the public sector it was at 73 per cent. It was also, then, a feature of larger workplaces, with 44 per cent of those with 25 or more employees covered whereas only 12 per cent of the smaller workplaces were. This reflected a weakness of trade unionism, that employers did not feel the need to negotiate. It was also a cause, weakness making it less attractive to join or remain a member.

While the overall picture was of substantial membership losses, these were less severe among female workers. Whereas in 1946 18 per cent of British trade unionists were female, in 2002 47 per cent were. Between 1946 and 1979 female trade union density rose from 24.5 to 40.4 per cent. This was due to such features of the labour market as fewer women were employed in the industries affected by severe job losses and more were in the service sectors; women were more often part time and paid less, so being more attractive to employers seeking cheap and flexible labour.

The very serious fall in membership also strongly encouraged unions not to be dilatory in recruiting workers from ethnic communities. While many trade union leaders and activists had been involved in local community relations councils formed from the late 1960s and anti-racist campaigns, matters had not always been so positive, especially on the shopfloor. By the mid-1990s union densities among black male and female workers were higher than among white workers. According to the *Labour Force Survey* data 42 per cent of black female and 39 per cent of male black workers were in unions compared to 29 per cent of white female and 35 per cent of white male workers; with the figures for Indian workers being 27 per cent for women and 30 per cent for men.

In the years of decline the trade unions also made greater efforts for equality on behalf of other workers. The TUC held a series of disability forums, was a supporter of the Disability Rights Commission (formed in 2000) and its *Louder than Words* campaign, and ran an annual disability conference from 2001. The TUC also made efforts to secure greater equality of treatment for lesbian and gay workers, setting up a Lesbian and Gay Committee to secure anti-discrimination legislation and held annual delegate conferences from 1998.

So by the early years of the twenty-first century British trade unionism had declined very substantially. Yet it was still substantial, compared to past trade union strength in France and some other countries. It had also moved a long way from being overwhelmingly male, with the dominant tone set by 'the big battalions' in classic industrial sectors such as iron and steel, engineering, coal mining, textiles, docks and railways. While gender and racial equality had a long way to go at the top of union hierarchies, the remaining trade union membership was a better reflection of the composition of the labour force.

However, the decline was nevertheless very serious. With the decline in collective bargaining, the trade unions had lost a major role. British industrial relations in much of the private sector and in increasing parts of the diminished public sector was marked by employers bringing in individualized patterns of pay and conditions of employment. While the Blair governments provided some protection for the poorest paid with minimum pay and some employment protection rights, they responded to globalization with insistence on labour flexibility and economic policies intended to minimize inflation. As a result, the trade unions looked to legal rights and their enforcement rather than to voluntaryism to protect their members and potential members.

Explaining decline: after 1979

In Britain the political climate became strongly anti-trade union from 1979. The Conservative party had seen the 1971 Trade Union Act discredited by concerted trade union opposition and Edward Heath's government had fallen when it clashed with the National Union of Miners (NUM) in early 1974. The British public increasingly believed during the 1970s that the trade union leaders were overpowerful and the widespread industrial unrest of 1979, most of which was a revolt against the Labour government's tightening incomes policy, outraged many people. As a result, Margaret Thatcher, the Conservative party leader, cast aside cautiousness on trade unions and made it clear that should she form a government the powers of the trade unions would be limited. This was carried out by a series of eight legislative measures which dealt with trade unions and employment laws between 1980 and (under her successor, John Major) 1993.

This legislation undoubtedly had a considerable impact on the trade unions. It affected the way trade unions could engage in industrial disputes. Under the Employment Act 1980, picketing was only lawful at the strikers' own workplace. Later legislation required secret ballots before strikes could be held, while the Trade Union Reform and Employment Rights Act 1993 required that employers should not only be given seven days' notice of strikes but be provided with lists of employees involved. There were also measures giving dissatisfied union members financial help to take legal action against their union, restricted employee rights against employers and ended various help to extend collective bargaining.

The 1980–93 Conservative governments' legislation marked a major shift away from the predominantly voluntary system of industrial relations which had evolved from at least the 1890s and had been underpinned by the Trade Disputes Act 1906. Other than during the two World Wars, the British system was based on free collective bargaining and relatively little direct state intervention. In contrast, after 1979 there was an extensive legal framework and clear government disapproval of trade unionism and collective bargaining.

However, a major part of the legislation's impact was the signal it gave that the government was hostile to the trade unions. While many employers, as with the earlier Conservative government's Industrial Relations Act 1971, did not use the provisions of the new laws, others did. In such a political climate there were more dangers and fewer

Table 18.4 Trade union membership in European countries, 1950–1980 (membership in thousands, density in %)

	1950		1960		1970		1980	
	Membership	Density	Membership	Density	Membership	Density	Membership	Density
Austria	12,90.6	62.3	1,501.0	63.4	1,520.3	62.1	1,661.0	58.4
Denmark	777.1	58.1	968.9	63.1	1,195.1	64.4	1,801.5	79.8
France	3,861	–	2,592	–	3,549	21.3	3,374	17.3
Germany (W)	5,751.1	34.7	7,778.6	38.3	8,232.9	37.6	9,590.0	41.0
Italy	5,830.4	49.0	3,907.6	29.6	5,530.1	38.3	9,005.8	54.4
Netherlands	1,214.6	43.0	1,398.8	41.8	1,575.8	39.7	1,722.3	35.5
Norway	488.4	50.2	662.8	62.8	764.0	62.9	1,056.9	62.7
Sweden	1,612.8	67.7	1,971.7	73.0	2,557.4	73.2	3,502.6	88.0
UK	9,289	44.1	9,835	44.2	11,187	48.5	12,947	52.9

Note: The union density represents the proportion of the workforce who legally could join a union (with unemployed included). The West Germany, Italy, Netherlands and Sweden figures include retired members.

Source: Based on Visser, 1989: 22, 42, 71, 96, 120, 152, 175, 197 and 241.

advantages in trade union membership. Moreover, the Conservative political ascendancy was buttressed by much support for free market economic theories which deemed trade unions to be impediments to economic growth.

Nevertheless, it would be a mistake to ascribe trade union decline to Margaret Thatcher's ability to 'tame the trade unions'. For similar developments were occurring not only in countries with similar Right governments, notably President Reagan's USA, but also in others of very different political complexions. Just as trade unionism had grown in a range of industrial countries during the 'golden years' of the international economy (1950–73), so it declined in most industrial countries from the late 1970s (see Table 18.4).

The British economy, like those of other early industrialized nations, was diversifying; its structure changing from large units of industrial production to smaller companies, more professional services and, by the early twenty-first century, very large numbers of people (as many as 4 million) working mostly from home. There were also increased numbers of part-time workers, who were predominantly female. These were all developments likely to result in lower rates of unionization, though the trade unions were trying to recruit in these areas.

While the return of a Labour government under Tony Blair in 1997 lifted outright political hostility to the trade unions, there remained a government ethos of praising and encouraging labour flexibility. Most employees did not feel an economic pressure to join a union, especially if membership was frowned upon, as was the case in much of the private sector. Also, just as success bred success, decline was a disincentive for some people in some sectors of the economy to join a trade union. So by the early years of the twenty-first century the rate of trade union decline had become slow but appeared not to have been halted, let alone reversed. It remained the case that disabled, black, female and low-paid male labour in unions secured higher pay ('the trade union mark-up') and better conditions of work than did non-unionized labour. British trade unionism retained a core membership, especially in the public sector of the economy.

In Focus

The 1984–85 coal-mining dispute

The 1984–85 coal dispute centred on the National Union of Miners' (NUM) determination to try to stop the closure of a substantial number of pits.

In this there were echoes of the major disputes of 1921 and 1926 when the miners had to try to lessen proposed substantial pay cuts at a time when prices for coal were falling. These disputes of 1921, 1926 and 1984–5 contrasted with 1972 and 1974 when oil was scarce and energy prices generally were rising. Then the NUM was able to secure its demands in spite of a hostile Conservative government, the Heath government losing office in 1974 after a poor general election result in an election centred on the mining dispute.

In March 1982 Arthur Scargill, who had come to prominence as a notably militant miners' leader in the 1972 dispute, became President of the NUM. He soon campaigned on the National Coal Board's (NCB) plans to close pits, specifically claiming in December 1982 that 'over an eight-year period the Board appears to be planning to close 95 pits with the loss of 70–100,000 jobs'. The NCB's view was that it was trying to reduce surplus capacity, thereby bringing output into line with the anticipated future demand for coal. In the early 1980s there was a fall in demand for coal. The consumption of coal by power stations fell from 89.1 to 80.8 million tonnes while other domestic users' consumption fell from 39.3 to 29.6 million tonnes in 1979/80 to 1982/3. By 1983 there were losses, not profits, in the deep-mining sector, though the opencast operations remained profitable.

Margaret Thatcher's Conservative government (1979–1990) was against subsidizing nationalized industries as far as possible. Moreover, from 1978 Margaret Thatcher and her colleagues were prepared to defeat the NUM if there was a further confrontation as in 1974. This came in March 1984.

Earlier, Scargill failed three times to secure sufficient support in the NUM for a national strike. Under the chairmanship of Norman Siddall, the NCB rationalized production gradually by closing collieries one by one after local negotiations. However, he was succeeded in September 1983 by Ian MacGregor, who had won plaudits from the government for the tough way he had cut the labour force at the British Steel Corporation.

The 1984–85 coal-mining dispute

The dispute was sparked off by the local announcement of the closure of Cortonwood pit (located between Barnsley and Doncaster). There was anger that over £1 million had recently been invested in the pit by the NCB and that the announcement breached the agreed closure procedure. The Cortonwood miners went on strike on 4 March with many other pits following the next day. The dispute ended a year later, on 5 March 1985 without an agreed settlement.

The NUM was defeated for several major reasons. Ian MacGregor and the government were determined to win and the government readily deployed the state's financial and law-and-order resources to achieve this. The NCB and the government took great pains to put their case to the public, the NCB spending £4,566,000 on press advertising. Another crucial aspect was that the government had large stockpiles of coal and was ready to import more, as well as demonstrating its ability to move coal by road to the power stations.

The coal dispute brought out the inherent sectionalism within the NUM. Areas such as Nottingham, the Midlands, Leicestershire and South Derbyshire had richer coal reserves and seemed less at risk. The miners were not united in anger as they had been in 1972 and 1974 over the erosion of their real wages. Indeed, many of the older miners were attracted by the £1000 per year of service redundancy terms on offer. The failure to hold a national ballot (on the basis that those in safe areas could vote others out of their jobs) undermined the legitimacy of the strike in some miners' and many of the public's views. The working miners formed the breakaway Union of Democratic Miners (UDM), which failed to gain as much support as initially expected. It was based on the Nottinghamshire and South Derbyshire miners and the 1300 strong Colliery Workers and Allied Trades Association.

In the other mining areas there was notable support for the strike. Women's support groups played a major role in sustaining the strike. The real threat of mass pit closures threatened not just male jobs, but also whole communities. After the strike, the remaining mines were privatized. By early 2005 there were only eight major deep mines in production, one in south Wales and seven in the Midlands and Yorkshire. In some areas the closure of the mines led not only to unemployment, but also a variety of social problems.

Debates and Interpretations

One major area of controversy has been whether the state should play a major role in industrial relations and, historically, whether it has.

For over three decades after the Second World War the British system of industrial relations, like the British Parliament, was praised as an especially effective model. Otto Kahn-Freund, a refugee from Nazi Germany and an eminent legal scholar, wrote in

Alan Flanders and Hugh Clegg's highly influential 1954 book, *The System of Industrial Relations in Britain*:

> The desire of both sides of industry to provide for, and to operate, an effective system of collective bargaining is a stronger guarantee of industrial peace and of smooth functioning of labour-management relations than any action legislators or courts or enforcement officers can ever hope to undertake . . . there exists something like an inverse correlation between the practical significance of legal sanctions and the degree to which industrial relations have reached a state of maturity . . . There is, perhaps, no major country in the world in which the law has played a less significant role in the shaping of these relations then in Great Britain and in which today the law and the legal profession have less to do with labour relations.

With rising inflation and high-profile wildcat strikes in some strike-prone industries, such as in motor-car manufacturing, Harold Wilson's Labour government (1964–70) proposed taking some legislative action (with its White Paper *In Place of Strife*, 1969) and Edward Heath's Conservative government (1970–74) did, with the Industrial Relations Act 1971. While that was repealed, as we have seen, substantial legislation was brought in by Conservative governments in 1980 to 1993.

Yet, there was more to state intervention affecting industrial relations and so the unions than laws. Free collective bargaining was substantially affected by a series of incomes policies from 1961 to 1979. These policies were strongly opposed at the time by trade union leaders such as Frank Cousins, Secretary of the Transport and General Workers Union. At the same time as Harold Macmillan's Conservative government (1957–63) pressed ahead with an incomes policy, it institutionalized consultations with the trade unions in the National Economic Development Council (NEDC) which operated from 1962 to 1992 (but with less influence after 1979). At the NEDC the government discussed broad economic issues with representatives of the Confederation of British Industry (CBI), the employers' organization, and the TUC.

Professor Keith Middlemas aroused considerable controversy when, in 1979, he published *Politics in Industrial Society*, which argued that British governments since the First World War had exhibited 'corporate bias'. He suggested that the trade unions and employers' organizations had become part of the 'governing institutions' of the country, although unlike governments they had not been democratically elected by the population as a whole. He also suggested that such 'corporate bias' played a part in Britain avoiding the extreme unrest experienced between the wars in the rest of Europe. While governments did consult both sides of industry, especially in the late 1930s with rearmament, historians generally have rejected notions of 'corporation' or 'corporate bias' in these years or, indeed, for 1945–60. The more substantial involvement came in 1962–79. However, even when the powerful trade union leaders Jack Jones, General Secretary of the Transport and General Workers Union, and Hugh Scanlon, General Secretary of the Amalgamated Engineering Union, played a major role in constructing 'the Social Contract' in the 1970s, they did not have a substantial wider impact on the Labour government's economic policies. With 'the Social Contract', the trade unions agreed to lower wage increases and annual agreements (not more frequent ones), thereby bringing about much of the fall in the rate of inflation from 24 to 8 per cent while the government delivered more on 'the social wage' (better housing, welfare, pensions and tax reductions), thereby helping to protect real standards of living. While this trade union cooperation was important in 1975–77, it was not extended, the Labour government unilaterally imposing its incomes policy thereafter. With the coming to power of the Conservatives in 1979, Margaret Thatcher made it very clear that she had no wish to involve the trade unions, or employers' organizations, in decision making.

In the Thatcher and Major era the political hostility to the trade unions was grounded in economic theories which believed that they distorted the workings of the free market. One notable way it was argued that the trade unions did this was through 'the trade union mark-up', which was the difference in pay and other benefits between union and non-union labour. The higher wage costs were deemed liable to make the firms with union labour less competitive and ultimately likely to lead to higher unemployment. While few would argue against higher costs endangering the viability of firms, there have long been discussions of whether cheap labour is truly cheap. By this, people have meant that cheap labour may not be efficient and also, in periods of ready alternative work, it can be costly to have a high labour turnover and so have to train new employees for the work.

A US study, edited by Mishel and Voos, argued that trade unions and collective bargaining were not responsible for the decline of US competitiveness. In some cases where the USA had a trade deficit, such as Germany and Canada, wages were higher than in the USA. In other cases, where wages were lower, such as Korea, Taiwan and Mexico, the pay gap between them and the USA had 'very little to do with union wage premiums in the US'.

A British survey, by writers critical of the trade unions, observed that the unions could 'adversely affect investment, innovation, productivity growth and the cost-structure of industry'. However, Aldcroft and Oliver balanced such views with such observations as:

> Strong wage pressure in highly unionised plants may also encourage employers to increase capital intensity and introduce more efficient work methods, both of which will raise productivity.

The considerable weakening of trade unionism generally in the USA and in the private sector in the UK has made it increasingly hard to ascribe declining economic competitiveness largely to the trade unions.

Moreover, the 'union mark-up' has often been seen as securing greater equalization of incomes for disadvantaged groups, including labour from ethnic communities and disabled people. In 1982 union pressure was estimated to have narrowed the wage gap between black and white workers by 5 per cent and, in the late 1990s, it was deemed to have narrowed the wage gap between female and male workers by 3 per cent. David Metcalf, a leading authority on British industrial relations, has taken up a suggestion by Alan Flanders that the trade unions not only have a 'vested interest' effect in looking after their members, but also 'a sword of justice' role in pushing for a wages mark-up for less advantaged employees.

Further reading

For those wanting a knowledgeable survey of the political controversies involving trade unions since the Second World War, there is Robert Taylor, *The Trade Union Question in British Politics* (Oxford, 1993). For a succinct economic and political survey see Chris Wrigley, *British Trade Unions Since 1933* (Cambridge, 2002) and for a collection of documents primarily about trade unions and the state see his *British Trade Unions 1945–1995* (Manchester, 1997). For a recent reinterpretation, arguing that the role of the state was greater in Britain than usually suggested, there is Chris Howell, *Trade Unions and the State* (Princeton, 2005).

For a very critical reassessment of the trade unions see D.H. Aldcroft and M.J. Oliver, *Trade Unions and the Economy* (Aldershot, 2000). For a more favourable US assessment see L. Mishel and P.B. Voos, *Unions and Economic Competitiveness* (New York, 1992), sponsored by the Economic Policy Institute, Washington, DC. For an example of David Metcalf's work see the *British Journal of Industrial Relations*, 31, 1993, for 'Industrial relations and economic performance'. There are many important essays in A. Campbell, N. Fishman and J. McIlroy (eds) *British Trade Unions and Industrial Politics*, 2 vols (Aldershot, 1999).

For the problems of the coal industry in the 1980s see M.J. Parker, *Thatcherism and the Fall of Coal* (Oxford, 2000). For the NUM see Andrew Taylor, *The NUM and British Politics*, vol. 2 (Aldershot, 2005). For the 1984–5 dispute, see M. Adeney and J. Lloyd, *The Miners' Strike 1984–85: Loss Without Limit* (London, 1986), H. Beynon (ed.) *Digging Deeper: Issues in the Miners' Strike* (London, 1985) and J. Winterton and R. Winterton, *Coal, Crisis and Conflict: The 1984–85 Miners' Strike in Yorkshire* (Manchester, 1989). More generally, see A. Charlesworth *et al.*, *An Atlas of Industrial Protest in Britain 1750–1990* (London, 1996).

For a comparative study of British and other European countries' industrial relations there is Colin Crouch, *Industrial Relations and European State Traditions* (Oxford, 1993). For reliable statistics on British and other countries' trade unions see G.S. Bain and R. Price, *Profiles of Union Growth* (Oxford, 1980) and J. Visser, *European Trade Unions in Figures* (Deventer, 1989).

References

Bain, G. and Price, R. (1980) *Profiles of Union Growth*. Oxford: Blackwell.

Flanders, A., and Clegg, H. (1954) *The System of Industrial Relations in Britain*. Oxford: Basil Blackwell.

Visser, B. (1989) *European Trade Unions in Figures*. Deventer: Kluwer.

Western, Bruce (1999) *Between Class and Market: Postwar Unionization in the Capitalist Democracies*. Princeton, N.J./Chichester: Princeton University Press.

19

Sexuality

Rebecca Jennings

THE TWENTIETH CENTURY WITNESSED a shift in attitudes to, and experiences of, sexuality for both men and women. Notably, the century was characterized by a growing sense of liberalism towards sexuality, although it should be emphasized that this was never straightforward and the twentieth century cannot be viewed as a simple story of progressive reform. There were, however, key social, medical and legal changes that, focusing on the second half of the century, this chapter will address. Contraception became increasingly available throughout the period, freeing heterosexual women from the burden of multiple and, sometimes, unwanted pregnancies. Similarly, sex manuals and sex education, targeted at specific audiences, were aimed at freeing men and women from a culture of ignorance and fear while presenting them with new ways of understanding and talking about their sexuality. The twentieth century also saw key shifts in popular and official attitudes towards homosexuality, with homosexual acts being decriminalized in 1967. Indeed, the 1960s have often been perceived as the decade of a sexual revolution. As this chapter demonstrates, however, sex was not 'discovered' in the 1960s and the decade neither quashed clashes between conservatives and liberals nor signalled the end of prejudices against homosexuality.

The population question

One of the central issues shaping attitudes to sexuality in the immediate aftermath of the Second World War was the population question. Birth rates had been in decline since the beginning of the twentieth century, reaching a historic low in the early 1930s. Although they began to rise again in 1942, the downward trend in the birth rate continued to be a major source of political concern during and after the war. A number of reports published in the 1940s identified the falling birth rate as a serious issue facing the nation. In 1942, William Beveridge expressed the fear, in his report on social insurance, that 'with its present rate of reproduction the British race cannot continue' (Beveridge, 1942: 154). Mass Observation, the social survey organization, endorsed the view that the birth rate was falling at an alarming rate in its 1945 report, *Britain and Her Birth-Rate* and in 1944 a Royal Commission was established to look into the issue. A number of causes for this trend were identified: Mass Observation suggested that pessimism about the future was putting people off having children, while the Royal Commission accepted that the emancipation of women had resulted in a rejection of the excessive childbearing which had dominated women's lives in the previous century. Eugenic ideas about the 'quality' of the British race prompted further concerns that the 'responsible' members of British society were reproducing at a much slower rate than 'social problem groups'.

The creation of the welfare state in the 1940s appeared to offer an opportunity to create a social and economic environment which might encourage socially responsible parenthood and the introduction of family allowances during the war was widely regarded as a financial incentive to prospective parents. Nevertheless, Mass Observation's survey found that most women not only regarded smaller families as bringing benefits to their children in terms of quality of life, education and opportunities, but were also aware of and using birth control to plan their families. By the 1950s, anxieties about population decline were beginning to be allayed. The birth rate had begun to stabilize and there was a growing realization that Britain had simply been experiencing a period of transition from the model of high birth and death rates which had characterized the nineteenth-century population, to a modern pattern of low birth rates and longer life expectancy. However, the debates which had surrounded the question of population decline were important in shaping attitudes to the family and motherhood, especially in the decades after the war.

Marriage and divorce

The population debates of the 1940s encouraged a cultural emphasis on marriage and the family and, in particular, an assumption that children should be brought up in an appropriate and stable domestic environment. Illegitimacy was strongly discouraged in the 1940s and 50s and marriage was increasingly described as a 'career' for women. Women's magazines, which were becoming more popular in the post-war decades, played a key role in propagating this culture of feminine domesticity: marriage and domesticity were dominant themes in *Woman*, *Woman's Own* and *Woman's Weekly* in the period 1949 to 1974. The two primary themes, 'getting and keeping your man' (which accounted for 59 per cent of all non-beauty themes in this period) and 'the happy family', promoted the ideals of romantic love within marriage and family solidarity and stability. Heterosexual love, either leading to or within marriage, was represented as a basic precondition for femininity and prompted much debate on the nature of 'true love'.

Expectations of marriage changed after the war with the emergence of the companionate marriage. Marriage was increasingly regarded as a partnership of equals with complementary roles and mutual sexual satisfaction was considered an essential component of a happy marriage. Marie Stopes's best-selling work, *Married Love*, had first emphasized the importance of sexual satisfaction within marriage for women as well as men in 1918. Geoffrey Gorer's *Exploring English Character* found that, by the post-war period, most of the respondents to his survey thought sexual love either very or fairly important in marriage and only 6 per cent thought it unimportant (Gorer, 1955: 94–116). Advice literature explored sexual relations in marriage in increasingly explicit terms and created an expectation that both husband and wife could and should be able to obtain sexual pleasure from their spouse. The Marriage Guidance Council's booklet *Sex in Marriage*, published in 1947, had sold over half a million copies by the late 1960s (Weeks, 1981: 237). Established in 1938 and expanding rapidly in the 1940s and 50s, the Marriage Guidance Council reflected a new belief that marriages needed to be worked at in order to be successful. The war was widely perceived to have had a negative impact on the family, destabilizing marriages by separating spouses and, inadvertently, encouraging sexual activity outside marriage. Divorce rates increased considerably in the late 1940s assisted by the Legal Aid system and the further extension of divorce jurisdiction to provincial courts. However, the number of divorces peaked in 1947 and then dropped dramatically, halving by 1954. The grounds on which couples could seek divorce also remained limited and it was not until 1969 that divorce by mutual consent became available. Despite widespread concerns about the instability of the institution, marriage was extremely popular in the 1950s, with increasing numbers marrying and at an earlier age.

Homosexuality and the law

The cultural emphasis on the family and heterosexual marital love highlighted the perceived deviance of alternative sexual practices such as prostitution and homosexuality. Acts of 'gross indecency' between men had been illegal since the Criminal Law Amendment Act 1885, but the 1950s witnessed a new wave of official and tabloid anxiety about moral decline. The decade began with a series of moral panics surrounding the public visibility of vice on the streets of London during the Festival of Britain in 1951 and Coronation Year in 1953. Homosexuality in particular was linked with a general Cold War paranoia about spies. Following the 1950 defection to Russia of two British spies, Guy Burgess and Donald Maclean, who were widely believed to be homosexual, the government came under increasing pressure from the US State Department to clamp down on homosexuals. The Home Office launched a campaign to tighten up on vice and the Home Secretary, Sir David Maxwell-Fyffe, said that homosexuals were 'exhibitionists and proselytisers, and a danger to others, especially the young. So long as I hold the office of Home Secretary, I shall give no countenance to the view that they should not be prevented from being such a danger' (Hyde, 1972:

240). From 1953 onwards, the newly appointed Metropolitan Police Commissioner, Sir John Nott-Bower, enforced stiffer sentences and prosecutions increased, supported by the popular press.

Social opinion was divided in its attitude toward homosexuality. A Mass Observation survey found that prejudice against homosexuality was much more deeply rooted than hostility to prostitution. However, increasing discussion of sexual issues meant that public opinion was beginning to change in favour of reform. Notably, a debate developed in the 1950s on the role of the state in policing private behaviour. Scientific research had created a more tolerant view and the explanation of homosexuality as a 'disease' was becoming widely accepted. In 1948, Kinsey's *Sexual Behaviour in the Human Male*, researched in America, revealed the extent of homosexual behaviour. His conclusions suggested that 4 per cent of the male population were exclusively homosexual; 8 per cent were almost exclusively homosexual for at least three years between the ages of 16 and 65; and 37 per cent had at least some overt homosexual experience leading to orgasm in their lifetime. Kinsey's research suggested that the assumption of a clear distinction between the sexually 'normal' and the sexually 'deviant' was unfounded. In 1952 the Church of England set up a pioneering committee to assess whether homosexual acts, although a sin, ought also to be a criminal offence. The report of this committee, *The Problem of Homosexuality: An Interim Report*, published in 1954, supported legal reform.

The sensational trial of Lord Montagu of Beaulieu and Peter Wildeblood, diplomatic correspondent for the *Daily Mail*, marked an important turning point in public opinion. The men were convicted of gross indecency solely on the testimony of the two airmen with whom the acts had been committed and the trial exposed various unsavoury facts concerning police tactics, such as the practice of searching premises without a warrant, the use of witnesses who were granted immunity and the use of police agents provocateurs. As a result, there were calls for legal reform in Parliament. Sir Robert Boothby MP said the duty of the state was 'to protect youth from corruption and the public from indecency and nuisance. What consenting adults do in privacy may be a moral issue between them and their Maker, but . . . it is not a legal issue between them and the State' (Haste, 1994: 171). The Wolfenden Committee was established to consider the issue and in 1957 its report concluded in favour of legal reform. Public debate revealed that seven national newspapers also supported legal reform, as did 40 per cent of the general public questioned in an opinion poll. However, conservative elements in the government resisted reform and it was to be another decade before new legislation was passed.

Despite widespread support for change, legal reform in the Sexual Offences Act 1967 was limited, largely due to the failure of Lord Arran, the chief architect of the Act, to involve reformers in the drafting of the Bill. The Act decriminalized homosexual acts between consenting adults in private but the definition of 'private' remained very narrow and the age of consent was fixed at 21, in comparison to a heterosexual age of consent of 16. In addition to these reforms, the Act also tightened up the law on offences involving minors and importuning. The sentence for an adult found guilty of committing 'gross indecency' with another male aged 16 to 21 was increased from two to five years' imprisonment.

A permissive society?

The Sexual Offences Act 1967 was part of a broader raft of liberalizing legislation enacted by the Wilson government, which has led contemporaries and historians to represent the 1960s as a decade of sexual reform. In 1967, the NHS (Family Planning) Act enabled local authorities to provide contraception on the NHS to any person who requested it, regardless of marital status. The same year, the Abortion Act extended the permissible grounds for abortion, allowing doctors to carry out abortions on social grounds and in the event of potential foetal abnormalities. The law concerning divorce came under increasing scrutiny in the 1960s and both the Law Commission and the Archbishop of Canterbury's working party advocated reform. Divorce law, which had previously relied upon the concept of assigning blame to one party for a matrimonial offence such as adultery, cruelty or desertion, was reformed in the Divorce Law Reform Act 1969. The new law depended on the idea of divorce as a response to the irretrievable breakdown of a marriage and was now available by the mutual consent of both parties after two years' separation or, without one party's consent, after five years' apart. The Act, dubbed Casanova's Charter amid fears that it would enable husbands to abandon older, financially dependent wives in favour of younger women, was highly controversial and did not take effect until 1970, when the Matrimonial Proceedings and Property Act had secured the financial position of women (Hall, 2000: 175–6).

Further legislation, enacted from the late 1950s onward, fostered a culture of more open discussion about sexuality. The Obscene Publications Act 1959 introduced 'literary merit' as a defence for the publication of 'obscene' material. The following year, to mark the thirtieth anniversary of the author's death, Penguin decided to issue D.H. Lawrence's *Lady Chatterley's Lover* as a test case. The Director of Public Prosecutions attempted to prosecute the novel for obscenity, but the publishers called on a number of well-known authors and intellectuals to testify to the book's literary merit, and a jury acquitted. The novel became an instant best-seller, selling 2 million copies in the first year of publication. In the late 1960s, the censorship laws were liberalized further with the Theatres Act 1968, which removed the powers of the Lord Chamberlain to censor serious, experimental plays and liberalized the standards of the British Board of Film Censors.

However, for many contemporary commentators, the clearest sign of a liberalization of social attitudes was in the emerging youth culture of the 1960s. In 1966, New York's *Time* magazine coined the phrase 'Swinging London' in reference to a range of new styles appearing in the capital. Music such as rock 'n' roll, with its explicitly sexual lyrics, provided a new cultural context for dating and became a symbol of sexual freedom. Fashions, such as the miniskirts modelled by 1960s' icon Twiggy, implied a loosening of sexual morality, while a range of working-class subcultures, from teddy boys and mods and rockers to punk, developed unique youth styles. At the root of these cultural changes lay a significant post-war shift in the social and economic position of young people. The baby boom of the 1940s meant that there were 1 million more unmarried 15–24-year-olds in 1960 than there had been in 1950. These young people were exceptionally affluent, having experienced a wage increase of 50 per cent between 1938 and 1958, double the national average, and became key consumers in a new market in leisure and fashion goods. Greater prosperity and health provision also meant that young people were reaching sexual maturity earlier and the sexual activities of the young became a major cause of public concern.

For women, in particular, the 1960s witnessed a greater discussion of sexuality. The contraceptive pill became widely available in the UK in 1961, prompting more open discussion about contraception. Unlike previous methods of birth control, the Pill was simple to use and enabled women to take decisions regarding contraception independently of their partners. The manufacturers advertised the Pill extensively and it was widely covered in the media, with the result that discussion about, and use of, contraception became more acceptable. Contraceptive advice also became more readily available. In 1963, the Brooke Advisory Centre began to offer advice to unmarried girls and by 1969, under the provisions of the NHS (Family Planning) Act, contraception became accessible to all on the NHS. A number of new magazines, such as *Cosmopolitan*, also began to appear in the 1960s. Marketed at younger women, the magazines tackled the subject of sex more openly and, by the late 1960s, female sexuality was increasingly discussed in terms of pleasure, rather than as a means of cementing a marital relationship.

The extent to which sexual practices reflected these shifts in the cultural representation of sexuality is difficult to assess. A rise in illegitimate birth and venereal disease infection rates suggest that young people were increasingly sexually active. Venereal disease infection rates rose significantly between the 1950s and the 1970s. Much of this increase reflected a rise in rates of gonorrhoea, which the advent of penicillin in the 1940s had made treatable. Attendance rates at clinics were also increasing, although this was perhaps more significant as an indication of the growing cultural openness about sexuality, as many of those seeking help were found to be healthy. A number of studies published in the early 1970s suggested that young people's sexual behaviour had not changed significantly. Michael Schofield's study, *The Sexual Behaviour of Young People*, published in 1973, found that only a minority of young people were engaged in sexual activity, although increasing numbers engaged in 'petting'. Geoffrey Gorer's *Sex and Marriage in England Today: A Study of the Views and Experience of the Under-45s* (1971) echoed the view that social attitudes remained chaste. A quarter of the male respondents to the survey and two-thirds of women remained virgins on marriage. Moreover, despite the sexual references of 1960s youth culture, young people remained widely ignorant on sexual matters, reflecting the continued absence of organized, formal sex education in schools and the reluctance of parents to discuss sexual issues with their children.

The Gateways and lesbian bar culture

The decades after the Second World War were a crucial period in the emergence of a lesbian bar culture in Britain. Although lesbians had been frequenting particular bars alongside male homosexuals, the bohemian avant garde and prostitutes in the interwar period, after the war a number of specifically lesbian bars began to appear. Lesbians became part of a homosexual scene at the New Union pub in Manchester, the Spotted Dog and Pigott's Bar in Brighton and across London and other cities in the 1950s and 1960s. However, the most famous of these was the Gateways nightclub in Chelsea, London. The Gateways had been owned by a retired colonel in the 1930s, when it was a sedate club frequented by local Chelsea residents. However, in the 1940s, it was taken over by Ted Ware and his wife Gina. By the 1950s, it was being run by Gina with her lesbian friend, an ex-US Air Force woman, known as Smithy. Lesbians had visited the club since the 1930s, but by the late 1950s it was almost exclusively lesbian. Like most gay bars in this period, the club had a low profile and did not advertise in the press, so it was difficult to find. The Gateways was located in a basement, which visitors entered through a door on a side street, off the King's Road; inside, the venue was small and dimly lit.

The Gateways was a members-only club and most of the clientele was made up of a few hundred regulars, many of whom visited the club several times a week. The behaviour and dress of these women was defined throughout the 1940s, 50s and early 60s by the lesbian culture of butch/femme. Newcomers to the bar scene were expected to choose either a butch or a femme identity before being fully accepted by the other women. Butch lesbians in this period wore suits with trousers, shirts and ties and had cropped hair, while femme lesbians adopted the ultra-feminine glamorous look of a dress, high heels, make-up, jewellery and a handbag. Butch/femme provided a code of behaviour within the bar culture, prescribing that femmes should only be attracted to butches and vice versa, and that butches had to ask the permission of other butches before dancing with another's femme girlfriend. In the USA, lesbian bars in this period were predominantly working class, but in the UK there is evidence of a wider social spread. However, when *Arena Three*, the first British lesbian magazine, began to be produced in 1964, its primarily middle-class readers tended to regard the bar culture as 'seedy' and 'underground'.

In the late 1960s, the Gateways opened up to wider social influences. Robert Aldrich's 1969 film, *The Killing of Sister George*, depicting a lesbian relationship between the two central characters, George and Childie, included a scene filmed in the Gateways. Regulars were used as extras in the Gateways scene and the film attracted both public attention and new members to the club. In the early 1970s,

> ### The Gateways and lesbian bar culture
>
> the club was the site of political conflict between the newly founded Gay Liberation
> Front and the long-standing culture of butch/femme. However, the club remained
> extremely popular, and despite the increasing numbers of bars and clubs opening
> across London in the 1970s, the Gateways remained a key lesbian venue until it
> closed in 1985.

Sexual politics

By the late 1960s, the liberalism characterized by legislative reform and more open
discussion of sexuality was facing a number of challenges. During the Lords debate on
the Sexual Offences Bill 1967, Lord Arran had asked homosexual men to 'show their
thanks by comporting themselves quietly and with dignity' (Hyde, 1972: 303). The
response to the legislation was muted, reflecting the limited scope of reforms which
only addressed the concerns of middle-class professional homosexuals whose relationships were conducted in the private domain. Sexual encounters between men in the
public domain remained illegal and increased policing meant that the number of
prosecutions for indecency between males trebled in the period 1967–1972. In 1970 a
new, aggressive form of gay political activism emerged with the establishment of the
Gay Liberation Front. The movement originated in the USA, developing out of riots
sparked by a police raid on the Stonewall Inn, a gay bar in Greenwich Village. The
first meeting of the British GLF was held at the London School of Economics in
October 1970 and the organization was initially dominated by students, but grew
fairly rapidly. Seeking to challenge the liberal notion that sexuality was an individual,
private concern, the movement emphasized publicity and stressed that gay people
should 'come out of the closet' and be open about their sexual identity.

Sexuality was also a central concern of the Women's Liberation Movement in the
early 1970s. The Abortion Act 1967 was one of the most controversial of the legislative
reforms introduced in the 1960s and it faced almost annual challenges throughout the
late 1960s and 1970s. Nevertheless, its scope was, in reality, rather limited. Abortions
were only available at the discretion of doctors and, although the Act provided for
abortions to be carried out on the NHS, regional variations in the provision of the service forced some women to rely on private clinics. Free contraception and abortion on
demand became one of the four demands of the Women's Liberation Movement
formulated in 1971 and the movement formed the Women's Abortion and Contraception Campaign in 1972 to campaign on this issue. To a certain extent, lesbians
were marginalized by these emerging sexual politics in the early 1970s. At a GLF conference in early 1972, the women members of GLF walked out in protest at the lack of
attention being paid to women's issues. Many of them put their energies into the
Women's Liberation Movement instead, feeling that they had more in common with

other women than with gay men. However, the Women's Liberation Movement was not initially supportive of lesbians either. Its early list of objectives made no mention of fighting for lesbian rights and many of its members saw lesbians as a threat which could potentially discredit the feminist cause. Betty Friedan, author of the seminal feminist text *The Feminine Mystique* (1963) described lesbians as 'the lavender menace', a dangerous fifth column who might destroy the political integrity of heterosexual feminists. However, the women's movement provided women-only spaces which facilitated intimacy between women, and many women came out as lesbians through the women's movement. In the late 1970s, new strands of feminist politics were emerging which were more supportive of lesbianism, the most influential of which was lesbian-feminism. Lesbian feminists argued that the formation of lesbian bonds between women posed a crucial challenge to the sexual oppression of women which they regarded as inescapable in heterosexual relationships.

New moralism

By the late 1960s, liberalism was facing a further challenge from the political right, vocalizing an increasing public concern with, and sense of alienation from, the social changes of the 1950s and 60s. A key representative of this viewpoint was Mary Whitehouse, a deeply religious former teacher, who campaigned for the restoration of the moral standards and sense of personal responsibility which she felt had been destroyed by the social welfare culture of post-war society. For Mary Whitehouse and others, the recent changes in sexual attitudes were symbolic of a wider disintegration of the moral order. In particular, she regarded the increasingly open discussion of sexuality in the media and the spread of pornography as bringing something which should be a private and sacred aspect of family life into the destructive glare of the public gaze.

Mary Whitehouse began campaigning in 1963, when she launched the Clean Up TV Campaign (later renamed the National Viewers and Listeners Association) and throughout the 1960s she clashed with Sir Hugh Greene, Director General of the BBC, in his attempt to represent a broader diversity of British society in the media. By the 1970s, Whitehouse had become a major international figure, but she presented herself as a spokesperson for popular opinion and used petitions and letters to demonstrate the widespread public support for her arguments. Others were voicing similar concerns, and in March 1971, the Festival of Light was founded to warn of a growing 'moral pollution' in Britain and to promote a Christian moral order. The following year, the Earl of Longford produced his *Longford Report on Pornography*, in which he argued for tighter regulation of pornography. At the heart of these campaigns for a new moral order was a concern with protecting the morality of children and young people. In the early 1970s a series of obscenity prosecutions were conducted which hinged on the issue of a corruption of young people's morals. In 1971, *The Little Red Schoolbook*, a Marxist book advocating pupil power and offering advice to young people on sex and drugs, was prosecuted. In the same year, the underground magazine *Oz* published a 'Schoolkids' Issue', edited by under-18s. Although the content of the issue was determined by the young people, the adult staff were prosecuted for obscenity and received harsh sentences, including a 15-month prison sentence followed by deportation for the magazine's Australian founder, Richard Neville. Some charges were, however, quashed or reduced on appeal.

In the 1980s, the dominance of religious campaigners in right-wing morality campaigns began to give way to a new political approach. From the mid-1980s, the Conservative party under Margaret Thatcher (first elected to government in 1979 and subsequently re-elected throughout the following decade) developed a New Right moral agenda. This was defined by hostility to the so-called 'sexual revolution' of the 1960s and a concern that 'the family' was under attack. The central aim of the New Right agenda was a return to traditional, family-centred sexual attitudes, frequently referred to as 'Victorian values'. In 1986, the government sought to bring control over sex education within the scope of the family through the Education Act, which placed decisions in the hands of school governors, assumed to be parents, rather than teachers. Two years later, the government again intervened in sex education with the enactment of the highly controversial Section 28 of the Local Government Act 1988. Section 28 made it unlawful for local authorities to 'intentionally promote homosexuality' and for maintained schools to promote the acceptability of homosexuality as a 'pretended family relationship'. The legislation has been seen in a political context as an attack by a Conservative central government on the power of left-wing local authorities. However, the specific focus of the legislation on homosexuality was undoubtedly enabled by a growing public hostility towards the gay community in the context of the AIDS crisis. Such attitudes allowed the government to present homosexuality as a factor in the undermining of the family and to argue for a return to the approach enshrined in the Sexual Offences Act 1967: homosexuality could be tolerated between consenting adults in private, but should not be presented as an acceptable way of life in the public domain.

Despite the dominance of right-wing attitudes which such legislation indicated, the gradual liberalization of attitudes toward sex continued in some areas in the 1980s. Rates of divorce, marriage and remarriage and cohabitation all increased during the decade, continuing the shift in models of the family which had become apparent in the 1970s. After decades of attempts to restrict legislation legalizing abortion, public support for abortion remained high. A number of new sexual issues also appeared in the public domain in the 1980s. Developments in reproductive technology meant that *in vitro* fertilisation (IVF), artificial insemination (AI) and surrogacy raised new moral questions about the relationship between sexuality and the family. Child sexual abuse was a cause of growing concern during the decade, culminating in the 1987 Cleveland child abuse scandal. The high numbers of children from a wide range of social backgrounds across Cleveland who were apparently showing signs of sexual abuse prompted a questioning of the ability of the medical profession to accurately recognize cases of abuse and of the rights of local authorities to remove children from the care of their parents.

In Focus

The AIDS crisis

Sexual politics in the 1980s were dominated by the emergence of a new sexually transmitted disease known as Acquired Immune Deficiency Syndrome (AIDS). The disease was first noticed in gay men in the USA and was reported in British medical journals and the gay press in 1981. The first British fatality occurred in the same year. However, the official response to the disease was muted in the early stages due to a belief that the disease was confined to homosexuals. The first British conference on the subject did not take place until 1983, by which time there had only been 14 diagnosed cases in the UK. Awareness of the disease was therefore primarily limited to the gay community and a number of voluntary organizations, such as the Terrence Higgins Trust, were established to provide support to those affected. However, by the mid-1980s, the disease had spread, rising to 241 cases by October 1985, and the first heterosexual cases began to appear.

As it became apparent that the disease was not confined to the gay community and that heterosexuals were also at risk, public concern rose. The process by which the disease was transmitted had not yet been clearly established and in this climate of uncertainty, the tabloid press fanned widespread hysteria about those infected and referred to AIDS as a 'gay plague'. The disease came to be associated with promiscuous behaviour and marginal sexual groups and was explained as the inevitable result of lax morality, provoking growing hostility towards the gay community and those suffering from the illness. The official response was limited throughout this period of panic and it was not until 1986 that the government first debated the issue. By this point, research had improved understandings of the nature and spread of the disease. In 1986 it had been discovered that AIDS originated in a virus, named the Human Immunodeficiency Virus (HIV). The appearance of the virus in haemophiliacs, intravenous drug users and heterosexuals, as well as gay men, had demonstrated early on that it was not spread by factors unique to the gay community, or solely by sexual activity, and it was gradually becoming apparent that the virus was spread through the exchange of bodily fluids.

Although a test for the virus had been developed in 1985, there was little sign of a cure or vaccine being developed in the immediate future and the only means of halting the disease appeared to be a public education campaign aimed at changing people's behaviour. The Chief Medical Officer at the Department of Health, Dr Donald Acheson, recommended targeted health education for high-risk groups and more generalized education for the wider public, and in November 1986 the government launched a major health education campaign. Advertisements were placed in the press, on the radio and television and leaflets were dropped at

The AIDS crisis

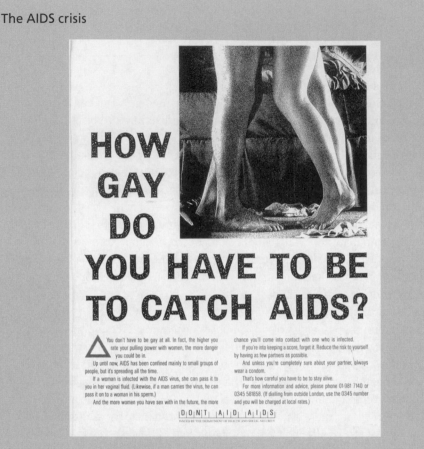

Plate 19.1 A government-sponsored image from the television and media advertising campaign in the 1980s to educate the public about the risks of AIDS (© The Advertising Archives).

23 million households, advising the public to restrict the number of their sexual partners and promoting 'safe sex' through the use of a condom. But the campaign lacked clarity and was hampered by the public's limited knowledge of sexual matters and the reluctance of politicians to discuss sexual behaviour. Nevertheless, the campaign represented an unprecedented discussion of sexual practices in government material and by ministers themselves.

Queer politics

The hostility directed at the gay community in the wake of the AIDS crisis and Section 28 led to the emergence of a new militancy in gay politics in the early 1990s. The first meeting of a new activist group, Queer Nation, took place in New York in

April 1990 and alongside other groups, including ACT-UP in the US and Outrage in the UK, redefined gay politics. The queer movement adopted a defiant political stance which sought to appeal beyond lesbians and gay men to embrace newly politicized groups such as transsexuals, transvestites and all those who experienced themselves as sexually deviant. In the lesbian community, new styles emerged as a new generation rejected the feminist definition of lesbianism as a political refusal of male sexual power. So-called 'lipstick lesbians' asserted the importance of sexual desire between women as central to lesbian identity and reclaimed feminine fashions as a means of attracting other women.

Feminist sexual politics were also changing in the 1990s. During the 1980s, feminists had been split on the issue of pornography. In 1986, the Labour MP Clare Short moved a Commons motion to ban 'Page three girls', the practice of showing topless images of women in tabloid newspapers. The motion failed, but represented part of a widespread campaign against pornography by many feminists in the 1980s, who argued that pornography was a cause of sexism and could lead to rape and violence against women. Other feminists, however, were reluctant to campaign on an issue which was associated with right-wing moral politics of repression. By the 1990s, a market in pornography for women was beginning to emerge and the pornography trade flourished as part of a broader commercialization of sex. Sex toys and lingerie became available to women in their own and their friends' homes through Ann Summers parties, and sex phone lines also became increasingly popular. Feminist campaigning in the 1990s became focused on supporting women who were the victims of violent or sexual assaults in the home through the establishment of women's refuges and support organizations like 'Women's Aid'. In 1991, the law recognized the crime of marital rape and the concept of date rape developed out of a recognition that rape victims frequently knew their attackers. An increasing willingness to acknowledge that men could be victims of rape also resulted in male rape becoming a crime under the Criminal Justice and Public Order Act 1994.

Debates and Interpretations

The history of sexuality has conventionally been viewed as a succession of alternating shifts between periods of sexual permissiveness and sexual repression. From this perspective, the post-war period has been constructed as beginning with an era of sexual conservatism in the 1940s and 1950s, followed by liberalism in the 1960s and early 1970s, brought to an end by a backlash in the late 1970s and 1980s. This perspective is encouraged by the representation of the 1960s as a period of sexual revolution in which sexual attitudes and behaviour underwent a major and dramatic change. However, many of the changes which took place in the 1960s and 70s clearly originated earlier in our period and the overall picture of post-war sexuality is therefore considerably more complex than the notion of alternating periods of repression and permissiveness allows. Throughout the second half of the twentieth century, the nature of the family underwent considerable change, as a result of rising rates of divorce, marriage and remarriage and cohabitation. The immediate post-war emphasis on mutually pleasurable sex as a means of cementing marriage was an early manifestation of a discourse prioritizing sexual pleasure and experience which became increasingly influential as the century wore on. Much of the legislation enacted in the 1960s was the product of long-term political lobbying and reflected shifts in public attitudes which had largely already occurred. Equally, while the 1980s have been identified as a period of sexual repression, symbolized by a backlash against gay men and lesbians in particular, the gay community successfully regrouped during this period, forging new supportive networks to combat the threat posed by AIDS. Within gay history, the influence of lesbian and gay political attitudes, articulated in the 1970s, on histories of sexuality has led to an emphasis on the late 1960s and 70s as a dramatic moment of liberation. However, as the existence of lesbian bar cultures in the 1950s and early 60s demonstrates, the history of lesbians forging communities and collective identities pre-dates this moment.

Many other issues have remained contentious throughout the period. Abortion, although partially legalized by the Abortion Act 1967, continued to be the subject of heated debate for the remainder of the decade, focusing the different concerns of both feminists and right-wing moralists. Sexually transmitted diseases, which seemed almost a concern of the past with the discovery of penicillin in the immediate post-war decades, again became a major source of concern with the advent of AIDS in the 1980s. Despite the renewed fears raised by HIV and AIDS, the most significant shift in sexuality since 1945 has perhaps been the decline in marriage as the primary site of sexual behaviour and the development of a cultural emphasis on personal sexual pleasure and diversity.

Further reading

The history of sexuality has only recently attracted the attention and interest of historians and publishing in this field remains limited. Nevertheless, there are a small number of surveys of twentieth-century sexuality available, including Jeffrey Weeks, *Sex, Politics and Society: The Regulation of Sexuality Since 1800* (London, 1981) and Lesley Hall, *Sex, Gender and Social Change in Britain Since 1880* (Basingstoke, 2000). Pat Thane's article, 'Population Politics in Post-war British Culture', in Becky Conekin, Frank Mort and Chris Waters, *Moments of Modernity: Reconstructing Britain 1945–1964* (London, 1999), explores the debates about the birth rate in the 1940s and 50s. Frank Mort, 'Mapping sexual London: the Wolfenden Committee on Homosexual Offences and Prostitution 1954–57', *New Formations*, 37 (1999) discusses the debates concerning homosexuality prior to the Sexual Offences Act 1967. On female sexuality and contraception, see Hera Cook, *The Long Sexual Revolution: British Women, Sex and Contraception in the Twentieth Century* (Oxford, 2003) and on the AIDS crisis in Britain, see Anna Marie Smith, *New Right Discourse on Race and Sexuality: Britain 1968–1990* (Cambridge, 1994). Most recently, Matt Houlbrook's *Queer London: Perils and Pleasures in the Sexual Metropolis, 1918–1957* (Chicago, 2005) and Matt

Houlbrook and Harry Cocks (eds) *The Modern History of Sexuality* (Basingstoke, 2005) provide overviews of cutting-edge research in the field.

References

Beveridge, William (1942) *Social Insurance and Allied Services*. London: HMSO.

Gorer, Geoffrey (1955) *Exploring English Character*. London: Cresset Press.

Hall, Lesley (2000) *Sex, Gender and Social Change in Britain Since 1880*. London: Macmillan.

Haste, Cate (1994) *Rules of Desire: Sex in Britain: World War 1 to the Present*. London: Pimlico.

Hyde, H. Montgomery (1972) *The Other Love: An Historical and Contemporary Survey of Homosexuality in Britain*. London: Granada Publishing.

Weeks, Jeffrey (1981) *Sex, Politics and Society: The Regulation of Sexuality Since 1800*. London: Longman.

20

Poverty and social exclusion

Julie Rugg

IN 1942, WILLIAM BEVERIDGE'S *Report on Social Insurance and Allied Services* outlined a comprehensive scheme to attack 'five giant evils: upon the physical Want with which it is directly concerned, upon Disease which often causes that Want and brings many other troubles in its train, upon Ignorance which no democracy can afford among its citizens, upon Squalor . . . and upon the Idleness which destroys wealth and corrupts men' (1942: 170). In 1997, Prime Minister Tony Blair announced the introduction of the Social Exclusion Unit (SEU), proclaiming New Labour's intention to tackle multiple indicators of deprivation. 'Social exclusion' redefined poverty as a problem that was not just about income, but was deemed 'a short-hand label for what can happen when individuals or areas suffer from a combination of linked problems such as unemployment, poor skills, low incomes, poor housing, high crime environments, bad health, and family breakdown' (DSS, 1999). In some senses, the setting up of the SEU was an indication that Beveridge's 1942 welfare plans had failed: the 'giants' of want, disease, ignorance, squalor and idleness had not been slain. The 1997 Labour government had inherited levels of poverty unprecedented since the end of the Second World War: more than 25 per cent of children lived in relative poverty, as did 21 per cent of pensioners (DWP, 2004). It could be argued that much of the history of poverty in the twentieth century describes a circle, which very nearly ends where it begins.

In its consideration of poverty in post-war Britain, this chapter reviews the arm of welfare known as 'social security': the financial assistance given to people who are unemployed or whose incomes are affected by old age, disability or family circumstances. The chapter gives a basic and necessarily selective chronological and narrative framework of policy developments and, in doing so, refers both to tensions in the economics of paying for welfare and to the changing interpretations of poverty. The chapter also contains three 'In Focus' case studies: homelessness, policy relating to young people, and life below the poverty line. Both these groups are marginal to the mainstream interests of social policy, but represent illuminating examples of attempts to define and tackle need among the more vulnerable members of society. The chapter's conclusion visits the notion that, in essential aspects, the experience of the 'socially excluded' in contemporary Britain bears comparison with those 'in want' prior to the beginning of the Second World War.

The Liberal welfare reforms

In reviewing the progress of policy responses to poverty in the post-war period, it is necessary to step back a little and consider earlier context. It is for this reason that the following review begins at the start of the twentieth century. A message underlies this long narrative: that policy response to poverty in any context, in any country, and at any time rests on two closely interlinked factors: the ability of a society's national economy to alleviate poverty through giving financial assistance or assistance in kind to those deemed poor; and the *meaning* that society assigns to poverty, in terms of it being more or less the responsibility of the individual involved.

The Liberal welfare reforms of the period immediately prior to the First World War reflected a government 'determined to lay the ugly spectre of poverty' (Bruce, 1973: 127–8). A slew of major studies of deprivation in the second half of the nineteenth century had begun to undermine notions that poverty was in some degree a moral failing of the poor. Further illumination was afforded to Oxbridge students who were given the opportunity to take up voluntary work at Toynbee Hall. This educational establishment was set up in 1884 in the East End of London and gave students direct contact with those in need. Students carried their experiences into the higher echelons of the civil service and Whitehall, and the influence of Toynbee Hall was reflected in the efforts of many policy makers, including William Beveridge, to alleviate poverty.

At the beginning of the twentieth century, two measures were of particular note in setting both principle and precedent for later welfare interventions. The first was the introduction in 1908 of assistance for older people. The Old Age Pension Act was non-contributory, in that it did not require its recipients to have made a payment into any sort of scheme in order to benefit. All pensioners with income of less than £21 a week were given 5s a week which they collected at the Post Office. In addition, the Liberal government introduced, in 1911, the National Insurance Act. This Act combined insurance against both unemployment and ill health. The unemployment insurance covered workers in trades most subject to cyclical unemployment, such as shipbuilding and work in the iron industry. It was a contributory scheme: while they were in employment, the workers paid in 2d a week. The fund was boosted by an additional 2d paid by their employee and a further small sum by the government. During times of unemployment, the worker could draw from the scheme around 7s a week. Health insurance covered all manual workers on low incomes between the ages of 16 and 70.

On signing up with a friendly society, the worker paid 4d a week; their employer paid 3d and the government provided an additional 2d. The scheme paid out sickness and disability benefit and paid for access to medical services.

The 1930s and the means test

The Great Depression of the 1930s brought mass unemployment to industrial regions and undermined the actuarial basis of the unemployment insurance scheme, which by the 1920s had been extended to cover two-thirds of the workforce. Crucially, more payments were drawn than went into the scheme. The government, faced with the need to make stringent budget cuts, increased the contributions required from workers and cut benefits to those unemployed in order to balance the books. As the economic crisis intensified, successive governments further attempted to contain the cost of unemployment by introducing restrictions on those eligible for assistance. Of great cultural significance was the introduction in 1931, through the blandly titled Unemployment Insurance (National Economy) No. 2 Order, of the 'means test'. Under the Order, entitlement to unemployment benefit was restricted to a period of 26 weeks. After that time, 'transitional payments' would be available. These payments were to be overseen by local public assistance committees (PACs) which also administered the poor law. Applicants were subjected to detailed and intrusive enquiry into their domestic circumstances, since the payments would only be made following stringent examination of household income. A father's transitional payments could be reduced on account of his aged mother's pension, if they lived under the same roof. Many PACs routinely awarded low transition payments, or disallowed them altogether. Walter Greenwood's 1933 novel *Love on the Dole* is a fine description of the impact of the regulations in one northern town.

William Beveridge and the universal principle

It has been routinely asserted that the Second World War, the 'People's War' affecting civilians throughout Britain, was the catalyst for the introduction of a whole programme of social reforms implemented during and in the years immediately after the conflict. The war fostered a sense of solidarity and set precedents for state interference in all aspects of life, even including what was eaten and worn. The year 1942 saw the publication of *Social Insurance and Allied Services* by William Beveridge. The report reflected a belief that social security should rest on *universalism*, that is, that every member of society should have access to assistance as a right, with the implicit assumption that no one could be blamed for their poor economic circumstances. The report recognized three key causes of poverty – large families, ill health and unemployment – and the basic policy assumptions were, therefore, the introduction of some kind of family allowance; the development of a National Health Service; and a commitment by the government to maintain full employment. Fuller, more detailed and comprehensive recommendations were included, which for social security rested on six fundamental principles: that the principal benefit would be set at such a rate that it would cover basic living expenses; there would be a flat rate of benefit that did not take into account the previous income of the recipient; all contributors would pay into the scheme the same rate; the scheme would be national, but administered through local offices; and the scheme would take into account different needs among different sections of the population, for example, the self-employed and housewives without paid employment (Timmins, 1995).

Legislation to tackle 'want' followed. In 1945, the Family Allowances Act granted a 5s weekly payment to all children excepting the first child, a restriction introduced as a means of containing the cost of the scheme. The 1946 National Insurance Act reflected Beveridge's social security proposals, in introducing a comprehensive scheme of unemployment and sickness insurance, including additional one-off payments for eventualities such as the birth of children and funerals. Contributions to the cost of the scheme were made by individuals, employers and the state. In 1948 the National Assistance Act laid down benefit regulations for people who were outside the scope of the general insurance scheme including those who were long-term disabled and so had never been in employment. The poor law was abolished but some services were still to be administered at a local level, including encouragement to local authorities to provide services to support people with disabilities and to manage residential accommodation for those unable to live independently.

The 1960s and the rediscovery of poverty

It was thought at first that the new legislative measures were effective but, on reflection, general improvements were more likely to have reflected an extended period of low unemployment. In the mid-1960s, social policy experts 'rediscovered poverty'. In 1965, Brian Abel-Smith and Peter Townsend published *The Poor and the Poorest*. Using a base measure set at 140 per cent of the national assistance rate plus rent, Abel-Smith and Townsend found that in 1953/4, 7.8 per cent of families could be interpreted as being in relative poverty; by 1960 this figure had nearly doubled to 14.2 per cent. It became evident that certain portions of the population were falling through the welfare 'net', including older people who did not like to claim means-tested benefits; young children in large families, whose incomes had been affected by failures to increase child benefits in line with inflation; and households reliant on low-paid work, whose limited income precluded them from applying for means-tested benefits.

Paradoxically, the 1950s and 60s also saw successive increases in government welfare spending: indeed, by the mid-1960s, it became the highest single item of expenditure. Multiple small changes to the system – including the introduction of income-linked contributions in 1966 – undermined some of the key principles of Beveridge's scheme. In addition, the ongoing task of plugging gaps and making small refinements

Plate 20.1 An unemployed man and his family in Northern Ireland, taken from the *Picture Post's* 'One Man in Five is Out of Work' feature, December 1955 (© Hulton Archive/Getty).

added substantially to its complexity: in 1968 it was calculated that some 3000 different means tests were in operation, guiding the allocation of funds and tokens for one-off items, such as school uniforms and medical equipment, and more substantial and routine costs, such as rent and rate charges.

Poverty under Thatcher

Policies introduced by the Conservative government that came into power in 1979 reflected the development of new thinking on welfare. Of particular influence was theory that came from the United States. In his 1984 book, *Losing Ground*, Charles Murray, a US academic, claimed the existence of an 'underclass' of poor people who could be distinguished by their conscious unwillingness to conform to society standards but who were quite willing to rely on benefit payment rather than seek employment. In 1989, Murray was invited by the *Sunday Times* to extend his analysis to developments in the UK. In particular, Murray claimed to recognize the existence of young women who considered it advantageous to live on benefits while bringing up their children alone and young men who preferred not to work rather than to take up unskilled and low-paid work. In his view, the existence of benefits had – paradoxically – *created* poor households who chose dependency (Lister, 1996).

This kind of thinking contributed to the general desire to 'roll back the state' in all aspects of welfare policy. The continuing rise of expenditure on social security was met with stringent budget cuts, but more substantial alteration was introduced with the Social Security Act of 1986 (which came into force in April 1988). Under the Act, individuals were encouraged to opt out of the universal state pension scheme and set up their own pension arrangements, using service providers in the open marketplace. The Act also introduced the Social Fund. This fund replaced single payments of supplementary benefit (now renamed income support) for items such as clothing and larger furniture items that people on low incomes would normally be unable to pay for outright. Under the Social Fund, the applicant would be eligible only for a loan, the repayment of which would be removed automatically from the ongoing benefit payment. The Act also clarified the process of housing benefit – which met some or all the rent liability of the claimant. This benefit was simplified and harmonized with income support. Finally, some claimants lost entitlement altogether, including 16–18-year-olds living in the parental home and students.

In Focus

Cathy Come Home

Shown on BBC1 on 16 November 1966, *Cathy Come Home* remains the most influential documentary in the history of poverty in the UK. The screenplay was written by journalist and homelessness activist Jeremy Sandford. Shot in a vivid, semi-documentary style, the film told the story of Cathy, whose husband loses his job following a motorcycling accident. The sudden reduction in income means that the couple and their children lose their home. The family stays in successively poor-quality accommodation and in hostels, and Cathy is separated from her husband. In a heart-rending final scene, shot on the streets, Cathy's young children are taken into care by the social services. A special screening of the documentary was arranged for Parliament, and further publicity campaigns using the film led to the creation of the homeless charities Shelter and Crisis.

Cathy Come Home can be viewed as part of a series of campaigning works that highlighted both the nature of homelessness and the inadequacy of policy responses. For example, George Orwell's *Down and Out in Paris and London* (1933) describes the author's stay in a succession of 'spikes'. Spikes, or 'casual wards' were provided under poor law regulations and were intended to provide overnight accommodation for people who were moving around to find work. Their regimes were deliberately punitive: men were allowed into the spike only in the evening, and they were ejected in the morning after being given a meagre breakfast. A similar account of

> ### Cathy Come Home

life in temporary hostels was written in 1981 by the journalist Tony Wilkinson working for the BBC1 *Nationwide* programme, indicating that little had changed since the 1930s.

Following the massed homelessness that had been created in some areas by aerial bombardment, homelessness was deemed more an issue for families after the Second World War. Part III of the National Assistance Act 1948 Section 2(1)(b) acknowledged the need to provide statutory assistance to people deemed homeless. The Act placed responsibility for dealing with homelessness in the realms of welfare departments in local authorities, underlining the fact that the inability to secure accommodation often reflected personal or family difficulties. However, in order to provide accommodation, families were often split up, with wives separated from their husbands and parents from their children, again reflecting the old poor law regulations. This was the situation reflected so starkly in the *Cathy Come Home* documentary.

During the 1970s and 1980s, homelessness increased substantially and by the 1990s 'sleeping rough' had become a visible and endemic problem. The stereotype of aged 'dossers' sleeping on the streets under sheets of newspaper was challenged by successive waves of research on the characteristics of homeless people. In 1991, a survey of single homeless people found substantial variation in the ages and circumstances among its sample. Young people, people with a history of living in different types of institution, and people from ethnic minorities were all evident (Anderson *et al.*, 1993).

Unemployment rates soared from the mid-to-late 1970s. Indeed, the Conservatives had come into power under the banner slogan 'Labour isn't working'. The situation worsened during the 1980s. The numbers of individuals out of work and claiming benefit increased from 4 per cent in 1979 to 10 per cent in 1983, topping 3 million at the highest peak (Nickell, 1999). In some senses, the unemployed were blamed for their plight and the 'benefit scrounger' became a regular feature of newspaper exposés. Employment Secretary Norman Tebbitt pandered to popular prejudice in 1981, when he declared that such people should 'get on their bikes' and look for work, as his father had done in the 1930s. Again, as in the interwar years, rapidly rising unemployment rates provoked the need to target benefits further for those out of work. Successive changes increased the amount of time required for payment into the scheme in order for claimants to receive unemployment benefit. Greater penalties were applied to those who left work without good reason: they were made ineligible for full assistance for six months. Fuller revision to the system came in the 1990s.

Under John Major, the Conservatives introduced the jobseeker's allowance (JSA) in December 1993; in 2006 this benefit was still in operation. The JSA replaced previous payments to those who were unemployed and reduced the period of payment from twelve to six months. Receipt of JSA is tied strongly to the production of evidence that the recipient is actively seeking employment. A 'jobseeker's agreement' sets out the steps that will be taken to find work, and periodic interviews take place at the job-centre in order to keep track of progress. A failure to meet the requirements of the scheme could lead to JSA payments being suspended.

In Focus

The 'Costa del Dole' scandal

The ambiguities inherent within welfare policies for young people were highlighted in the summer of 1985 when newspapers became full of what was termed the 'Costa del Dole' scandal. Policy makers have always faced problems in framing legislation that will offer financial support to young people, since it is assumed that where benefit regimes are generous, young people will be encouraged to leave the parental home and live independently, wholly subsidized by the state.

This argument came to the fore when in 1985 sudden concern was attached to the use of board and lodgings by young people. Use of such accommodation had massively increased from 23,000 in 1982 to 85,000 in 1985. The media reported that young people were using the benefit to subsidize life in hotels at seaside resorts – the so-called 'Costa del Dole'. MPs in the House of Commons referred to 'schoolgirl daughters . . . paid for by the DSS' living in Morecambe with their boyfriends. New regulations were introduced that set a time limit on the period for which board and lodgings payments would be made, with particularly stringent limits set for the 'resort' areas. More substantially, at this time a change was made with regard to the householder/non-householder distinction that had allowed a higher level of benefit to be paid to people who were living independently. Instead, all recipients under the age of 25 – whatever their circumstances – would receive a lower level of benefit on the assumption that most under-25s would be living with their parents.

A final alteration, introduced in 1996, restricted the amount of housing benefit that would be paid to under-25s, so that it would always be equivalent to the average cost of a room in a shared house, no matter if the young person lived in another type of accommodation with a higher cost. Arguments against the cut highlighted the poor basis of the assumption that young people's housing behaviour was being influenced by the availability of benefit. In fact, leaving the parental home early is often a sign of family breakdown: many such young people are no longer able to secure financial support from their parents. Indeed, young people living alone needed *more* not less support since they were often ill prepared for the responsibility of being a householder.

> ### The 'Costa del Dole' scandal
>
> Housing benefit regulations have been supplemented by other regulations to further disadvantage young people. New Labour's 'welfare to work' programme introduced, in 1998, a 'New Deal for Young People'. New Deal is compulsory to everyone under the age of 25 if they have been unemployed for more than six months. Under the programme, extended efforts would be made to assist young people to gain employment, after which one of four options would be available: full-time education or training; subsidized employment; work with the Environment Task Force or unpaid work (but still supported by benefit) in the voluntary sector. Financial support is only available for young people taking up one of these options. Changes to benefit entitlement have been cited as a major reason for the increased evidence of youth homelessness in the 1980s and 90s.

New Labour, new solutions?

The advent of New Labour in 1997 brought no substantially new ideas to the administration of social security. However, policies became more tightly focused on the need to encourage people back into work, and it was declared that Labour would rebuild the welfare state around the work ethic. There was a change to both unemployment policy and to benefit support for low-paid families. A programme of 'New Deal' initiatives targeted sub-groups within the wider population of unemployed people, including young people, people with disabilities, lone parents, people in long-term unemployment and the partners of people who were unemployed. An essential element of New Deal was for the receipt of benefit to be more strongly linked to action on behalf of the recipient, with government agencies taking greater responsibility for delivering intensive advice, training and education packages to get people back into work. As with earlier Conservative policies, benefit reductions were a consequence if recipients did not meet their obligations, but under Labour these reductions could be applied to any benefit received by the entire household.

For people in low-paid work, there were two new developments. First, the government introduced – for the first time in the UK – a national minimum wage of £4.85 per hour, applicable across all industry sectors. Second, a working families tax credit became available to households with dependent children, with earnings below a certain income level and where the recipient worked at least 16 hours per week. The payment would be made not as a benefit, but through the wage packet, with the rationale that such a measure would 'associate the payment in the recipient's mind with the fact of working, a potentially valuable psychological change' (HM Treasury, 1998: 8).

Although social security administration had not changed substantially, New Labour embraced the notion of 'social exclusion'. The phrase has never clearly been defined by policy makers, but reflected attempts to view poverty in terms of multiple deprivations: those who were deemed 'socially excluded' had low incomes, poor health and limited education. They lived in areas blighted by high levels of long-term unemployment, with above-average crime rates. All these factors were thought to feed into each other, exacerbating a household's 'exclusion' from society norms: limited employment opportunities led to low spending on nutritious food, which led to ill health; a lack of interest in education led to young people aimlessly hanging around streets, increasing the incidence of petty crime. The introduction of the Social Exclusion Unit in 1997 was a means by which policy could be 'joined up' to ensure that social exclusion could be tackled from a number of angles simultaneously (Hills and Stewart, 2005). However, it is telling that on 1 October 1997, social policy commentators wrote to the *Financial Times* praising the scheme but also criticizing the Labour government for failing to include any reassessment of benefit levels in its new social exclusion agenda.

Poverty: an enduring problem

There is general agreement that, during the final quarter of the twentieth century, poverty has become more pronounced and has defied the ability of policy makers to arrive at adequate solutions. In 1979, around one-tenth of the British population could be defined as being poor. In 1995/6, the comparable figure was one in five. These figures relate to *relative poverty*, that is, the number of households whose incomes are less than half that of the average household income. Overall, incomes have increased for the majority of households, but the gap between the richest and poorest has become wider. Many reasons have been cited for the continued incidence of poverty, despite ever-increasing expenditure on social security measures.

For many commentators, the incidence of poverty reflects a number of changes that have taken place to family structures in the post-war period. It has always been the case that poverty relates to 'lifecycles' and that households are more vulnerable at certain times: for example, where there are young children and so mothers cannot take paid employment, or when an individual is no longer able to work because of old age. Changes in demographics have increased the numbers of people who are more likely to be poor. First, there has been an increase in the number of single parent households and – in particular – a growing number of single parent households where the parent is not in work. During the 1960s in particular, there was a substantial growth in the incidence of divorce. In 1961, UK divorces numbered around 27,200; by 1991 this figure had increased to 158,700 (Rowlinson, 2003). The number of divorces, together with growth in the number of births outside marriage, has led to expansion in the proportion of households in which a single adult is taking care of dependent children. For many such households, it is difficult for the parent to secure work that will also cover the costs of childcare, or to secure employment that would accommodate the school day. As a consequence, within the lowest income group, the single parent has increased from being 5 per cent of that cluster in 1961–3, to 15 per cent in 1991–3. A second substantial shift has been the growing number of pensioner households. For men, life expectancy increased from 59.4 in 1940 to 73.2 in 1991. As with the population more generally, income distribution among pensioners is wide: those with occupational pensions generally have higher incomes, and younger pensioners generally fare better than older. However, many faced decades reliant on the state retirement pension. In 1979, 16 per cent of pensioner couples had incomes below the contemporary mean; by 1992–3, this figure had increased to 25 per cent (Burgess and Propper, 1999).

Shifts in the labour market have also had a substantial impact on the incidence of poverty. In the post-war economy, traditionally male-dominated industries – such as mining, shipbuilding, steel and iron production – have declined and, in some areas, disappeared altogether. These changes have led to a disproportionate incidence of unemployment among men without formal qualifications. In 1979, the unemployment rate was 7 per cent for those with no qualifications; in 1998, the figure was 15.6 per cent (Nickell, 1999). A greater proportion of women are entering the labour market, but traditionally women's work has tended to be in lower-paid, part-time and insecure work. Indeed, the lowest-paid occupations continue to be dominated by those in which female employment is high, such as care work, catering, hairdressing and retail. However, poor conditions have begun to percolate into the male labour market. For example, in the period from 1975 to the 1990s, the incidence of low pay for men in the labour market has doubled (Stewart, 1999).

These basic, structural, social and economic changes have undermined the operation of a social security system that was initially based on a number of assumptions: that governments would always be committed to maintaining full employment, that men would be the main breadwinner in the majority of households, and that they would be able to contribute to a national system in order to meet their household's costs in the limited periods in which they would be out of work. Since the end of the Second World War successive minor amendments to the social security system have been unable to mitigate the failure to meet these assumptions. Nevertheless, it could still be argued that the use of *relative* poverty measures masks the fact that, overall, 'want' in Britain – as understood by men such as Beveridge – has disappeared. Sir Keith Joseph, later a minister in Thatcher's Conservative government, claimed in 1976 that 'A family is poor if it cannot afford to eat. By any absolute standards there is very little poverty in Britain today.' Much of the discussion of poverty in the 1990s reflected increases in *income inequality*, rather than absolute need (Gordon, 2000).

Nevertheless, the idea that the current social security system affords even a basic 'safety net' for households on low incomes is denied by reports that underline the difficulties for families seeking to exist on state benefits. Quantitative studies that use various measures to assess the incidence of poverty fail to convey the qualitative experience of living on a low income, below whatever version of the poverty line is currently in vogue. For those on low incomes, there remains a difficult decision-making process on how to stretch limited funds between the competing imperatives of providing shelter capable of being heated, of feeding the family, and of providing adequate clothing.

In 1996, Kempson produced the report *Life on a Low Income*, which used a series of qualitative studies to describe how families coped. For many, diet was filling rather than nutritious; the use of gas and electric heating was cautious, with many having to budget using the more expensive method of coin metres; and there was a fear that expenditure may be required on clothing – particularly if there was damage to shoes and winter coats. These findings bore comparison with the earlier work of Peter Townsend in the 1960s (chairman of the Child Poverty Action Group from 1969) and even with Seebohm Rowntree's poverty survey of 1950. It is, perhaps, also worth noting the findings of a 1997 study that indicated that the least healthy areas – those having the highest mortality rates – were also those in which the indicators of poverty were the greatest (Dorling, 1997).

In Focus

Life below the minimum

Man 79 and wife 80 . . . Because they buy no clothes, they can just manage on their income, but there is no money for pleasure. They both suffer from the cold, and if they had more money it would be spent on coal in preference to anything else.

B. Seebohm Rowntree and G.R. Lavers, *Poverty and the Welfare State* (1951)

'If the wife doesn't get some shoes soon she won't be able to go out. What will happen to the little one then? . . . Look at how we have to manage. We drew £7.50 today. There was £6.10 for food at the shop and from the rest we can get one bag of coal. We can't get two bags.' They buy all their clothing through clothing clubs, and have been missing payments lately. Mrs Agnew has not had a new winter coat in the last three years.

Peter Townsend, *Poverty in the United Kingdom* (1979)

'I try to cut down on the electric. Many a Sunday afternoon our electric has gone. We've just waited 'til Monday [the day she collected her benefit].'

Elaine Kempson, *Life on a Low Income* (1996)

In reviewing the incidence of, and meanings ascribed to, poverty over the course of the second half of the twentieth century, it is appropriate to conclude that developments have been cyclical. Beveridge recognized that effective measures to tackle poverty would require a broad assault on unemployment, ill health, poor educational attainment and low-standard housing. His solution was the implementation of a universalist scheme that introduced a national system of education, the National Health Service and a social security system that aimed to deliver a basic level of income to all households. Changes in demography and in the labour force have undermined the ability of the system to deliver on its promise. There has been difference in opinion on the methods of measurement, definitions of and meanings that can be ascribed to poverty, but it was incontrovertible that in 2001 New Labour was faced with well-established evidence of a growing incidence of multiple deprivation requiring solutions on a number of fronts. In contemporary Britain, it is still the case that a substantial number of persons experience homelessness, go without adequate food, and/or do not have sufficient incomes to buy appropriate clothing or heat their homes in the winter.

Debates and Interpretations

The progress of social policy in the post-war period spans the disciplines of both history and social policy, with much of the relevant documentation falling in the latter field. However, in terms of historiography, a great deal of writing on post-war poverty has focussed on questions that relate to the degree of political consensus attached to the passage of welfare legislation in the post-war period. The contention that there was universal support for the notion of a 'welfare state', bolstered by war experience, is highlighted by Paul Addison. Alternative approaches indicate pre-war policy developments that were a necessary precursor. Shifting objectives for welfare and the degree to which the 1979 Conservative government introduced a radical challenge to general consensus on welfare principles remains subject to debate, as does the extent to which New Labour continued the development of essentially Thatcherite policies.

A common evaluatory device with regard to sociology and social policy is to consider the competing claims of 'structure' and 'agency' explanations for personal experiences. With regard to poverty, structural arguments would pinpoint the wider market forces that engineer outcomes that individuals are unable to escape: for example, broader labour market changes that reduce demand for unskilled labourers so increase unemployment rates for that group. Agency explanations are more likely to focus on an individual's responses to these contexts, and so would perhaps consider welfare dependency as an active choice. For some commentators, the existence of welfare support in itself undermines recipients' ability to seek and retain a degree of financial independence.

It is worth remembering that while, for a significant number of people, poverty is a lived experience, it is also an abstract concept. Definitions of poverty, along with notions of a 'poverty line', did not remain static through the twentieth century and were far from value free, often incorporating middle-class understandings of idleness and 'deserving' poverty. In addition, arbitrary notions of deprivation tend to be bound with multi-sensory perceptions of what poverty looked, smelt and sounded like. The middle-class bias of studies of poverty began to be redressed in the second half of the century. Indeed, one of the more recent streams within both historiography and social policy is the increasing attention given to the voices of the underprivileged, through oral history interviews and by revisiting official policy-related documentation in an attempt to construct a historical understanding of the experience of poverty.

Further reading

For debates concerning the degree of consensus with regard to the formulation of a welfare state, compare Paul Addison's classic consensus text, *The Road to 1945: British Politics and the Second World War* (London, 1975), with Pat Thane's *The Foundations of the Welfare State* (Harlow, 1996), which advances a case for the importance of pre-war policy in shaping the fabric of the 1945 welfare reforms. To situate debates concerning poverty within the broader context of welfare reforms, Margaret Jones and Rodney Lower's (eds) excellent *From Beveridge to Blair: The First Fifty Years of Britain's Welfare State 1948–1998* (Manchester, 2002) provides an overview of key facets of welfare reform: health care, education, social security, personal social services and housing. Utilizing a wide range of documentary evidence (from government papers to newspaper stories and personal testimony), the book posits welfare initiatives within the context of the vision-shaping reforms and examines the outcomes of those reforms.

A history of poverty in the post-war period is encompassed within the much broader debate attached to the rise and fall of the 'welfare state'. For many commentators, the best summary of this history is given in Nicholas Timmins' *The Five Giants: A Biography of the Welfare State* (London, 2001), which outlines much of the political manoeuvring that underpinned social policy change in the 50 years following Beveridge's report. Useful succinct summaries are available in David Gladstone's *The Twentieth Century Welfare State* (Basingstoke, 1999) and Helen Fawcett, 'The Welfare State since 1945', in Jonathan Hollowell (ed.) *Britain Since 1945* (Oxford, 2003: 442–60). Joan C. Brown's chapter 'Poverty in Post-War Britain', in James Obelkevich and Peter Catterall's *Understanding Post-War British Society* (London, 1994), considers poverty by testing later policy developments against the principles underlying support for Beveridge's proposals, including the desire to ensure that benefits were set at an adequate level and that dignity should be afforded to those in financial difficulties. An alternative approach is taken in P. Alcock's 'Poverty and Social Security', in Robert Payne and Richard Silburn's *British Social Welfare in the Twentieth Century* (Basingstoke, 1999). David Vincent's *Poor Citizens: The State and the Poor in Twentieth Century Britain* (London, 1991) summarizes a great deal of material in a readily accessible narrative. For overviews of particular aspects of the welfare state, see Paul Johnson, 'The Welfare State, Income and Living Standards', in Roderick Floud and Paul Johnson (eds) *The Cambridge Economic History of Modern Britain: Structural Change and Growth, 1939–2000*, Vol. 3 (Cambridge, 2004: 213–37) and Rodney Lower, 'Modernizing Britain's Welfare State: The Influence of Affluence, 1957–64', in Lawrence Black and Hugh Pemberton (eds) *An Affluent Society? Britain's Post-War 'Golden Age'* (Aldershot, 2004: 35–51).

Research into the policies of late-twentieth-century governments can be found in Rodney Lower's *The Welfare State in Britain Since 1945* (Basingstoke, 2005) and M. Hewitt, 'New Labour and Social Security', in M. Powell (ed.) *New Labour, New Welfare State?* (Bristol, 1999). P. Toynbee and D. Walker's *Did Things Get Better: An Audit of Labour's Successes and Failures* (London, 2001) indicates the difficulties in establishing just how far more recent social security initiatives have had a redistributive effect in taxing the rich to ensure better standards for those on lower incomes. For material addressing the structures of poverty, see William Julius Wilson's *When Work Disappears: The World of the New Urban Poor* (New

York, 1996), which describes the impact of a global downturn in demand for blue-collar workers on inner-city communities. The arguments are played out within the UK context by H. Dean and Taylor-Gooby's *Dependency Culture: The Explosion of a Myth* (London, 1992).

Attempts to locate the agency of those designated poor are best represented in T. Hitchcock, Peter King and Pamela Sharpe (eds) *Chronicling Poverty: The Voices and Strategies of the English Poor, 1640–1840* (Basingstoke, 1997). Referring to an earlier period, this collection of essays indicates the value of using policy-related documentary evidence to understand the experience of poverty. A contemporary social policy analogue is Carol Walker's *Managing Poverty: The Limits of Social Assistance* (London, 1993), which included interviews with social security claimants.

References

Anderson, I., Kemp, P. and Quilgars, D. (1993) *Single Homeless People*. London: HMSO.

Bruce, Maurice (1973) *The Rise of the Welfare State*. London: Weidenfeld & Nicolson.

Burgess, Simon and Propper, Carol (1999) 'Poverty in Britain', in Paul Gregg and Jonathan Wadsworth (eds) *The State of Working Britain*. Manchester: Manchester University Press.

Department of Social Security (1999) *Opportunity for All: Tackling Poverty and Social Exclusion*. London: DSS.

Department for Work and Pensions (2004) *Households Below Average Income: An Analysis of Income Distribution 1994/5–2003/4*. Leeds: Corporate Document Services.

Dorling, Danny (1997) 'Changing mortality ratios in local areas of Britain 1950s–1990s', *Joseph Rowntree Findings: Social Policy Research*, 126.

Gordon, David (2000) *Poverty and Social Exclusion in Britain*. York: Joseph Rowntree Foundation.

Hills, John and Stewart, Kitty (eds) (2005) *A More Equal Society: New Labour, Poverty, Inequality and Exclusion*. Bristol: The Policy Press.

HM Treasury (1998) *The Modernisation of Britain's Tax and Benefit System Number 2: Work Incentives: A Report by Martin Taylor*. London: HMSO.

Lister, Ruth (ed.) (1996) *Charles Murray and the Underclass: The Developing Debate*. London: Institute for Economic Affairs.

Nickell, Stephen (1999) 'Unemployment in Britain', in Paul Gregg and Jonathan Wadsworth (eds) *The State of Working Britain*. Manchester: Manchester University Press.

Rowlingson, Karen (2003) ' "From Cradle to Grave": Social Security over the Life Cycle', in Jane Millar (ed.) *Understanding Social Security*. Bristol: The Policy Press.

Stewart, M.B. (1999) 'Low Pay in Britain', in Paul Gregg and Jonathan Wadsworth (eds) *The State of Working Britain*. Manchester: Manchester University Press.

Timmins, Nicholas (1995) *The Five Giants: A Biography of the Welfare State*. London: Fontana.

21

Religion and 'secularization'

John Wolffe

SHORTLY AFTER THE END OF THE Second World War, Mass Observation (1947) conducted a study of popular attitudes to religion in an unspecified London borough. It was concluded that:

> Not more than one person in ten . . . is at all closely associated with any of the churches, and about two-thirds never or practically never go to Church. The majority, however – four out of five women and two out of three men – give at least verbal assent to the possibility of there being a God, and most of the rest express doubt rather than disbelief. Uncompromising disbelievers in a Deity amount to about one in twenty.

The somewhat negative tone with which this quotation opens illustrates the widespread perception of the twentieth century as a period in which religion became marginal to everyday life. However, almost any other activity that attracted the committed involvement of up to a tenth of the population, the passive sympathy of two-thirds to four-fifths of a sample, and was totally rejected by only one-twentieth of respondents, would be regarded as a successful and influential historical force. Thus we confront immediately the problem of how to interpret the evidence regarding the place of religion in the life of the people of Britain during the decades after 1939: should we dwell on how far the 'tide of faith' had gone out, or concentrate our attention rather on how much water remained in the sea?

The view of the twentieth century as an era of decline in organized religion is one that can superficially be supported by sequences of statistics such as those in Table 21.1 (p. 324). During the first half of the century near stability in absolute numbers in the Church of England masked significant decline in its proportional support in the population. From the 1960s falls in both absolute and relative terms were steep and unmistakable. The sequences for the Roman Catholic Church show, however, a rather

Table 21.1 Membership of selected religious denominations, 1900–2000
(in m with % of total population in brackets)

	Church of England		Church of Scotland		Roman Catholic	
1900	2.90*	(8.9)	1.15	(25.7)	1.91*	(4.9)
1925	3.60	(9.2)	1.30	(26.2)	2.18*	(4.8)
1940	3.39	(8.2)	1.28	(25.8)	2.23*	(4.6)
1950	2.96	(6.7)	1.27	(24.9)	2.43*	(4.8)
1960	2.86	(6.2)	1.30	(25.1)	2.85*	(5.4)
1970	2.56	(5.6)	1.15	(22.0)	2.75	(5.0)
1980	1.82	(3.7)	0.96	(18.7)	2.46	(4.3)
1990	1.40	(2.7)	0.79	(15.6)	2.20	(3.8)
2000	1.34*	(2.5)	0.61	(11.9)	1.72*	(2.8)

Notes: (a) Asterixed figures are estimates.
(b) The figures for the Church of England are calculated as a percentage of the population of England and Wales, but do not include the Church in Wales. Apart from the estimated figure for 1900 they are electoral roll numbers, which first became available in 1924. Figures for the Church of Scotland are given as a percentage of the population of Scotland; those for Roman Catholics are mass attendances, relating to the whole of the United Kingdom, including Northern Ireland with its relatively very large Catholic population.
(c) Calculations are based on the nearest available census data; that for 1925 is the mean of the 1921 and 1931 censuses, that for 1940 is the mean of the 1931 and 1951 censuses.
(d) Figures for the Church of Scotland for 1900 and 1925 include the United Free Church which amalgamated with it in 1929.

different pattern: here numbers advanced throughout the first half of the century, and the peak was not reached until 1960. The Church of Scotland was much stronger relative to population than the Church of England and, like the Roman Catholic Church, its position remained stable until the 1960s. All three churches declined seriously in the last quarter of the century, although for the Church of England, which had led the trend, there were indications that the fall was bottoming out by 2000. Regional and national contrasts were very marked: in Northern Ireland in 1971 more than 90 per cent of the population identified with a particular denominational group (Fulton, 1991). There were also significant gender differences: around 1980, female churchgoers comprised 55 per cent of the total in England, 62 per cent in Scotland and 63 per cent in Wales. We shall explore further below the difficulty of interpreting such statistics, but for the moment they represent an important caution against viewing trends in religious commitment in a uniform fashion.

The early twentieth century

Nevertheless, there had been important changes in the period between 1900 and 1945. The Victorian era had seen a great flowering of religious energies, still apparent today in its massive legacy of church buildings. This did not produce anything approaching universal churchgoing, but in the face of the challenges of industrialization, urbanization, and rapid population growth, the proportion of commitment and observance remained approximately constant at least until the 1880s. Thereafter, especially among nonconformists, relative decline set in, but the Church of England proved to be initially more resilient, and it was not until after the turn of the century that absolute numbers declined.

Explanations of the loss of Victorian momentum are numerous and can only be noted briefly here. It is frequently argued that the cultural impact of Darwinian ideas of human origins, and historical and moral criticism of the Bible progressively undermined the ideological credibility of Christianity. From the perspective of social history the relative success of the churches in the nineteenth century has been attributed to their importance as 'midwives' of the transition to an industrialized, class-based society, and their subsequent decline to social redundancy once that process was complete. A related argument is to point to the growing importance of the state in taking over administrative, educational and social welfare functions previously exercised by religious organizations. Explanation is also couched in terms of a crisis of morale within organized Christianity itself, with theological uncertainty and institutional ossification feeding off each other.

On the other hand, especially outside England, significant signs of religious vitality remained. The continuing loyalty of around a quarter of the Scottish population to the Church of Scotland was probably assisted by the completion in 1929 of a process of Presbyterian reunification which facilitated the identification of church and nation. Similarly the disestablishment of the (Anglican) Church in Wales in 1920 freed it from the appearance of being an alien English institution and its communicant numbers had increased by more than 20 per cent by 1939. The Roman Catholic Church also benefited from an enduring sense of community identity among the Irish population in Britain. In a more diffuse and limited fashion the Church of England was also shielded somewhat from decline by the patriotic loyalties it inspired as a national church.

The impact of the two world wars on religious life was an ambivalent one. To a limited extent a sense of spiritual crusade rekindled a form of Christian devotion in both 1914 and 1939–40. The observances of Armistice Day and Remembrance Sunday were to provide an enduring link between the churches and the wider community. The Second World War also gave a prophetic status and national prominence to Christian leaders such as William Temple, briefly Archbishop of Canterbury from 1942 to 1944, and George Bell, Bishop of Chichester, a vigorous opponent of the bombing of German cities by the Royal Air Force. On the other hand, not only did the wars disrupt the normal habits of Christian practice, but for many they also challenged conventional theological assumptions. Experience of the Western Front in the First World War tested to the limit belief in the providence and care of God; the horror of the Nazi concentration camps in the Second World War again led many to doubt either God's omnipotence or His goodness. It is certainly observable that the 1940s saw rather sharper falls in denominational memberships than the interwar period had done, although the situation stabilized again in the 1950s.

The limitations of statistics

How much do the dry bones of the figures for membership really tell us about the religious life of the British people since 1945? Certainly they indicate significant trends over time, but the information that, say, 6.7 per cent of the population of England and Wales in 1950 had their names on the electoral roll of a Church of England parish tells us little if it is taken in isolation from other evidence. On the one hand, people could identify themselves with a Christian denomination for social rather than spiritual reasons (although this is in itself an interesting phenomenon for the historian); on the other, the widespread perception that 'You do not need to go to church to be a Christian' suggests that membership statistics may significantly understate popular religious belief. Certainly such figures routinely excluded one very significant group: children judged too young to make a formal profession of faith or undertake the responsibilities of church membership. Their attendance at religious worship was often involuntary and frequently ceased in the mid-to-late teens, but not before it had left them with a certain deposit of diffuse Christian ideas.

Influence of this kind helps to explain the high proportion of vaguely theistic belief noted by the Mass Observation researchers in 1947, and also evident in the opinion poll and survey evidence summarized in Table 21.2. This has to be regarded with caution because a great deal depends on the phrasing of questions, which differed slightly between the sources used in the table. The general impression is of downward drift in the extent of belief, especially in the perception regarding the nature of Jesus that defines a broadly orthodox Christian. It is true that a substantial majority of the popu-

Table 21.2 Opinion poll and survey returns on religious belief (%)

	God	Belief in Jesus as Son of God	Life after death
1947	84		49
1957	78	71	54
1963	71	60	53
1973	74		37
1982	73	43	40
1990s	67		44

Source: Based on Gallup, 1976: I: 166, 405, 682; II: 1250–1; Gill, 1999: 70; Krarup, 1982: 46, 48–9.

lation continued to believe in some kind of god. However, when people were asked more specifically about God, it transpired that although belief in an impersonal life force remained very constant at around 40 per cent, belief in a distinctively Christian personal god declined from 43 per cent in the 1940s and 50s to 31 per cent in the 1990s. The slight upturn in the 1980s and 90s in belief in life after death is interesting, but suggests more a generalized renewal of interest in spiritual matters than a return to Christianity as such.

Quantitative evidence is helpful in pointing up both significant changes and notable continuities in the history of religion in Britain since the Second World War. Even more than in other fields of social history, however, it is ultimately something of a blunt and potentially treacherous instrument. It accordingly needs to be complemented by a brief survey of other major developments.

The 1950s and 60s

As the figures in the tables indicate, the 1950s were indeed a period of near stability in religious life. Geoffrey Fisher, Archbishop of Canterbury from 1945 to 1961, was distinguished more by administrative acumen than prophetic vision, a make-up shared by his Roman Catholic counterparts, Cardinals Griffin and Godfrey. Such leaders generally seemed well suited to their times. The machinery of institutional Christianity was kept in fairly good order, and the loyalty of the faithful was nourished and retained. The Billy Graham crusades in the middle of the decade were a serious attempt to evangelize the unchurched, but their most enduring result was probably a reawakening of spiritual fervour among existing congregations. Meanwhile, Christianity seemed assured of a prominent place in national and cultural life: in 1953 Elizabeth II was crowned queen amidst the glories of Anglican ceremonial; the novels and theological writings of C.S. Lewis enjoyed great popularity; while the building of a new Coventry cathedral, consecrated in 1962, became a potent symbol of reconstruction after the horrors of war.

Before the end of the decade, however, signs of change were in the air. In January 1959 the recently elected Pope John XXIII announced the summoning of a general council of the Roman Catholic Church, which eventually convened in Rome in October 1962, and lasted until the end of 1965. The Council transformed the nature of Roman Catholic liturgy and in 1967 Pope Paul VI authorized the saying of Mass in the vernacular. There was a general softening of the Roman Catholic Church's authoritarian ethos and a reformulation of doctrine in terms that drew closer to other Christians and hence stimulated ecumenical activity. In 1968, however, the publication of Paul VI's encyclical *Humanae Vitae*, condemning artificial methods of contraception, indicated that the process of reform had its limits and gave rise to widespread conflict and demoralization in the Roman Catholic Church. In the meantime, controversy of a rather different kind had been stirred by the publication in 1963 of a short book by the Anglican Bishop of Woolwich, John Robinson, entitled *Honest to God*. Faced with the secularity of south London, Robinson argued for a new theological language that would make sense for men and women outside the churches and implied a fundamental rethinking of traditional images of God and the supernatural. Moreover such change and controversy in the religious world both reflected and contributed to the general social and cultural climate of radical questioning and reform characteristic of the 1960s. In particular, the arguments over *Humanae Vitae* related to a much more widespread secular climate of change in sexual mores, in which relationships outside marriage lost much of their social stigma, and abortion and homosexual relations between consenting adults were legalized. In this environment even more liberal Christians struggled not to seem out of touch.

Britain's final retreat from empire in the 1960s also had important implications for religious consciousness. During the late nineteenth and early twentieth centuries a sense of imperial civilizing mission had combined potently with Christian evangelistic zeal to give ideological legitimation to British control over non-European territories. In 1947 the granting of independence to India and Pakistan had removed a key support of this structure of cultural assumptions; in the 1960s the 'wind of change' in Africa took this process much further. Britain was left less sure of herself, her identity and her role in the world, and, given the extent to which religion had earlier been bound up with patriotism, national uncertainty contributed to the climate of religious questioning. Meanwhile, ever-increasing facility of travel and communication heightened awareness of religions other than Christianity in Britain, as in the West generally. Buddhism, in particular, gained a following among the indigenous population of the United Kingdom.

Religious minorities and Christian reassertion

Moreover, one important legacy of empire remained to challenge traditional assumptions at home. Up to the 1950s Britain had been a 'Christian' country in the sense that for the vast majority of the population Christianity was the only obvious organized religious option. True, there was a long-standing Jewish community, numbering about 300,000 in 1920 and rising to about 450,000 by the 1960s, but this was religiously self-contained and did not expect or seek converts from the majority population. By the mid-1960s, however, substantial numbers of Hindus, Muslims and Sikhs had arrived in Britain, mainly from the Indian subcontinent and East Africa. Initially at least, these groups were relatively isolated from 'mainstream' religion and culture, but gradually their presence began to diversify the range of religious options apparent to the people of Britain. Until the census of 2001 for the first time included a question on religious identification, it was impossible to calculate numbers of adherents to minority religions with any precision. Table 21.3 (p. 329) gives estimates for the size of these communities in 1975 and the actual numbers returned in the 2001 census. Estimates of other smaller communities in 1988 were 5000 Ba'hais, 20,000 Jains, and 5000 Zoroastrians (Knott, 1988). It should be borne in mind, however, that these figures (unlike Table 21.1) are

Table 21.3 Minority religious populations in Britain

	1975 (estimates)	2001 (Eng + Wales)	2001 (Scotland)
Hindus	300,000	552,421	5564
Jews	400,000	259,927	6448
Muslims	400,000	1,546,626	42,557
Sikhs	200,000	329,358	6572
Buddhists		144,453	6830

Source: Based on *UK Christian Handbook Religious Trends No. 3 2002/2003* (London, 2001): 10.7; *Census 2001: National Report for England and Wales* (London, 2003): 182; *Scotland's Census 2001 Reference Volume* (Edinburgh, 2003): 279.

based on numbers identifying themselves with the respective religions, rather than those actively practising them, who were likely to have been significantly less numerous. Moreover, the extent of the impact of minority religions varied substantially over the country in reflection of the geography of settlement itself, concentrated in London and the other major cities, notably Birmingham, Bradford and Leicester. In rural and small-town Britain, it remained possible, even in the late 1980s, for people to live their daily lives without normally encountering an adherent of a religion other than Christianity. The presence of religious minorities was much less strong in Scotland than in England, with Muslims, the most numerous group, only making up 0.84 per cent of the population in 2001, whereas they were 2.97 per cent of the population of England and Wales. In Northern Ireland, census data indicate there were still, in 2001, only a total 5028 adherents of 'other religions and philosophies' in 2001, making up a tiny 0.3 per cent of the province's population.

The legacy of the 1960s proved to be an ambivalent one. Although, as we have seen, statistical measures of the overall extent of religious commitment and practice were set firmly on a downward trend, there were three important contrary tendencies. First, among those still identifying with organized religion, levels of commitment tended to increase. In particular, among Christians there was a resurgence of evangelical forms of belief and practice, characterized by strong emphasis on the authority of the Bible, and a stress on personal conversion and commitment. During the 1970s evangelicalism gained further stimulus from the charismatic movement which claimed the direct inspiration and prompting of the Holy Spirit, and contributed to a wider trend to freer and more culturally 'relevant' forms of worship. Thus, while overall church membership declined, support for evangelical and charismatic churches grew substantially, masking an even steeper falling off in numbers affiliated to 'Catholic' and 'liberal' churches. The informal charismatic 'new churches' (also known as house churches), which only originated in the 1970s, had a membership of 140,000 at the end of the century. The overall strength of Christianity was also reinforced by the relatively high levels of commitment among Afro-Caribbean settlers in Britain. These often felt themselves 'frozen out' of existing 'white' churches, but developed their own

Plate 21.1 The Tooting New Testament Assembly, 1993. Since the 1970s evangelical and charismatic churches have bucked the declining trend in Christian worship. Afro-Caribbean immigrants have been particularly influential in establishing new charismatic churches (Open University).

forms of vigorous religious expression, predominantly, but not exclusively, charismatic or Pentecostal in character. Their presence was a major factor in the growth of Pentecostal membership in the UK from 37,000 in 1950 to 86,000 in 1970 and 233,000 in 2000. The Orthodox churches, swelled both by migration from Cyprus and gaining converts in Britain, more than doubled from 81,000 in 1950 to 208,000 in 2000. Parallel developments were evident among Muslims (see below), Hindus, Sikhs and others, who during the 1970s and 1980s increasingly developed formal religious organizations, publications and buildings. These helped to stimulate and sustain higher levels of practice and commitment (*UK Christian Handbook*, 1999).

Second, the period after 1970 was one of considerable religious innovation. In addition to novel developments within Christianity there were also numerous new religious movements: 450 or so between the mid-1940s and the mid-1980s (Knott, 1988). These became even more diverse and conspicuous in the last quarter of the century, although still small in number compared to 'mainstream' religions, with total active membership estimated at 5630 in 1985 and 21,336 in 2000 (*UK Christian Handbook*, 1999; 2001). The adherents of organizations such as the Unification Church ('Moonies') and the Hare Krishna movement were widely in evidence witnessing on the streets in the 1970s and 80s. Considerable controversy followed, partly because of various well-publicized cases of alleged 'brain-washing' of recruits, but also because the absolute claims to the loyalty of their devotees made by such bodies were an implicit challenge to the secularity and conventional Christianity of the majority of the population. These two groups declined in the 1990s, and by 2000 the largest single grouping was the Pagan Federation, with an estimated 11,000 members, having grown rapidly in the 1980s and 90s. In the meantime, religious innovation had taken a further turn with the emergence of the loose network of spiritualities and worldviews collectively known as the New Age.

Third, in the 1980s religion gained increasing prominence in public life. In 1982 Pope John Paul II made a high-profile visit to Britain which attracted considerable interest from the media. In 1984 widespread controversy was stirred when David Jenkins, the bishop-designate of Durham, publicly expressed doubts regarding the Virgin birth and bodily resurrection of Christ. The drama was heightened when a major fire broke out at York Minster during a thunderstorm shortly after Jenkins's consecration in the building, provoking not altogether flippant suggestions that divine wrath was being manifested. The interesting feature of the Jenkins affair was not that a bishop was rethinking central Christian doctrines – Bishop Robinson had said more radical things two decades before – but that the media and its audience still seemed to find such episcopal utterances to be worthy of note. Similarly, discussions over the role of women in religious organizations attracted widespread public interest, above all the controversy over their ordination to the Anglican priesthood, finally agreed in 1992. Religion acquired greater prominence in political life, notably in disagreements between church leaders and supporters of the Conservative government over the most appropriate means of marking victory in the Falklands War of 1982, and over the relative merits of schemes to regenerate the inner cities. In 1988 Margaret Thatcher took a step without obvious precedent among post-war prime ministers in setting out the religious basis of her approach to politics in a speech to the General Assembly of the Church of Scotland. Then, in 1989, hostile Muslim reaction to Salman Rushdie's novel *The Satanic Verses* stirred a controversy which raised profound questions about the nature of British culture, the place of minority groups within it, the role of religion in the contemporary world, and the standing of Britain abroad. The 1990s saw intriguing crosscurrents: in Britain there was growing positive acceptance and affirmation of religious diversity, at the very time that politico-religious conflicts elsewhere in the world, notably in Bosnia, South Asia and the Middle East, heightened consciousness of religious tensions. These complexities increased after 2000, particularly with the 11 September 2001 attacks on the United States, the subsequent occupations of Afghanistan and Iraq, and the terrorist attacks on London on 7 July 2005. The effect has been to highlight among Muslims a tension between a 'moderate' majority able to make an accommodation with British society, and an 'extremist' minority that perceives itself to be ideologically in conflict with the West.

In Focus

Muslims in Britain

As the largest single religious minority in post-war Britain, Muslims serve as a particularly good example of the social and historiographical issues raised by the presence of substantial non-Christian groups in Britain. It should be noted that a resident Muslim presence in this country can be traced back to the late nineteenth century. A mosque was built in Woking in 1889 and one opened in Liverpool in 1891. Communities developed in several ports, notably Cardiff, London and South Shields, as a result of the settlement of seamen from the Middle East and India. After the Second World War immigration from South Asia massively increased Muslim numbers. Estimates of the total size of the population varied enormously, a reflection of the difficulty of obtaining reliable figures in the absence until 2001 of any census question on religious affiliation and a lack of the kind of membership figures for mosques that exist for Christian denominations. Calculations were normally based on the numbers born in such predominantly Muslim countries as Pakistan, a basis that became less reliable with the passing years, as a second and third generation were born in Britain. Furthermore such estimates could not measure actual religious practice, although inferences can be drawn from samples such as that of Muslim householders in Handsworth (Birmingham) in 1981, 45 per cent of whom attended public worship at least once a week, a substantially higher proportion than for any major Christian group outside Northern Ireland (Ratcliffe, 1981).

Muslims arrived in Britain with a legacy of historic division among themselves, partly from the traditional divergences of Islam, between Sunni and Shi'a, Sufi and legalist; partly from the range of movements that developed in the Indian subcontinent during the nineteenth century aiming to preserve the faith intact in the face of British rule; partly from the linguistic and cultural variations among those coming from different parts of the world, and different regions of India, Pakistan, and Bangladesh. Faced with the fragmented nature of a religion whose adherents made a great virtue of their professed solidarity, Muslim leaders – often self-appointed – took a number of initiatives designed to develop some united organization. Such attempts, however, often compounded the problem that they were designed to solve, as organizations like the Union of Muslim Organizations, the Islamic Foundation, and the Muslim Institute were unable to gain anything approaching universal support. The Muslim Council of Britain, formed in 1996, seems more successful than such predecessors, but not all Muslims have accepted its leadership.

The growth of mosque registrations is a good indicator not so much of the numbers of nominal Muslims as of the extent of organized religious activity. Up to 1965 there had only been 13 mosque registrations in Britain, but by 1985 this total

Muslims in Britain

Plate 21.2 Inside the Bristol Jamia mosque. Mosque registration figures almost certainly understate actual numbers, given the likely existence of numerous unofficial house mosques. By the 1980s more purpose-built mosques were appearing, an indication of the increasing stability of Muslim communities and of their growing economic resources (© Mark Simmons).

> ### Muslims in Britain
>
> had swelled to 338; 239 of which had occurred in the decade since 1976 (Nielsen, 1987). In 2000 there were 672 registered mosques, and it is likely there were several hundred other buildings also used for worship. The typical mosque was not purpose built, but was rather a converted terrace house, hall or warehouse. By the 1980s larger traditionally Islamic mosques began to be built, giving enhanced dignity and stability to the community, but in some cases, such as the Regent's Park Mosque in London (1978), these were – at the time – somewhat remote from the lives of ordinary Muslims.
>
> For Muslims, as for other recently settled religious groups, the surrounding society and culture presented serious challenges. Were they to isolate themselves indefinitely from a Britain that increasingly looked like a permanent home, or to run the risk of their religion being eroded by assimilation to Christianity or secularity? The issues were complicated by the difficulty of distinguishing clearly between Muslim religious teaching and cultural practice, a confusion which was most apparent in relation to the emotive interlocked issues of the regulation of sexuality and the status of women. Education too became a controversial matter, as children of different religions went to school alongside each other and Muslim parents grew more articulate in their demands for distinctively Islamic instruction.
>
> By the 1980s Muslims had become a major force in the religious life of Britain, but *The Satanic Verses* affair was to underscore their own sense of insecurity and, conversely, the feeling of the rest of the population that Islam had become a 'threat'. This last perception was a revealing one because it points up the extent to which a predominantly secular society still felt itself challenged by religion. During the 1990s and early 2000s the radicalization of an unrepresentative small minority of Muslims contributed to the growth of misplaced and generalized Islamophobia.

Debates and Interpretations
Secularization and the 'death of Christian Britain'

During the 1970s and 80s the concept of secularization was widely accepted as a general model for explaining and describing what is portrayed as the gradual marginalization of religion in 'modern' society, providing a wider context for immediately obvious processes such as declining church attendance and membership. Secularization, it was suggested, is inherent in the long-term reorganization of society and culture consequent upon the 'Enlightenment' and the 'Industrial Revolution'. Eighteenth- and nineteenth-century intellectuals dethroned theology from her position as 'queen of the sciences' and developed modes of understanding the world that did not need resort to supernatural agency. Meanwhile, industrialization and urbanization were removing the great majority of the population from an environment subject to the vagaries of nature, and substituting the artificial rhythms and rationality of the factory and the office. Even though death remained ultimately inescapable, medical advance meant that it was for most people postponed until remote old age and removed from the family circle into the clinical environment of hospitals. The twentieth century saw the mushrooming of alternative forms of leisure – the cinema, professional sport, the motor car, television – that distracted people from church attendance on Sundays and filled their consciousness to the exclusion of spiritual concerns. All these factors meant that for the majority of the population religious ideas and activities became much less prominent. Moreover, the argument runs, even the church itself became secularized, in that it came to accept the values of the surrounding culture and adjusted its teaching to suit its audience. Where there was continuing religious vitality and activity this was only a subcultural phenomenon, sustained by those who had opted out of the mainstream of society in order to continue a supernaturalist view of the world whose credibility could not be supported by any other means.

At first sight the argument is a persuasive commonsense one, which provides a satisfactory general framework for understanding the decline of organized religion in modern Britain. Doubts begin to arise, however, when the case is pushed further and it is proposed that there is an inherent contradiction between 'modernity' and religion, which has condemned the latter to marginalization in the contemporary world, whereas it had been central to life in a 'pre-modern' culture. Broader chronological and geographical perspectives render such a hypothesis questionable. The medieval and early modern eras cannot be simplistically described as a golden age of faith; while in the Victorian period organized religion initially flourished during the transition to an industrial economy. Moreover, in Britain, as we saw at the beginning of this chapter, institutional Christianity continued strong even in the first half of the twentieth century. The secularization hypothesis is also – at least in its crude form – inadequate for explaining the case of the United States where, in one of the most developed and technologically advanced societies in the world, organized religion remained in the second half of the twentieth century substantially stronger than in Britain.

During the 1990s, while some scholars continued vigorously to advocate the secularization hypothesis, others came to find it an unsatisfactory model for interpreting religious change in modern Britain. The debate was given a major new turn with the publication in 2001 of Callum Brown's book *The Death of Christian Britain*. Brown agreed that Christian influence had declined – indeed he subtitled the book 'Understanding secularization 1800–2000' – but he rejected many of the premises of the secularization thesis as previously advanced. In particular he argued that even though secularization as an intellectual concept originated in the eighteenth century, Christianity as a social and cultural reality remained central to British life until around 1960. The 1960s, however, saw abrupt and catastrophic change, attributable in particular to the changing roles and self-images of women who had hitherto been the mainstay of religious observance. Although churches continued to exist and people continued to believe in

God, British culture as a whole was, according to Brown, no longer distinctively Christian.

Brown's thesis of 'revolution' in the 1960s provides an alternative reading of the early and mid-twentieth century that fits the facts rather better than does the hypothesis of longer-term continuous secularization. On the other hand, both approaches risk overstating the secularity of the late twentieth century. It is unsatisfactory simply to regard signs of continuing religious vitality as isolationist exceptions that prove the rule. The growing charismatic churches of the 1970s and 80s in important respects – such as their use of music – reflected the surrounding culture rather than rejecting it; ethnic minority groups became more loyal to their religions even as in other respects they became more integrated into British life. Even among those who did not regularly practise any religion rates of nominal identification remained high: in 1974, 41.6 per cent of an English sample considered themselves to be 'Church of England'; in 1988 more than two-thirds of first marriages were still being celebrated in church (Medhurst and Moyser, 1988). Nearly all deaths were still followed by some kind of religious ceremony. Opinion polls might detect a drift away from the boundaries of Christian orthodoxy, but by the 1980s there were signs that the movement was towards Eastern and New Age religious ideas as well as towards secularity. Public reactions to the death of Diana, Princess of Wales, on 31 August 1997 were evidence of widespread spiritual interest, albeit not directed towards particular religious institutions.

Moreover, the historian of post-war Britain should not ignore the case of Northern Ireland where, in a 1973 sample, 92 per cent of Roman Catholics and 34 per cent of Protestants claimed to attend church at least once a week (McAllister, 1982). The province is often dismissed as a somewhat embarrassing anomaly, but in terms of the history of religion, it may well better be regarded as an indication of potentialities that remained in other parts of the country. Although Northern Ireland has been economically and socially one of the less well developed parts of the United Kingdom, its degree of 'backwardness' was insufficient to explain its continuing religiosity on the basis of the secularization hypothesis. It represented rather an extreme case of a situation where culture and history combined to support religion as an important part of personal and community identities in an essentially 'modern' society. A similar tendency can be observed in ethnic minority religions and theologically conservative Christian groups elsewhere. For a significant minority of the British people the contemporary secular world seemed not so much secure and rational as unstable and irrational. Accordingly religious structures of meaning – whether in charismatic Christianity, resurgent Islam, or the New Age – continued to provide a satisfying basis on which to find and develop an identity. At a more diffuse level, religious rituals continued to appeal as a means of marking the passing of time, and the joys and griefs of personal and national life, and thereby providing some overall framework for human experience. A rounded account of the history of religion in Britain between 1945 and 2000, therefore, needs to balance the language of secularization and the 'death of Christian Britain' with an awareness of continuity, adaptation and new beginnings. These processes have considerable relevance to an understanding of the wider course of social and cultural history.

Further reading

Statistical data on organized religious activity has been derived (unless otherwise indicated in footnotes) from Robert Currie, Alan Gilbert and Lee Horsley, *Churches and Churchgoers: Patterns of Church Growth in the British Isles since 1700* (Oxford, 1977) and Peter Brierley, *'Christian' England: What the 1989 English Church Census Reveals* (London, 1991). The biennial *UK Christian Handbook* and its companion *UKCH Religious Trends*, published by Christian Research, is a valuable source of statistical data on recent decades, while the 2001 Census provides a snapshot of religious identification at the turn of the millennium.

Study of religion in post-war Britain has been somewhat fragmentary, with the historian's interest in change over time often overshadowed by the contemporary preoccupations of sociologists with religion and religious practitioners. The most authoritative overview of Christianity is Adrian Hastings, *A History of English Christianity 1920–1990* (London, 1991), which can usefully be supplemented for particular traditions by P.A. Welsby, *A History of the Church of England 1945–1980* (Oxford, 1984), D.W. Bebbington, *Evangelicalism in Modern Britain: A History from the 1730s to the 1980s* (London, 1989) and M.P. Hornsby-Smith, *Roman Catholics in England: Studies in Social Structure since the Second World War* (Cambridge, 1987). On Scotland, see Callum G. Brown, *Religion and Society in Scotland since 1707* (Edinburgh, 1997) and on Wales, D. Densil Morgan, *The Span of the Cross: Christian Religion and Society in Wales 1914–2000* (Cardiff, 1999). There is a large literature concerned with religion in Northern Ireland, but no satisfactory overview: Steve Bruce, *God Save Ulster: The Religion and Politics of Paisleyism* (Oxford, 1986) provides an insightful and readable analysis of one aspect.

For overviews of minority religions, see Paul Badham (ed.) *Religion, State, and Society in Modern Britain* (Lampeter, 1989); Gerald Parsons (ed.) *The Growth of Religious Diversity: Britain from 1945: Vol. I, Traditions; Vol. II, Issues* (London, 1993); Terence Thomas (ed.) *The British: Their Religious Beliefs and Practices 1800–1986* (London, 1988); and an anthology of sources and comment edited by John Wolffe, *The Growth of Religious Diversity in Britain from 1945: A Reader* (London, 1993). For accounts of particular religions see Geoffrey Alderman, *Modern British Jewry* (Oxford, 1998); and Humayun Ansari *'The Infidel Within': Muslims in Britain since 1800* (London, 2004). Other traditions as yet lack such overviews but for valuable insights see Richard Burghart (ed.) *Hinduism in Great Britain: The Perpetuation of Religion in an Alien Cultural Milieu* (London, 1987); David N. Kay, *Tibetan and Zen Buddhism in Britain: Transplantation, Development and Adaptation* (London, 2004); and Ramindar Singh, *Sikhs and Sikhism in Britain Fifty Years On: The Bradford Perspective* (Bradford, 2000).

For statements of the secularization thesis, see Alan D. Gilbert, *The Making of Post-Christian Britain* (London, 1980), and more recently, Steve Bruce, *Religion in Modern Britain* (Oxford, 1995). A range of perspectives is provided by Steve Bruce (ed.) *Religion and Modernization: Sociologists and Historians Debate the Secularization Thesis* (Oxford, 1992). Grace Davie, *Religion in Britain since 1945: Believing without Belonging* (Oxford, 1994) is an interpretation from a sociologist critical of the hypothesis of inexorable secularization. John Wolffe (ed.) *Religion in History: Conflict, Conversion and Coexistence* (Manchester, 2004) contains both an extended critique by Gerald Parsons of Callum G. Brown *The Death of Christian Britain* (London, 2001) and a chapter by David Herbert and John Wolffe that explores the international context of British religion at the turn of the millennium.

References

Brown, Callum (2001) *The Death of Christian Britain: Understanding Secularisation, 1800–2000*. London: Routledge.

Fulton, John (1991) *The Tragedy of Belief: Division, Politics and Religion in Ireland*. Oxford: Clarendon.

Gallup, George H. (1976) *The Gallup International Public Opinion Polls: Great Britain: 1937–1975*. New York: Random House.

Gill, Robin (1999) *Churchgoing and Christian Ethics*. Cambridge: Cambridge University Press.

Griffin, Tom (1990) *Social Trends*, vol. 20. London: HMSO.

Knott, Kim (1988) 'Other Major Religious Traditions' and 'New Religious Movements', in Terence Thomas (ed.) *The British: Their Religious Beliefs and Practices 1800–1986*. London: Routledge & Kegan Paul.

Krarup, Helen (1982) 'Conventional religion and common religion in Leeds, interview schedule: basic frequencies by question', University of Leeds, *Religious Research Papers*, 12.

McAllister, Ian (1982) 'The devil, miracles and the afterlife: the political sociology of religion in Northern Ireland', *British Journal of Sociology*, 33.

Medhurst, K. and Moyser, G. (1988) *Church and Politics in a Secular Age*. Oxford: Clarendon.

Nielsen, J. (1987) 'Muslims in Britain: searching for an identity?', *New Community*, 13.

Ratcliffe, P. (1981) *Racism and Reaction: A Profile of Handsworth*. London: Routledge & Kegan Paul.

UK Christian Handbook Religious Trends No 2 2000/01 (1999; 2001). London: Christian Research.

22

Britain and Europe

Neil Rollings

BRITAIN HAS OFTEN BEEN CALLED 'a reluctant European' and after it joined the European Community in 1973 'an awkward partner'. Britain's relationship with European integration has been fraught but this should not be surprising: European integration has been a complex and wide-ranging phenomenon and can be approached from a variety of perspectives: economic, social, cultural, political and strategic, for example. Britain's response to European integration raised all sorts of issues about the country's past and its future. With whom would it be best to form trading links? How could Britain best maintain its status in the world? With whom did it feel most comfortable associating? Who should decide government policy? These were (and remain) just some of the questions raised by the subject and help to explain why it has been such a contentious issue for Britain since 1945.

From the end of the Second World War to British membership of the European Community 1945–73

The Marshall Plan and the Schuman Plan

After the Second World War Britain saw itself as lying at the centre of three separate spheres of influence: the United States, the Commonwealth and Europe. In British eyes at least, the Second World War had strengthened both the first of these – in the form of 'the special relationship' between Britain and the USA – and the second – with Commonwealth soldiers standing side by side with their British counterparts. Given this, Britain's relationship with the rest of Europe was seen as important but very much the third ranked of these relationships: there was a commitment to building relations with the rest of Europe but not to the extent that it harmed the other two spheres of influence. Accordingly, when the Marshall Plan insisted on some form of European integration in return for American funds to aid European economic recovery, the British were reluctant to be tied too closely to Europe in return for the financial support on offer. They believed that Britain deserved a special status. As Ernest Bevin, the Foreign Secretary in the Labour government after the war, put it: Britain 'was not simply a Luxembourg' (Plowden, 1989: 94). With such views there was little support for any form of integration which involved ceding national sovereignty by Britain and this was a clear constraint on efforts to develop European integration within the framework of the Marshall Plan.

It was in this context that Jean Monnet and other French officials drafted proposals aimed at securing lasting reconciliation between France and Germany and with it set out the idea of creating a new Europe. The starting point, announced by Robert Schuman, the French Foreign Minister, on 9 May 1950, which became known as the Schuman Plan, was the proposal to pool coal and steel resources equally between the two countries, plus any others that wished to participate. This would prevent any single member state using its steel and coal industries for war purposes; that is, national governments would hand over control, or sovereignty, of policy in these two industries to a supranational body operating above national governments. The British government were given no warning of the proposal and despite serious consideration felt unable to join the ensuing negotiations. This was because of French insistence on the need for a supranational body to which Britain would have to cede sovereignty if it joined. As the coal industry had just been nationalized and the steel industry was about to be nationalized and taken under government control, this seemed at odds with the British government's policy. Accordingly, Britain played no role in the talks which led to the signing of the Treaty of Paris in April 1951 and the resulting creation of the European Coal and Steel Community (ECSC). Those that did become members of the ECSC were France, West Germany, Italy, Luxembourg, the Netherlands and Belgium, otherwise known as 'the Six'. Setting the tone for Britain's sustained ambivalence towards European integration, the government was not willing to sign up to full membership but was afraid of the consequences of being completely excluded. Instead, Britain sought a halfway house and in 1955 became 'associated' with the ECSC.

The creation of the European Economic Community (EEC)[1]

After the success of establishing the ECSC, European integration then faltered with two initiatives in the fields of political and defence cooperation failing to come to fruition. In response the Six returned to the field of economic integration in the mid-1950s to try to move European integration forward. A conference was held in June 1955 at Messina in Sicily. Following the conference the Six began negotiations which were to lead to the signing of the Treaty of Rome in March 1957 and the creation of the EEC in January 1958. Britain sent a representative to these negotiations but he withdrew in November 1955, unable to countenance the required loss of sovereignty to the proposed new supranational institutions and unwilling to commit Britain to participating in the creation of a body which would harm trade with the Commonwealth. However, again Britain was afraid of exclusion: if Germany, Britain's main economic rival at the time, was a member and Britain was not then there was a potential threat to Britain's economic competitiveness. Britain responded with its own 'alternative' proposal, a free trade area consisting of all the countries of Western Europe that had received Marshall Aid; that is, most of Western Europe.

Ultimately, the British proposal failed and with the EEC in operation the British government had to adopt the fall-back position of helping to create the European Free Trade Association (EFTA), consisting of Britain, Ireland, Portugal, Denmark, Sweden, Norway and Austria. EFTA came into operation in 1960 but was always regarded as a second-best means to an end – Britain still hoped for a wider and looser form of integration covering both the Six and the EFTA countries. EFTA was a way for the non-EEC member states to keep together to strengthen their bargaining position with the EEC.

It soon became clear that a bridge was not going to be built between EFTA and the EEC in the near future: the Six seemed more intent on deepening integration among themselves. In addition, elements in British industry were becoming convinced of Britain's need to join the EEC. It can be misleading to try to depict firms or industries as pro- or anti-European integration because European integration could mean different things – the free trade area, EFTA and the common market all had different features – it was dynamic in the sense that it was changing and developing all the time, particularly the EEC as its policies began to emerge, and views on a subject like European integration were not always based on a rational assessment of the likely impact on the particular sector or firm. Nevertheless, large firms, responsible for a significant proportion of Britain's exports and seeing opportunities to exploit economies of scale, were an important voice pushing for British entry into the EEC in the early 1960s. From a sectoral perspective, the chemical industry and the car industry were in favour of British entry while opposition came from those industries fearing that they could not compete against their continental counterparts.

More generally, informed opinion was moving in favour of British membership of the EEC: trade with Western Europe was growing while that with the Commonwealth was stagnating, even if it was still larger than trade with Western Europe (see Table 22.1, p. 342), and with growing concerns over Britain's economic performance there was a strengthening belief that joining the EEC would not only offer 'a cold shower of competition' but would impose the same institutions on Britain and that this might be economically beneficial. Politically, as well, there was a feeling that swapping the Commonwealth and EFTA for the EEC would enhance Britain's influence in the world. Accordingly, in July 1961, less than two years after Britain had signed the convention which created EFTA, Harold Macmillan, the Prime Minister, announced the government's intention to open negotiations with the Six about the possibility of applying to join the EEC. Negotiations lasted until January 1963 at which point President de Gaulle, the French President, famously vetoed Britain's application, in part because France wanted to ensure it was the leading country in the EEC but also because he remained unconvinced of Britain's commitment to European integration.

Table 22.1 Distribution of UK merchandise trade by area, 1950–1996 (%)

Area	1950	1960	1965	1970	1975	1979	1987	1996
Imports								
EC total[b]		15	15	18	34	45	53	54[a]
EC6	13[a]	15	15	18	30	38	44	40[a]
Rest of Western Europe[b]	12	15	16	16	15	17	14	6
United States	8	12	12	13	10	10	10	13
Commonwealth	40	31	29	23	14	11	8	
Exports								
EC total[b]		15	19	21	32	42	50	57[a]
EC6	11[a]	15	19	21	20	34	39	41[a]
Rest of Western Europe[b]	14	14	17	20	17	14	9	4
United States	5	9	11	12	9	10	14	12
Commonwealth	38	34	26	20	16	12	11	

Notes:
a Includes all Germany.
b The shifts in these figures in part reflect the enlargements of the EC.

Source: Based on Moore, 1999: Table 4.1.

Britain was still a member of EFTA and the Commonwealth and had to try to mend bridges with these two and try to put pressure on the EEC to reduce its barriers to trade with the rest of the world so that British exporters could gain access to the markets of EEC member states. This was really a policy of simply picking up the pieces – there was no real fall-back position if Britain did not gain entry, as most people had simply expected Britain's application to be accepted. However, the ultimate goal remained EEC entry and so Britain was left to tread water in the meantime. A second application was launched in 1967 by the Labour government but it was again vetoed by de Gaulle, though it did help to show that Britain's desire to join the EEC was genuine. It was only after de Gaulle had lost power in 1969, dying soon after, that a new application from Britain stood any chance of success. It was Britain's third application, with formal negotiations opening in the autumn of 1970, which after some hiccups finally led to Britain joining the EEC in January 1973, eleven and a half years after the first application.

Britain as a member of the European Community (EC) and its successors since 1973

Denmark and Ireland became members of the EC at the same time as Britain, transforming the Six into 'the Nine'. Membership for Britain did not, however, end the issue of Britain's relationship to the EC. A significant body of opposition to membership had developed. More generally, the early 1970s were not a propitious time to join the EC for a number of reasons. First, the outstanding economic growth rates achieved since the early 1950s were coming to an end, the Bretton Woods system was beginning to fall apart and, in addition, the oil crisis was about to break. But it was not just the general economic environment that was becoming less favourable. The EEC itself did not look so enticing. Its policies had developed over the 1960s without British input and, in particular, it was feared that the Common Agricultural Policy would impose a considerable burden on Britain, both financially in terms of Britain's contribution to the Community's budget and in terms of an increase in the cost of living through higher food prices. Given rising wage demands and industrial militancy it was feared that this would set off a spiral of increasing wages and prices.

In the February 1974 election the Labour party campaigned successfully on the basis of renegotiating Britain's terms of entry in order to reduce Britain's financial contribution and that, if elected, it would hold a popular vote on membership. Back in power, Harold Wilson, the Prime Minister, had to avoid splitting the party over the issue of Europe and so a rather tortuous but relatively limited process of negotiation was embarked upon. In addition, after some internal disagreement a referendum on EEC membership was held in June 1975 with both those in favour and against maintaining EEC membership carrying out extensive lobbying of public opinion. The public were asked if they wished to stay in the EEC and, in part because of the way the question was phrased and in part because of the relative strength of the pro-EEC campaign, public opinion began to shift in favour of maintaining Britain's membership. On a relatively high turnout of nearly 65 per cent of the electorate, over two-thirds voted in favour of continued membership. Support was strongest in the south-east of England and weakest in Scotland but only in the Shetlands and Western Isles were there majorities against.

This endorsement of membership did little to resolve Britain's position and it was no more supportive of initiatives to further European integration after the referendum. First, one of the last acts of the Labour government before it lost power in 1979 was to refuse to join the Exchange Rate Mechanism (ERM). Second, in the first direct elections to the European Parliament held in June 1979 Britain had the lowest percentage turnout of voters. Finally, the new Prime Minister, the Conservative Margaret Thatcher, was determined to renegotiate Britain's financial contribution to the Community, once more on the grounds that Britain continued to contribute heavily to the EEC budget and got relatively little in return. It took four years to resolve the issue of a British rebate during which time further integration stalled.

With the issue finally resolved in 1984 progress was once more possible. Most crucial in this respect was the emergence of the Single Market Programme. The idea of creating a single market had widespread political and business support, though which was the original source of the idea is disputed. It was seen as a way of relaunching European integration, it offered a potential solution to Europe's declining competitiveness and it chimed with liberal notions of removing barriers to trade and increasing competition by freeing market forces. In many ways there was nothing new with the notion of a single market – the idea underpinned the removal of tariffs which lay at the heart of the Treaty of Rome – but many other barriers relating, for example, to differences in taxation and in technical standards remained, and had even increased during the 1970s. There was a broad consensus within Europe, including Margaret Thatcher and the British government, that such barriers needed to be removed and this was aim of the Single Market Programme. To achieve a single market among member countries the 1986 Single European Act (SEA) was drafted. This set out a programme of measures to create a single market by the end of 1992 but also revised the Treaty of Rome with the aim of speeding up decision-making within the European Community.

What was still unclear, however, and remained a source of contention, was the extent to which the creation of a single market required the adoption of common practices and policies. To some member states it seemed logical that a single market required considerable tax harmonization and a single currency; others, such as the British, saw no need for deeper integration of this sort. Consensus, therefore, was short-lived, with divisions emerging once more over proposals for economic and monetary union (EMU). These proposals were published in 1989 in what has become known as the Delors Report, after Jacques Delors, the President of the European Commission and chairman of the committee that drafted the report. Not long after this the EC Commission also published a 'social charter' to protect worker rights. Like EMU this was again at odds with Thatcher's view of European integration – in general she favoured the removal of barriers to trade and some degree of foreign policy cooperation, but opposed increased spending and increased powers being given to EC institutions (and hence was also against the extension of EC-level interventionist policies). A further challenge to Thatcher's line on Europe came from her own ministers who were pushing for Britain to join the ERM, which it finally did in 1990. This was symptomatic of the Prime Minister's increasingly weak position in the Conservative Party and later that year she was replaced by John Major.

Major was now faced with the situation of maintaining unity in his party between the Eurosceptics, those opposed to further integration, and the Euroenthusiasts, while also negotiating with his counterparts from other member states about how best to take European integration forward. At the Maastricht summit in December 1991 talks on the future of Europe came to a head. Out of the summit came the Treaty of European Union, signed on 7 February 1992. This turned the European Community into the European Union by taking further steps to political integration and also agreed a programme to bring about EMU. Major regarded these negotiations as a great success for Britain as there were limits on the extension of supranationalism. In addition, Britain negotiated two opt outs from the treaty – to the final stage of economic and monetary union and to the social chapter. However, within the Conservative party this outcome only papered over the cracks between the Eurosceptic and Euroenthusiast factions. These divisions became steadily more obvious, particularly after 'Black Wednesday', 16 September 1992, when Britain was forced out of the ERM. Pressure on sterling had forced the British government to increase interest rates markedly at a time when the domestic economy was already depressed. These measures failed to remove the pressure on sterling to devalue and the government had little choice but to withdraw from the ERM. Thereafter British policy consisted of pushing for enlargement and emphasizing that there was no single model of European integration which fitted all member countries. It was, in Major's own words, 'multi-track, multi-speed, multi-layered', a concept which resonated with Britain's position in the 1950s when proposing the free trade area, and which not only allowed flexibility but could also mean almost anything one liked (Young, 2000: 165).

With the election of Tony Blair's Labour government in May 1997 rhetoric and policy became more positive towards European integration. One of the first tasks of the new government was to sign the social chapter and there was much talk about Britain wanting to be a leading country at the heart of Europe. In practice, the shift was more of tone than substance. On the central issue of economic and monetary union Britain continued to opt out, one of only three member states to follow this route. Britain did not, therefore, join the Eurozone, the group of EU countries covering most of Western Europe that introduced economic and monetary union in 1999; nor did euros, the new currency of the Eurozone, enter into public circulation in Britain in 2002, and there is little indication at present that the promised referendum on the subject is imminent. Indeed, at the time of writing the future of the EU is in the air. The enlargement of the EU into Eastern Europe in 2004, so that it now consists of 25 members, and with the prospect of further accessions to follow, was inevitably going to create considerable stresses for the EU and to push the EU into new directions. The failure of France and the Netherlands to ratify the European Constitution, the reopening of the issue of the British rebate and, in return, Britain's call for a fundamental review of the EU's expenditure, particularly that on the Common Agricultural Policy, have all quickly followed. As a result, the future path of European integration is currently less certain now than it has been for a number of years.

To sum up, the story of Britain's relationship with the European Union and its predecessors is one of both continuity and change. It is undeniable that much has changed – Britain is a member of the European Union which has itself developed considerably over time, while the Commonwealth is now regarded as largely irrelevant; over 50 per cent of British trade was with other EU member states in 1996, whereas in the 1950s trade with Western Europe was far exceeded by that with the Commonwealth (see Table 22.1); and, with regard to everyday life, while considerable public antipathy towards the EU still exists, few would deny its influence over our lives. Yet, at the same time, it is clear that there are considerable similarities in British policy now to that in the 1950s – there is a preference for looser and wider forms of integration in particular, and this continues to put Britain at odds with some of its European partners, notably France.

In Focus

'Plan G' and the alternative route to integration

It is sometimes helpful to think of historical events as road maps. Having arrived at where we are today it is possible to trace back from now the route taken to whatever seems an appropriate starting point. However, it has to be remembered that adopting this approach uses the benefits of hindsight and that a clear road of progress seems obvious and inevitable. One of the main contributions of historians can be to put themselves back at the apparent starting point and look forward. In this way one gets a better understanding of the uncertainties and choices – the bridges, crossroads, dead ends, etc. – that those involved in the events experienced. Studies of the history of European integration have often adopted a backward-looking approach as it helps to explain how the European Union has taken the form that it has today. This way of thinking also lies behind the argument that Britain's unwillingness to participate in the early history was a missed opportunity.

One of the dangers of this way of looking at the history of European integration is that it focuses on what succeeded – that is, the EU and its predecessors – and downplays all other proposed forms of European integration which fell by the wayside. In looking at the creation of the EEC and the British response to it, historians have played a valuable role by showing how uncertain the situation was and providing an understanding of the rationale behind British policy.

First, few individuals at the time in Britain realized the significance of the talks at Messina in June 1955. Yet it has become clear that the government did take the initiative seriously, but that it was felt that Britain could not join. Why not? One aspect was the issue of losing national sovereignty to the institutions of the EEC, but this was not all. A second problem was that the EEC covered agricultural goods as well as manufactures. This was a problem with regard to the Commonwealth, which was Britain's main external supplier of foodstuffs, as explained below, but was also an issue for the British agricultural industry, the structure of which was very different from that on the continent. The third, and final, problem was that the EEC had the aim of establishing a common market; that is, a market in which there would be free movement of goods, services, labour and capital between the member states, but common barriers to such movement from the rest of the world. The first objective of the EEC was to create a customs union, a lesser form of integration in that it only creates free movement of goods and services among the member states and establishes a common external tariff on imports from the rest of the world. In other words, there would be no barriers to trade within the customs union and every member state would have the same level of duty on any particular good coming from outside the EC.

Joining such a customs union was a problem for Britain because of the common external tariff. In the 1950s Britain had preferential trading relations with the Commonwealth and remaining colonies; that is, Britain could export goods to

'Plan G' and the alternative route to integration

Commonwealth countries and pay a lower import duty than its competitors and, equally, Commonwealth countries could export to Britain with similar preferences. Having to establish a common external tariff would remove that preferential arrangement. This was seen as particularly important to Britain because the Commonwealth supplied Britain with most of its imported foodstuffs and many raw materials and most of these entered Britain free of any import duty. If Britain became a member of the common market then the common external tariff would be imposed on these goods, making them more expensive.

Having quickly ruled out the possibility of Britain joining for these reasons, it was nevertheless clear from an early date that if the proposals were successful then there would be serious consequences for Britain as a non-member. Politically, Britain could be marginalized as US attention would shift to the Six and, economically, exclusion from an economic grouping which included Germany would not only give German business an advantage in the member states' markets but also increase the competitive position of German exporters in other markets, including the Commonwealth. Accordingly, the British government set about finding a suitable alternative proposal to that of a common market. In 1956 it opted for what was called 'Plan G'. This was to be a free trade area covering all OEEC countries for industrial products only. The key differences from the common market were that agriculture was excluded completely, it would be a much wider body, covering virtually the whole of Western Europe, and it would be a free trade area rather than a customs union. In other words, internal barriers to trade would still be removed but, unlike a customs union, there would be no common external tariff. Instead, each member state would be allowed to maintain their own external tariffs and, in the British case, this meant the retention of imperial preference.

A range of motives for the British proposals have been put forward by historians, from a scheme aimed at wrecking the creation of the EEC to one with the objective of building a bridge between the Six and the rest of Europe. It seems increasingly clear that even if the initial motive was malicious this did not last long: from a British perspective the free trade area proposals appeared the most suitable compromise available, moving Britain closer to Europe but without giving up on the Commonwealth. Although formal negotiations over the proposals were long-delayed and short-lived, the proposals remained government policy until the end of 1958 and even after that date underpinned the creation of EFTA as a potential bridge between the EEC and the rest of Western Europe. It is unlikely that Britain would ever have made the free trade area proposals on its own initiative except as an alternative to other proposals for European integration and it is also probable that the French would never have been in a position to accept the proposals. However, this does not mean that the episode was an irrelevance or a distraction from the 'true' path of European integration. Rather, it was an important element not only of the history of Britain and Europe but also of European integration more generally by illustrating contesting notions of what European integration could look like.

Debates and Interpretations
Europe: A missed opportunity?

Euroenthusiasts point to Britain's post-war history as one of missed opportunities, particularly in rejecting the initial steps towards European integration in the 1950s. As Tony Blair put it in 2001: 'The tragedy for British politics – for Britain – has been that politicians of both parties have consistently failed, not just in the 1950s but on up to the present day, to appreciate the emerging reality of European integration. And in doing so, they have failed Britain's interests.'[2] Thus Roy Denman, a civil servant who was involved in the negotiations for British entry, entitled his book on the subject *Missed Chances*, and other titles of works in this vein are 'Missing the boat at Messina and other times?' 'How (and why) Britain lost the leadership of Europe', and *The Schuman Plan and the British Abdication of Leadership in Europe* (Camps, 1993; Charlton, 1981; Dell, 1995; Denman, 1996). Nor is this simply related to politics: it is also common to argue, as Geoffrey Owen does, that earlier membership of the EC would have improved Britain's economic performance just at the time when Britain's relative economic decline was at its most problematic (Owen, 1999). Entering the EEC in the 1950s, it is argued, would not only have given British manufacturers open access to the large markets of the Six but would also have removed protection at home and that this increased competition would have improved economic performance by breaking down 'the cosy relationship' between business and labour. Underpinning all of this 'if only' school of thinking is criticism of past policy. Similarly, once Britain became a member of the EC, the same thought lies behind Stephen George's influential work *An Awkward Partner*, which is typical of those critical, implicitly or explicitly, of Britain's policy on Europe (George, 1998).

Such critical views of Britain's policy towards European integration were also the starting point for the historiography of the subject but since the 1980s it has tended to move away from this position. Consulting the records of the key government departments, notably those of the Foreign Office, and of Cabinet discussions has led to the emergence of a more sympathetic picture. A better understanding of British policy has emerged, in particular there has been a recognition that the 'missed opportunities' argument is too simplistic: the argument ignored the realities of the post-war world, underestimated the constraints that these imposed on British policy and downplayed the complexity of the situation. It has also become accepted that Britain did not turn its back on Europe after the war but that British policy was based on cooperation between governments rather than via supranational bodies.

This view has developed as records have become available to historians: not joining the ECSC was first to be given this more sympathetic treatment – it was not a missed opportunity. Indeed, Greenwood went so far as to suggest that it was Jean Monnet who missed the opportunity: his tactics of not informing Britain in advance limited European integration to only six nations (Greenwood, 1992: 39). This may not be a typical view but illustrates how far academic debate had moved since the early 1980s. Similarly, more sympathetic treatments of the free trade area proposals, Britain's decision not to join the EEC and the failure to gain entry in the 1961–63 negotiations have emerged, though critics of each of these still remain. In this more positive interpretation, rather than the 1961 application being regarded as too late it is seen as surprisingly early given existing interests – British policy changed radically and moved quickly away from being unwilling to make any commitment to Europe which impinged on other interests to one where it was willing to ditch the Commonwealth. The delay in achieving entry caused by de Gaulle's vetoes then becomes the key issue.

One key feature of the literature is also its narrowness. Until recently the historical study of Britain and Europe has been dominated by diplomatic historians who have focused their studies on a small elite of government ministers and officials in which strategic and geopolitical considerations have dominated and a narrow selection of records have been studied. Alan Milward, an economic historian who has written one of the most influential books on European integration, has been highly critical of this work as little more than 'preliminary comments' on the subject. His work and an equally influential, but controversial, book by Andrew Moravcsik have argued that European integration has been driven by economic forces (and in Moravcsik's case, even more narrowly defined commercial considerations). Partly in response to this, more recent work by historians has moved towards considering the views and records of the economic departments of British government, notably the Treasury and the Board of Trade, and it is significant that Milward has written the official history of Britain's relations with Europe, the first volume of which has been published and the second is currently being drafted. Slowly, attention is also moving away from government records and historians are beginning to build up a picture of public attitudes and of the views and actions of interest groups such as business and, to a lesser extent, trade unions, towards European integration. The picture that is emerging is inevitably more complex and raises many new issues, but it is certainly clear, for example in the case of business, that even among Euroenthusiast elements in Britain there was no clear and sustained commitment to European integration simply for its own sake. Thus it is hard to argue that there was a missed opportunity in the sense of government policy not responding to the calls of industry to join. At the same time, it is becoming clear that it is too simple to argue that it was a missed opportunity to shake up business and challenge its generally defensive and protectionist outlook. Industry, after all, was in favour of a free trade area which would have opened the domestic market to more competition than simply joining the EEC because of the larger number of member states. In addition, from a different angle recent research has shown that, despite the creation of the EEC, member states were able to maintain barriers between national markets in key industries such as cars. In other words, joining the EEC might have exposed British industry to more competition but not offered access to European markets in return, raising a serious question mark about whether earlier entry was a missed opportunity to have improved Britain's economic performance.

Costs of EC membership

While the popular debate on the period before Britain became a member of the EC has been dominated by Euroenthusiasts, the same cannot be said of the period since 1973. Contemporary popular debate is generally critical of the EU, fed by media attacks on the institutions of the EU. *The Sun*'s famous reaction to the Delors Report on EMU was the front page headline 'Up Yours Delors'.

Yet, it is important to note that at the time of the 1975 referendum the paper was staunchly in favour of staying in and that its reporting reflects the tastes of its readership. For example, its coverage of the launch of the euro into public circulation was completely different in the Republic of Ireland compared to that in the UK edition of the paper – the former full of praise, the latter simply condemning. Over the years it has been easy journalism to create scare stories about the EU, be it about bent cucumbers, sausages or even condoms, all stressing 'Brussels bureaucracy' and the loss of British sovereignty to it. History has often played a central role in this popular debate. Eurosceptics point to Britain's global history, it being an island nation and its ties to the Commonwealth: Hugh Gaitskell, the Labour party leader in 1961, saw Britain's possible entry into the EEC as 'the end of a thousand years of history' (Young, 1998: 163).

Academic work on Britain and European integration, by way of contrast, is often at odds with this popular discourse. In part this has been a consequence of the position that most historians working on European integration being interested in the topic because they are sympathetic to the cause of European integration and of Britain's involvement in that process. However, the situation is changing and this factor alone does not explain one significant difference between the historiography and popular debates. A key theoretical debate among historians and political scientists has been over the driving force behind European integration and, therefore, what European integration may look like in the future. One group emphasize the growing powers of the supranational institutions of the EU and its predecessors. Apart from seeing this generally in a positive light there is little difference between this body of research and popular debate. However, the argument of the second group is at odds with popular perceptions. This group, often called inter-governmentalists, believe that European integration has been, and remains, controlled by national governments, only handing over sovereignty to supranational bodies on their terms and in their own interests: European integration has been an inter-governmental process. Alan Milward has played a crucial role in the development of these ideas, building up his argument from research on the start of European integration, and entitling his key work *The European Rescue of the Nation-State* (1992 and 2000). He argued that post-war European integration was just one part of the post-war reconstruction of the state in Western Europe. This reconstruction centred upon the notion of a strong national government which managed the economy and provided a welfare state, among other things. However, it was not possible for national governments on the continent to achieve this solely by their own actions because of their interdependence with other nations – by the 1950s, for example, 40 per cent of the national income of the Netherlands was earned

Plate 22.1 Tabloid newspaper *The Sun* urges its readers to express open antipathy to the French Minister's 'Delors Report' on European Economic and Monetary Union (© NI Syndication).

outside its national frontiers. European integration provided a solution, Milward suggests, to this problem of interdependence by helping to provide increased security and greater prosperity. In other words, national governments in the Six were willing to hand over a small amount of sovereignty to supranational institutions in return for this extra security and prosperity which followed from European integration and which, in turn, then buttressed the popular allegiance and legitimacy of these national governments.

Milward's conclusions, along with those of other inter-governmentalists, are disputed but they remain highly influential as a corrective to the view that European integration inevitably meant the emergence of a supranational European state. Rather, the institutions of the EU are seen to have created a new level of decision making *in addition* to local, regional and national governments, what is called multilevel governance. If nothing else this debate has shown that it cannot be taken for granted that 'Brussels bureaucracy' has simply taken over a wide range of powers from Westminster and other national governments across Europe and will inevitably continue to do so until a European state has been created, as is commonly presented in popular discussion of Britain and European integration.

Further reading

There are many popular accounts of the history of Britain and European integration but one of the best recent ones is Hugo Young's *This Blessed Plot* (London, 1998). A more personal account, drawing on his own experiences as a civil servant involved in the negotiations, is supplied in Denman's *Missed Chances* (London, 1996). A brief account of Euroscepticism can be found in Anthony Forster's *Euroscepticism in Contemporary British Politics* (London, 2002). The best academic overview of the whole post-war period has been provided by John W. Young in *Britain and European Unity 1945–1999* (Basingstoke, 2000) but there is also D. Gowland and H. Turner, *Reluctant Europeans* (Harlow, 2000). More detailed historical analyses of the period for which records have been available have been provided on the Schuman Plan – Edmund Dell, *The Schuman Plan and the British Abdication of Leadership in Europe* (Oxford, 1995) and Christopher Lord, *Absent at the Creation* (Aldershot, 1996). On the free trade area negotiations there is James Ellison, *Threatening Europe* (Basingstoke, 2000) and on the first application there is G. Wilkes's edited collection, *Britain's Failure to Enter the European Community, 1961–63* (London, 1997). To some extent these have been superseded by Alan Milward's official history, *The Rise and Fall of a National Strategy, 1945–1963* (London, 2002). On the second application there is Daddow's edited volume, *Harold Wilson and European Integration* (London, 2003). Little work has been published on the third application to date. Beyond broad surveys already mentioned, historians have written little on the period after 1973 and the field is dominated by political scientists. The seminal work here is Stephen George's *An Awkward Partner* (Oxford, various editions). The two most influential recent books on the history of European integration are Milward, *The European Rescue of the Nation-State* (1992 and 2000) and Moravcsik's, *The Choice for Europe* (1998).

References

Camps, M. (1993) 'Missing the Boat at Messina and Other Times?' in B. Brivati and H. Jones (eds) *From Reconstruction to Integration: Britain and Europe since 1945*, Leicester: Leicester University Press.

Charlton, M. (1981) 'How (and why) Britain lost the leadership of Europe', *Encounter*, 57: 1–3.

Dell, E. (1995) *The Schuman Plan and the British Abdication of Leadership in Europe*, Oxford: Oxford University Press.

Denman, R. (1996) *Missed chances: Britain and Europe in the twentieth century*, London.

George, S. (1998) *An awkward partner: Britain in the European Community*, Oxford: Oxford University Press.

Greenwood, S. (1992) *Britain and European co-operation since 1945*, Oxford: Blackwell Press.

Moore, L. (1999) *Britain's trade and economic structure: The impact of the European Union*, London: Routledge.

Owen, G. (1999) *From empire to Europe: The decline and revival of British industry since the Second World War*, London: HarperCollins.

Plowden, E. (1989) *An industrialist in the Treasury: The post-war years*, London: Deutsch.

Young, H. (1998) *This blessed plot*, London: Macmillan.

Young, J.W. (2000) *Britain and European unity 1945–1999*, Basingstoke: Macmillan.

Notes

1   At the same time as the EEC was created, Euratom was also created. With the ECSC this made three communities and so it was common to refer to the EEC or the European Communities. In 1967 the three communities were merged and so there was then just one European Community (EC). This then became the European Union (EU) in 1992.

2   Tony Blair, 23 November 2001 on opening the European Research Institute, University of Birmingham http://www.eri.bham.ac.uk/eriopening.htm (accessed 15 June 2003).

23

Education and opportunity

Katherine Watson

ON HIS APPOINTMENT AS PRESIDENT of the Board of Education in 1941, R.A. Butler faced several challenges: the economic and social impetus for innovation in secondary education was significant, yet he inherited a system in which reform had been stifled by a combination of fiscal stringency and institutional obstacles. The 1918 Fisher Act formalized the school leaving age at 14 (achieved by 1922), but the ambition to raise this further to 15 and to provide continuation schooling for 16–18-year-olds foundered under the economic and budgetary pressures of the 1920s. Hadow's recommendation in 1926 that schooling should be reorganized to establish distinct infant, junior and senior schools, with admission to different types of secondary school determined, at least in part, by ability, had been similarly frustrated by public expenditure cuts. The 1936 Education Act nominally reinforced these aims (although it still permitted employment exemptions from the proposed leaving age of 15), as did, more forcefully, the 1938 Spens Report of the Consultative Committee to the Board of Education, but, this time, war obstructed implementation. By 1938, 88 per cent of children educated in the maintained sector in England and Wales were still being taught in elementary schools and very few achieved formal qualifications or had any real opportunity to remain in education beyond 14 (Simon, 1999: 26).

In this context, it is perhaps not surprising that Butler's 1944 Education Act was heralded as such a significant reform (Dent, 1947: 3). At the heart of the Act lay the determination to provide compulsory, free education for all children aged 5–15. Children above the age of 11 were to receive at least four years of secondary education in schools designated for the purpose, and the intention was to raise the school leaving age to 16 as soon as practicable. A new Ministry of Education would oversee the assimilation of many voluntary church schools into the maintained sector and significant new investment in educational infrastructure. From 1947 secondary schools would no longer be permitted to levy fees. The previously under-utilized talents of the intelligent working class were expected to flourish, reaping economic as well as cultural benefits.

Conflict and compromise

An important challenge facing education reformers was how to manage conflicting religious interests in the management and funding of schools. Equality of opportunity required schools to be organized on the same terms, not least because few schools outside the maintained sector could afford to implement the required reforms in secondary provision. Local authorities seemed best placed to assume control of voluntary schools, yet the churches would only support the 1944 Act if their schools retained religious autonomy and this was politically difficult as their funding would depend on taxation of those who did not necessarily share their beliefs (Gosden, 1976: 260). Voluntary-aided schools supported by partial grants from local authorities, but under limited church control, was the compromise solution: if churches failed to maintain schools to national standards, local authority control could be imposed. Conflict between the churches was also difficult to resolve: Nonconformists feared, particularly in rural areas, that children would have no choice but to attend Catholic or Anglican church-aided

Plate 23.1 Cartoon by David Low, 'Religious conflict', *The Evening Standard*, 17 January 1931 (supplied by the Centre for the Study of Cartoons and Caricature at the University of Kent, reproduced courtesy of Solo Syndication).

schools, and Catholic schools, typically located in areas of urban deprivation, were often under-resourced and more vulnerable to withdrawal of voluntary-aided status (Gosden, 1976: 291). Even with compromise, it was difficult to create a nationally coherent system of education.

Further conflict emerged over the organization of secondary schooling. Much interwar advice advocated transfer at 11+ to grammar schools for those destined for the professions, and the development of new institutions for those for whom technical or relatively unskilled work was more appropriate (the technical and modern schools respectively). But the capacity of local authorities to implement change was variously affected by their existing stock of schools, as well as by attitudes to the timing and accuracy of selection. Ultimately, pressure to impose a rigid structure for secondary education was resisted. Local authorities were free to propose alternative development plans for review by the Minister for Education, including the creation of multilateral (comprehensive) schools: these were developed in some areas for principled reasons and in others because regional demography made it economically inefficient to offer a range of distinct secondary schools. Nevertheless, in embracing the Norwood Report of 1943, which suggested children's predisposition to a particular type of education could be identified, the government provided a clear steer towards the tripartite system, encouraging most local authorities to develop selective secondary education (Simon, 1999: 61).

Dissatisfaction with the organization of secondary schooling was reinforced by the lack of investment in technical schools so that they failed to develop into the strong third strand of the system initially envisaged. By 1960 there were just 266 secondary technical schools (compared to 248 in 1938): although 63 new schools had been established between 1945 and 1960, many counties sought to establish technical streams within secondary grammar and modern schools and actually reduced their separate technical provision (Sanderson, 1987: 59–60; Sanderson, 1999). In 1954, just 5 per cent of secondary schoolchildren were being educated in maintained technical schools (Lowe, 1988: 114). Similarly, only 536 new secondary modern schools were built between 1945 and 1956 and there remained 1026 all-age schools that had still not been subjected to Hadow reorganization. Only about 10 per cent of the total modern school stock had been established with this purpose in mind, exacerbating the perception that these tiers could not sustain parity of esteem with the grammar schools (Sanderson, 1987: 56).

Many smaller public schools feared erosion of their market as state schools improved, but integration of the independent, direct grant and maintained sectors proved intractable. Many direct grant schools were former endowed grammar schools, drawing a small proportion of their intake from local elementary schools in exchange for payment of a grant direct from the Board of Education in respect of fees. Once maintained fees were abolished, it was difficult to justify the continued financial support of what were in effect local authority places at schools operating outside their control. The 1942 Fleming Committee reviewed these issues, ultimately advocating increased access to the independent schools via a means-tested bursary funded by the local authority for those who had attended local primary schools. However, the report was not published until shortly before the Education Bill received Royal Assent and far too late to implement these proposals formally within it. Post-war prosperity saw the recovery of demand for independent school places, and the impetus for radical reform seemed to have gone (Gosden, 1976: 366).

The task facing Butler and his team of civil servants was immense: in order to guide his Bill to the statute books he had to secure the cooperation of a diverse set of institutions, themselves a legacy of nineteenth- and early twentieth-century compromise. Further compromise was almost inevitable. As Kenneth Baker (architect of the 1988 education reforms) argued, what emerged was 'an education system which had grown up via addition and adaption' and was ultimately 'a bit of a muddle' (Timmins, 1995: 94).

Progress and restraint

Initial progress in implementing the 1944 reforms was slow. Additional teachers and school buildings were vital if there was any prospect of securing the agreed increase in school leaving age to 15 by 1947. Progress was achieved against the tide of labour and materials shortages and the competing pressures for public spending, including the urgent demand for new housing. The tenacity of Ellen Wilkinson, Minister of Education, was critical in maintaining the programme for reform; she resisted strongly her Cabinet colleagues' fears that the practical obstacles were insurmountable and that labour shortages would only be aggravated further by the withdrawal of 15-year-olds from employment. Temporary buildings, large classes and the recruitment of emergency teaching staff addressed the immediate problem of increasing school places (see Figure 23.1, p. 358), but few new secondary schools were completed before the mid-1950s, with the greatest expansion in the later 1950s (see Figure 23.2, p. 358) (Gosden, 1983: 1–18).

The proportion of national income spent on education grew minimally from 2 per cent in 1938 to 2.2 per cent by 1951, but the 10 per cent increase in the school population undermined the real impact of this growth (Simon, 1999: 169). Conflicting pressures of rearmament in the wake of the Korean crisis and the mounting sterling and balance of payments crises, combined with Conservative commitment to reduce taxation, demanded stringent control of education spending. Ironically, it was Butler himself, now in his capacity as Chancellor of the Exchequer, who imposed restraint on the education minister, Florence Horsbrugh. Discussion even took place regarding reversal of the decision to increase the school leaving age to 16, or raising the age at which school started to six, and serious consideration was given to reintroduction of fees for secondary education at least for those staying at school beyond statutory age. Although these measures were ultimately rejected, their contemplation is indicative of the restrictions of this period (Lowe, 1988: 88–90; Simon, 1999: 163–4).

The post-war recovery in the birth rate intensified pressure to increase school places during the early 1950s. From 1954, the new education minister, David Eccles, recognized more clearly the political imperative for increased real investment in

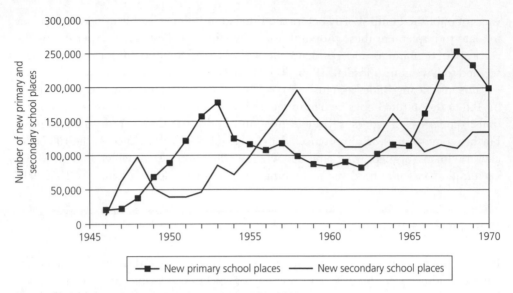

Figure 23.1 Number of school places created, 1945–1970
Source: Based on Gosden, 1983: 18.

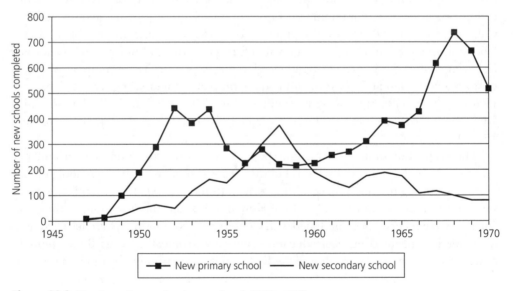

Figure 23.2 Number of new schools completed, 1945–1970
Source: Based on Gosden, 1983: 18.

education (see Figure 23.3, p. 359) (Simon, 1999: 182). He also reasserted Conservative commitment to the grammar schools and to selection at 11, but acknowledged growing disquiet about the inability to establish parity of esteem for different schools within the tripartite system. As a consequence, he advocated enhancing the opportunities for transfer between modern, technical and grammar schools at 15 or 16 and

Figure 23.3 Public spending on education as a percentage of GDP, 1953–2003
Source: Based on 1953–86: Simon, 1999: Table 15; 1987–2003: National Statistics (2003) *Public Expenditure Statistical Analyses 2005*, Cm 6521: Table 3.4.

increasing the prospects for children in these schools to secure formal qualifications. The limited growth of technical schools was to be tackled by developing these opportunities for children with appropriate abilities *within* existing secondary modern and grammar schools. At best, central support for new technical schools was ambivalent

Plate 23.2 Metalwork class in progress, demonstrating the emphasis on vocational careers for working-class students and the gendering of education (© Liverpool Record Office).

from the mid-1950s and, in reality, technical institutional growth was very sparse. By 1960 the tripartite system had virtually become bipartite, with approximately 75 per cent of children destined for secondary modern schools at the age of 11 (Lowe, 1988: 114–116).

Education enjoyed a welcome elevation in the ranks of public priorities as the economy prospered between the mid-1950s and the early 1970s. Yet, it was becoming increasingly clear that inconsistency in the management and delivery of reforms undermined claims that the 1944 Act marked the advent of equality of opportunity in education.

Challenging continuity

One of the challenges facing British education was how to manage the improved opportunities for all envisaged in 1944 within a system where local providers largely retained autonomy over resource allocation, subject to development plans being approved by the Education Minister. Some areas elected to pursue comprehensive education, and among those choosing selective secondary schooling, the probability of accessing grammar schools varied widely by region, gender and also by social class. For example, while Westmoreland offered 42 per cent of their secondary school places in grammar schools, Gateshead could manage just 9 per cent. Even within authorities the probability of accessing grammar schools still varied widely, especially where single-sex schools dominated: Birmingham boys were twice as likely to secure a grammar school place as their female contemporaries simply because the number of places available was greater for boys than girls (Lowe, 1988: 107–8).

The 1958 National Foundation for Educational Research study of the selection process and its outcomes concluded that at least 10 per cent of children in any cohort were selected for the 'wrong' school at the age of 11, adding to the pressure for more flexible transfer arrangements (Simon, 1999: 209–10). Even if the inequities of the selection process itself were ignored, the obstacles to transfer between schools, the rigidities in the curriculum, and the unequal prospects for taking public examinations in different types of school meant that these wide variations in access probabilities in effect consigned many children to poorer life and employment chances on grounds that even the most enthusiastic supporter of selection had to concede was unjust.

Floud, Halsey and Martin's 1956 study of social class and social opportunity in Middlesbrough and south-west Hertfordshire also questioned the extent of the benefits which the 1944 Education Act had secured for working-class children. The increased likelihood that working-class boys would transfer to grammar schools during the 1920s was eroded by the economic downturn and public expenditure cuts of the 1930s. After the war, free grammar school places were disproportionately secured by middle-class pupils who would formerly have paid fees, suggesting that the 1944 Act had simply consolidated middle-class advantage. Once the distribution of ability had been considered, working-class boys seemed to secure only slightly less than their expected quota of free grammar school places (Floud et al., 1956: 58). However, a crucial difference was in the benefits boys from different social backgrounds gained from selective education: a far higher proportion of working-class pupils failed to complete the full secondary school curriculum and left either before public examination at 16 or without progressing to sixth form courses and university. It seemed considerable talent was still being under-utilized, the 1944 reforms notwithstanding.

Further doubt was cast on the validity of selection once the examination system altered in 1951. The School Certificate was replaced with the General Certificate of Education at Ordinary level, examined via independent subject papers, providing opportunities for more able secondary modern pupils to study specialist examination courses. Pupils who had been assessed at 11 as having an IQ well below average succeeded in passing five or more of these examinations, undermining confidence in the validity of 11+ selection. The variability in effectiveness of different schools was also questioned: Why were some secondary modern pupils able to achieve examination performances far superior to those of their supposedly more academic contemporaries in grammar schools?

As the 1950s progressed, several local authorities proposed that as new schools were built, they should accept a comprehensive intake. By proposing secondary modern schools should become high schools for 11- to 14-year-olds and the grammar schools open-access comprehensives for 14- to 18-year-olds, the 1957 Leicestershire Plan provided a new strategy for converting existing school stock more quickly to achieve multilateral schooling. Although there were still only 130 comprehensive schools in 1960, the prospects for further expansion seemed strong (Simon, 1999: 208–9). By 1963, the Conservative Minister of Education, Sir Edward Boyle, estimated that 90 of the 163 local education authorities were actively considering plans for comprehensive reorganization. His broad sympathy with local government initiatives to diminish selection helped to steer the 1964 Education Act through Parliament, thereby permitting LEAs optionally to develop comprehensive middle schools (Simon, 1999: 274).

The election of a Labour government in 1964 with a mandate to reorganize secondary schooling along comprehensive lines and to extend grammar school provision to those formerly arbitrarily denied access to it by selection at 11 (Labour Party, 1964), provided a further impetus for reform. However, instead of legislating for change, Department of Education and Science circulars 10/65 and 600 were issued to local education authorities in England and Wales, and in Scotland respectively, requesting that they submit schemes for reorganization within a year. In practice, with the absence of clear time constraints for implementation, and an unwillingness initially to supply extra resources to finance reorganization, recalcitrant local authorities were able to ignore this request. The conflict between national and local political interests was difficult to resolve without greater formal commitment to reform. The weakness of the 1964 parliamentary majority arguably undermined Labour's capacity to enforce their proposals, but the scale of the party's national political advantage between 1966 and 1970 was such that this lack of action was much harder to understand (Benn and Chitty, 1996: 9). From 1966 capital grants for new secondary buildings became conditional on reorganization, providing some incentive for LEAs to coalesce with Labour policy, but in the wake of the sterling crisis of 1967, expenditure cuts once more dampened progress. The long-awaited increase in the school leaving age to 16 was postponed again from 1970 to 1972, delaying the building programme in schools needed to accommodate additional pupils in their fifth year of secondary education and rejecting a further opportunity to use expansion as a means to proceed with reorganization. It was not until 1969 that the Labour party began drafting an act to abolish selection at 11, but they lost office in 1970 before these plans could come to fruition.

Between 1960 and 1970, the proportion of children in English and Welsh maintained secondary schools receiving their education in comprehensive schools increased from less than 5 per cent to almost a third, but for supporters of reorganization, progress was frustratingly slow. More than half of these schools coexisted with grammar schools and were unable to recruit pupils from the full ability range. Even within these schools, many of the principles underpinning the old selective system typically remained, including differentiating pupils by ability and streaming them into academic and less academic classes.

Ironically the amendments to the public examination system also created obstacles to real reform. The development of the new Certificate of Secondary Education (CSE) examination from 1962 and first sat in 1965 had been designed to motivate and reward the more able secondary modern school pupils. The General Certificate of Education (Ordinary level) was deemed appropriate for the top 20 per cent of the ability range, typically to be found in grammar schools; the new CSE was felt to be attainable by the next 40 per cent of the ability range with half aiming for at least four CSE passes and half attempting fewer subjects. This divisive examination system almost immediately appeared incongruous alongside the move towards comprehensive schooling since it inevitably prompted division of pupils within these schools into three groups, the O-level, CSE and non-examination streams, and required comprehensive schools to administer more than one examination system simultaneously.

By the end of the 1960s it was clear that simply maintaining existing provision in education was unacceptable, yet the path to significant reform was uneven. Economic, political and institutional constraints perpetuated the pattern of piecemeal progress, with pragmatism often triumphing over radicalism.

Resisting resistance

The year 1970 saw the election of a Conservative government committed to protecting grammar schools. In June 1970 the DES issued a circular permitting those authorities that had not yet introduced comprehensive schools to retreat from reorganization. Emphasis shifted too from building new secondary schools to improving primary accommodation. Comprehensive reorganization now had to be pursued much more contentiously using existing school stock, intensifying political conflict between national and local government. Although Margaret Thatcher rejected some proposals for reform, local resistance permitted comprehensive reorganization to continue in most counties, but critically these plans were often undermined by her insistence that existing grammar schools should also survive, thereby violating the principle that pupils should be admitted from the full ability range.

The election of a Labour government in 1974, albeit with a very slim majority, allowed reorganization to be pursued with greater conviction. From March 1975 support was withdrawn from direct grant schools, requiring them either to move into the state sector as comprehensive schools or go independent: a large majority opted for independence. Finally, the government resorted to compulsion in relation to comprehensive reorganization with the passage of the 1976 Education Act. By 1980 about 80 per cent of UK secondary school pupils were being taught in comprehensive schools (ONS, 2006: 35). Yet, by then, optimism was dwindling that comprehensive schools alone could generate the improved standards in education Britain needed to sustain economic growth and compete effectively with other advanced economies. Just as the structure of schooling ought to have become a diminishing focus for political conflict, curriculum content and delivery moved centre-stage, with the Labour Prime Minister Jim Callaghan leading this debate.

Fighting 'failure' with radical reform

Callaghan asked the new Secretary of State for Education and Science, Fred Mulley, to report on the weaknesses in state education and the changes needed to restore public confidence in the nation's schools. The resulting Yellow Book was ostensibly a confidential document, but key elements of it were leaked to the press. These advocated stronger commitment to formal core skills teaching at primary level and the development of vocational courses to motivate lower-ability secondary children and prepare them more effectively for employment. In a famous speech delivered at Ruskin College in October 1976, Callaghan emphasized the economic importance of scientific and technical training and the need to raise educational standards. Attention shifted from the capacity and structure of the education sector to the evaluation of the efficiency with which education resources were used. By the time Margaret Thatcher's Conservative government was elected in 1979, these issues had assumed even greater importance as rising unemployment and, in particular, youth unemployment focused attention on how education might affect economic security.

Almost immediately, the Conservative government revoked the 1976 Act. Several authorities, including Kent and Essex, were permitted to withdraw their reorganization proposals and retain selection. Introduction of the Assisted Places Scheme, which in effect subsidized independent schools by paying school fees directly on behalf of selected pupils, was supposed to enhance opportunities for the able working classes, but children from semi-professional and professional families often secured these places. In a bid to cut costs, the burden on local authorities to provide school meals, milk and transport was also relaxed, and they were required to prioritize parental choice in allocating school places. As far as practicable, parents would be permitted to choose the school their child would attend, even where they lived outside the relevant catchment area. The aim was to strengthen successful schools, while weaker schools would fail to recruit sufficient pupils to survive.

In 1984, Keith Joseph finally sought to tackle the problems of the divided examination system. The new General Certificate of Secondary Education (GCSE) was initially conceived as an umbrella qualification in which differentiated papers were available: able children would sit examinations administered by the university examinations boards to secure an A–C grade and the remainder would take CSE papers to secure grades in the range D–G. This was far from the integrated system envisaged by the pioneers of comprehensive education.

Six months after his appointment as Secretary of State for Education and Science in 1986, Kenneth Baker announced his intention to establish 20 'pilot' city technology colleges in urban areas of relative deprivation. These schools would operate outside local authority control, but would be funded in part by the state. The remainder of their capital would be raised from private business sponsorship. They were permitted to select pupils believed to be most able to benefit from the opportunities available. Although there had been a promise that the success of these pilot schools could see hundreds being formed after the election, it proved difficult to secure suitable sites or the sponsorship needed and ultimately just 15 had been established by 1990 (Chitty, 2004: 52).

The return of the Conservatives to office in 1987 with a majority exceeding 100 encouraged bold policy making. Along with the poll tax, the Great Education Reform Bill ('Gerbill') was presented to the House as 'flagship' legislation. Parental choice was elevated and funds were permitted to follow pupils. Schools were pitted against each other in competition for children and the funding they brought with them. In addition, schools were expected to manage their own budgets and were able to fix their own admission quotas. Governing bodies could ballot parents to opt out of local authority management, creating grant-maintained schools funded directly from central government. Teachers were required to follow a national curriculum covering ten subjects, and pupil performance would be assessed at each of four key stages. Pupils were expected to achieve level 2 by the age of seven at the end of Key Stage 1, level 4 by the age of 11, level 5 by 14 and pass GCSE examinations by the end of Key Stage 4. Publication of examination results would provide a 'signal of quality' for parents seeking to choose between schools.

The national curriculum provoked considerable consternation among educationalists, parent groups and politicians. Consultation papers had been issued in the development of the Bill, but these were despatched in July for return by September, severely curtailing the capacity of most educational establishments to respond effectively. Criticism was largely dismissed as vested interest lobbying: the commitment of trade unions, local authorities and Left-leaning universities to the chimera of egalitarianism had to be broken down if educational standards were to be raised and Britain's economic standing restored (Tomlinson, 2001: 47). Schools choosing grant-maintained

(GM) status would be able to pursue selective admissions policies, thereby undermining the progress achieved towards comprehensive education. In addition, there was concern that the Secretary of State assumed responsibility for setting the national curriculum: for many critics, what had been presented as the liberation of schools actually represented a massive swing towards central control with the role for local authorities decimated. Concern too was expressed for the children whose education might be blighted while their school 'failed'. Ted Heath was the only Conservative to abstain as the Education Bill passed its second reading, attacking the proposals for parental choice as a 'confidence trick' and predicting the impact of the Bill would be 'socially divisive' and would 'destroy the educational system' (Simon, 1999: 543).

Subsequent Conservative education reforms sought to reinforce the market agenda. The 1993 Act aimed to increase the number of GM schools, changing the balloting arrangements to make it easier for schools to opt out. It also established a procedure for identifying failing schools and placing them in special measures. If LEA support was unable to turn these schools around, it was expected they would convert to GM status.

Reforming the market for education

In 1997, Andrew Adonis and Stephen Pollard presented a depressing picture of persistent social and educational segregation, arguing that the gap between the privileged and the disadvantaged had actually widened since the 1960s. Although in the mid-1990s just 7 per cent of children were independently educated, they commanded a quarter of university places (Adonis and Pollard, 1997: 45). The gap between average achievement in independent and state schools was wide, but so too was the gap between the highest and lowest achieving state schools. The wealthiest families opted out of state education altogether and the middle classes typically moved to more affluent areas in search of academic security for their children. The badly managed transition to comprehensive schooling had simply replaced selection according to ability with 'selection' by social class and house price.

The year 1997 also saw the election of a Labour government for the first time in 18 years, bringing with it another torrent of education reforms. New Labour advocated inclusion, the promotion of lifelong learning, zero tolerance of failing schools, and a commitment to providing additional support for deprived urban areas (via education action zones). They promised to increase spending on education, reduce class sizes and set targets for raising standards in schools. They withdrew the assisted places scheme and defined three types of maintained school: community schools (formerly county schools), aided schools, and foundation schools which were intended to encompass all LEA and grant-maintained schools. New Labour affirmed its commitment to comprehensive schooling, but proposed 'modernizing' comprehensive schools, permitting differentiation by ability within schools and selection of up to 10 per cent of a specialist school's intake by aptitude. (More recent conflict over this issue has seen interviewing banned as part of the admissions process and the rejection of new selection by ability reaffirmed in the 2006 Education Bill.) Specialist schools were to remain and be developed, raising fears among critics that this would undermine the comprehensive ethos, their brief to undertake outreach work with local primary schools notwithstanding. National literacy and numeracy strategies were introduced to focus attention on core skills. Attention was also drawn to progress within schools rather than final attainment: introduction of baseline assessment in schools and the development of value-added measures of performance aimed to control for social advantage in judging the quality of schools. From 2000, the new post-16 curriculum included development of modular A-levels and a transitional AS qualification to be completed in Year 12, ostensibly making post-statutory schooling more attractive and encouraging more students to pursue higher education (see, for example, Chitty, 2004; Lawton, 2005).

Evaluation of these measures has been mixed. Critics have focused on the continued commitment to market principles and the entrenchment of inequalities this is believed to have generated. Success has also been highlighted in the form of improved attainment at Key Stages 2 and 4, but critics have worried that this has been achieved by narrowing the curriculum to the detriment of arts and humanities and the loss of extension activities. By 2000, 75 per cent of children achieved at least level 4 in English at the age of 11 compared to 57 per cent in 1996 and in mathematics the improvement was from 54 to 72 per cent over the same period (Chitty, 2004: 73). In the last five years, progress has slowed, but 79 per cent achieved at least level 4 in English and 75 per cent in mathematics. In 2005 about 55 per cent of pupils achieved five A*–C GCSE passes (compared with 46 per cent in 1995/6 and 63 per cent in 2001/02), but this dropped to 42.5 per cent if English and Maths were included. Just 3 per cent of pupils left school without any GCSE qualification in the A*–G range (DfES, 2005). In general, the expansion in funding in schools has been acknowledged and the commitment to urban improvement accepted, but inequalities in achievement and in opportunity remain significant. The government has been accused of timidity in failing to endorse the Tomlinson proposals for 14–19 curriculum and assessment reform and has thereby perhaps lost an opportunity to redeem past weaknesses in the domain of technical education.

In Focus

Further and higher education

During the later 1950s, as secondary provision improved, attention turned to further and higher education as ministers became more aware of Britain's technical limitations and of the growing mismatch between those students qualified to pursue degree courses but unable to secure places. In 1959, The Crowther Report re-emphasized the need for growth in post-compulsory education during the 1960s beyond what was already being discussed. Between 1957 and 1963, the number of

Further and higher education

students in higher education, including teacher-training colleges in Great Britain, increased by almost 50 per cent, to about 217,000 (Simons, 1999: 223). Publication of the Robbins Report in 1963 heralded further expansion, the aim being to double student numbers by 1977 and treble them by 1985. In order to achieve this aim, it advocated founding new universities and streamlining administration into a unitary system, encompassing colleges of advanced technology as new universities and integrating teacher training-colleges as schools of education within universities.

Significant progress was achieved as more students achieved the two A-level passes required for university entrance. By 1968 approximately 376,000 students were in higher education. Expansion exceeded Robbins's targets, although the pattern of reform did not match the structure he envisaged. Instead of adopting the unitary system Robbins advocated, the Labour Secretary of State for Education and Science, Tony Crosland, proposed a binary system in which the different, and ostensibly complementary, contributions of university and college education would be recognized. The proposal to create polytechnics was implemented in 1969, generating anxiety that an opportunity to consolidate the administration of higher education and remove academic hierarchies had been lost.

Although the growth of higher education was significant, new places went disproportionately to the socially advantaged. The children of manual workers remained stubbornly at about 3 per cent of the university population and widening access particularly benefited middle-class girls and mature students. Worryingly too, attempts to strengthen science and technology fell a long way short of securing the intended two-thirds of additional university places in these disciplines, much of the growth actually taking place in social sciences and humanities. Although the fantastically innovative 'University of the Air', which, as the Open University, recruited its first students in 1971, offered opportunities for students in employment to study part time, easing working-class access to higher education, it attracted large numbers of teachers and clerical workers to its courses. Open University course fees soon increased to maintain the institution's viability, further undermining its success in widening social participation.

Between 1988 and 1992, significant changes in higher education included the ending of local authority funding of polytechnics and the withdrawal of academic tenure in higher education. Student loans were introduced as the grant system for student support decayed. Polytechnics were permitted to issue their own degrees and adopt the title of 'university', but they were to compete with existing universities for funds allocated on the basis of teaching and research assessments. The market became the dominant mechanism determining the allocation of education resources at all levels of provision. The introduction of means-tested tuition fees from 1998 and the growth of student loans have consolidated the perception of higher education as a commodity. Transition to higher-level fees from 2006 has been pursued with a stronger commitment to bursaries and widening participation, and is levied as an

> ### Further and higher education

income-related graduate tax rather than an entry charge, but optimism that improved funding will enhance the quality of Britain's higher education sector is tempered by anxiety that social disadvantage may be consolidated.

Higher education has continued to expand rapidly in pursuit of the target for half of Britain's school leavers to be able to access degree-level study. Between 1990 and 2003, the numbers in higher education doubled from about 1.1 million to more than 2.4 million students. Almost seven times as many women attended higher education courses in 2003 than in 1970, while for men the growth has been 250 per cent (ONS, 2006: 38). Participation rates for 18 to 19-year-olds have increased from about 6 per cent in 1960 to about one-third by 2000, with much of this growth occurring since 1990 (Machin and Vignoles, 2004).

Yet concerns about the persistence of socio-economic factors as determinants of education success remain. By 2000, the Sutton Trust reported that the 7 per cent of children attending independent schools were now securing 18 per cent of university places, but they also noted that the probability of a candidate from an independent school achieving a place at one of the top 13 universities was about 25 times greater than for a candidate from a poor social background. They noted that independent schools tended to produce one-third of the top grades at A-level while state schools produced two-thirds, with, of course, state schools entering far more candidates. Evidence has increased that pupils admitted from disadvantaged schools with lower A-levels could still achieve very good degrees on graduation, suggesting that considerable talent was being wasted (Sutton Trust, 2000). This problem has been compounded by the league-table culture which has afflicted universities as much as schools in recent years, as one of the 'quality' indicators is the grade point average at A-level of new students. By raising grades, many popular courses have sought to consolidate their competitive position, but in so doing have risked alienating large proportions of socially disadvantaged candidates, and simultaneously undermined their own investment in widening participation schemes designed to attract this talent.

Debates and Interpretations
Education and social opportunity

So, where has 60 years of educational reform – undertaken at particularly blistering pace during the last 20 years – left Britain in terms of the educational and social opportunities it offers its citizens? Have Butler's goals been achieved?

Fundamental changes have, of course, taken place in terms of entitlement to secondary schooling from the ages of 11 to 16 and in the range of experiences that can be accessed by most children. Yet questions remain as to the impact these changes have had on relative life chances for children from different backgrounds as the twentieth century progressed. Dispiritingly, social class remains a persistent barrier to educational success. Taking a crude measure of deprivation, just short of 30 per cent of children eligible for free school meals completed Year 11 with five A*–C GCSE passes, compared to 59 per cent of those who were not eligible (DfES, 2005). A recent Sutton Trust study of rates of free school meal (FSM) eligibility at the 'top 200' state schools noted that these schools had an average rate of FSM eligibility of 3.0 per cent, compared to a national average of 14.3 per cent. Furthermore, these schools were found not to reflect the social composition of their immediate social areas: FSM eligibility was much greater for the postcode sectors ostensibly serving these schools than it was for the schools themselves. This observation was true for both the grammar schools and the comprehensive schools in the top 200. The implication is that equality of access to the highest achieving maintained schools has yet to be achieved (Sutton Trust, 2005).

Far from liberating the disadvantaged, increased reliance on the market seems to have deepened inequalities. The costs of maintaining the market infrastructure alone have represented a huge financial burden covering, for example, publication of statistical tables and school expense on marketing and promotion, let alone the assimilation and implementation of successive curriculum changes and initiatives etc. Funding formulae are stacked against schools located in the poorest areas: opportunities for parents to subsidize school budgets with fund raising are likely to be reduced and the claims on that budget tend to be greater (e.g. more rapid staff turnover, higher expenditure on supply cover, greater maintenance costs, etc.). Additional evidence exists to suggest that since urban schools disproportionately feature among the least advantaged and ethnic minority populations tend to be concentrated in these areas, they bear a significant burden of underachievement, with the market system serving to intensify racial segregation within cities (Tomlinson, 1997: 63–76).

Inevitably the market for education struggles to work as predicted in situations where there is either no choice of school (e.g. in rural areas), or where particular schools are substantially oversubscribed. It seems that accessing the information necessary to make an informed choice and, if necessary, financing your child to travel out of the area to attend a chosen school, are all factors which favour the socially advantaged, aggravating social segregation and reinforcing perceptions of institutional success and failure. In essence, a choice is not really a choice if you have no opportunity to express it.

Institutional reorganization seems often to have exacerbated inequalities, albeit not always intentionally. In trying to establish various types of school, funding incentives have followed initiatives by successive governments: grant-maintained schools, City technology colleges, specialist schools, etc. have all been offered additional funding, which inevitably has diverted additional funds from other schools. Since, in some cases, achieving this status depended on the capacity of local communities to hold a ballot and raise private funding to bolster the new school's capital, the tendency has been for initiatives largely to favour more affluent areas. The Labour party has sought

" *This appalling compre-
hensive scheme may
mean that all pupils are
equal — but remember
that some will always be
more equal than others.*"

Plate 23.3 Cartoon by Margaret Belsky, 'The challenge of ending selection', *The Sun*, 22 May 1965 (supplied by the Centre for the Study of Cartoons and Caricature at the University of Kent, reproduced courtesy of NI Syndication).

to redress this with its urban development schemes, but it remains the case that few comprehensive schools can truly claim an intake which reflects the full ability range, with many schools still subjected to 'creaming' by neighbouring selective schools, by competitor 'comprehensives', or from the independent sector.

Even within higher education where expansion has been particularly significant, widening participation is not happening quickly enough. Evidence combining data from the National Child Development Study for children born in one week in March in 1958, plus the British Cohort Study covering those born in one week in April 1970 and the British Household Panel Survey, demonstrates a decline in intergenerational mobility between 1958 and 1970. The prospects for students from all backgrounds achieving a degree has increased as a consequence of the massive growth in higher education, but the wealthiest have benefited far more than the poorest. Between 1958, 1970 and the 1980s, the trend has been one of parental income increasingly affecting higher education access probabilities and educational ability at 11 becoming relatively less important (Machin and Vignoles, 2004).

The pursuit of Butler's goals has confounded successive governments for more than 60 years. A persistent theme has been how to manage change while accommodating existing interests. Education has ebbed and flowed in the ranks of government priorities and many good intentions have faltered in the face of economic pressure. Pragmatism has often defeated radicalism, and opportunities where significant change might have been secured have sometimes been missed. Educational opportunities have increased massively since 1945, but they remain disproportionately accessible by the most advantaged members of British society. While education remains the key to social mobility for the least-advantaged, persistent inequalities within the system still represent an obstacle that the poorest must overcome if they are to develop their talents to the full. To the extent that we fail to utilize these talents fully, we continue too to impose a cost on the whole of society.

Further reading

Essential reading on education since 1945 includes Brian Simon's *Education and the Social Order, British Education Since 1944* (London, 1999). Useful survey texts include Roy Lowe's *Education in the Post-War Years: A Social History* (London, 1988); C. Chitty, *Education Policy in Britain* (Basingstoke, 2004); C. Knight, *The Making of Tory Education Policy in Post-war Britain, 1950–1986* (London, 1990); D. Lawton, *Education and Labour Party Ideologies, 1900–2001 and Beyond* (London, 2005); S. Tomlinson, *Education in a Post-welfare Society* (Buckingham, 2001).

Useful sources on the 1944 Act, its development and impact remain: P.H.J.H. Gosden, *Education in the Second World War* (London, 1976); P. Gosden, *The Education System since 1944* (Oxford, 1983); G. McCulloch, *Educational Reconstruction, The 1944 Education Act and the Twenty-first Century* (Ilford, 1994).

The weakness of innovations relating to science and technology are best covered by Michael Sanderson in *Educational Opportunity and Social Change in England* (London, 1987) and *The Missing Stratum, Technical School Education in England, 1900–1990s* (London, 1994).

On comprehensive schools, see C. Benn and B. Simon, *Halfway There: Report on the British Comprehensive School Reform* (London, 1970); C. Benn and C. Chitty, *Thirty Years On* (London, 1997); D. Rubinstein and B. Simon, *The Evolution of the Comprehensive School, 1926–1972* (London, 1973).

The literature on social mobility is vast and a serious consideration of it should take in more recent journal articles. A useful survey can be found in A.H. Halsey (ed.) *British Social Trends since 1900: A Guide to the Changing Social Structure of Britain*, 2nd edition (Basingstoke, 1988).

References

Adonis, A. and Pollard, S. (1997) *A Class Act*. London: Penguin.

Benn, C. and Chitty, C. (1996) *Thirty Years On*. London: Penguin.

Chitty, C. (2004) *Education Policy in Britain*. Basingstoke: Palgrave Macmillan.

Dent, H. (1947) *The Education Act, 1944*, 3rd edn. London: University of London Press.

DfES (2005) *Education Statistics*.

Floud, J.E., Halsey, A.H., and Martin, F.M. (1956) *Social Class and Educational Opportunity*. London: William Heinemann.

Gosden, P.H.J.H. (1976) *Education in the Second World War*. London: Methuen.

Gosden, P. (1983) *The Education System since 1944*. Oxford: Martin Robertson.

Labour Party (1964) *The New Britain*. General Election Manifesto.

Lawton, D. (2005) *Education and Labour Party Ideologies 1900–2001 and Beyond*. Abingdon: RoutledgeFarmer.

Lowe, R. (1988) *Education in the Post-War Years, A Social History*. London: Routledge.

Machin, S. and Vignoles, A. (2004) 'Educational inequality: the widening socio-economic gap', *Fiscal Studies*, 25: 107–128.

Office for National Statistics (2006) *Social Trends*, 36.

Sanderson, M. (1987) *Educational Opportunity and Social Change in England*. London: Faber & Faber.

Sanderson, M. (1999) *Education and Economic Decline in Britain, 1870s to the 1990s*. Cambridge: Cambridge University Press.

Simon, B. (1999) *Education and the Social Order, British Education Since 1944*. London: Lawrence & Wishart.

Sutton Trust (2000) *Entry to Leading Universities*.

Sutton Trust (2005) *Rates of Eligibility for Free School Meals at the Top State Schools*.

Timmins, N. (1995) *The Five Giants, A Biography of the Welfare State*. London: Fontana.

Tomlinson, S. (1997) 'Diversity, choice and ethnicity: the effects of educational markets on ethnic minorities', *Oxford Review of Education*, 23: 63–76.

Tomlinson, S. (2001) *Education in a Post-welfare Society*. Buckingham: Open University Press.

Notes on contributors

Stephen Brooke is Associate Professor of History at York University, Toronto. He is the author of *Labour's War: The Labour Party During the Second World War* (1992) and has published articles on class, gender and sexuality in *Past and Present*, the *American Historical Review* and the *Journal of British Studies*.

Francesca Carnevali is Senior Lecturer in Economic History at the University of Birmingham. Her publications include *Europe's Advantage. Banks and Small Firms in Britain, France, Germany and Italy since 1918* (2005).

Harry Cocks is Lecturer in History at Birkbeck College, University of London, and the author of *Nameless Offences: Homosexual Desire in 19th Century England* (2003), and co-editor of *The Modern History of Sexuality* (2005).

Nick Crafts is Professor of Economic History, University of Warwick. Publications include *Britain's Relative Economic Performance, 1870–1999* (2002).

Martin Daunton is Professor of Economic History in the University of Cambridge, and Master of Trinity Hall. His most recent book is *Wealth and Welfare: An Economic and Social History of Britain, 1850–1950* (2007). He is now working on the taxation of the British Empire and on Britain's engagement in the international economy since 1850.

Julian Greaves is Lecturer in Economic History at the University of Birmingham. The focus of his research is state/industry relations in Britain during the interwar period. His latest publication is entitled *Industrial Reorganization and Government Policy in Interwar Britain* (2005).

Rebecca Jennings is a researcher at Macquarie University, Sydney, Australia. Her interests include the history of gender and sexuality in modern Britain, with a particular focus on post-war lesbian history, and her book, *Tomboys and Bachelor Girls: A Lesbian History of Post-war Britain* will be published by Manchester University Press in 2007.

Max Jones is Director of the MA Programme in Modern British History at the University of Manchester. He is the author of *The Last Great Quest: Captain Scott's*

Antarctic Sacrifice (2003) and editor of Scott's *Journals: Captain Scott's Last Expedition* (2005). His latest research project investigates the rise and fall of the national hero.

Sean O'Connell is Senior Lecturer at Queen's University Belfast. His publications include *The Car in British Society* (1998) and *Mail Order Retailing in Britain: A Business and Social History* (2005). He is currently writing a second book for OUP, on working-class experiences of credit and debt since 1880, and researching the history of joyriding.

Michael Oliver is Professor of Economics at École Supérieure de Commerce de Rennes and a director of Lombard Street Associates (part of Lombard Street Research, UK). He is the author and editor of several books, including two on economic policy-making post-1979. His most recent publication is *Economic Disasters of the Twentieth Century* (edited with Derek H. Aldcroft, 2007).

Panikos Panayi is Professor of European History at De Montfort University. He has written widely on the history of immigrants and minorities in Britain, Germany and Europe. He is currently completing a book entitled *Spicing Up English Life: The Multiculturalization of Food in Britain*.

Christopher Price is Lecturer in Economic History at the University of Liverpool. He specializes in the interwar British economy, rearmament and Anglo-American relations. His publications include *Britain, America and Rearmament: The Cost of Failure* (2001) and most recently 'A Very Peculiar Practice: Under-employment in Britain During the Interwar Years', *European Review of Economic History*, 10 (1), April 2006, with Sue Bowden and David Higgins.

Martin Pugh was Professor of Modern British History at Newcastle University until 1999 and Research Professor in History at Liverpool John Moores University 1999–2002. He is the author of several books including *The Pankhursts* (2001) and *'Hurrah for the Blackshirts!': Fascists and Fascism in Britain Between the Wars* (2005).

Neil Rollings is Senior Lecturer in the Department of Economic and Social History at the University of Glasgow. He has written widely on British economic policy after the Second World War and also on British industry and European integration, on which he is currently writing a monograph. His latest book (co-authored with A. Ringe and R. Middleton) is *Economic Policy Under the Conservatives, 1951–64* (2004).

Julie Rugg is Senior Research Fellow at the Centre for Housing Policy, University of York. Although much of her current work comprises contemporary policy analysis, she also completes historical studies: one of her recent projects was a study of the management of death in the post-war period in the UK. Her current research interests include private rented housing, housing benefit and all aspects of cemeteries from 1740 to the present day.

Catherine Schenk is Professor of International Economic History at the University of Glasgow. She has published widely on international economic relations in the post-war period. Her recent publications include: 'The Empire strikes back: Hong Kong and the decline of sterling in the 1960s', *Economic History Review*, 2004 and 'Finance of industry in Hong Kong 1950–70: a case of market failure?' *Business History*, 2004.

Peter Scott is Reader in International Business History at the University of Reading Business School. He is also Director of the University's *Centre for International Business History* (CIBH) and a trustee of the Business Archives Council. His current research examines the growth of the mass market and mass consumption in interwar Britain.

Julie-Marie Strange is Lecturer in Modern British History at the University of Manchester. Her work includes the monograph *Death, Grief and Poverty, 1870–1914* (2005). New research is on the cultural history of menstruation, 1800–1960 and fatherhood in working-class culture.

Penny Tinkler is Senior Lecturer in Sociology at the University of Manchester. Her publications include *Constructing Girlhood: Popular magazines for girls growing up in England, 1920–50* (1995) and *Smoke Signals: Women, Smoking and Visual Culture in Britain* (2006).

Jim Tomlinson is Bonar Professor of Modern History at the University of Dundee. He has published books on the economic policies of both the Attlee and 1960s' Wilson government. He is currently working with Ben Clift of Warwick University on historical and comparative developments in economic policy in Britain and France and on a project on: 'Managing the economy, managing the people: Britain 1940–1997'.

Katherine Watson is Lecturer in Modern History at the University of Birmingham. Her research interests include British economic development, financial services and public and private institutional change since the nineteenth century.

John Wolffe is Professor of Religious History at the Open University. He has published widely in religion in modern Britain. His recent publications include an edited volume, *Religion in History: Conflict, Conversion and Coexistence* (2004) and *The Expansion of Evangelicalism: The Age of Wilberforce, More, Chalmers and Finney* (2006).

Chris Wrigley is Professor of Modern British History at Nottingham University. His publications include *David Lloyd George and the British Labour Movement* (1976) and *British Trade Unions Since 1933* (2002). The books he has edited include three volumes of *A History of British Industrial Relations* (1982–96) and *A Companion to Early Twentieth Century British History* (2003).

Index

employment (*continued*)
  hours of work 17–18
  low-paid jobs 318
  and masculinity 52
  structure 11–13
  and trade union membership 279–81,
    284–5
  women 3, 13, 50, 268, 318
    in domestic service 221–2
    and equal pay 51–2
    and the First World War 137
    and protective legislation 50, 51
  working hours 137, 142, 198
  young people and work 219–22
  see also labour market; unemployment
EMU (Economic and Monetary Union)
  344–5, 351
Enlightenment project 27, 29
equality *see* inequalities
ERM (Exchange Rate Mechanism) 70–1,
  266, 343, 344–5
ethnic minorities
  and integration 252–3
  and racism 256–9
  and religion 328–31
  and trade unions 285
  see also immigration
eugenics 185, 294
Europe 339–52
  EEC 19, 70, 237, 246, 339, 340–2, 347,
    348–9
  and the ERM 70–1, 266, 343, 344–5
  and the Marshall Plan 339–40, 341
  and the Schuman Plan 340
European integration 2, 339, 341, 344, 345
  debates and interpretations 348–52
  and Plan G 346–7
European Union 91, 342–7
Exchange Rate Mechanism (ERM) 70–1,
  266, 343, 344–5
exchange rates 68–71, 72–4

Falklands War 89, 90, 331
family allowances 311
family planning 294, 297
FDI (foreign direct investment) 64–6

feminism 51, 54, 103, 300–1, 305
feminization of the nation 84–5
Festival of Britain (1951) 39, 295
Festival of Light 301
films
  and national identity 89, 90, 92
  Second World War propaganda 88
  on trade unions 283–4
financial sector
  expansion 8, 13
  and the First World War 133–4
  international investment 63–6
  international monetary system 68–74
  and the interwar depression 149–50
First World War 127–43
  and the Bloomsbury Group 37
  and class 48
  deaths 86, 136–7
  debate on the post-war legacy 136–40
  debts and reparations 150–1
  demobilization and reconstruction 132–4
  and the economy 63, 69, 133–4, 138–40,
    149, 233–4
  effects of total war 127–9
  and the General Strike 134–6
  housing 165
  and modernism/modernity 27, 30, 31,
    32–8
  and national identity 80–2, 85, 90–1
  rationing 128–9
  and religion 325
  state control 129–32
  and welfare reforms 188–92
  and women 3, 33–4, 101–3, 117, 118,
    129–31, 137
flapper vote 105–7
food
  curry in Britain 253–5
  rationing 128–9
football 211
Ford, Henry 113
Forster, E.M. 36, 37
free trade 58, 74, 75, 139, 148, 154
  and welfare reform 185
French welfare policy 194
Freud, Sigmund 31